Palgrave Studies in Economic History

Series Editor
Kent Deng, London School of Economics, London, UK

Palgrave Studies in Economic History is designed to illuminate and enrich our understanding of economies and economic phenomena of the past. The series covers a vast range of topics including financial history, labour history, development economics, commercialisation, urbanisation, industrialisation, modernisation, globalisation, and changes in world economic orders.

More information about this series at
https://link.springer.com/bookseries/14632

Hamish Maxwell-Stewart · Michael Quinlan

Unfree Workers

Insubordination and Resistance in Convict Australia, 1788–1860

palgrave
macmillan

Hamish Maxwell-Stewart
School of Humanities, Arts and Social Science
University of New England
Armidale, NSW, Australia

Michael Quinlan
School of Management, Business School
UNSW Sydney
Sydney, NSW, Australia

ISSN 2662-6497 ISSN 2662-6500 (electronic)
Palgrave Studies in Economic History
ISBN 978-981-16-7557-7 ISBN 978-981-16-7558-4 (eBook)
https://doi.org/10.1007/978-981-16-7558-4

Cover illustration: Ian Beattie/AUSCAPE/Alamy Stock Photo

This Palgrave Macmillan imprint is published by the registered company Springer Nature Singapore Pte Ltd.
The registered company address is: 152 Beach Road, #21-01/04 Gateway East, Singapore 189721, Singapore

In memory of

Kay Daniels, Ian Duffield and Bill Robbins

ACKNOWLEDGEMENTS

We would like to thank Trudy Cowley, the database manager for Digital History Tasmania who together with Melissa Gibbs and Kelsey Priestman helped wrangle much of the evidence used to populate this book. We are also very grateful to all the Archivists and Librarians in the Tasmanian Archives, New South Wales State Archives and State Library New South Wales who have put up with our requests over decades. We owe a particular debt of thanks to Ross Latham, Caroline Homer, Ian and Vicki Pearce, Jessica Walters, Fiona McFarlane, Mark Dunn, Danielle Thyer, Robyn Hollander, Peter Akers, Liang Li, Richard Croucher and Kim Pearce. We would also like to thank our fellow academics who have encouraged us to keep counting protests and protestors despite the scale of the task, especially Julie Gough, Adrian Graves, Richard Tuffin, Deb Malor, Stefan Petrow, Martin Gibbs, Tony Moore, Monika Schwarz, Nick Carter, Mike Davis, Ruth Barton, Barrie Dyster, Deborah Oxley, David Meredith, Barry Godfrey, Kris Inwood, Clare Anderson, Marcus Rediker and Tamsin O'Connor. We are very much in the debt of Greg Patmore, Terry Irving, Tom Dunning, David Roberts and Lucy Frost who were kind enough to read a draft of this book and suggest changes that have immeasurably helped to strengthen it.

We also acknowledge the indefatigable Female Convict Research Centre whose volunteers transcribed the Tasmanian female convict records. This book owes a huge debt of thanks to them and the many other family and citizen researchers, who provided their personal knowledge and time to help correct the text of digitised newspapers, transcribe, code and link tens of thousands of records. They have helped us to identify and trace many important sources and connections which have immeasurably enriched our own scholarly endeavours. This book is dedicated to the following volunteers and all the others who have worked to improve access to Australia's convict past.

Denise Adamson, Gillian Balgowan, Giselda Bannister, Raelene Beazley, Nathan Beer, Vanessa Bland, Michelle Blake, Anne Blythe Cooper, Katie Bonsar, Rhoda Copeland, Caroline Corrigan, Christine Crawford, Judith Cross, Pamela Dilworth, Debbie Domingo, Nicole Don, Margaret Dousset, Heather Ewings, Eugenia Farrell, Karen Filewood, Chris Gallagher, Kris Gatenby,Lauren Hanson-Viney, Michael Heath, Aileen Higgins, Julie Holmes, Irene Hunt, Tracey Hurd, Katrina Ingpen, Regina Knight, Chris Lehman, Cally Lott, Megan Luhrs, Gillian Macdougall, Jennifer Macfarlane, , Colette McAlpine, Shauna McGlone, Thelma McKay, Jacinta Marr, Helen Menard, Emma Morrison, Jude Moyle, Lois Newham, Stephen Newham, Tanja Nussbaumer, Jodie Ombao, June Pongratz, Jane Pryor, Sandy Pullen, Sally Rickman, Jennifer Robinson, Maree Rowley, Catherine Ruhz, Allistair Scott, Jude Smith, Vanessa Smith, Marion Stoneman, Margaret Strike,Narelle Sullivan, Rose Wade, Anne Waller, Julia Webb, Karen Welsh, Sarah White, Ann William Fitzgerald, Colleen Wilson.

This research was supported partially by the Australian Government through the Australian Research Council's Linkage scheme (project LP180101048).

Contents

List of Figures

List of Tables

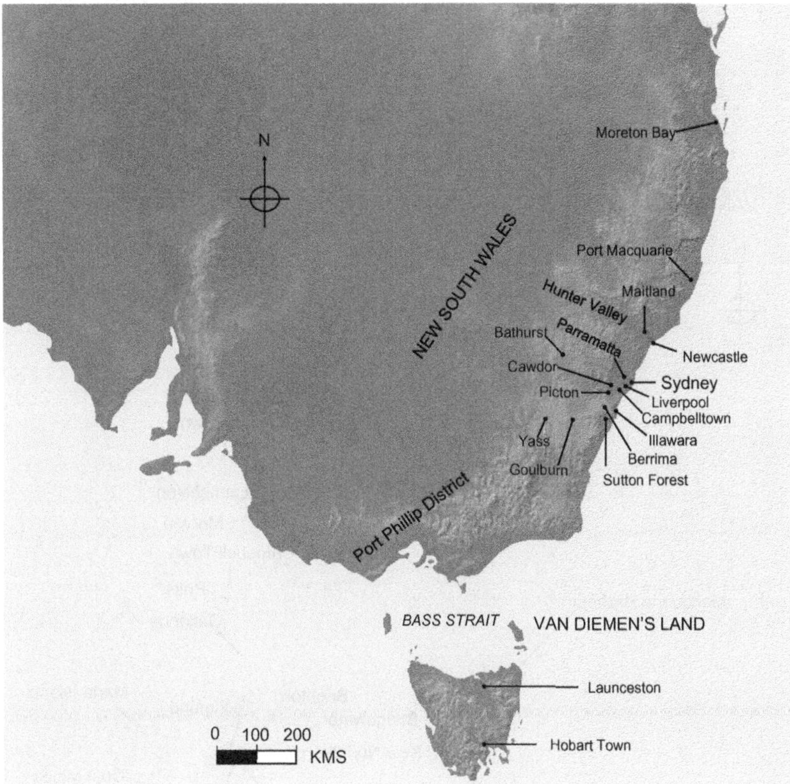

New South Wales

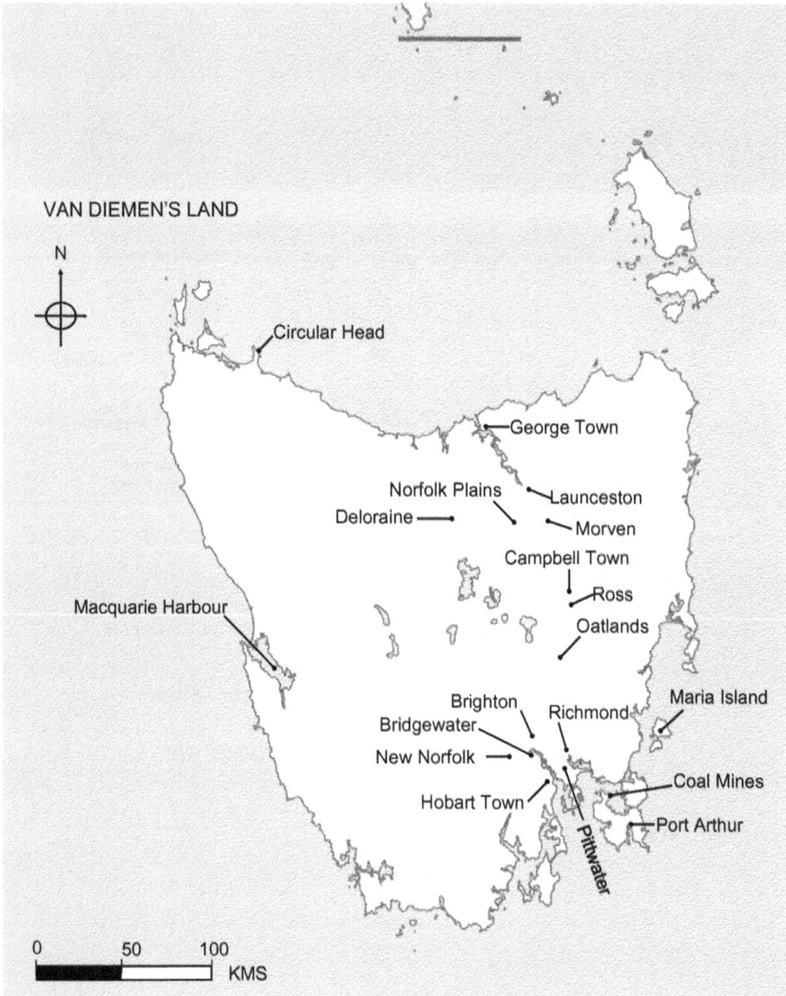

Van Diemen's Land

PART I

Incarceration—Convicts, Unfree Labour and Colonial Capitalism

CHAPTER 1

Unfree Labour, Dissent, Convict-Transportation and the Building of Colonial Capital

This is a book on the subordination and resistance of convicts, by far the biggest and most important category of unfree labour in Australia's history. As such it tries to place this Antipodean workplace struggle within a global context of capitalist development. This chapter sets the context for the book by examining the history and role of penal transportation as a tool designed to further the ends of criminal justice while simultaneously promoting colonization. It starts with a review of the history of resistance and collective action in the metropolitan and colonial world before moving on to map the use of convict labour as a tool of British imperialism. A key purpose of the chapter is to introduce the concept of 'convictism' and to explore the similarities between this and other means of justifying labour exploitation, including plantation racism. The chapter concludes by outlining a number of arguments central to the book. These include the manner in which the history of penal transportation can further understandings of the development of capitalism as a global system of exchange as well as the many ways in which that process was resisted.

H. Maxwell-Stewart and M. Quinlan, *Unfree Workers*, Palgrave Studies in Economic History,
https://doi.org/10.1007/978-981-16-7558-4_1

Unfree Labour and Dissent

Over the past three decades there has been a substantial expansion of global research into the regulation and management of work and everyday lived experiences of various categories of unfree and semi-free labour included slaves, indentured workers and convict labour.[1] While illuminating in many regards relatively little of this research has entailed a systematic examination of collective dissent by unfree labour. On occasion groups of unfree workers, especially slaves, engaged in small or large-scale revolts, or violent rebellions, and a number of these have been the subject of detailed investigations.[2] Scholars like Turner have also pointed to tacit bargaining by slaves which entailed a degree of informal collective organisation. An extensive literature also refers to absconding by unfree labour, identifying it—correctly in our view—as perhaps the single most pervasive form of work-related dissent and one which could have a collective dimension (though the latter has seldom been explored systematically).[3] Other studies point to the extent of temporary absences from work and the ways that these could be used as a bargaining tool.[4] The extent and characteristics of other forms of collective actions like strikes, go-slows,

[1] See for example, Craton, M. (1982) *Testing the Chains: Resistance to Slavery in the British West Indies*, Cornell University Press, Ithaca; Beckles, H. (1988) *Afro-Caribbean Women and Resistance to Slavery in Barbados*, Karnak House, Trenton; Franklin, J. and Schweninger, L. (1999) *Runaway Slaves: Rebels on the Plantation*, Oxford University Press, Oxford; Rivers, L. (2012) *Rebels and Runaways: Slave Resistance in Nineteenth-Century Florida*, University of Illinois Press, Urbana; Horne, G. (2014) *The Counter Revolution of 1776: Slave Resistance and the Origins of the United States*, New York University Press, New York.

[2] See for example, Smith, M. ed. (2005) *Stono: Documenting and Interpreting a Southern Slave Revolt*, University of Southern Carolina Press, Columbia; Greenburg, K. ed. (2006) *Nat Turner: A Slave Rebellion in History and Memory*, Oxford University Press, Oxford; Finch, A. (2015) *Rethinking Slave Rebellion in Cuba: La Escalera and the Insurgencies of 1841–1844*, University of North Carolina Press, Chapel Hill.

[3] Turner, M. ed. (1995) *From Chattel Slaves to Wages Slaves: The Dynamics of Labour Bargaining in the Americas*, Indiana University Press, Bloomington and Indianapolis.

[4] Atkinson, A. (1979) Four Patterns of Convict Protest, *Labour History*, 37, 28–51; Wood, B. (1987) Some Aspects of Female Resistance to Chattel Slavery in Low County Georgia 1763–1815, *The Historical Journal*, 30(3), 603–622; Smith, B. (2008) *A Cargo of Women: Susannah Watson and the Convicts of the Princess Royal*, Allen & Unwin, Sydney; Quinlan, M. (2018) *The Origins of Worker Mobilisation: Australia 1788–1850*, Routledge, New York.

collective demands, threats, petitioning, small scale assaults on supervisors and managers and sabotage, however, have received comparatively little attention. It is sometimes argued that 'day-to-day' forms of protest did not constitute resistance as those who participated in such actions sought to ameliorate local conditions rather than directly challenge the circumstances that held them in bondage.[5] Tacit bargaining should not in the opinion of some be seen as an expression of organised resistance. Others maintain, however, that any attempt to address inequality at work should count as a form of industrial action.[6] Within the literature of unfree labour there have been few attempts to explore the manner in which different forms of action are linked, or how forms of action differed by sex or across different landscapes of exploitation.

This neglect becomes even more striking when placed in the wider context of worker organisation and mobilisation. Early writers and theorists on the rise of organised labour focused on formal organisation of free workers (notably unions but also political bodies and community organisations like anti-sweating leagues).[7] In conjunction with the work of a number of other scholars like George Rudé, E.P. Thompson's *Making of the English Working Class* signalled a major shift in historical scholarship and understanding of worker organisation and action.[8] Thompson argued that the working class was not just a structure or thing, but a process. In his view agency was intrinsic to class formation and the working class was the most active participant in its own making. This process occurred over a longer timeframe than the industrial revolution that preoccupied institutional analysts. Thompson pointed to the importance of ideas, informal organisation and the fluidity of both the flow of concepts within emerging networks, but also of organisational forms.

[5] For a summary see McGary, H. (1992) Resistance and Slavery, in McGary, H. and Lawson, B. eds. *Between Slavery and Freedom*, Indiana University Press, Bloomington, 35–54.

[6] Kelly, J. (1998) *Rethinking Industrial Relations: Mobilization, Collectivism and Long Waves*, Routledge, London.

[7] See for example Webb, S. and Webb, B. (1914) *Industrial Democracy*, Longman Green & Co, London.

[8] Rudé, G. (1964) *The Crowd in History: A Study of Popular Disturbances in France and England 1730–1848*, John Wiley & Sons, New York; Thompson, E. (1968) *The Making of the English Working Class*, Penguin, Harmondsworth; Thompson, E. (1991) *Customs in Common*, Merlin Press, London, 187–188; Hobsbawm, E. and Rudé, G. (1972) *Captain Swing*, Penguin, Harmondsworth.

At the same time, Thompson along with Linebaugh and Hay pointed to the critical role of the state in class formation, especially the use of the law and courts to suppress popular dissent.[9] This approach, and particularly the role of countervailing informal organisation and networks, was taken up by other scholars perhaps most notably the joint and individual work of Peter Linebaugh and Markus Rediker. They argued for a larger network of ideas and actions exchanged across the Atlantic which encompassed a diverse array of workers including seamen, soldiers and slaves and former slaves.[10] Rediker and others have also emphasised the degree to which such systems of labour classification are fluid. Many West Africans served as soldiers before becoming enslaved plantation workers while some eventually moving into maritime industries.[11]

More recently their notion of collaboration across wider spatial domains has drawn the attention of social geographers. Reconstructing the geography of resistance across the eastern Australian colonies is one of the significant themes if not objectives of the current book.[12] For example, we examine not only the transfer of ideas via transported radicals like the Luddites, but also the more informal modes of resistance like the centuries' old practices of incendiarism in rural districts and customary entitlements at harvest time or during traditional holidays. We also trace the origin of collective action to bonds formed while on hulks and other British and Irish penitentiaries and gaols as well as the voyage to Australia. Following Thompson, this book highlights the centrality of the state apparatus, both imperial and colonial, in seeking to subordinate workers and the considerable resistance this sparked.

[9] Hay, D. Linebaugh, P. Rule, J. Thompson, E. and Winslow, C. eds. (1977) *Albion's Fatal Tree: Crime and Society in Eighteenth Century England*, Penguin, Harmondsworth; Thompson, E.P. (1977) *Whigs and Hunters: The Origin of the Black Act*, Penguin, Harmondsworth; Linebaugh, P. (1991) *The London Hanged: Crime and Civil Society in the Eighteenth Century*, Penguin, London.

[10] Linebaugh, P. and Rediker, M. (1990) The Many-Headed Hydra: Sailors, Slaves, and the Atlantic Working Class in the Eighteenth Century, *Journal of Historical Sociology*, 3(3), 225–252.

[11] Rediker, M. (2007) *The Slave Ship: A Human History*, Viking, New York; Thornton, J. (1991) African Soldiers in the Haitian Revolution, *Journal of Caribbean History*, 25(1), 58.

[12] Featherstone, D. and Griffin, P. (2016) Spatial Relations, Histories from Below and the Makings of Agency: Reflections on the Making of the English Working Class at 50, *Progress in Human Geography*, 40(3), 375–393.

Markus Rediker in particular has pointed to widespread informal organisation by workers, including those like merchant seamen and soldiers bound under forms of servitude. A central purpose of this work has been to emphasise that the differences between free and unfree labour are neither static nor sharply delineated, but better viewed as a shifting spectrum of arrangements.[13] His work has encouraged others to re-visit global labour history, uncovering evidence of widespread collective action by precarious workers, whether they were indigenous or free or unfree immigrants.[14] There is also a growing recognition that unfree labour has been a critical and ongoing component of global capitalism. A number of studies examine the degrees of coercive control in different types of unfree labour including slaves, indentured workers and convicts. Many of these acknowledge that even free labour was (and sometimes remains) heavily subordinated through state instruments.[15] Others like Brass have explored the implications for class formation in particular countries and regions of complex combinations of race, ethnicity and labour subordination in different locations.[16]

The question that arises, however, is the extent to which unfree and semi-free labour acted collectively and the implications of this for wider understandings of worker mobilisation. In recent decades there has been a substantial expansion of research into various categories of unfree labour including slaves and indentured workers. Much of this work has focussed on non-European workers and has sought to examine their experiences through the lens of systemic racism or other forms of identity analysis.

[13] Rediker, M. (1987) *Between the Devil and the Deep Blue Sea: Merchant Seamen, Pirates and the Anglo-American World, 1700–1750*, Cambridge University Press, Cambridge.

[14] Linebaugh, P. and Rediker, M. (1990) The Many-Headed Hydra: Sailors, Slaves, and the Atlantic Working Class in the Eighteenth Century, *Journal of Historical Sociology*, 3(3), 225–252; Breman, J. and Van der Linden, M. (2014) Informalizing the Economy: The Return of the Social Question at Global Level, *Development and Change*, 45(5), 920–940.

[15] See for example Rao, J. (1999) Freedom, Equality, Property and Bentham: The Debate Over Unfree Labour, *The Journal of Peasant Studies*, 27(1), 97–12; Banaji, J. (2003) The Fictions of Free Labour: Contract, Coercion, and So-Called Unfree Labour, *Historical Materialism*, 11(3), 69–95; Hay, D. and Craven, P. eds. (2004) *Masters, Servants, and Magistrates in Britain and the Empire 1562–1955*, University of North Carolina Press, Chapel Hill.

[16] Brass, T. (1994) Some Observations on Unfree Labour, Capitalist Restructuring, and Deproletarianization, *International Review of Social History*, 39(2), 255–275.

This literature has deepened our understanding of the experience and views of these workers especially through reference to their resistance to oppression by masters and the state apparatus both individually and collectively. For example, paralleling developments in research into free labour (and unions) and slavery, there is recognition that the overseas deployment of convict labour needs to be viewed in a longer historical time-frame stretching back before the fifteenth century rather than as a series of studies limited to particular colonial moments.[17]

Yet, while various modes of resistance have been examined within this burgeoning literature detailed and systemic examinations of resistance within particular jurisdictions and regions are less common than might be expected—perhaps reflecting a wider decline in studies of collective action by workers per se and the rise of more individualised perspectives.[18] Several authors have identified the need for more research on

[17] De Vito, C. and Lichtenstein, A. (2013) Writing a Global History of Convict Labour, *International Review of Social History*, 58(2), 285–325; Maxwell-Stewart, H. (2016) The Rise and Fall of Penal Transportation, in Johansen, A. ed. *Oxford Handbook of the History of Crime and Criminal Justice*, Oxford, Oxford UP, 335–654.

[18] For studies examining resistance see Wells, A. (1981) Social Conflict and Protest in the English Countryside in the Early Nineteenth Century: A Rejoinder, *The Journal of Peasant Studies*, 8(4), 514–530; Scott, J. (1985) *Weapons of the Weak: Everyday Forms of Resistance*, Yale University Press, New Haven; Scott, J. and Tria Kerkvliet, B. eds. (1986) *Everyday Forms of Peasant Resistance in South-East Asia*, Frank Cass, London; Colburn F. ed. (1989) *Everyday Forms of Resistance*, M.E. Sharp, New York; Haynes, D. and Prakash, G. eds. (1991) *Contesting Power: Resistance to Everyday Social Relations in South Asia*, University of California Press, Berkeley; Casanovas, J. (1995) Slavery, the Labour Movement and Spanish Colonialism in Cuba, 1850–1890, *International Review of Social History*, 40(3), 367–382; Lichtenstein, A. (1996) *Twice the Work of Free Labor: The Political Economy of Convict Labor in the New South*, New York; O'Laughlin, B. (2002) Proletarianization, Agency and Changing Rural Livelihoods: Forced Labour and Resistance in Colonial Mozambique, *Journal of Southern African Studies*, 28, 511–530; Chase, R. (2012) Slaves of the State Revolt: Southern Prison Labor and a Prison-Made Civil Rights Movement, 1945–1980, in Zieger, R. ed. *Life and Labor in the New South*; Reid, K. (1998) "Contumacious, Ungovernable and Incorrigible": Convict Women and Workplace Resistance; Van Diemen's Land, 1820–1839, in Duffield, I. and Bradley, J. eds. *Representing Convicts: New Perspectives on Convict Forced Labour Migration*, Leicester University Press, London, 106–123; Anderson, C. (1998) The Genealogy of the Modern Subject: Indian Convicts in Mauritius 1814–1853, in Duffield, I. and Bradley, J. eds. *Representing Convicts: New Perspectives on Convict Forced Labour Migration*, Leicester University Press, London, 162–184.

unfree worker agency.[19] Mary Turner's pioneering use of a nuanced control and resistance model to elucidate patterns of tacit bargaining amongst slaves provides a good illustration of this form of study. Even after slavery was abolished, former slaves in Jamaica, Trinidad and elsewhere in the Caribbean responded to their emancipation with widespread refusals to work and revolts as they discovered the degree to which waged employment entailed substantial subordination.[20] Others examined female resistance to chattel slavery as well as particular slave revolts and conspiracies in the United States, Caribbean and elsewhere.[21] In Australia, Nichols explored the labour process in a large convict workplace, highlighting an ongoing control and resistance struggle.[22] As Roberts' review of perspectives on convicts in Australia indicates, the question of agency and resistance is not just something to be added to the narrative of unfree labour, its nature and extent can shape fundamental understandings of labour history, if not history more generally.[23]

Recent research has found slave societies and production regimes differed markedly across time and geographical regions. Particular product requirements (for example the varying labour intensity required

[19] De Vito, C. and Lichtenstein, A. (2013) Writing a Global History of Convict Labour, *International Review of Social History*, 58(2), 285–325; Brass, T. and Bernstein, H. (1992) Introduction: Proletarianisation and Deproletarianisation on the Colonial Plantation, *The Journal of Peasant Studies*, 19(3–4), 1–40.

[20] Turner, M. ed. (1995) *From Chattel Slaves to Wages Slaves: The Dynamics of Labour Bargaining in the Americas*, Indiana University Press, Bloomington and Indianapolis; Turner, M. (2004) The British Caribbean, 1823–1838: The Transition from Slave to Free Legal Status, in Hay, D. and Craven, P. eds. *Masters, Servants and Magistrates*, University of North Carolina Press, Chapel Hill, 303–322.

[21] Wood, B. (1987) Some Aspects of Female Resistance to Chattel Slavery in Low County Georgia 1763–1815, *The Historical Journal*, 30(3), 603–622; Rashid, I. (1998) "Do Dady Nor Lef Me Make Dem Carry Me": Slave Resistance and Emancipation in Sierra Leone, 1894–1928, *Slavery & Abolition*, 19(2), 208–231; Nash, G. (1998) Reverberations of Haiti in the American North: Black Saint Dominguans in Philadelphia, *A Journal of Mid-Atlantic Studies*, 65, 44–73; Levy, C. (1970) Slavery and the Emancipation Movement in Barbados 1650–1833, *The Journal of Negro History*, 55(1), 1–14; Gaspar, D. (1978) The Antigua Slave Conspiracy of 1736: A Case Study of the Origins of Collective Resistance, *The William and Mary Quarterly*, 35(2), 308–323.

[22] Nichol, W. (1984) Malingering and Convict Protest, *Labour History*, 47, 18–27.

[23] Roberts, D. (2011) The 'Knotted Hands That Set Us High': Labour History and the Study of Convict Australia, *Labour History* (100), 33–50.

in sugar production compared to coffee), differences in labour management regimes (including living space, opportunities to work for themselves and other incentives) and the use of punishments for dissent varied widely. These differences seem to have influenced the likelihood of violent revolts although in general absconding, neglect, temporary absence and work refusals, feigning illness, insolence and revenge and sabotage were far more endemic forms of slave resistance.[24] Absconding (sometimes termed marronage or petit marronage for temporary absence) was often collective and perhaps the most-costly form of resistance. Slave-owners attempted to curb it by posting notices offering significant rewards to encourage recapture—analogous to efforts to combat convict absconding in Australia.[25] The level of absconding was influenced by sex, climate and season. Opportunities to abscond, for example, were restricted on remote islands. Surveillance costs, alternative food sources and work intensity also varied across slave societies.[26]

As with slavery, there has been growing research into the transportation and treatment of convict workers in North America, the Caribbean,

[24] Campbell, G. and Alpers, E. (2004) Introduction: Slavery, Forced Labour and Resistance in Indian Ocean Africa and Asia, *Slavery & Abolition*, 25(2), 9–27; Kay, M. and Cary, L. (1976) "The Planters Suffer Little or Nothing": North Carolina Compensations for Executed Slaves, 1748–1772, *Science & Society*, 40(3), 288–306; Lack, P. (1982) An Urban Slave Community: Little Rock, 1831–1862, *The Arkansas Historical Quarterly*, 41(3), 258–287; Bush, B. (1984) Towards Emancipation: Slave Women and Resistance to Coercive Labour Regimes in the British West Indian Colonies, 1790–1838, *Slavery & Abolition*, 5(3), 222–243; Beckles, H. (1985) From Land to Sea: Runaway Barbados Slaves and Servants, 1630–1700, *Slavery & Abolition*, 6(3), 79–94; Handler, J. (1997) Escaping Slavery in a Caribbean Plantation Society: Marronage in Barbardos, 1650s–1830s, *New West Indian Guide*, 71(3), 183–225; Kyles, P. (2008) Resistance and Collaboration: Political Strategies Within the Afro-Carolinian Slave Community, 1700–1750, *The Journal of African American History*, 93(4), 497–508.

[25] Morris, R. (1948) Labor Controls in Maryland in the Nineteenth Century, *The Journal of Southern History*, 14(3), 385–400; Bly, A. (2012) A Prince Among Pretending Free Men: Runaway Slaves in Colonial New England Revisited, *Massachusetts Historical Review*, 4, 87–118.

[26] Wood, B. (1987) Some Aspects of Female Resistance to Chattel Slavery in Low County Georgia 1763–1815, *The Historical Journal*, 30(3), 603–622; Rashid, I. (1998) "Do Dady Nor Lef Me Make Dem Carry Me": Slave Resistance and Emancipation in Sierra Leone, 1894–1928, *Slavery & Abolition*, 19(2), 208–231; Nash, G. (1998) Reverberations of Haiti in the American North: Black Saint Dominguans in Philadelphia, *Journal of Mid-Atlantic Studies*, 65, 44–73.

Australia and elsewhere since the seventeenth century but, again, relatively few studies have systematically examined the extent and forms of resistance. Available research indicates that, as with slaves, absconding was widespread. Using employer notices and other sources Morgan calculated that 29 percent of absconding by convict servants in eighteenth-century Maryland was collective. He also determined that those with marketable skills were more likely to run and that they generally took their tools with them as well as food and extra clothing. On occasion convicts absconded with slaves, although this could increase risk of recapture, as did having tattoos or physical disfigurement like pox marks.[27] Johan Heinsen has also revealed how high levels of resistance amongst transported Scandinavian convicts in the seventeenth-century, forced a rethink of Danish use of penal labour in its Caribbean possessions.[28]

In Australia a pioneering study by Atkinson (1978) identified four forms of convict protest: attack; appeal to authority; withdrawal of labour; and compensatory retribution.[29] The last three of these he saw as evidence that convicts operated within a form of moral economy. That is, that while they might accept the terms under which they were bound to serve, they perceived the powers invested in the state or master as having prescribed limits. Since then, a growing number of published and unpublished studies have referred to (mostly) small-scale revolts, convict strikes and collective absconding making clear by implication these were not isolated activities.[30] As yet, however, there have been few attempts to

[27] Morgan, G. and Rushton, P. (2003) Running Away and Returning Home: The Fate of English Convicts in the American Colonies, *Crime, Histoire & Sociétés*, 7(2), 61–80, 47; Morgan, K. (1989) Convict Runaways in Maryland, 1745–1775, *Journal of American Studies*, 23(2), 253–268.

[28] Heinsen, J. (2018) The Scandinavian Empires in the Seventeenth and Eighteenth Centuries, in Anderson C. ed. *A Global History of Convicts and Penal Colonies*, Bloomsbury, London, 97–121.

[29] Atkinson, A. (1979) Four Patterns of Convict Protest, *Labour History*, 37, 28–51.

[30] O'Connor, T. (1994) Power and Punishment: The Limits of Resistance, Moreton Bay Penal Station 1824–1842, Hons Thesis, University of Queensland; Hindmarsh, B. (2001) *Yoked to the Plough: Male Convict Labour, Culture and Resistance in Rural Van Diemen's Land, 1820–1840*, Ph.D. Thesis, University of Edinburgh; Dunning, T. and Maxwell-Stewart, H. (2002), Mutiny at Deloraine: Ganging and Convict Resistance in 1840s Van Diemen's Land, *Labour History*, 82, 35–47; Roberts, D. (2005) A "Change of Place": Illegal Movement on the Bathurst Frontier, 1822–1825, *Journal of Australian Colonial History*, 7, 97–122; Smith, B. (2008) *A Cargo of Women: Susannah Watson and the Convicts of the Princess Royal*, Allen & Unwin, Sydney; Duffield, I. (2013)

try and assess the extent and nature of collective action by convicts and to link this back to their work experiences. This book tries to fill some gaps in previous research by providing a detailed and systematic examination of convict resistance in eastern Australia. In contrast to single colony studies, this book examines all forms of resistance by convicts in New South Wales and Van Diemen's Land. Further, the book explores the origins, nature and interrelationships of this array of dissent using both qualitative and quantitative techniques based on the analysis of 'big data' sets. The study also evaluates the relationship of convict dissent to that by free labour and the overall importance of convict resistance to the industrial relations and socio-political history of Australia.

The Centrality of Convicts to Colonial Capitalism

In order to understand the scale and form of convict resistance in Eastern Australia it is important to place the history of penal transportation to New South Wales and Van Diemen's Land within a wider transnational context. The overseas deployment of convicts in pursuit of imperial economic interests was neither exclusive to Britain nor limited in scale. All of the Western empires utilised convict labour, shipping well over a million penal labourers to colonial destinations in the period 1415–1954.[31] The British alone transported at least 379,000 convicts in the years 1619–1939—only 45 percent of whom were sent to the Australian colonies.[32] Convicted labourers were often deployed alongside slaves and indentured servants or were used interchangeably with other

Cutting Out and Taking Liberties: Australia's Convict Pirates, 1790–1829, in Anderson, C. Frykman, N. van Voss, L. and Rediker, M. eds. *Mutiny and Maritime Radicalism in the Age of Revolution: A Global Survey*, Cambridge University Press, Cambridge, 197–228; Smith, B. (2014) *Luck of the Irish*, Allen & Unwin, Sydney; Reid, K. (1997), "Contumacious, Ungovernable and Incorrigible": Convict Women and Workplace Resistance, Van Diemen's Land 1820–1839, in Duffield, I. and Bradley, J. eds. *Representing Convicts: New Perspectives on Forced Labour Migration*, Leicester University Press, London, 106–123.

[31] Anderson, C. and Maxwell-Stewart, H. (2014) Convict Labour and the Western Empires, 1415–1954, in Aldrich, R. and McKenzie, K. eds. *Routledge History of Western Empires*, Routledge, London, 165–183.

[32] Anderson, C. (2016) Transnational Histories of Penal Transportation: Punishment, Labour and Governance in the British Imperial World, 1788–1939, *Australian Historical Studies*, 47(3), 382.

forms of unfree labour, including conscripts.[33] They formed, in effect, an important flow of unwilling migrants that played a critical role in the development and defence of overseas colonial possessions.

There were three distinctive features which collectively shaped the British overseas deployment of penal labour. These were traits that might individually be shared with other unfree migrations systems, but collectively help to distinguish the trans-global movement of convicts from other unfree labour management practices. First, the length of time that a convict was ordered to serve was fixed by a sentence passed by a court. Second, the transported were removed from the place where they were sentenced to an overseas colony where they were subjected to forced labour. Third, it was the rights to the labour of the convict that was transferred between parties, not ownership of the body of the convict per se. This last distinction had important intergenerational implications. The children of convicts were, at least in a technical sense, born free. This was the case even when the convict had been sentenced to transportation for life. As the length of servitude was fixed by a sentence, judicially imposed unfreedom could not be transferred from one individual to another, as was the case with chattel slavery.[34]

In practice, however, all of these boundaries could be muddied. There are plenty of examples of other categories of unfree labour being treated in similar ways to convicts and vice versa. In part this is precisely because British penal transportation practice evolved in tandem with other unfree labour systems. It was critically informed by indenture, slavery and military service, yet it also helped to shape these experiences too. An encounter with a court could result in other forms of unfreedom—not just penal transportation. An examination of the origins of slaves taken in British early nineteenth-century West African anti-slaving operations revealed, for example, that just over 10 percent had become enslaved as a result of judicial sentence. In short, West African courts minted slaves

[33] In the case of Mauritius see Anderson, C. (1997) The Genealogy of the Modern Subject: Indian Convicts in Mauritius 1814–1853, in Duffield, I. and Bradley, J. eds. *Representing Convicts: New Perspectives on Convict Forced Labour Migration*, 164–182; Croucher, R. and Didier, M. (2014) "Legal at the Time?": Companies, Governments and Reparations for Mauritian Slavery, *Journal of African Law*, 58(1), 89–108.

[34] Evans, R. (2009) 19 June 1822, Creating an 'Object of Real Terror': The Tabling of the First Bigge Report, in Crotty, M. and Roberts, D.A. *Turning Points in Australian History*, UNSW Press, Sydney, 53–54.

in the same way as British courts produced convicts.[35] While these judicial institutions did not operate under English (or Scottish) law, prior to 1807 the labour of the condemned was sold to British slaving interests and shipped across the Atlantic in British registered vessels. The point is far from esoteric. Convict service is often distinguished from slavery on the grounds that a person enters slavery through no fault of their own, while loss of freedom for the convicted was the result of past indiscretions.[36] In the case of a significant number of slaves, this turns out to be a false dichotomy.

A court encounter could also convert a slave into a convict. There are many examples of slaves being sentenced to transportation in courts located in both the West Indies and Mauritius.[37] Those convicted in Jamaican courts were sold to Spanish traders. This was a practice that was largely driven by economics. If a slave was executed the slave's master was due compensation. Sale provided a convenient means of providing financial redress for the loss of property that resulted from conviction.[38] The criminal justice system could also provide a route into military service or indenture. While on occasion English and Welsh courts sentenced individuals directly to military service, many more recruits were sourced from the prison system before their case came to trial. The army even had a name for those that entered the service via this peculiar form of plea bargaining. They were termed 'culprits'—a label that could be applied to anyone charged with an offence, although not necessarily convicted. It has been estimated that 20 percent of the British army serving in the West Indies in the years 1799–1802 were recruited as a direct result of encounter with the criminal justice system.[39] Similar mechanisms could be used to secure the services of indentured labourers. County gaols formed fertile

[35] Emmer, P. (2005) *The Dutch Slave Trade, 1500–1850*, Berghahn Books, New York, 6, 51–4.

[36] Neal, D. (1991) *The Rule of the Law in a Penal Colony: Law and Power in Early New South Wales*, Cambridge University Press, Cambridge, 36.

[37] Hordvik, E. (2016) Mauritius—Caught in the Web of Empire: The Legal System, Crime Punishment and Labour 1825–1845, Ph.D. Thesis, University of Tasmania; Duffield, I. (1986) From Slave Colonies to Penal Colonies: The West Indian Convict Transportees to Australia, *Slavery and Abolition*, 7(1), 25–45.

[38] Paton, D. (2001) Punishment, Crime and the Bodies of Slaves in Eighteenth-Century Jamaica, *Journal of Social History*, 34(4), 923–945.

[39] Buckley, R. (1988) *The British Army in the West Indies: Society and the Military in the Revolutionary Age*, University Press of Florida, Gainesville, 87, 96–97.

grounds for recruiting unfree servants in the seventeenth and eighteenth-century, many of whom were crimped into indentured or military service by their gaolers as a means of clearing prison debts. As Clare Anderson has shown, the same was true of the later recruitment of indentured servants in the Indian sub-continent. As she put it: 'In nineteenth-century India, there was a close association between convict transportation and indentured migration, discursively, institutionally, and imaginatively'. The two systems were organised in similar ways and were often confused in popular imagination, an illustration of the degree to which the boundaries between different categories of labour were in practice 'fuzzy and ill-defined'.[40]

The similarities and differences between various forms of bondage were a frequent topic of conversation in early colonial Australia. Alfred Stephen, who had been brought up in St Kitts and later served as attorney general in Van Diemen's Land, thought for example that West Indian slavery 'was infinitely milder than in these Colonies.' Alexander Maconochie contrasted the assignment system with slavery as masters 'disliked, coerced and inveighed' against their assigned servants 'because they only possessed temporary power in them and no long-term interest in their well-being.'[41] There are echoes here of the contrasting experience of convicts and slaves in the seventeenth and eighteenth century Atlantic. Expendable convict labour was sometimes substituted for expensive slave labour. The Spanish replaced slaves used to construct harbour defences in San Juan and Havana with convicts, since high death rates had driven up the costs of maintaining a slave labour force.[42] In the seventeenth century the French galley fleet came to rely increasingly on convicts, as opposed to slaves, for similar reasons. Where 'Turkish' slaves were retained, it was to perform specific skilled tasks—for example, to serve as first oarsmen and therefore set the pace and control timing of the stroke, with the remaining power being delivered by unskilled and expendable convicts.[43]

[40] Anderson, C. (2009) Convicts and Coolies: Rethinking Indentured Labour in the Nineteenth Century, *Slavery and Abolition*, 30(1), 93–109.

[41] Maconochie, A. (1838) *Thoughts on Convict Management: And Other Subjects Connected With the Australian Penal Colonies*, MacDougall, London, 8.

[42] Pike, R. (1978) Penal Servitude in the Spanish Empire: Presidio Labor in the Eighteenth Century, *Hispanic American Historical Review*, 58(1), 21–40.

[43] Bamford, P. (1956) The Procurement of Oarsmen for French Galleys, 1660–1748, *American Historical Review*, 65(1), 31–48.

Others drew parallels with slavery in order to justify the treatment meted out to convicts. George Arthur, a former superintendent of Honduras who later served as lieutenant-governor of Van Diemen's Land argued that the master of convict labour 'may draw from his knowledge of their crimes, a sanction, quite as satisfactory as that arising from difference of colour, for any severity he would practice against them.'[44] His succinct appraisal captures the essence of 'convictism'—the means by which the past moral failings of transported workers were used to justify labour exploitation. Here the important issue is not the similarity between the two conditions. It would be a mistake to argue, for example, that 'convictism' was the direct equivalent of plantation racism. Rather, the point is that the ideological underpinnings of these two unfree labour systems were based on assertions of inferiority. The extent to which criminality (in addition to sexuality in the case of female convicts) was used to justify both forcing convicts to work for no or low pay, and the punishment of those who refused to do their master's or the state's bidding, is critical to the arguments presented in this book. In this sense the New South Wales convict master, James Mudie, was right to argue that the transported constituted a special category of labour which he termed the 'felonry'.[45]

It is in the interests of capital to separate different workers into categories. Classification is essential if the 'deserving' are to be divided from the 'undeserving', and in this sense, the convicts transported in large numbers across the Western empires formed the ideal workforce. The felonry set to work in the Australian penal colonies could easily be distinguished from the deserving poor who remained behind, or were selected for passage to the colonies as assisted migrants. This was a division that sat as comfortably in the mind of the reformer as it did with the administrator and settler colonists. Few cared about the flesh cut from the backs of recalcitrant convicts, or at least if they did, they cared much less than they did about the treatment of slaves, or children employed in factories, simply because those transported to the penal colonies were morally

[44] Arthur, G. (1835) *Defence of Transportation in Reply to the Remarks of the Archbishop of Dublin in his Second Letter to Early Grey by Colonel George Arthur*, George Cowie, London, 18.

[45] Mudie, J. (1837) *The Felonry of New South Wales: Being a Faithful Picture of the Real Romance of Life in Botany Bay: With Anecdotes of Botany Bay Society*, Whaley and Co, London.

responsible for their own condition.[46] It is of no wonder that the very word 'convict' was so disliked by the men and women who arrived in irons in Australia. They preferred more neutral terms such as prisoner that implied someone held against their will, rather than a term which emphasised the weight of the ideological chains that helped to keep them in place.[47]

Just as a slave was at risk of being essentialised in ways that obliterated their previous lives as farmers, soldiers, traders, mothers and children—so convicts were at risk on conviction of losing their prior history. They ceased to be agricultural workers, sailors, butchers and domestic servants and became thieves, 'whores' and robbers. Thieves are also not traditionally thought of as good workers. It was therefore easy to argue that the employer of convict labour was engaged in an act designed to result in a public good. Rather than profiteering, they sought to relieve the colonial government from the burden of feeding and housing shoddy, work-shy criminals. Of course, in the process they could also argue that they created an additional benefit by inculcating criminals with the habits of industry. Again, there are clear ideological parallels with common justifications for slavery. Yet, as the plight of convicts attracted little sympathy and their labour was not regarded as valuable, it is perhaps little surprise that the history of transportation has been comparatively neglected compared to slavery and indenture.

Despite the widespread use of the practice, penal transportation has also been the subject of comparatively little study by historical criminologists. Ever since the publication of Michel Foucault's *Discipline and Punish* most European accounts of the evolution of criminal justice systems have centred on the rise of the prison.[48] In stark contrast to the nineteenth-century penitentiary, the systems of control that characterised the Australian penal colonies lacked walls. The decision to despatch the First Fleet to the far side of the world, rather than construct a system of panopticons as advocated by the philosopher Jeremy Bentham, might be regarded as a backward step. The aim of the prison was to architecturally

[46] Lydon J. (2021) *Anti-Slavery and Australia: No Slavery in a Free Land?* Routledge, London, 91.

[47] Laugesen, A. (2002) The Politics of Language in Convict Australia, 1788–1850, *Journal of Australian Colonial History*, 4(1), 26.

[48] Foucault, M. (1977) *Discipline and Punish: The Birth of the Prison*, Pantheon, New York.

seclude the offender—to wall them up in a space where, separated from the company of the dissolute, they could be reshaped. By contrast transportation appeared to hark back to early modern systems of law and order that sought to combat crime through the public infliction of pain. The association of penal transportation with the lash, leg irons and toil in the open air reinforced the perception that it was an anachronistic system of punishment out of step with the general thrust of penal reform.

A reliance on whip cord to keep convicts in line has also helped to associate penal transportation with pre-capitalist modes of production. As Stephen Nicholas once memorably put it, there is perhaps no greater symbol of inefficiency at work than the lash.[49] There has been a long-standing consensus that capitalism is underpinned by free wages. As Adam Smith wrote: 'A person who can acquire no property can have no other interest but to eat as much, and to labour as little as possible.'[50] For many the violence of both the slave trade and systems of exploitation that sought to extract labour from the unwilling bodies of criminals belonged to an inefficient mercantilist world later superseded by the rapid growth of a free economy underpinned by wage labour.[51] In more recent years that consensus has been challenged by an emergent new history of capitalism.

Writing in the 1940s, Eric Williams first argued that the Atlantic slave trade catalysed the development of industrial capital. While mercantilism masked the inefficiencies of slavery, he pointed to the many ways in which the profits derived from plantation economies were reinvested in other critical industries including shipbuilding, canal construction and coal mining. Once the Atlantic slave trade had pump-primed an industrial revolution, it was in the interests of the British to abandon their former slaving interests, switching over to a capitalist system proper.[52] Williams' many critics have pointed out that the Iberian investment in plantation economies matched that of the British, but failed to stimulate the industrial growth of Spain and Portugal. They also argued that the profits from slavery were dwarfed by those derived from other sectors of the economy,

[49] Nicholas, S. (1988) The Convict Labour Market, in Nicholas, S. ed. *Convict Workers: Reinterpreting Australia's Past*, Cambridge University Press, Cambridge, 113.

[50] Smith, A. (1766) *The Wealth of Nations* 1970 edition, 488.

[51] Lydon, *Anti-Slavery and Australia*, 68.

[52] Williams, E. (1964) *Capitalism and Slavery*, Andre Deutsch, London.

disputing the role that slavery played in accelerating industrial development.[53] As Harvey points out, however, none of these accounts explore the reverse question. In his words they fail to ask 'whether mass plantation slavery and subsequent forms of servile, non-free wage labour would have developed in the absence of capitalist wage-labour industrialisation'.[54]

One of the illustrations he provides is the synergies that developed between the colonial world and the Birmingham gun industry. While colonial conflicts stimulated firearm production, the enormous peacetime demand for muskets in the West African slave trade was crucial to the long-term development of the industry. Between 1750 and 1807 a staggering 20 million muskets were produced to be exchanged for slaves. While non-wartime demand played a large part in refining production to the point where a musket could be assembled in a minute, the militarisation of West Africa also transformed the business of slaving. While the slaves produced by this exchange mechanism were not waged, they were certainly commodified. They were held in place not just by physical restraints, but by the laws that protected property. They could be insured and traded and when the British finally abolished slavery, their owners were generously compensated. In short this was two systems working in parallel—a British waged economy that was inextricably linked to the unfreedom of the Atlantic.[55] The model also helps to explain why West Africa, and for that matter Iberia, failed to benefit from the slave trade to the same extent as Britain. Some societies invested the profits from slave trading in imports, while others took advantage of new market opportunities to stimulate industrial growth. In contrast to the Birmingham gun trade, craftsmen were unable to complete with the influx of cheap manufactured goods that flooded into West Africa as a result of the slave trade.[56]

[53] Solow, B. (1987) Capitalism and Slavery in the Exceedingly Long Run, *Journal of Interdisciplinary History*, 17(4), 711–737; Eltis, D. and Engerman, S. (2000) The Importance of Slavery and the Slave Trade to Industrializing Britain, *Journal of Economic History*, 60(1), 123–144.

[54] Harvey, M. (2019) Slavery, Indenture and the Development of British Industrial Capitalism, *History Workshop Journal*, 88, 66–88.

[55] Harvey, M. Slavery, Indenture and the Development of British Industrial Capitalism, 71–77.

[56] Green, T. (2020) *A Fistful of Shells: West Africa from the Rise of the slave Trade to the Age of Revolution*, Penguin, Milton Keynes, 143–148.

A similar argument can be used to explain the evolution of penal transportation. The development of overseas plantation economies was not possible in the absence of compulsion. Few migrants could either afford the cost of a trans-Atlantic passage or wished an encounter with scurvy or yellow fever, merely to swap waged work at home for waged work abroad. In the absence of a workforce, the cost of colonial labour would have remained high and growth slow. Penal transportation developed as a means of killing two birds with one stone. On the one hand it encouraged the growth of waged labour in Britain and Ireland by punishing the idle and dissolute (as well as protecting the interests of property) while simultaneously supplying manpower to the colonies. The origins of convict transportation are bound up with the evolution of waged labour. The transition from payment in-kind to waged labour was underpinned by the law, which progressively criminalised access to workplace perks.[57] Like the arms manufactured in Birmingham, however, those laws were not bound by national borders. They too circulated through the wider colonial world.

In fact, the history of penal transportation is entirely consistent with Foucault's account of the way in which the criminal justice system was adapted to suit a wider industrial need for docile labour. Indeed, an understanding of the role played by transportation helps to solve a conundrum that has plagued conventional accounts of the rise of the prison. Until the completion of Millbank in 1821 there was no national prison system. Most county gaols were designed to hold short-term prisoners and debtors. Before the American Revolution disrupted the trans-Atlantic supply of condemned labour to the colonial world, courts rarely passed terms of imprisonment. Between January 1674 and December 1780 a total of 26,546 verdicts were recorded in the proceedings of the Old Bailey. Less than five percent of these resulted in a custodial sentence compared to 47 percent of cases where the defendant was sentenced to transportation (see Table 1.1). The data from the Old Bailey underscores the extent to which eighteenth-century courts were reluctant to imprison offenders found guilty of indictable offences. In short, there was no straight line connecting the creation of workhouses for the indolent poor in the later sixteenth-century and the construction of the nineteenth-century penitentiary.

[57] Linebaugh, P. (2003) *The London Hanged: Crime and Civil Society in the Eighteenth Century*, Verso, London, 225–255.

Table 1.1 Sentences recorded in Old Bailey Proceedings January 1674–December 1780

Sentence	*Number*	*Percent*
Death	5125	19.31
Transportation	12,550	47.28
Imprisonment	1287	4.85
Branding	3343	12.59
Corporal Punishment	2942	11.08
Military duties	125	0.47
Fines, sureties etc	793	2.99
Pardoned or sentence respited	381	1.44
	26,546	100.00

Tim Hitchcock, Robert Shoemaker, Clive Emsley, Sharon Howard and Jamie McLaughlin, et al., *The Old Bailey Proceedings Online, 1674–1913* (www.oldbaileyonline.org, version 7.0, 24 March 2012)

Moreover, the minority of prisoners confined in county gaols were generally subjected to short-term stays, usually under three-months. By contrast the minimum sentence to transportation was set at seven years. This was fixed to suit commercial outcomes—it helped to position penal transportation within the trans-Atlantic market for indentured labour. The longer the sentence, the longer a colonial buyer could acquire the service of the condemned. Other colonial practices foreshadowed later metropolitan surveillance systems. This included the circulation of the descriptions of prisoners as an aid to identification, a process that started in the eighteenth-century Atlantic but reached its apogee in the Australian penal colonies.[58] The ship itself formed a convenient floating prison. Rather than merely forming a way of transporting the labour of prisoners to the colony, it evolved into a system of discipline in its own right. The convict transports that conveyed penal labour to the Australian colonies, for example, were organised in ways that were remarkably similar to Bentham's design for regulating work within the confines of the panopticon. Indeed, many of the systems developed to manage convict labour in the colonies were later incorporated into the British and Irish penitentiary system. In fact, there is a strong argument that, rather than an anachronistic alternative to the development of the modern prison, penal

[58] Shoemaker, R. and Ward, R. (2017) Understanding the Criminal: Record-Keeping, Statistics and the Early History of Criminology in England, *British Journal of Criminology*, 57, 1442–1461; Bradley, J. and Maxwell-Stewart, H. (1997), 'Behold the Man': Power, Observation and the Tattooed Convict, *Australian Studies*, 12(1), 71–97.

transportation was critical to the way in which experimentation within the criminal justice system developed a blueprint for the management of a range of other institutions including the school, hospital and factory. The creation of an 'off-shore' carceral archipelago in effect informed the development of European systems of surveillance, or at the least, was marked by an exchange of ideas and technologies.[59] In order to explore this in more detail it is necessary to outline the way in which British transportation practice evolved.

Imprisonment is wildly expensive. By way of illustration, the cost of placing a child in secure custody is considerably more than the fees charged by an élite private school.[60] Historically, the expense of incarceration placed it beyond the means of most governments. Instead, judicial authorities resorted to public spectacle, maiming and or executing offenders in the hope that this would deter others. Elites who possessed the means to travel could also be ordered into exile, a relatively inexpensive alternative to the state sanctioned public exercise of terror. In those societies where property rights were held in others, judicial slavery presented a further means of limiting the costs associated with the exercise of the law. The sale of the convicted was common in early medieval Europe, although such sanctions became less widespread as the use of slavery declined. They became rare in the West after the twelfth century and thereafter penal enslavement was increasingly replaced with punishments which mutilated or otherwise marked the body of the offender.[61]

The decline in penal enslavement coincided with a general reduction in the use of slave labour in European societies. By the fifteenth century slavery had ceased to exist in England and was uncommon elsewhere in Western Europe. Mixed agriculture, with its high seasonal variations in demand for labour, is not particularly suited to the use of chattel slaves. The introduction of horse- and ox-drawn ploughs exacerbated

[59] Anderson, C. (2018) Introduction: A global History of Convicts and Penal Colonies, in Anderson, C. ed. *A Global History of Convicts and Penal Colonies*, Bloomsbury, London, 9.

[60] Langen, N. (2019) Prisons, *The Justice Gap*, 15 May 2019, https://www.thejusticegap.com/the-cost-of-a-year-in-prison-is-greater-than-fees-for-eton-perhaps-we-should-be-more-ambitious-about-what-we-expect/ (accessed 10 January 2020).

[61] Rio, A. (2015) Penal Enslavement in the Early Middle Ages, in De Vito, C. and Lichtenstein, A. eds. *Global Convict Labour*, Brill, Leiden, 79–107.

the issue, reducing ganging at the expense of the employment of skilled teams of workers. The majority of agricultural work undertaken in Europe was more suited to the use of serf labour rather than slaves.[62] Feudal lords allowed common and even private ownership, of land in return for labour services, which over time were increasingly substituted for rents. Exceptions included mining and mono-cultivation of plantation crops. A Scottish Act of 1672, for example, empowered the owners of coal mines to use vagrants and those who had 'escaped hanging for thefts' as unfree labour.[63] The development of New World plantation economies, however, rekindled demand for unfree labour and European legal systems quickly responded.

In England plans to transport the unproductive members of society first emerged in the late sixteenth century. Richard Hakluyt wrote to Elizabeth I in 1584 to suggest that 'loyterers and idle vagabondes' should be condemned to service in Newfoundland and other parts of the Americas where they could be employed in a number of tasks including: felling timber; manufacturing pitch and tar; mining metals; planting sugarcane and gathering cotton ('whereof there is plenty').[64] Following an appeal by Governor Dale of Virginia, in 1615 James I decreed that prisoners sentenced to death 'whoe for strength of bodie or other abilities shall be thought fitt to be ymploied in forraine discoveries' could be spared on condition of overseas service.[65] The first convicts were transported in the same year. The number of capital and other offenders formally sentenced by courts to transportation, however, remained modest until the passage of the Transportation Act in 1717.[66]

62 Blackburn, R. (1997) The Old World Background to European Colonial Slavery, *William and Mary Quarterly*, 54(1), 65–102.

63 Eltis, D. (1993) Europeans and the Rise and Fall of African Slavery in the Americas: An Interpretation, *American Historical Review*, 98(5), 1404; Morgan, G. and Rushton, P. eds. *Banishment in the Early Atlantic World: Convicts, Rebels and Slaves*, Bloomsbury, London, 30–31.

64 Hakluyt, R. (1877) A Discourse Concerning Western Planting, 1584, in Deanne, C. ed. *Collections of the Maine Historical Society*, 2nd series, ed., John Wilson, Cambridge, 36–38.

65 Konig, D. (1984) "Dale's Laws" and the Non-Common Law Origins of Criminal Justice in Virginia, *The American Journal of Legal History*, 26(4), 366.

66 Meredith, D. and Oxley, D. (2007) Condemned to the Colonies: Penal Transportation as the Solution to Britain's Law and Order Proble, *Leidschrift*, 22(1), 21–22.

Yet, there were many other ways in which the criminal justice system could be used to generate coerced Atlantic workers. Inundated by the tide of vagrants, London's Bridewell turned Hakluyt's proposal for transportation for the idle poor into a reality in the early seventeenth century. Between 1617 and 1648 the Bridewell Court books contain orders for the sale of over a thousand criminals and vagabonds who were condemned to service in Barbados, Virginia and Bermuda.[67] The practice continued until well after the Restoration precisely because apprenticing the convicted poor to merchants proved to be a cost-efficient way of dealing with petty offenders.[68] It was also widely copied by houses of correction in other counties.

Other unfree workers were 'produced' by war. The bloody civil war fought to put an end to Stuart tyranny ironically led to a dramatic increase in the number held in bondage in the wider Atlantic world. Several thousand Royalist sympathisers and prisoners of war were transported.[69] In 1654 the Parliamentary commander in Highland Scotland was empowered to transport all those he encountered under arms to the plantations. Thereafter further transportations occurred in the wake of the Argyle and Monmouth rebellions of 1685 and the 1715 and 1745 Jacobite uprisings.[70] Many others were transported out of Ireland in the aftermath of the Cromwellian invasion of 1649–1653. Contemporary accounts put the number of felons, vagrants and prisoners of war conveyed to Barbados in the 1640s and 1650s at 12,000.[71] Even accounting for exaggerations, it is apparent that during the Interregnum substantial numbers of individuals were forcibly transported to the New World by one means or another. Between 1645 and 1650 at least 8000 indentured servants

[67] Beier, A. (1978) Social Problems in Elizabethan England, *The Journal of Interdisciplinary History*, 9(2), 219; Waring, J. (2017) *Indentured Migration and the Servant Trade from London to America, 1618–1718*, Oxford University Press, Oxford, 33.

[68] Morgan and Rushton, *Banishment*, 9 and 15–17.

[69] Pestana, C. (2004) *The English Atlantic in the Age of Revolution 1640–1661*, Harvard University Press, Cambridge, MA, 183–189 .

[70] Sankey, M. (2005) *Jacobite Prisoners of the 1715 Rebellion: Preventing and Punishing Insurrection in Early Hanoverian Britain*, Ashgate, Aldershot, 56; Butler, J. (1896) British Convicts Shipped to American Colonies, *American Historical Review*, 2(1), 13–14; Morgan and Rushton, *Banishment*, 36.

[71] Gragg, L. (2003) *Englishmen Transplanted: The English Colonization of Barbados, 1627–1660*, Oxford University Press, Oxford, 142.

arrived in Barbados, many of whom were transported.[72] Indeed, so common was the practice that to be 'Barbado'ed' became a verb. This was a period when voluntary migration to the colonies declined while New World demand for labour rose.[73] The capture of Jamaica as part of Cromwell's Western Design in 1655 more than doubled the amount of Caribbean acreage in English hands.[74] While this paved the way for British domination of sugar production in the long-run, it increased immediate demand for labour—a problem exacerbated by limited English access to West African slaving markets in the mid-seventeenth century, still largely dominated by the Dutch and Portuguese.[75]

The gap in supply and demand was bridged by shipping those that the Puritan rulers regarded as 'the degenerate poor'.[76] By 1652 justices of the peace were empowered to apprehend beggars and vagrants and send them to ports for trans-shipment to the New World.[77] Four years later judges were ordered to send lists of criminals convicted in assizes to London in order to identify suitable recruits. In the same year a thousand London poor were sent to Barbados.[78] Seventeenth and eighteenth-century county gaols were poorly funded and gaolers relied on fees levied upon inmates to supplement meagre or non-existent salaries. Prisoners regularly had to pay for the use of their cell, bedding, food and even their release.[79] Many prisoners were incarcerated beyond the expiration

[72] Beckles, H. (1985) Plantation Production and "White Proto-Slavery": White Indentured Servants and the Colonisation of the English West Indies 1624–1645, *The Americas*, 41(3), 35–36.

[73] Donoghue, John (2010) "Out of the Land of Bondage": The English Revolution and the Atlantic Origins of Abolition, *The American Historical Review*, 115(4), 950.

[74] Pestana, C. (2005) English Character and the Fiasco of the Western Design, *Early American Studies: An Interdisciplinary Journal*, 3(1), 1.

[75] Beckles, Plantation Production and "White Proto-Slavery", 23 and 30–31.

[76] Donoghue, Out of the Land of Bondage, 958.

[77] Gragg, *Englishmen Transplanted*, 142.

[78] Donoghue, Out of the Land of Bondage, 966.

[79] McConville, S. (1981) *A History of English Prison Administration, Vol. 1 1750–1877*, Routledge, London, 66–73; Devereaux, S. (1999) The Making of the Penitentiary Act, 1775–1779, *The Historical Journal*, 42(2), 409; Willis, Transportation versus Imprisonment, 186.

of their sentence as a result of becoming indebted to their gaoler.[80] This rendered them liable to transportation as gaolers, like the Governors of Bridewell, stood to profit from the sale of indebted prisoners to shipping contractors.

In the long run the experience of indenture and convict transportation in the seventeenth-century Caribbean helped to shape later attitudes to labour. In the short, it aided the shift to chattel slavery.[81] Following a collapse in the London price of cotton and indigo in 1641 to 1642, planters in Barbados experimented with sugar production resulting in a marked increase in work intensity. The clearing of new ground in particular was undertaken by indentured labour (much of it transported). Indentured servants were cheaper than slaves because they were contracted to work for shorter periods of time—an average of six years in mid-sixteenth century. Transported labour was particularly cheap and, in this period, abundant. The prevalence of former prisoners and vagrants prompted Henry Whistler to describe Barbados as a 'Dunghill.'[82]

Barbados was a place that quickly developed a reputation for brutality. The owners of European labour had little vested interest in their charges after their term of servitude had expired and accordingly treated many as disposable assets. Conditions of service further deteriorated following the introduction of sugar. Whereas apprentices and servants in England remained in control of their leisure time outside of the hours they laboured for their masters, in Barbados all of the servant's time was owned. The Servant and Slave code of 1661 all but eliminated 'freedom dues'—the customary payments made to servants who survived their contracted period of service. Long before this Barbadian courts became adept at using the indiscretions of servants to extend periods of service. Even those who had not been judicially transported were at risk of being converted into convicted labour by colonial courts.[83] Treatment of Europeans working on Barbadian plantations in the period 1645–1660 shocked visitors. As Richard Ligon, noted, 'I have seen such cruelty there done to servants, as I did not think one Christian could have done

[80] Baine, R. (1993) New Perspectives on Debtors in Colonial Georgia, *The Georgia Historical Quarterly*, 77(1), 1–19.

[81] Beckles, Plantation Production and "White Proto-Slavery", 37.

[82] As quoted in Winthrop, D. (2012) *White Over Black: American Attitudes Toward the Negro, 1550–1812*, University of North Carolina Press, Chapel Hill, 65.

[83] Newman, In Great Slavery and Bondage, 72–76.

to another.' Tellingly he thought that indentured servants were treated worse than slaves who are 'kept and preserv'd with greater care'. Servants had, in his words, 'the worser lives, for they are put to very hard labor, ill lodging and their dyet [is] very sleight'.[84]

Despite these levels of brutality, work-orientated punishments could be justified as they returned a public good. As Thomas Moore argued, the use of convicts as 'slave' labour was an appropriate penalty for a major crime since it resulted in a greater benefit to society than execution.[85] The influential eighteenth-century jurist, Beccaria, made a similar observation in 1764. He maintained that the strongest deterrent to crime would be 'the long and painful example of a man deprived of his freedom and become a beast of burden, repaying with his toil the society he has offended.'[86] Because their workforce was largely drawn from the idle, dissolute and dangerous, planters could rationalise the ill-usage to which their servants were subjected. It was easy to argue that those condemned into service by magistrates, higher courts and military tribunals were paying for past indiscretions. As we have seen, the owners of convict labour could maintain that they were engaged in a public good in that plantation work was an ideal mechanism for inculcating the idle and disorderly with the habits of industry. As Newman put it, this was a class-based system of exploitation shaped by ethnic and religious prejudices, one in which 'English, Scottish and Irish convicts, vagrants, rebels and prisoners of war whose lives were forfeit, ... could be treated as disposable labour.'[87] Barbados provides a vivid example of how 'convictism' was the ideological precursor of plantation racism.

The profits generated through the employment of indentured labour enabled planters to accumulate the necessary capital to transition to slave labour.[88] After 1650, substitution with African unfree labour became increasingly common. After 1660 the demand for European labour in the Caribbean as a whole started to decline. Whereas in 1640 there were thirty European servants to every slave, by 1680 there were seventeen

[84] As quoted in Newman, In Great Slavery and Bondage, 72.

[85] Blackburn, The Old World Background to European Colonial Slavery, 85–86.

[86] Sellin, J. (1976) *Slavery and the Penal System*, Elsevier, Amsterdam, 66.

[87] As quoted in Newman, In Great Slavery and Bondage, 69–71.

[88] Beckles, Plantation Production and "White Proto-Slavery", 37.

slaves for every servant.[89] By the end of the seventeenth century it became uncommon for European bonded labour to be employed in field work as labour exploitation became increasingly racialized.

Changes in the Atlantic demand for European unfree labour meant that almost all criminals sold into service in the eighteenth century were purchased by employers in the American colonies. The supply of convict labour was further shaped by changes to the criminal justice system. Seventeenth-century penal transportation was constrained by its reliance on private interests. From the start it had been dependent on the market in Atlantic indentured labour, but market demand fluctuated. Some criminals were also worth more than others. Sex, age, skill and state of health could all affect cost, as could the offence for which the prisoner had been convicted. Arsonists, for example, commanded a particularly low price as employers weighed up the potential costs of industrial sabotage.[90] The crippled could be especially difficult to sell, and yet those afflicted with conditions that restricted their ability to work were over-represented amongst prison populations. In order to better utilize the Atlantic market for labour as a means of disposing of the bodies of the idle, dissolute and dangerous, greater state regulation was required.

The rise in conviction rates which accompanied the 1697 and 1713 partial demobilization of the armed forces provided further impulse for change.[91] As bridewells filled with an influx of felons sentenced to hard labour new legislation was prepared.[92] The Transportation Act of 1717 ushered in two important changes. It extended the scope of penal transportation to cover felonies other than those reprieved from the gallows. Second, it provided a financial incentive to merchants in the form of a subsidy to ensure that transportation sentences were actually carried into effect.[93] At least in theory, it was no longer possible for those seeking to

[89] Beckles, H. and Downes, A. (1987) The Economics of Transition to the Black Labor System in Barbados, 1630–1680, *The Journal of Interdisciplinary History*, 18(2), 228.

[90] Grubb, F. (2001) The Market Evaluation of Criminality: Evidence from the Auction of British Convict Labor in America, 1767–1775, *The American Economic History Review*, 91(1), 297.

[91] Meredith and Oxley, Condemned to the Colonies, 25.

[92] Throness, L. (2016) *A Protestant Purgatory: Theological Origins of the Penitentiary Act, 1779*, Ashgate, Abingdon, 134.

[93] Meredith and Oxley, Condemned to the Colonies, 28.

purchase the labour of prisoners to pick the most valuable and leave the remainder.

While 50,000 convicts were shipped to the American colonies in the years 1718–1777 colonial opposition to the importation of penal labour increased. Transportation was unpopular with colonial free workers as competition with unfree labour reduced wage rates, providing a powerful illustration of the ways in which free and unfree labour systems can be connected. In the end the American Revolution forced the issue. The war put an end to continued transportation and the new American Republic introduced legislation banning further imports. No convicts were sent to the Americas from English ports between 1777 and 1782 and while a small number were despatched from Ireland subsequent to this, the trade was soon abandoned.[94]

With no place to send convicts the British government warehoused those sentenced to transportation in hulks anchored in the Solent and Thames estuaries. The Hulk Act of 1776 was initially passed for two years in the belief that the trans-Atlantic trade in convicts would soon resume. With the loss of Britain's former colonies, it became apparent that a more permanent solution would have to be sought. The British government could at this stage have decided to embark on a national penitentiary programme of the sort advocated by Jeremy Bentham. Instead, it baulked at the costs, attempting instead to find alternative sites to deploy convict labour, settling in the end on Botany Bay.

The Botany Bay 'experiment' was shaped by a long prior history of the use of convicted labour in colonial settings. The scale of penal transportation to Australia, however, was unprecedented. In effect the British state used the labour of convicts to steal a continent. That act of theft was enabled by sentencing strategies. By the early nineteenth-century a substantial discrepancy had emerged in the terms served by prisoners sentenced to be transported and imprisonment. As convicts were questioned about their previous encounters with the courts on arrival in the Australian penal colonies, it is possible to use this confessional data to compare the variation in transportation and imprisonment sentence lengths (see Table 1.2).

Counting life as 21 years the mean length of a transportation sentence was 13 years compared to just 0.39 years for all previous convictions that

[94] Ekirch, A. (1984) Britain's Secret Convict Trade to America, 1783–1784, *American Historical Review*, 89(5), 1285–1291.

Table 1.2 Mean sentence length comparisons

	Sentenced to imprisonment		*Sentenced to Transportation*	
	Number	*Mean sentence length (years)*	*Number*	*Mean sentence length (years)*
Offences against the person	2987	0.22	1490	15.41
Offences against property	29,327	0.51	40,456	11.12
Forgery and offences against currency	326	0.90	947	13.82
Offences against good order	4467	0.15	215	10.54
Other civil offences	1317	0.24	1127	13.77
Offences against military discipline	1450	0.32	856	13.00
All	39,874	0.39	45,091	12.94

Note a sentence for Life was calculated at 21 years. Sources: Tasmanian Archives (henceforth T.A.), Con 31, 33, 40 and 41

resulted in a sentence to imprisonment. Even prosecutions for forgery and other offences against the currency, an offence which Georgian and early Victorian courts tended to treat with some severity, resulted in mean prison terms of under a year compared to nearly 14 years transportation. Some of the discrepancies in sentence tariffs in Table 1.2 can be explained by differences in sentencing court. Many of the former convictions reported by transported convicts are likely to have been awarded by magistrates' benches or petty sessions. While such summary courts were empowered to sentence an offender to a term of imprisonment in a house of correction, periods of confinement in these institutions were usually short—a matter of weeks or even days. The data nevertheless highlights the huge increase in tariff between sentences to imprisonment and transportation.

This difference in sentencing patterns was driven by economics. As imprisonment was costly, terms were kept short. This was true of both houses of correction and county gaols. By contrast, the minimum sentence to transportation was fixed at seven years in the seventeenth century that is much longer than any custodial based form of punishment. Unlike in the Atlantic economies of the seventeenth and eighteenth centuries, the labour of convicts was not sold to private sector buyers in the Australian colonies. Nevertheless, sentence length continued to be an important driver of the colonial economy. While the work performed by prisoners built the infrastructure upon which an expanding colonial economy depended, settlers further benefited from the labour of prisoners assigned to the private sector for free prior to 1840 and lent out at minimal rates thereafter. Although masters had to house, clothe and feed their convict servants, in the 1830s these costs amounted to an estimated 59 percent of a free wage (although, as we shall see convict resistance impacted on profit margins). While the amount of saving to the private sector fluctuated over time, the foregone earnings of convicts effectively subsidized the income of their masters.[95] In effect, the advantages derived from the colonial deployment of convicts were even greater since they competed with free labour, severely curtailing the bargaining power of the later. The manner in which convict labour and free labour intersected reveals the flaw in Smith's logic. It may not have been in the interests of the convicts to bend their backs for their masters in the absence of a wage, but those masters did not just benefit from the exploitation of convict labour. They also profited too from the manner in which the supply of unfree labour dragged down wider colonial wage rates. In any account, there were many ways in which labour could be coaxed out of the unwilling bodies of convicts and many of those systems proved useful in managing other descriptions of workers. Far from being an unprofitable pre-capitalist from of production, convict Australia rapidly developed into a vibrant economy in ways that would not have been possible without the technologies of surveillance and management that arrived in the wake of the First Fleet.

It is no surprise that in most years the demand for convict labour outstripped supply.[96] Available labour depended not just upon the number of convicts landed in the Australian colonies, but also on the length of time they were bound to serve without wages. Although the property rights the state acquired in the body of a convict were no longer sold as in the seventeenth and eighteenth-century Atlantic, the scale of profits that accrued from their exploitation still depended upon the length of

[95] Panza, L. and Williamson, J. (2019) Australian Squatters, Convicts and Capitalists: Dividing-up a Fast Growing Frontier Pie, 1821–1871, *Economic History Review*, 72(2), 582–583.

[96] Reid, Contumacious, Ungovernable and Incorrigible, 108.

time they were unfree. The upshot of this was that a recidivist's first encounters with the court system were likely to result in very short custodial terms followed by a 3318 percent increase in tariff severity when the court decided on a transportation sentence, rather than another term of imprisonment. That increase in time was necessary in order to make transportation profitable. In short, variations in sentencing were a court-based strategy aimed at commodifying convict labour.

Just as early flows of convict labour had catalysed Atlantic tobacco production and played a critical role in the mid-seventeenth-century sugar revolution, the deployment of convict labour in the Australian colonies generated considerable economic opportunities. Kenneth Pomeranz has argued that the scale of British colonial land acquisition played an important role in facilitating industrial development by overcoming a series of ecological constraints that would have otherwise blunted economic expansion. The seizure of colonial 'ghost acres' provided Britain with access to resources that could not be produced locally. A good illustration of this is the rapidly expanding Australian pastoral frontier.[97] By 1840 a third of all British wool imports were sourced from the Australian colonies.[98] In effect convict transportation provided the British wool industry with access to 23 million acres of pasture, significantly more than the 17 million acres of land under domestic agricultural production. Without the cheap labour of thieves minted through the operation of British and Irish courts it would have been have been difficult to secure those lands from their First Nation custodians, or put them into productive use.

Charting Convict Resistance

The purpose of this book is to identify the different ways in which convict workers sought to modify or challenge the systems of labour control they encountered in New South Wales and Van Diemen's Land. In the process we attempt to chart the scale of convict action in early colonial Australia. A count of convict worker organisation based on a survey of surviving court records, newspaper and absconding notices identified

[97] Pomeranz, K. (2000) *The Great Divergence: China Europe and the Making of the Modern Economy*, Princeton University Press, Princeton, NJ, 209–285.

[98] Southey, T. (1848) *The Rise and Present State of Colonial Wools*, Smith Elder & Co., London, 54–55.

over 10,903 instances of collective action (some taking multiple forms)—6433 instances in New South Wales and 4470 in Van Diemen's Land. While the book constitutes the first attempt to both quantify and analyse collective resistance by unfree labour for entire jurisdictions over a considerable timespan, it will not be the last word. Other researchers will find more cases than we have been able to unearth. Our research endeavours have also been curtailed by the constraints of the record systems at our disposal. The vast majority of cases that we have examined were documented because the collective action they detail was the target of some legal response. Many successful actions are likely to have escaped recording altogether.

Information about other cases has been lost as a result of gaps in the archival record. Many New South Wales benchbooks for the period 1820 to 1840 are no longer extant, including those of major urban centres including Sydney and Maitland. Surviving benchbooks afford an indication of the extent of action that we have been unable to enumerate. For example, the Campbelltown (New South Wales) benchbook for 1832–1837 contains over 130 instances of collective action by convicts. Although many Van Demonian benchbooks survive there are conspicuous gaps prior to 1820 and between 1826 and 1832. Indications of the lost instances are evident, again, from those that survive. The Launceston benchbook contained over 40 cases of collective action in 1825 suggesting that for this one police district we are 280 missing cases across this seven-year gap. If, as is likely, the trend in actions for Van Diemen's Land broadly follow those in New South Wales we estimate we are missing about 700 instances of collective action across Van Diemen's Land as a whole. As Fig. 1.1 shows there is a very noticeable dip in the number of cases we have identified for Van Diemen's Land in the late 1820s and early 1830s. Of course, the New South Wales records are themselves incomplete. Our conservative estimate is that our count is missing at least 2500 cases.

In the future it may be possible to plug some of these gaps. The digitisation of the Van Demonian conduct records should make it possible to reconstruct all collective prosecutions in that colony. This remarkable record series contains summaries of every charge brought against every convict. At time of writing digitised transcripts of all female conduct records are available, but only around ten percent of male convicts have been transcribed. Nevertheless, the broad trends are evident from the research we have completed to date. These are plotted in Fig. 1.1. While,

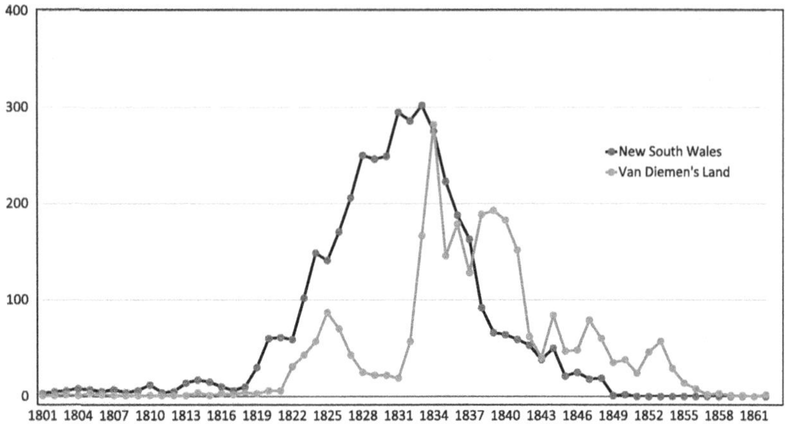

Fig. 1.1 Instances of prosecution for convict organisation by year 1801–1862

for all of the reasons that we have outlined above, the actual levels of resistance are likely to have been a good deal higher still, the chart graphically illustrates the sharp upturn in the number of convicts prosecuted for collective resistance in the years following the ending of the Napoleonic wars.

As we will outline in more detail in the next chapter, it is possible to use absconding notices placed in government newspapers to plug some of these gaps. In terms of the numbers of convicts involved, collective absconding was a constant problem faced by administrators in both colonies. Adding those who ran in company to the convicts collectively prosecuted for dissent, we found that convicts in Eastern Australia took part in at least 10,903 instances of collective action involving over 43,000 protesters. While many engaged in multiple actions and are thus counted several times in this total, it is still evident that a large proportion of those transported to Australia challenged their penal managers. In the first part of this book we detail the ways in which the colonial state attempted to incarcerate its charges. In the second we explore how the unfree sought to 'excarcerate' themselves by testing the conditions of service imposed upon them.

CHAPTER 2

Approach, Sources and Methods

This book focuses on Eastern Australia and particularly the colonies of New South Wales and Van Diemen's Land. While the vast majority of convicts arriving prior to 1850 were transported to these colonies a handful of skilled prisoners were sent to King George Sound in Western Australia in 1826 on the promise of indulgences. Despite the small size of this outpost, convicts colluded in an attempt to set work norms—threatening those who started their allotted task early and finished too quickly. Others absconded in the hopes of reaching the Swan River settlement where there were acute labour shortages or of joining sealing gangs.[1] One group left in protest, claiming never to have received the indulgences they were promised on joining the expedition. Listed as absconders in April 1830, five of the missing men were finally apprehended on the schooner *Eagle* in Hobart in June 1831.[2]

The small settlement at King George Sound aside, Western Australia's engagement with transported labour started later than the Eastern colonies. The first transport vessels to depart from Britain did not reach

[1] Young, D. (2020) Layers of Visibility: Convict Discipline, Crime and Punishment, King George's Sound, Western Australia, 1826–1831, *Studies in Western Australian History*, 34, 41–77.

[2] *Sydney Gazette* 13 April and 21 October 1830; ML Tas Papers 265, Hobart Police Office Letter book, correspondence 29 June 1831.

H. Maxwell-Stewart and M. Quinlan, *Unfree Workers*,
Palgrave Studies in Economic History,
https://doi.org/10.1007/978-981-16-7558-4_2

Fremantle until 1850. The 9719 convicts sent to the colony in the years to 1868 were selected in ways that differed from earlier transportation flows. Unlike the attempts to use convict labour to shape development in the eastern colonies, no women were landed in Western Australia.[3] Furthermore, all male convicts despatched to the colony had undergone periods of confinement in British and Irish penitentiaries or had served time in the Royal Naval administered convict stations located in Bermuda and Gibraltar. Many were disembarked already in receipt of tickets of leave, having served the bulk of their sentence confined elsewhere. Those that were not in receipt of tickets were more likely to be barracked in the confines of purpose-built depots and subjected to solitary confinement and other sensory deprivation punishments.[4] There are other indications that the experience of Western Australian convicts differed from those in the east. Mortality rates amongst ticket-of-leave-holders were surprisingly high, a reflection of poor pay rates and conditions of service.[5] This may explain the high rate of interactions between former convicts and the court system.[6] The ways in which these different experiences impacted upon both the form and scale of convict protest is deserving of further study in its own right.

The way in which transportation to Western Australian was foreshadowed by other attempts to mobilise unfree labour is also of interest. These included the deployment of child apprentices who had already served sentences as juvenile convicts in Parkhurst, as well as experimentation

[3] Hyland, J. (2020) 'The Vilest and Most Degraded of Human Beings': An Investigation into Why Female Convicts Were Not Transported to Western Australia, *Studies in Western Australian History*, 34, 147–163.

[4] Meinzer, N. (2015) The Western Australian Convicts, *Australian Economic History Review*, 55(2), 163–186; Winter, S. (2013) Legislation, Ideology and Personal Agency in the Western Australian Penal Colony, *World Archaeology*, 45(5), 802–811; Gibbs, M. (2006) The Convict Places of Western Australia, *Studies in Western Australian History*, 24, 71–97; Marshall, L. (2018) Surviving the Colony, the Impact of the Western Australian Convict System on Prisoner Health, 1850–1877, Ph.D. Thesis, University of Western Australia.

[5] Marshall, L. (2020) The Ticketer's Plight: Living Standards and Mortality Among Ticket-of-Leave Convicts in Western Australia, 1850–1877, *Studies in Western Australian History*, 34, 98–121.

[6] Godfrey, B. and Cox, D. (2008) 'The Last Fleet': Crime, Reformation, and Punishment in Western Australia after 1868, *The Australian and New Zealand Journal of Criminology*, 41(2), 236–258.

with Indian and Chinese indentured labour.[7] A distinctive feature of the Western Australian engagement with unfree labour is the manner in which the imposition of British law was used to mobilise and coerce Aboriginal labour. This preceded the arrival of European convicts, operated in parallel with that system, and lasted long after 1868—the date usually used to mark the ending of Australia's transportation era.[8] While these interactions lie beyond the scope of this book, they illustrate the ways in which the convict era continued to shape many aspects of labour organisation and control, including settler-Aboriginal relations, long after the arrival of the last convict vessel.

In Eastern Australia two colonies were hived off New South Wales, Victoria in 1851 and Queensland in 1859. Both regions received convict labour prior to this date. Moreton Bay penal station located on the banks of the Brisbane River was a particularly important site of secondary punishment. The Port Phillip district of New South Wales, which later became Victoria, was also first settled using convict labour. While some convicts moved into the area from New South Wales as part of the 1830s pastoral expansion, more crossed the Bass Strait as assigned servants and ticket-of-leave-holders in the employ of settlers from Van Diemen's Land. These played a critical role in the dispossession and disruption of Aboriginal societies in the years leading up to the establishment of Victoria.[9] Convict actions enumerated in these regions prior to the creation of the new colonies have been added to the totals for New South Wales.

Approach

The book examines convict dissent in its widest sense and tries to situate over 10,000 instances of collective action within the broader context of the hundreds of thousands of prosecutions of individual convicts for

[7] Moss, K. (2020) The Swan River Experiment: Coerced Labour in Western Australia 1829–1868, *Studies in Western Australian History*, 34, 23–39.

[8] Moss, K. (2020) The Swan River Experiment; Curthoys, A. (2020) The Beginnings of Transportation in Western Australia: Banishment, Forced Labour, and Punishment at the Aboriginal Prison on Rottnest Island before 1850, *Studies in Western Australian History*, 34, 59–77; Roscoe, K. (2020) Work on Wadjemup: Entanglements Between Aboriginal Prison Labour and the Imperial Convict System in Western Australia, *Studies in Western Australian History*, 34, 79–95.

[9] Boyce, J. (2013) *The Founding of Melbourne and the Conquest of Australia*, Black Inc, Melbourne.

Table 2.1 Five patterns of convict protest

Main category	*Sub-category*
Issue of demands	Demands
	Demands accompanied by threats
Appeal to authority	Petitioning
	Court action
Withdrawal of labour	Go-slows
	Bans and strikes
	Absenteeism and absconding
Compensatory retribution	Sabotage
	Theft
	Assault on individuals
Attack	Riot
	Mutiny, armed rebellion and bushranging
	Piracy

work-related dissent. We point to some of the inter-linkages between individual dissent and collective dissent, although there are many opportunities for further exploration of this issue. Once a sufficiently large database of individual cases has been created, it will prove possible, for example, to examine the relationship between the proclivity of particular employers to prosecute their servants and levels of resulting collective action.

In broad terms we have structured the book's analysis and chapters according to types, and to a lesser degree the location, of dissent (as in the case of attempted mutinies on transport vessels). Any organising principle has strengths and weaknesses, but we judged this approach most elucidating as well as facilitating comparison with dissent by unfree workers in other contexts. It also has an added strength in that it enables us to build on Atkinson's existing typology. He identified four patterns of convict dissent: attack (both verbal and physical); appeal to authority; withdrawal of labour and compensatory retribution.[10] We have added a fifth category—the issuing of demands—as well as a series of sub-categories (see Table 2.1). We have also reordered Atkinson's typology to reflect the manner in which convict action could escalate, one form of protest being followed by another if the first failed to achieve its objectives.

[10] Atkinson, Four Patterns, 28–51.

As E.P. Thompson pointed out, the poor are often observed only when they collide with the law. Reflecting this court records form a rich source of documentation for this book.[11] As a tool of historical enquiry, however, archival descriptions of the administration of justice are blinded in important respects. While court records capture details that might otherwise escape documentation, their coverage is limited to instances where relations between employers and their convicts became sufficiently fractured for one or other party to resort to the courts. That party was usually the state or the master. Further, it was not uncommon for prosecutions to be limited to ringleaders or a selection of those involved.[12] Thus, the court record only documents the tip of a wider phenomenon. Moreover, the way in which cases enter the archival record reflects the distribution of power relations, which were heavily tilted against convict defendants. The problem is two-fold—court records capture only fragments of convict relations with employers and the state, and they do so in ways that were both informed by—and designed to reinforce—the ideological underpinnings of a system of labour exploitation based on criminal conviction history. The court knew that each convict defendant (and for that matter convict prosecutor) had a tainted past—knowledge that shaped court outcomes in ways similar to the manner in which the operation of the law within plantation societies was underpinned by notions of race.

This said, a survey of all surviving court records is useful. To borrow Ann Laura Stoler's phrase, we have first attempted to read the colonial judicial archive along the grain before using the record of convict court interactions to estimate levels of protest.[13] Levels of litigation are indicative of the central role of the law in shaping labour relations, as well as documenting the nature and level of disputes. While the sheer number of cases provides a strong evidentiary base for identifying key issues, patterns and trends, the manner in which those cases are documented is also important. Usefully, court cases make frequent reference to wider

[11] Thompson, E. (1977) *Whigs and Hunters: The Origin of the Black Act*, Penguin, Harmondsworth; Hay, D. Linebaugh, P. Rule, J. Thompson, E. and Winslow, C. (1977) *Albion's Fatal Tree: Crime and Society in Eighteenth Century England*, Penguin, Harmondsworth.

[12] Byrne, P. (1993) *Criminal Law and Colonial Subject: New South Wales 1810–1830*, Cambridge University Press, Cambridge, 33.

[13] Stoler, A. (2008) *Along the Archival Grain: Epistemic Anxieties and Colonial Common Sense*, Princeton University Press, Princeton, NJ.

issues and patterns of dissent leading up to a prosecution. Instances where masters charged their servants for repeated insolence, neglect and disobedience were common and indicative of growing tensions built up over time. Such information is detailed in enough cases to elucidate a broader understanding of the extent to which rates of prosecution reflect both wider levels of dispute and particular chains of events. Typical was the case of Ralph Adams charged by Broadmarsh farmer William Stanfield with 'neglect of duty on Monday, insolence yesterday and repeatedly insolent to him for the past month'.[14] Similarly, in October 1835 when Sutton Forest farmer John Atkinson prosecuted Thomas Saile and John Morris for absence he complained that two days earlier they had been insolent, disobeyed orders and used abusive language. Atkinson also alleged that Morris had told him 'damned little work I'll do.'[15]

Importantly, we were also able to draw on an array of other sources that helped to place the record of prosecution contained in surviving benchbooks within wider perspective. The deployment and administration of convicts in the Australian colonies was documented in an impressive range of overlapping and cross-referenced records. Read in parallel with court proceedings, these provide a powerful means of documenting gaps in the former, as well as placing the operation of the law within the context of shifting labour market demand and individual convict bargaining power. This wider record is also useful in that it enables the prosecution process to be thematically and spatially mapped. The location in which each convict was deployed could powerfully influence prosecution rates. In part this is because surveillance was easier to maintain in some locations. Indeed, taking all of these sources into account, we think it likely that the prosecution of convicts in colonial Australia was better documented than was the case for any other group of unfree or free workers in the Anglophone world in the period 1788–1860.

Police or magistrate's office correspondence and letter books provide additional insights into the administration of the law. These often include discussion about the interpretation of legislation and the appropriateness of particular penalties. Colonial authorities attempted to ensure consistency, or at least guard against the prospect of court decisions being unwound by appeal processes. Diaries and private correspondence also

[14] M.L., Tas Papers 2, Richmond and Brighton Benchbook 13, 14 May 1835.

[15] Sutton Forest Benchbook, 5 October 1835.

proved useful supplementary information. Some masters recorded details of labour disputes, which for one reason or another, were never brought to court. Others wrote to the colonial secretary wishing to bring details of a case not presented in court to the attention of the colonial administration. They might for example, seek to intervene post-trial in order to secure mitigation of a sentence—a way of seeking to rebuild bridges in an attempt to secure future labour participation by valued workers. In other cases, they sought to influence the process by which labour lost as a result of court prosecution was replaced. On occasion masters might argue that other convicts who had not been prosecuted should be replaced as they strongly suspected that they had been complicit in actions such as haystack burning and cattle maiming or had provided support to absconders, secretly supplying absent convict servants with food and other materials.[16]

Colonial newspapers regularly reported court proceedings, especially those that took place in urban centres. On occasion this has enabled us to plug gaps in missing benchbook series. Newspaper reporting proved important for other reasons too. While the divide between those that had come free to the colony and those that had 'left their country for their country's good' remained an important colonial delimitator of class, colonial elites were far from unified. Access to convict labour, land and government salaried positions were all hotly contested. In both New South Wales and Van Diemen's Land the differing political opinions that resulted from these contests were reflected in the pages of the colonial press. Some newspapers supported the government line while others provided a mouthpiece for the administration's opponents. A small number of newspaper editors had themselves been 'lagged to the colony', to use a popular colonial expression, and their former experiences of servitude shaped the content and tone of the printed material they put into circulation.[17] These differences of view are reflected in the ways in which individual trials were reported. On occasion, newspaper reporting

[16] Others have used these sources to flesh out incendiarism activities like those on the Archer Estates in Northern VDL. Hindmarsh, B. (2001) *Yoked to the Plough: Male Convict Labour, Culture and Resistance in Rural Van Diemen's Land, 1820–1840*, Ph.D. Thesis, University of Edinburgh, 139–143.

[17] Ihde, E. (2005) *A Manifesto for New South Wales: Edward Smith Hall and the Sydney Monitor 1826–1840*, Australian Scholarly Publishing, Sydney; Woodberry, J. (1972) *Andrew Bent and the Freedom of the Press in Van Diemen's Land*, Fullers, Hobart.

of cases provided background information on the circumstances leading to a trial absent in official proceedings. The *Monitor*'s 1833 coverage of a case brought by Mackay, a Williams' River landholder, against one of his convicts reveals that the man had in fact been the ringleader of a wider convict protest. In this case the defendant was sentenced to receive 50 lashes for insolence and abusive language, plus an additional 50 strokes for contempt in abusing the magistrate who heard the case.[18] In other instances court proceedings and newspapers refer to efforts to incite collective action or garner wider support.

The administrative systems used to regulate the daily operation of the penal colonies were also of considerable use. As well as a means of circulating information about appointments to public office, new laws and regulations and other routine information, the *Hobart Town Gazette*, *Sydney Gazette and New South Wales Advertiser* and *New South Wales Government Gazette* published lists of absconded convicts. These notices include identifying details of the missing convict and details of the place where they absconded from and date of absence. Using this information, it is possible to reconstruct a detailed picture of absconding patterns as well as the rate at which convicts absconded in company. While this helped to plug gaps in the benchbooks, it was of further use in that not all absconders were charged and the trials of those that were did not always specify the location the convict had absconded from.

Finally, in the case of Van Diemen's Land we were also able to draw upon the conduct records. This voluminous series once existed for both colonies, although the New South Wales registers are no longer extant. For their time, these were impressive surveillance documents. Each entry is ordered according to police number, an identification system that enabled records pertaining to individual convicts to be easily cross-referenced. Other identifying details include the convict's name, place and date of trial, sentence and ship of arrival. The body of each record consists of a summary of each colonial court appearance organised by date of trial. As well as a brief description of each charge, information about sentence outcomes and the initials or names of the magistrates who presided over the case are also included. Entries often contain additional information on the date that tickets of leave and pardons were awarded or revoked and details of death, especially where the deceased was still under

[18] *Monitor*, 20 April 1833.

sentence. Many records include entries that were added after the convict had become free, especially further encounters with the colonial courts.

The conduct records not only fill important gaps in other series but help uncover and provide insights into the otherwise hidden networks of convict communication. For example, on 4 October 1822 Macquarie Harbour convict Alexander McCurdy was charged with neglect in losing his shirt. On the following day John Flynn (alias Trevor alias George Keefe) was charged with 'raising false reports by saying that a person named Alexander McCurdy that was punished yesterday for losing or making away with his shirt was punished innocently.' The significance of these events is further heightened by other administrative records that reveal that Flynn was the settlement flagellator and was responsible for administering the punishment he subsequently denounced as unjust.[19]

We estimate that there are over 400,000 individual trial summaries contained in the male and female conduct series for Van Diemen's Land. At time of writing, 120,000 of these have been digitally transcribed, coded and linked. This includes all 71,000 female conduct records, a task undertaken by the indefatigable Female Convict Research Centre. Together with a four percent digitised longitudinal sample of the larger male series, this has enabled detailed reconstructions of prosecution patterns by age, sex and skill. The same data can be used to explore associations between fluctuations in the colonial business cycle and rates of prosecutions and sentencing outcomes. While the colonial administration sought to pin the blame for prosecution rates on the recidivist proclivities of transported workers, digital data enables a detailed analysis of the way in which the operation of the criminal justice system facilitated colonial labour exploitation.

The organisation of conduct records places constrains on their use. This is especially true of the analysis of rates of collective prosecution. The series was originally compiled to facilitate the management of individual convicts. To determine whether an applicant was worthy of an indulgence, for example, colonial officials required access to a list of their prior peccadillos. The conduct records were drawn up to suit this administrative requirement. They are an individual record of prosecutions, each entry providing few clues to the identity of any co-defendants who may have also been arraigned on the same charge. To determine if a convict

[19] Alexander McCurdy, per *Dromedary*, Police No. 215, Tasmanian Archives (henceforth T.A.), Con 31-1-29; John Flynn, per *Guildford*, Police No. 110, Con 31-1-13.

prosecuted for 'neglect of duty' or 'refusing to work' was tried in isolation or in company with others, it is necessary to digitally transcribe and link all conduct records for those serving at a particular work location at a particular time. To date this laborious task has been completed for a series of important punishment locations including the Cascades, Launceston and Ross female factories and Macquarie Harbour and Port Arthur penal stations. A comprehensive analysis of the scale of collective prosecutions across all public and private workplaces must necessarily await the digitisation of each of these UNESCO Memory of the World registered records.

In addition to historical records we have also drawn on a growing body of archaeological research. Fieldwork conducted on convict sites like the Port Arthur penal station, convict constructed road-works, particularly in New South Wales, as well as female factories has provided additional insights into the operation of individual sites.[20] This research has not only yielded a more detailed picture of the extent and shifting terrain of convict

[20] See for example Karskens, G. (1986) Defiance, Deference and Diligence: Three Views of Convicts in New South Wales Road-Gangs, *Australian Historical Archaeology*, 4, 17–28; Casella, E. (2001) To Watch or Restrain: Female Convict Prisons in 19th-Century Tasmania, *International Journal of Historical Archaeology*, 5(1), 45–72; Parham, D. and Noble, B. (1994) *Convict Probation Stations Archaeological Survey*, Tasmanian Archaeological Society, Hobart; Tuffin, R. Gibbs, M. Roberts, D. Maxwell-Stewart, H. Roe, D. Steele, J. Hood, S. and Godfrey, B. (2019) *Convict Labour Landscapes, Port Arthur 1830–1877*, www.convictlandscapes.com.au; Tuffin, R. and Gibbs, M. (2020) The Archaeology of the Convict Probation System: The Labor Landscapes of Port Arthur and the Cascades Probation Station, 1839–1855, *International Journal of Historical Archaeology*; Tuffin, R. and Gibbs, M. (2020) 'Uninformed and Impractical'? The Convict Probation System and Its Impact Upon the Landscape of 1840s Van Diemen's Land, *History Australia*, 17(1), 87–114; Tuffin, R. Roe, D. Gibbs, M. Clark, D. and Clark, M. (2020) Landscapes of Production and Punishment: LiDAR and the Process of Feature Identification and Analysis at a Tasmanian Convict Station, *Australian Archaeology*, 1–20; Tuffin, R. and Gibbs, M. (2019) Repopulating Landscapes: Using Offence Data to Recreate Landscapes of Incarceration and Labour at the Port Arthur Penal Station, 1830–1877, *International Journal of Humanities and Arts Computing*, 13(1–2), 155–118; Tuffin, R. and Gibbs, M. (2018) Early Port Arthur: Convict Colonization and the Formation of a Penal Station in Van Diemen's Land 1830–1835, *International Journal of Historical Archaeology*, 23(3), 568–595; Tuffin, R. Gibbs, M. Roberts, D. Maxwell-Stewart, H. and Roe, D. et al. (2018) Landscapes of Production and Punishment: Convict Labour in the Australian Context, *Journal of Social Archaeology*, 18(1), 50–76; Tuffin, R. (2018) Convicts of the "Proper Description": The Appropriation and Management of Skilled Convict Labour, *Labour History*, 114, 69–92; Tuffin, R. (2013) Australia's Industrious Convicts: A Reappraisal of Archaeological Approaches to Convict Labour, *Australian Archaeology*, 76(1), 1–12; Tuffin, R. (2008) 'Where the Vicissitudes of Day and Night Are Not Known': Convict

work activities, but has also enabled the mapping of digitised archival content. This physical and geographical dimension has been important in analysing differences in prosecution and punishment patterns across different landscapes of production and punishment. It has also enabled the ground truthing of many historical record series, particularly site and building plans. Our book draws on this work. We anticipate, however, that future work in this area will do much to improve understandings of the geography of control and resistance in colonial Australia.

This book largely focuses on collective action as this was invariably read by the colonial administration as a threatening act. This is not to say that many individual prosecutions stemmed from acts that might be regarded as a threat to the distribution of power relations or were in other ways designed to ameliorate working conditions. James Major, for example, was charged in September 1833 with insubordination and 'wickedly endeavouring to injure his Master and Family by charging a Log of Firewood with Gun powder'. The summary of the case entered in Major's conduct record does not reveal whether this nineteenth-century improvised incendiary device was discovered before or after detonation in the Patterson family grate. The act, however, attracted a sentence of three years hard labour at Port Arthur penal station, the maximum penalty that a magistrates' bench was empowered to award.[21] Other convicts were individually charged with supporting acts subversive to the maintenance of discipline. Typically, these were also severely punished. James Wall was sentenced to 12 months hard labour in chains at Port Arthur for 'absence without leave on several nights and a suspicion of harbouring a runaway friend, his master's servant.'[22] Note here the use of the word suspicion. While harbouring was an indictable crime, magistrates often took the decision not to refer such matters to a higher court since to do so would require a greater burden of proof. Lower courts provided a convenient way of dealing with suspects without the risks and costs associated with referring a case to higher judicial authority, although the Quarter Session

Coal Mining in Van Diemen's Land, 1822–1848, *Tasmanian Historical Studies*, 13, 35–61; Tuffin, R. (2007) The Evolution of Convict Labour Management in Van Diemen's Land: Placing the 'Penal Peninsula' in a Colonial Context, *Tasmanian Historical Research Association*, 54(2), 69–83; Tuffin, R. (2007) The Post-Mortem Treatment of Convicts in Van Diemen's Land, 1814–1874, *Journal of Australian Colonial History*, 9, 99–126.

[21] James Major, per *Bengal* Merchant, Police No. 656, TA, Con 31-1-29.

[22] M.L., Tas Papers 291, Benchbook, 24 April 1840.

and Supreme Court were empowered to pass a greater array of sentences including a further term of transportation.

While we use evidence drawn from individual prosecutions in order to illustrate particular points, we have not included these in our running total of actions. It is worth reminding readers, however, that for every collective prosecution for work-related dissent there are many other cases where individual workers were charged with similar offences. This includes being absent, refusing to work, insubordination, neglect of duty, idleness, insolence, threats, sabotage and assaults on masters and mistresses. We have little doubt that many of these charges also stemmed from protest actions.

An additional issue associated with our approach is that an emphasis on collective action is likely to lead to significant undercounts in some workplaces simply because local circumstances limited the ability of convicts to collectively organise. This is an issue that disproportionally applies to female convict prosecutions. Convict women were distributed across many different colonial households. With the exception of government houses of correction, hospitals and hiring depots, it was unusual for more than three women to be deployed to a single location at any time. While men and women did participate in the same actions, the work that they undertook was often different and was organised in distinctive ways hindering cross-sex workplace collaboration. As the vast majority of convict women were deployed as domestic servants, they were under the eye (and feet) of masters and mistresses to a greater extent than male outdoor workers. That they were usually quartered in the main house meant that they also faced greater movement restrictions. Being caught with a man in the wrong place could render them liable to prosecution for example. We are not surprised that we have found less evidence for collective prosecution for dissent for female convicts compared to male. Importantly, however, convict women were at greater overall risk of prosecution than men. They were particularly liable to be charged with absconding—indeed we argue that the rate at which women absconded compared to men was higher than for any other category of unfree labour in the eighteenth- and nineteenth-century British imperial world. Strikingly, however, female convicts were much less likely to run in company compared to their male counterparts.[23]

[23] Maxwell-Stewart, H. and Quinlan, M. (2017) Female Convict Labour and Absconding Rates in Colonial Australia, *Tasmanian Historical Studies*, 22, 19–36.

We suspect that the approach that we have adopted also underestimates the degree to which convict protests were assisted by others. While many convicts chose not to actively participate in protests, they also refused to render assistance to convict managers when requested to do so.[24] As it was difficult to prosecute inaction, tacit support of this nature is rarely documented in court cases. Masters often suspected that convict servants who were outwardly loyal, provided succour to absconders and other protestors behind their back. Many free individuals also supported convict labour withdrawals. There were incentives for harbouring convicts on the run who would often work for ultra-low wages. Many female convict absconders were undoubtedly assisted by free and unfree men. It was unusual for absconder and harbourer to be charged together. It can be difficult to see the collective nature of some acts without linking separate court actions. This is particularly the case with the many women who contested the colonial state's authority to police their sexuality to maximise the amount of cheap convict labour available to service the homes of free colonists.

Finally, it is also the case that modes of dissent are not mutually exclusive. For example, in late January early February 1834 Wanstead estate landholder, Richard Willis, charged four workers with having potatoes in their possession. Two of these received 50 lashes and another two, charged with being insolent or slandering their master, received terms of six and twelve months in Notman's road party.[25] On 28 February Willis charged two more servants with stealing potatoes and another two with disobedience. Just over a week later he charged another four servants with refusing work, drunkenness and insubordination. Of these eight workers, five received 50 lashes while the others were sentenced to between six and twelve months on the Long Meadows gang.[26] These actions were undoubtedly interconnected. Disputes over food were widespread in convict Australia. The court records, however, afford no explanatory details of the circumstance that led to the prosecution, merely the charges

[24] For evidence of this activity see Hindmarsh, B. (2001) *Yoked to the Plough: Male Convict Labour, Culture and Resistance in Rural Van Diemen's Land, 1820–1840*, Ph.D. Thesis, University of Edinburgh, 139–150.

[25] M.L., Tas Papers 195, Convict Records, Campbell Town magistrates' return, 30 January and 1, 3, 4 February 1834.

[26] M.L., Tas Papers 256, Campbell Town Prisoner Records and Sentences, 28 February and 8, 9 March 1834.

and sentences. Nonetheless, in many instances the interconnections can be found, enabling analysis of the relationship of absconding and neglect to other forms of protest including refusals to work, assaults and revolts. These relationships operated at both a micro and macro level. At the micro level workers who had been punished for striking or go-slows might abscond.[27] For example in July 1834 William Call and Joseph Geley both absconded after being punished for their involvement in group go-slows. At the macro level we explore the extent to which the rate of absconding at a colony level was associated with reductions or increases in the incidence of more violent protests including assaults, revolts and mutinies.

Methods

Two relational databases have been used to organise and analyse information on collective actions. The first of these was developed in order to explore worker mobilisation in Australia in the years 1788–1900.[28] This records each instance of organisation by a group of workers, both informal associations (which includes all convict organisations, but also informal groups of free workers) and formal organisations of free workers, both unions and political bodies. Informal bodies involve no formal institutional arrangements (a governing structure, constitution or rules) and were mostly short-lived (though the same applies to the many unions that collapsed soon after their formation). At present the database includes files for over 15,700 organisations (free and convict). The main file records: the organisation's name (where formal), location, known dates of existence, leading activists or officials, objectives (for example, to campaign for better working hours); methods (go-slow, strike action etc.); links to other bodies where known; and the information sources used (for example, formal records, court case, newspaper reports). Sub-files deal with instances of strikes or other collective action, court proceedings, petitions and deputations, charges, outcomes, numbers involved and sources. The database also includes an annual summary file for each instance

[27] M.L., Tas Papers 277, Launceston Benchbook 15, 16 July 1834.

[28] For information the database and its application see Quinlan, M. Gardner, M. and Akers, P. (2003) Reconsidering the Collective Impulse: Formal Organisation and Informal Associations Amongst Workers in the Australian Colonies 1795–1850, *Labour/Le Travail*, 52, 137–180.

of organisation recording information like membership or the numbers involved (where known) for each particular form of action in a given year. Organisations or actions can be broken down by gender, numbers involved, occupation, industry and location amongst other options. It is also possible to view sub-files independently of the main file, for example scrolling through all strikes or all court actions.

Finally, the main file and sub-files contain quantitative information (including the number of workers prosecuted and the details of sentences awarded). These also hold a considerable amount of qualitative information, including names of activists, details on action or organisation and copies of some source material like newspaper reports. The database can store up to 10,000 words of qualitative information for an organisation, although entries for most informal bodies usually only contain several hundred words, sometimes less.

The second dataset is focused on Van Diemen's Land and was originally put together to explore the impacts of punishments and enforced removal to Australia on convict life course outcomes. A desire to better understand the way the past can influence the lives of subsequent generations formed an important secondary agenda. In order to explore these complex issues the dataset includes many digitally transcribed, linked and coded convict and non-convict records. These include Tasmanian births, deaths and marriages, military service, property valuations, bank accounts and post-1865 convictions.[29]

The dataset also includes digitised admission registers for some British and Irish institutions including Grangegorman female penitentiary, Dublin, 1840–1852; Millbank convict prison, London, 1837–1846; Pentonville penitentiary London 1842–1847, and all British Hulks (prison ships used to accommodate prisoners sentenced to transportation) 1834–1845. Many entries in these series are for individuals who were sentenced to transportation, but instead served out their sentences in Britain or Ireland or were pardoned. Others are for convicts who were sent to penal colonies other than Van Diemen's Land. These entries are useful in that they can be used to explore administrative decision making

[29] Godfrey, B. Inwood, K. and Maxwell-Stewart, H. (2018) Exploring the Life Course and Intergenerational Impact of Convict Transportation, in Bijleveld, C. and S Weijer, S. eds. *Intergenerational Continuity of Criminal or Antisocial Behaviour*, Routledge, London, 61–75.

which determined whether a convict would be despatched overseas, and if so, the colony to which they should be sent.

Data has also been added from surgeons' journals for 289 convict voyages to Van Diemen's Land sailing in the period 1817–1853. In the context of this book, this information was useful in that it enabled a more detailed study of the conditions that contributed to shipboard protest including attempted mutinies. On landing each convict was provided with a police number—an early example of the use of identifiers to aid the tracking of individuals. This number, together with the details of the ship of arrival, the length of their sentence and place and date of trial, were used to index all records subsequently generated in the colony. Every convict was also interviewed prior to disembarkation. Together with a record of their past interactions with the court system forwarded on the same vessel that carried them into exile, these testimonies provide details of place of birth, age, next of kin, religion, occupation, level of literacy and a statement of previous life circumstances including the number of times each man and woman had been convicted. Each new initiate into the penal colony was also measured to the nearest quarter inch and described. This process included the documentation of scars, injuries and other deformities, as well as eye and hair colour and the documentation of any tattoos.

Many additional record series were generated in order to assist with the operation of this complex unfree labour system. The most important of these were the conduct records (also known as the black books). As well as a summary of each charge, these registers include a detailed enumeration of every punishment down to each stroke of the lash applied to a convict's back and each day spent in solitary confinement or at hard labour.

Other digitised records include notices of appointments to the colonial police (the latter was largely staffed by serving convicts), details of prisoners transferred to different private sector employers, descriptions of prisoners who had absconded, applications for permission to marry and information about the receipt of tickets of leave (an early form of probation) and the issue of pardons and certificates of freedom. Before 1840 convicts in private sector employment were not supposed to be paid a wage. After that date a system of payments was introduced to distance penal transportation from any association with slavery. We also argue that the reintroduction of wage payments represented a belated state attempt to regulate the system of clandestine payments conceded by most private sector masters in the face of sustained convict tacit bargaining and other protests. Such payments were tracked through a series of registers that specified the duration of each passholder contract and the amount the convict would be paid. Finally, the deaths of convicts who were still under sentence were not entered into the civil registration system. Instead, these were recorded in a separate series of convict death registers.

This large collection of data has been useful in that it has enabled a detailed reconstruction of the operation of an important British penal colony. We have used this opportunity to explore the issues that provoked convict unrest, including oscillations in the rate of punishment over time and across different workplaces. It has also provided the means to examine the manner in which male and female workers experienced life in a penal colony, as well as variations in prosecution rates across different skill levels. For the 1840s, where information about passholder lengths of contract and payments are available, it has provided an opportunity to examine variations in working conditions across different regional and economic sectors of the colonial economy.

Importantly linked life course data can be used to explore the ways in which relationships between convicts informed various protest movements. Were those who had shared experiences of the same transport vessel or workplace likely to be prosecuted in conjunction for workplace actions, for example? An issue of particular interest is the extent to which the same individuals, or networks, were responsible for multiple protests over time. Access to longitudinal data has also enabled us to explore the manner in which different forms of action were linked and, importantly, the relationship between prosecutions for charges not normally associated with political activism and more overt forms of protest. For example, a prosecution for theft of rations might be linked to subsequent attempts to abscond or follow charges for refusing to work. Finally, access to total count data has enabled us to explore the ways in which those prosecuted for protest actions differed from all transported convicts. It has been argued in the past, for example, that the roots of convict protest can be traced to worker experiences in Britain in Ireland. Indeed, it was alleged at the time that the Irish were more prone to bushranging and other acts of rebellion, than British convicts.[30] It is also conceivable that groups of

[30] Maxwell-Stewart, H. (2015) "And All My Great Hardships Endured"? Irish Convicts in Van Diemen's Land, in Whelehan, N. ed. *Beyond the Island: Transnational Perspectives in Modern Irish History*, Routledge, London, 72.

workers with a history of labour activism, such as maritime workers, were more likely to engage in political protests in Australia.

It is useful that these two datasets have different coverage. The one formed to chart levels of collective action contains more information for New South Wales (indeed 57.5 percent of all instances of convict organisation) while the convict longitudinal database is firmly focused on Van Diemen's Land. To some extent, the strengths in one cover the weakness of approach in the other. Combined we hope that they provide a demonstration of the ways in which the work of digitising, cleaning, coding and linking archival records can aid radical new understandings of the past. The ability to reconstruct long-runs of data and read across multiple record series forms an important part of the approach we have adopted.[31] There are, however, other ways in which we have used the systematic organisation of digitised record collections to piece together early colonial labour relations. This has included the use of many newspaper articles, diary entries and other qualitative sources. Rather than forming a distinct approach, the events and people named in these accounts have been linked to database entries, enabling us to place these descriptive accounts within the context of other reported events.

Evolving data handling and analytical techniques as well as skills that are more advanced than those that we have managed to acquire are likely to enable others to use these datasets to derive further insights. Much more could be done, for example, by way of spatial and network analysis. These techniques could be used to plot the intersections between different life courses, management techniques and shared life experiences. We hope that this study encourages others to explore these issues in greater depth than we have been able to do here and, to that end, are committed to making the data that underpins this account accessible to future researchers.

Finally, we are conscious that previous attempts to use quantitative techniques to shed light on Australia's convict origins have been criticised as 'statist', in that they have tended to take data produced by the

[31] Barker, J. (2016) A History of History through the Lens of Our Digital Present, the Traditions That Shape and Constrain Data-Driven Historical Research and What Librarians Can Do About IT, in White, J. and Gilbert, H. eds. *Laying the Foundation: Digital Humanities in Academic Libraries*, Purdue University Press, West Lafayette, IN, 15.

colonial administration at face value.[32] We argue that such 'statism' has not been restricted to quantitative approaches. The ideology that helped shape the colonial archive has powerfully shaped wider attitudes to the nation's past, blinding us all to both levels of labour exploitation and the widespread resistance encountered by convict managers. While we agree with those who argue that deep reading is an important part of the historical process, we would argue that in a digital age counting and charting form essential constituent components of reading.[33] By combining quantitative and qualitative modes of working, we hope that we have provided the necessary framework to read the nation's convict archive along its epistemological grain and use that reading to place the many traces of convict radicalism within narrative context.

[32] Evans, R. and Thorpe, W. (1992) Power, Punishment and Penal Labour: *Convict Workers* and Moreton Bay, *Australian Historical Studies*, 25(98), 100.

[33] Moretti, F. (2005) *Graphs, Maps, Trees: Abstract Models for a Literary History*, Verso, London; Godfrey, B. Homer, C. Inwood, K. Maxwell-Stewart, H. Read , R. and Tuffin, R. (2021) Crime, Penal Transportation and Digital Methodologies, *Journal of World History*, 32(2), 241–260.

CHAPTER 3

Convict Eastern Australia: Labour Bureaucracy or Police State?

This chapter provides a detailed description of the transportation process from hulks to the convict vessels sailing to Australia and their immediate reception. It describes the bureaucratic processes for organising labour exploitation included the ways in which convicts were described and monitored. It also explores the evolving structure of convict employment, the graduated scale of confinement and punishment and rationing levels. A particularly important part of the chapter will be its examination of the role of the convict police, overseers, watchmen, matrons and other unfree managers of convict labour. It will also describe the use of penal stations, road gangs and female factories as well as tickets of leave, and reward systems for apprehending absconders, bank accounts and other inducements and incentivisation mechanisms.

The Demise of the Commonwealth Thieves

Initially there was some debate about what a sentence to transportation meant. Prior to the decision to despatch the First Fleet to Botany Bay, the British Government had toyed with the idea of setting up a convict colony in the Gambia River on the West Coast of Africa. By the late eighteenth century, the deployment of European unfree labour in the Atlantic had become problematic. Putting white convicts to work challenged the racial

H. Maxwell-Stewart and M. Quinlan, *Unfree Workers*, Palgrave Studies in Economic History, https://doi.org/10.1007/978-981-16-7558-4_3

division of labour that lay at the heart of the plantation economy.[1] There was also the small matter that there were no planters on the Gambia River to sell the labour of prisoners to. The proposed settlement was planned as a commonwealth of thieves—a place where the transported could be left to their own devices. The government committee set up to evaluate the scheme was scathing. Its report derided the 'Idea of composing an Entire Colony of Male & Female Convicts, without any other Government or Control but what they may by Necessity be left to be Establish themselves …'. Instead, it recommended that the labour of convicts be in future put to productive use.[2]

While some speculated that the convicts transported to Botany Bay would be exiled, but otherwise placed under no compulsion to work, this is not what eventuated. From the start the government claimed property rights in the labour of each convict for the duration of their sentence. It also assumed rights to all the other resources of Eastern Australia which were claimed as Crown lands. Yet, as New World experience had shown, land was useless without labour. While convicts provided the 'knotted hands' that would perform the work required to put former First Nation land to productive use, those hands still had to be compelled or induced to work. There were two models that pointed to alternative futures. One was Barbados a place where convict labour was literally worked to death in order to pump-prime the establishment of a plantation economy. The second was a more parsimonious option, where the settlement would be encouraged to become a self-sufficient out-post on the edge of the Pacific that might act as a resupply point for British shipping, but otherwise demand little in the way of governance or resourcing. While in this more benign model convicts might not be left entirely to their own devices, they would have a great deal of say of how they utilised their time outside of the hours of government labour. After the end of their sentence, they might also look forward to the opportunity of becoming a land holder and thereby escape waged-labour.

At first the convicts at Sydney Cove were housed in lines of tents separated by sex and placed under the keen eye of the marine encampment

[1] Christopher E. and Maxwell-Stewart, H. (2013) Convict Transportation in Global Context, c. 1700–88, in Bashford, A. and McIntyre, S. eds. *Cambridge History of Australia*, vol. 1, Cambridge University Press, Cambridge, 88–89.

[2] McGillivray, A. (2004) Seaman's Greens and Imperial Designs at Port Jackson: A Maritime Perspective of British Settler Agriculture, *Agricultural History*, 73(3), 261–288.

that was located between them and the site where the governor and officers were quartered. It was here, between the rows of canvas that the first convict was executed. As buildings started to spring up, little heed was paid, however, to formal planning and the rows of tents gave way to more haphazard alignments. Convicts were given time off to construct their own accommodation in the form of wattle-and-daub huts. The 'Rocks', a district that bordered the west of Sydney Cove where many chose to erect buildings, developed into a maze of habitations intersected by pathways and alleys.[3] Where attempts were made to impose architectural order, these met resistance. The 1788–1789 construction of a barracks for the marines was effectively undermined by convict go-slows and loss of tools.[4]

Government control was further loosened in the years when the colony's military officers were left in temporary in charge. In the interregnum between the departure of one governor and the arrival of the next the settlement's officers sped up the privatisation of the one important colonial resource, land—alienating considerable tracts for their own use. In order to garner political support, they also made smaller blocks available to time-served convicts and the marine rank and file. This move was calculated to undermine any attempts to reverse this distribution of government assets since to do so would invoke the ire of the colony's lower orders. In a significant subsidiary move, they broke the government monopoly on the convict labour supply, distributing a proportion of the convicts to the private sector.

As the number of free settlers grew, the practice of 'assigning' convict labour to the private sector became firmly established. Over time, a series of regulations developed to govern the process. In 1800 orders were issued to clarify a series of misapprehensions held by those engaging convicts.[5] Private masters were also expected to clothe and maintain their convict servants, supplying them 'with a ration equal to that issued by government'.[6] Not only was there a distinct lack of enclosing walls in the

[3] Karskens, G. (2009) *The Colony: A History of Early Sydney*, Allen & Unwin, Sydney, 71–74.

[4] Robbins, W. (2005) Spatial Escape and the Hyde Park Convict Barracks, *Journal of Australian Colonial History*, 7, 84.

[5] Government Order, 26 December 1800, *HRA* 1:3, 43 cited in Huf, B. (2018) Making Things Economic: Theory and Government in New South Wales, 1788–1863, Ph.D. Thesis, Australian National University, 136.

[6] Mann, *The Present Picture of New South Wales*, 23–24.

new thief colony, but there were no uniforms either. Convicts and emancipists dressed alike, rendering it impossible to distinguish the free from the unfree. In lower order farms on the edges of settlement there was little distinction between master and convict servant. When employer and employee set out to work, they did so in the universal garb of the colonial lower orders, the kangaroo skin jacket.[7]

The lack of walls also impacted on the arrangements for housing new arrivals. There were no barracks or other institutions designed to accommodate the government's charges. Instead, they were left to find their own accommodation. The majority rented rooms—although the payment of rent meant that prisoners required access to income. Convicts were permitted to 'work on their own hands' after the end of government hours. This was in stark contrast to seventeenth-century Barbados where the over-supply of prisoners, vagrants and rebels enabled masters to acquire rights over the convicts' entire working day. By contrast, labour shortages in Botany Bay meant that the sentence affixed by British and Irish courts acquired daily limits. For part of the day the convict's labour belonged to government, or to whomever they had been assigned, and the rest was to do what they saw fit with.

Within a few years of the establishment of New South Wales, wages started to be paid to convicts for informal work largely undertaken outside of government hours. While in part this helped to solve a growing accommodation problem, such wage payments reflected the shortage of labour and the resultant growth in bargaining power. Orders setting reapers' wages were introduced as early as 1795, with further orders issued in 1797 and 1800 in an attempt to check wage inflation.[8] By 1806 an annual payment of £10 plus rations, clothing and accommodation had been semi-formalised for assigned workers, reflecting the degree to which the financial payments had become the norm. Additional incentives were provided to workers engaged in other activities like lambing. Indeed, a common means of incentivising those entrusted as stockkeepers was to provide them with a third of the natural increase. These early measures provide an indication of the degree to which serving convicts in early New

[7] Dixon, J. (1984) *Narrative of a Voyage to New South Wales and Van Diemen's Land in the Ship Skelton During the Year 1820*, Melanie, Hobart, 85.

[8] For details on these and other work-related convict regulations see Quinlan, M. (2018) *The Origins of Worker Mobilisation: Australia 1788–1850*, Routledge, New York, 36.

South Wales and Van Diemen's Land were able to flex their industrial muscle.

As Dyster has observed, the payment of convicts had important benefits for the colonial economy increasing consumption and the development of goods supplied to satisfy local demand. This helped to ensure that the colonies rapidly transitioned into vibrant capitalist economies rather than some form of southern gulag.[9] Humphrys argues, despite the early Australian colonies encompassing the extensive use of unfree convict labour and a virtual absence of wage-labour, the 'English relations of production' (definitively capitalist relations) were present from the start.[10]

The detritus thrown into the wells at the back of emancipist houses in the Rocks district of Sydney provides physical evidence of the extent of this. Fragments of Chinese export porcelain, glass decanters made in the English city of Newcastle and creamware from the Staffordshire potteries have been recovered by archaeologists.[11] These were objects that were beyond the means of the majority of the British and Irish poor, suggesting that forced relocation to the Australian colonies might result in material gains. The extent of property ownership amongst former convicts underscored the point. By the close of the Napoleonic Wars many hundreds had secured land grants of between 20 and 50 acres scattered along estuarine littorals and the banks of river systems.[12] This reflected Atlantic precedents. The practice of providing 'freedom dues', usually in the form of small blocks of land, to time-served convicts and indentured servants was common in many British seventeenth and eighteenth-century colonies. While enclosure severely diminished working-class access to land in the British Isles, transportation restored it in the colonies. Other emancipists

[9] Dyster, B. (1979) Argentine and Australian Development Compared, *Past and Present*, 84, 91–110; Dyster B. ed. (1996) *Beyond Convict Workers*, Department of Economic History, University of New South Wales, Sydney. For other research on the ongoing role of wages and cash in the convict economy see Dillon, M. (2008) Convict Labour and Colonial Society in the Campbell Town Police District, 1820–1839, Ph.D. Thesis, University of Tasmania.

[10] Humphrys, E. (2012) The Birth of Australia: Non-Capitalist Social Relations in a Capitalist Mode of Production? *Journal of Australian Political Economy*, 70, 111.

[11] Karskens, G. (1999) *Inside the Rocks: The Archaeology of a Neighbourhood*, Hale and Iremonger, Sydney, 48–74.

[12] Wegman, I. (2018) Water Wise: How Rivers Shaped a Colony, *Tasmanian Historical Research Association Papers and Proceedings*, 65(3), 45–60.

acquired property in urban areas where many were operating businesses as fishmongers, butchers, brewers, bakers, shoemakers or were otherwise engaged in commercial activity.

Property acquisition amongst serving convicts and emancipists was accelerated by shortages of hard currency which ensured that labour was often renumerated in-kind. An 1814 government order attempted to put a break on the practice, proscribing payment in goods in order to reduce the amount of private property, particularly livestock, controlled by convicts. This attempt at regulation appears to have been widely ignored.[13] Payments in kind were particularly common in the agricultural sector where workers were paid in wheat at harvest time or received a percentage of the natural increase in stock, in effect providing them with a share of the means of production. This was in distinct contrast to Britain where such payments rapidly reduced in the eighteenth and early nineteenth-century as waged labour became more prevalent. As others have pointed out, that many convicts were sentenced to transportation for stealing goods from the workplace was itself a reflection of the extent to which traditional ways of renumerating workers were increasingly criminalised.[14] It was ironic that the actions of the law could result in a reversal of that process.

The height of the colonially born provides an indication of the degree to which transportation could result in colonial advantages. A diet rich in protein and a relative absence of childhood disease ensured that, on average, the offspring of convicts grew up tall—so tall in fact that they were known as 'cornstalks'. For many, it seemed improbable that thieves could produce such fine progeny. As one commentator put it: 'All our six-feet high native boys and girls have sprung from these "reprobates"'.[15] The children of convicts looked athletic in comparison to free British migrants. As one press report had it, 'a native "cornstalk"' could take on 'any foreign sapling'.[16] This added further to the confusion of visitors to Botany Bay, as height could not be used as a gauge of class—as

[13] McKay, A. (1958) The Assignment System of Convict Labour, Van Diemen's Land 1824–1842, M.A. Thesis, University of Tasmania, 18.

[14] Nicholas, S. and Shergold, P. (1988) Convicts as Workers, in Nicholas, S. ed. *Convict Workers*, 64–65.

[15] Molloy, J. (2000) *The Native-Born: The First White Australians*, Melbourne University Press, Melbourne, 23.

[16] *Australian*, 7 January 1831.

was common in Europe. While the Australian penal colonies never quite became a Commonwealth of Thieves, they started out as places that enjoyed a surprising array of freedoms.

Those freedoms were not an inevitable outcome. From the first days of the colony there had been concerted efforts to drive its development in an altogether different direction. Governor Philip sought to establish a number of planned settlements. The first of these at Parramatta was, as Karskens points out, designed to mimic the geography of a British country estate. A new government house was erected on a hill surrounded by its own parklands with neat rows of whitewashed workers cottages forming an avenue that led up to the gates. This was an ordered geographical arrangement that stood in distinct contrast to the disorder of the Rocks.[17] In both New South Wales and Van Diemen's Land there were repeated attempts to count people, livestock and property and to otherwise measure the thief colony, placing it in charted space where the extent of property could be defined and protected in law. Regulations were first passed to number Sydney's houses in 1789 although the frequency with which these were repeated provides an indication of the degree to which the imposition of cadastral order was resisted.[18]

Philip used ganged labour to create public farms, the first of which was established at Toongabbie in 1791. The clearing of ground was particularly brutal work and the government attempted to use such public labour to set the official hours of work. Soon, however, the government was forced to revert to task-work, a system of labour organisation that incentivised convicts by providing the opportunity to gain access to greater amounts of free time. Tellingly the amount of land each convict was expected to hoe was first set at sixteen rods, subsequently halved to eight and then reduced still further to seven, after a convict deputation raised the issue directly with the governor. Public farming also proved unpopular with settlers (both those who had come free and emancipists) as it cut off supplies of labour and provided agricultural competition.

The public farms, however, had a wider utility. Despite the successful way in which ganged convicts managed to negotiate reductions in labour

[17] Karskens, *The Colony*, 80–81.

[18] Karskens, G. (1997) The Dialogue of Townscape: The Rocks and Sydney, 1788–1820, *Australian Historical Studies*, 27(108), 105.

load, Toongabbie emerged as the colony's first site of punishment. Organised on a plantation model, with barracked accommodation in tents and gangs supervised by overseers, it was a place that could be used to extract pain through toil. Work intensity was invariably greater on land that required breaking in, as opposed to established properties. Levels of violence against slaves in Jamaica peaked in the first half of the eighteenth-century, for example, when many new sugar plantations were being carved out from frontier land.[19] As well as providing a site where those who refused to toe the government line could be chastised, Toongabbie had the further advantage of being removed from the temptations of Sydney. Constant cropping, however, quickly depleted the soils and the site was soon turned over to pasture. The process of clearing land had to start anew.[20]

Castle Hill farm, an enormous undertaking that involved the labour of some six hundred convicts marked a conscious attempt to tilt the trajectory of the colony back in favour of government. The first convict barracks was erected there. A stone-built structure designed to contain the labour force at night, effectively controlled the use of their time at the end of the working day. As Karskens put it: 'convicts could now be locked up, watched and counted'. This effort to impose the state's will on convict bodies triggered Australia's first, and most serious, rebellion. When the soils at this settlement were exhausted, however, Castle Hill was wound down.[21]

There were other early attempts to increase the ways in which convicts were regulated. In 1816 Governor Macquarie issued an order specifying that assigned convicts were to be paid a wage of £10 per annum for men and £7 for women in addition to rations. A set of more specific task-based or piece rates were set for predominantly rural work like tree-felling, burning and stump removal, reaping, threshing, husking, splitting palings, shelling corn and planting. These regulations were a continuation of measures aimed at capping remuneration for convicts who possessed skills that were in demand. In his account of New South Wales and Van Diemen's Land published in 1819, Wentworth lamented that government

[19] Burnard, T. and Garrigus, J. (2018) *The Plantation Machine: Atlantic Capitalism in French Saint-Domingue and British Jamaica*, University of Pennsylvania Press, Philadelphia, 38.

[20] Karskens, *The Colony*, 84–88.

[21] Karskens, *The Colony*, 89–90.

demand for convict construction workers and mechanics such as blacksmiths, coopers, and harness-makers drove up private sector rates of pay. These could be as high as eight to ten shillings per day. Wentworth's suggestion that a cap be placed on payments to convicts prefigured later recommendations.[22]

In the short run, imposing controls on convict access to free time proved key to curbing convict wage inflation. One of Macquarie's first acts was to appoint a town crier and bell ringer. Drums and church bells were also used to mark the start and end of the working day, a means of curtailing attempts by convicts to strike different workplace deals aimed at negotiating greater time on their own hands.[23] The erection of Hyde Park Barracks in 1819 marked a further concerted government effort to wrest back control of time. Before its construction the norm for the convict working day was eight hours in summer and six in winter. After the completion of the barracks inmates had to work from sunup to sunset, or twelve hours in summer and nine in winter. They also lost the right to earn money by working in the private sector in what little time was left to them and were, for the first time, forced into uniform. When they left the confines of the institution in which they were confined outside of working hours they were clothed in government slops marked P. B. (short for Prison Barracks) and emblazoned with the broad arrow—the mark of government property. The completion of Hyde Park barracks helped to set a new labour standard. No wonder the front of the building was emblazoned with a clock, a monument to the building's success in imposing industrial work discipline. The building set the pace for what was to come.[24]

[22] Wentworth, W.C. (1819) *Statistical, Historical, and Political Description of the Colony of New South Wales and Its Dependent Settlements in Van Diemen's Land with a Particular Enumeration of the Advantages Which These Colonies Offer for Emigration, and Their Superiority in Many Respects Over Those Possessed by the United States of America*, G & WB Whittaker, London, 55–56 and 189.

[23] Karskens, The Dialogue of Townscape, 109.

[24] Robbins, Spatial Escape, 92.

Profiting from Pain

The rapid increase in convictions that followed the post-Napoleonic War demobilisation of the army and navy sorely tested the resources of the British government. As can be seen from Fig. 3.1, the unfree share of the European adult population of New South Wales rose from 21 percent in 1816 to 60 percent in 1820. Concerned about the rise in the numbers of transported convicts, the Secretary of State for the Colonies instigated an enquiry into the costs and efficacy of the Australian penal settlements. The man he appointed to conduct that review was John Thomas Bigge, a former chief justice of Trinidad. A sugar colony captured from the Spanish in 1797, Trinidad was unusual amongst Britain's early nineteenth-century Caribbean plantation economies.[25] Rather than suffering from depleted soils, the results of years of sugar monoculture, it remained surprisingly fertile and possessed large tracts of land ripe for cultivation. Accordingly, planters imported large numbers of slaves in the first decade of the nineteenth-century in order to capitalise on these advantages. The labour of these 'saltwater' arrivals was used to substantially increase the area under cane. The cutting-out of new land was always backbreaking work. During Bigge's four years in office the island could perhaps best be described as in the throws of a sugar revolution—a process catalysed by the exploitation of large amounts of bonded labour.[26]

By contrast early colonial Australia seemed backward and outdated. Bigge was shocked at the number of convicts who remained under the control of government and disapproved of previous policies aimed at reducing the resultant maintenance costs. Many convicts were pardoned after a few years of service, effectively throwing them on their own hands thereby forcing them to find the wherewithal to maintain themselves. The related policy of granting emancipists blocks of land of 50 acres or less was also aimed at ensuring self-sufficiency. Likewise, the small number of female convicts who arrived in the colony were encouraged to marry so that their husbands could provide for them—their labour not being

[25] Bigge almost certainly got his former job because of his knowledge of Spanish and Spanish law obtained as part of his training in Madeira. Bennett, J. (1966) Bigge, John Thomas (1780–1843), *Australian Dictionary of Biography*, Melbourne University Press, Melbourne, 99–100.

[26] Meredith, J. (1988) *The Plantation Slaves of Trinidad, 1783–1816: A Mathematical and Demographic Enquiry*, Cambridge University Press, Cambridge, 1–7 and 43–51.

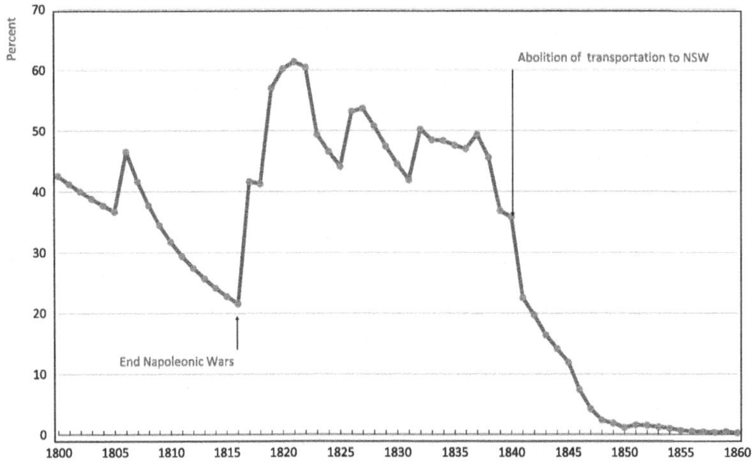

Fig. 3.1 Convicts as a percentage of adult European population of New South Wales (*Sources* Butlin, N. G. , Ginswick, J. and Statham, P. (1987) The Economy Before 1850, in W. Vamplew (ed.) *Australians Historical Statistics*, Cambridge University Press, Cambridge, 104; Sturma, M. (1983) *Vice in a Vicious Society: Crime and Convicts in Mid-Nineteenth Century New South Wales*, University of Queensland Press, St. Lucia, 188)

considered particularly useful. These cost cutting measures, together with the other concessions wrought by convicts, contrasted strongly with the condition of slaves in Trinidad.

Bigge particularly disapproved of the practise of assigning convict labour to emancipists. Appalled at the laxity of master, servant relationships on small-scale farms, he hoped that by encouraging an appropriate settlement pattern convicts could be placed in a more appropriate deferential environment—one that might be better calculated to affect their moral reformation. Impressed by the estates of some of the former officers of the military garrison, he recommended that future grants of land should only be made to settlers with at least £500 in capital. He also advocated an extension of the practice of 'assigning' convict labour, but only to private individuals of means. His hope was that cheap land and labour could be used to attract migrants with capital from the British Isles. Instead of sugar (which will not grow commercially in southeast

Australia), he thought that such a policy would encourage the production of fine wool, lessening the British woollen industry's dependence on European suppliers.[27] He perceived that the transplanting of a landed élite would reproduce the hierarchy and stability evident in both the British rural landscape and the world of the slave plantation. That is, a notion of hierarchy that embodied a social ordering which would seek to legitimize power through the exercise of local paternalism. In short, this would be a society that would reward the 'deserving' while expecting all those dependent on the master resident in the big house to curtsey, remove hat and touch forelock.[28]

In effect this was an expanded version of Philip's vision for Parramatta. A series of agricultural districts each of which might be administered by a genteel landed élite who would supervise the construction of 'substantial' ordered cottages for tenant farmers and neat barracks for estate workers. An Anglican church and a school, and perhaps even a benefit society, might sit at the heart of each settlement, alongside a courthouse, a watch-house and a range of solitary cells. From these rural centres 'concentric rings of economic clientship' might extend outwards encompassing all manner of service industries which depended on the business of the estate and its settlement annexe.[29] It was hoped that tight local control coupled with a system of obligations and acquired rights would extinguish the petty disputes, illicit distilling and stock theft which was thought to characterise the haphazard settlement fostered under the early governors. For, as E. P. Thompson argued, gentry everywhere make a habit of labelling the mass of common people who exist outside of their control as 'idle and disorderly'.[30]

Bigge believed that such an arrangement would not only save public money but would inculcate British and Irish criminals with an appropriate set of values. They would learn to respect their betters, while receiving guidance from their masters. In short, he wished to inject the paternalism

[27] Evans, Creating an 'Object of Real Terror', 48–61; Boyce, J. (2008) *Van Diemen's Land*, Black Inc., Melbourne, 145–174.

[28] Newby, H. (1975) The Deferential Dialectic, *Comparative Studies in Society and History*, 17, 151–153.

[29] Roe, M. (1965) *Quest for Authority in Eastern Australia, 1835–51*, Melbourne University Press, Melbourne, 48–50.

[30] Thompson, E.P. (1974) Patrician Society, Plebian Culture, *Journal of Social History*, 7(4), 385.

of the plantation into New South Wales and Van Diemen's Land. He was not averse to injecting a little terror either, advocating that the state should expand the number of road gangs, chain gangs, penal stations and female houses of correction. These would be places where recalcitrant convicts who refused to obey their masters' orders could be sent.

To this end he recommended an expansion in the number of penal stations, although in effect this was already underway. These were places of extreme toil, remote labour camps where the most disorderly elements of the convict population could be sent to suffer. The first such site had been established at Newcastle in the wake of the 1804 Castle Hill rebellion. The second was opened further up the New South Wales coast at Port Macquarie in 1821. This was followed by Wellington Valley in the Hunter region in 1823 and Norfolk Island and Moreton Bay the following year. A parallel system developed in Van Diemen's Land. Macquarie Harbour was established in 1822 on the remote west coast and Maria Island on the opposite side of the island in 1825. The last penal station to be established in Eastern Australia was at Port Arthur on the Tasman Peninsula. This was set up in 1830 following the decision to abandon Maria Island and Macquarie Harbour.[31] While a few women were sent to penal stations, the principal disciplinary device set up to control female convicts was a system of houses of corrections, or factories as they were commonly known. These complex institutions were composed of multiple yards or divisions, one of which was reserved for the 'crime class'—a term used to describe those sentenced to hard labour.

The intention was that convicts sent to these places of punishment would be kept at unremitting toil engaged in the most labour-intensive tasks. In convict parlance these sites constituted something of an underworld. Macquarie Harbour penal station was referred to as Pluto's Land.[32] Penal stations were designed to extract pain from convict bodies. The extent to which these sites of coercion succeeded in their objective can be measured in graves. The death rate for the convicts that laboured in the gangs at Port Arthur was four times greater than those engaged in

[31] Evans, Creating an Object of 'Real Terror', 59–60; Roberts, D. (2006) The Valley of the Swells, 'Special' or 'Educated' Convicts on the Wellington Valley Settlement, 1827–30, *History Australia*, 3, 11–21.

[32] Maxwell-Stewart, H. (2008) *Closing Hell's Gates: The Death of a Penal Station*, Allen and Unwin, Sydney, 1.

assigned service.[33] The penal stations and female factories were genuine innovations. It would have been impossible, for example, to implement such a system in Trinidad. No master would ever seek to extract labour from a slave beyond the point that it was economic to do so. The difference in the forms of unfreedom that anchored convict and slave in place enabled the establishment of a more complex system of labour extraction in the Australian penal colonies.

Unlike the Caribbean, it was the government who possessed property rights in the sentence that condemned each convict to colonial servitude. While the state chose to temporarily assign those property rights to masters where it suited their interests to do so, it also possessed the ability to absorb the costs associated with the production of pain. The post-Bigge penal landscape was populated by many different working experiences. The assigned servant who laboured on a country estate, or worked in an urban business, occupied one end of that scale, while the penal labourer, to use a phrase coined by Evans and Thorpe, condemned to a penal station or female factory washtub marked the other.[34] Behind the incentives that were primarily used to coax labour from assigned servants lurked the terrifying spectre of hard labour on 'short commons'. It did not matter if the majority of convicts never walked through the doors of the crime class yard or had irons hot-riveted to their legs in a penal station lumberyard, the threat was sufficient to make any prisoner think twice about answering back on not or performing their allotted task. As the Chief Justice of New South Wales put it, the object of a sentence to a penal station was not just to punish those who transgressed the law but 'to serve as a terror to others'.[35]

In between the extremes of the penal station and assigned service, Bigge also recommended an expansion of other, lesser forms of punishment. This included work in road parties and chain gangs. These were distributed the length and breadth of the settled districts. Men could be sent to such sites of coercion on a magistrate's order to labour for terms of up to three years under the ever-vigilant eye of an overseer. The work

[33] Maxwell-Stewart, H. (2012) Isles of the Dead: Convict Death Rates in Comparative Perspective, *Historic Environments*, 24(3), 26–34.

[34] Evans and Thorpe, Power, Punishment and Penal Labour, 90–111.

[35] Duffield, I. (1987) The Life and Death of "Black" John Goff: Aspects of the Black Contribution to Resistance Patterns During the Transportation Era in Eastern Australia, *Journal of Australian Politics and History*, 33(1), 30.

they performed built the colony's road system, as well as constructing its wharves and docks and supplying the brute labour required to develop the infrastructure that enabled the colony as a whole to turn a profit. Together with the female factories and penal stations these sites of coerced labour were calculated to induce 'obedient, productive and profitable' compliance in all convicts no matter where they were located.[36] This was a finally calibrated system that balanced the paternalism of the country estate with the pain of penal labour. Critically this landscape of punishment and obligation was underpinned by an expansion of the powers of the local bench. As Lauren Benton and Lisa Ford argue, magisterial jurisdiction in the Caribbean and Australian penal colonies became closely aligned post-Bigge.[37]

One of the key recommendations of the Bigge Report was the abolition of convict wages. Payments to prisoners were officially prohibited in 1824. Nonetheless, monetary incentives continued to be made to some who were still under sentence.[38] This was particularly the case for those whose services were crucial to the daily administration of the penal colonies. In both New South Wales and Van Diemen's Land the police were largely staffed by serving convicts. Convict constables were paid a small wage and were also permitted to supplement their income through rewards for apprehending absconders and other performance bonuses.[39] Government convicts lent out for harvest also continued to receive daily payments. Many masters found it convenient to make occasional financial rewards to convicts, even though these were proscribed by the rules governing assignment.[40] The aim of cutting convict access to ready cash proved hard to implement. Even public works convicts engaged in non-police work could gain access to money, although it was widely recognised that this could assist absconding and promote other activities that were frowned upon, especially gambling and drinking. Indeed, much of the

[36] Evans and Thorpe, Power, Punishment and Penal Labour, 101.

[37] Benton, L. and Ford, L. (2013) Magistrates in Empire: Convicts, Slaves and the Remaking of the Plural Legal Order in the British Empire, in Ross, R. ed. *Legal Pluralism and Empires, 1500–1850*, New York University Press, New York, 173–197.

[38] Lieut. Governor Arthur to Earl Bathurst, 7 July 1827, *HRA*, III, V:459.

[39] Petrow, S. (2000) Policing in a Penal Colony: Governor Arthur's Police System in Van Diemen's Land, 1826–1836, *Law and History and Review*, 18(2), 351–395.

[40] McKay, A. (1958) The Assignment System of Convict Labour, Van Diemen's Land 1824–1842, M.A. Thesis, University of Tasmania, 178.

evidence for the tacit ways in which convicts received pecuniary rewards comes from prosecutions for such activities. Two George Town Marine Department boatmen charged with gambling in the penitentiary courtyard at 2 p.m. on 15 September 1839 explained that they had obtained money for labour services. Johnson stated he was paid 18 pence to take some goods back to Launceston (boatmen typically travelled between this town and George Town). Although such payments were prohibited, they appear to have been commonplace.[41] It later emerged that pilots were in the habit of providing boat crews with payments if their work necessitated an overnight stay in Launceston.[42]

Rather than focussing on the total abolition of monetary rewards, the post-Bigge changes were designed to do two things. First, they attempted to remove the right to financial payments in return for work. There would be no more talk of a convict wage. Instead, financial incentives were provided as an indulgences—they were a reward for good behaviour not a right. Second, they sought to use such perks and rewards as a means of binding the interests of the convict to that of state and master. To this end the colonial administration established an elaborate system of convict bank accounts. Surgeon superintendents on board convict vessels bound for Australia were tasked with collecting any cash or property brought onboard by their convict charges. On arrival in Australia this money was entered into the Convict Savings Bank. Any sums subsequently earned by prisoners while still under sentence were supposed to be added to these accounts. This precursor of Samuel Smiles' self-help system was designed to prevent convicts from spending their accumulated petty cash in disorderly houses and taprooms while simultaneously providing a source of money from which fines could be paid.[43] It was one of a number of schemes calculated to encourage thrifty, prudent and deferential attitudes—the kind of behaviour that would prepare the convict for a post-sentence life as a free colonial worker.[44]

[41] Tas Papers 260 George Town Police Magistrate Letterbook, correspondence magistrate JP Davy to Chief Police Magistrate (CPM) Hobart, 15 September 1839 and sworn statement of John Johnson, 19 September 1839.

[42] Quinlan, M. (2018) *The Origins of Worker Mobilisation: Australia 1788–1850*, Routledge, New York, 244.

[43] Travers, T. (2016) *Samuel Smiles and the Victorian Work Ethic*, Routledge, London.

[44] Maxwell-Stewart, H. (2016) The State, Convicts and Longitudinal Analysis, *Australian Historical Studies*, 47(3), 417.

As the labour of convicts remained the property of the state and was subject to its direction and oversight, this meant that rations, bedding and clothing were all specified in official regulations. The organisation of labour in the public sector effectively set a benchmark for the private. At times these rules were altered following lobbying by private interests. For example, the regulation specifying that flour supplied to convicts should be made from wheat was amended in New South Wales in 1834 as a direct result of private sector pressure. The new regulations gave contractors the authority to substitute maize and barley for wheat.[45] In general, however, the masters of assigned labour were bound to conform to a series of government-imposed practices.

A network of commissariat stores was established to distribute clothing and food. Elaborate rules also governed ration levels in gangs and other public works, with an additional ration scale for those undertaking particularly strenuous tasks such as miners. This was the economics of Hyde Park Barracks writ large. While the post-Bigge reorganisation of the penal colonies led to a dramatic increase in the assignment of convicts, that process was anchored in the secure control over ration rates, working hours and other terms of service for convicts in government employ. After the publication of Bigge's recommendations it became unusual for convicts in government service to be accommodated in the private sector. In order to be granted the 'indulgence' of sleeping outside the walls of a government-controlled institution a prisoner had to apply for a special dispensation. This effectively removed the argument for convict control over the hours of their sentence that lay outside of the government working day.

As the prominent settler James McArthur put it to Bigge, 'A thief's most vulnerable part is his belly'.[46] Diet therefore played a prominent role in the landscape of terror installed across Eastern Australia in the 1820s. At one extreme, those condemned to solitary cells were restricted to bread and water—a diet that would have supplied an estimated 1400 calories a day. This was less than the basal metabolic rate for an adult male convict of average nineteenth-century height and weight. Even if they slept all day, a convict in solitary would be expected lose weight over the course of their punishment. The standard fare supplied to convicts in road parties,

[45] *New South Wales Government Gazette* No. 136, 8 October 1834.

[46] Quoted in Evans, Creating an Object of 'Real Terror', 57–58.

Table 3.1 Ration scale for male convicts in Van Diemen's Land

	Assigned servant	*Public works*	*Punishment*[a]	*Gaol*[b]	*Solitary*
Bread	1 lbs	1.25 lbs	1.25 lbs	1 lbs	1.25 lbs
Meat[c]	1 lbs	1 lbs	1 lbs	8 ozs	
Vegetables[c]	2 lbs	0.5 lbs	0.5 lbs	0.5 lbs	
Milk	2 pints				
Sugar	1 ozs	2 ozs			
Tea or coffee[c]	1 ozs	1 ozs			
Calorie estimate	4150	3250	3050	2050	1400

Source Tasmanian, 7 November 1834
[a]This was the standard ration supplied to punishment gangs, including chain gangs and those in penal stations
[b]A No. 2 punishment ration was commonly imposed as a sanction in road and chain gangs. We have assumed that this was equivalent to the goal ration
[c]Meat assumed to be boiled beef, vegetables to be boiled potatoes with skins, coffee scorched wheat

chain gangs and penal stations was substantially more generous, yielding over 3000 calories a day. While this compared favourably with British nineteenth-century diets, it was less than that required to sustain a convict engaged in very active labour, particularly in summer when the working day was at least ten hours.[47] Some convicts in punishment gangs were placed on a number two ration as a sanction. While the contents of this reduced diet are not specified in the standard scale, the suspicion is that this was akin to the gaol ration. If so, this was a substantial sanction. As the editor of the *Independent* put, it is perhaps little wonder that men on the No. 2 ration were frequently punished for plundering the potato fields of neighbouring settlers. As they noted: 'There is something very horrible in the idea of putting strong labouring men on half rations, and then punishing them for the cravings of nature'.[48] By contrast, the stipulated diet for assigned servants would have yielded around 4000 calories a day. The perversity of course was that work-intensity was inversely corelated with levels of energy supplied (see Table 3.1). As a result, hunger pinched the stomachs of the recalcitrant as surely as their backs were threatened by the scourge of the lash.

[47] *Historical Records of Australia*, III, 6, 101.

[48] *Independent*, 2 March 1833.

Salt meat was a particularly common dietary item in penal stations and remote road and chain gangs. Even when more centrally located, the supply of vegetables to convicts in punishment gangs was limited. Deficiency disorders were not uncommon and persisted largely because the conditions that gave rise to them were difficult to ameliorate without upsetting the carefully constructed ration scale on which the efficiency of colonial labour extraction relied.

In October 1832 an outbreak of scurvy occurred in the chain gang residing in the Hobart Town Hulk. An investigation by the Colonial Surgeon attributed the disease to the quantity and quality of food supplied, poor clothing (especially lack of shoes) and local sanitary conditions. He condemned the sleeping arrangements on the hulk in particular, foul bilge water having seeped into the convict bedding exposing the men to damp and cold conditions at night. The surgeon recommended the provision of a half-pound of 'potatoes or wholesome vegetables' per man and accommodation in a shed on land.[49] These recommendations were resisted by Roderic O'Connor, the Land and Roads Commissioner. O'Connor, who was also a prominent landholder and employer of assigned convict labour, opposed providing the Hulk gang with more rations than other parties, arguing that the issue was quality of the supplied ration (especially the flour) and not the quantity.[50] A hastily organised Board of Inquiry echoed O'Connor's views. Concerned at setting a dangerous precedent, the board recommended that any additional rations should only be supplied for a limited period.[51] Despite the implications for convict health, any local rise in the ration was likely to trigger convict demands for pro-rata increases elsewhere and was to be resisted no matter the medical advice to the contrary.

Breaches of orders on the supply of rations were accordingly treated as serious offences. In June 1833 James Littlejohn received six months hard labour for giving some of his master's flour to Charles Morgan, a convict in the Richmond Chain Gang who had been a former shipmate. In addition to sentencing Littlejohn, the court ordered Morgan to receive

[49] T.A., CSO1/1/618 14134, Correspondence Colonial Surgeon to Colonial Secretary, 29 October 1832.

[50] T.A., CSO1/1/618 14134, Correspondence Roderic O'Connor, 31 October 1832.

[51] T.A., CSO1/1/618 14134 Garrison Order and Report, 2 and 3 November 1832, and Correspondent O'Connor, 12 November 1832.

an additional 12 months' hard labour for receiving.[52] Two months later David Hardcastle, an assigned servant of David Lord, was prosecuted for supplying some meat and bread to a man on the chain gang. The bench rejected his plea for mercy, instead sentencing him to 50 lashes. In convict Australia charity could most definitely constitute a crime.[53]

Rather than the clandestine topping up of rations, a more constant problem was the way they were depleted by the operation of black economies. In the absence of wages, the ration became the means of convict exchange. Linus Miller reported, when stationed in the Hobart Penitentiary in 1841, that he traded nine evening meals for a pair of knee-breeches with a convict known as 'Timothy Greedy'.[54] On the then current government ration scale, this would have amounted to 3 lbs. 6 ounces of bread and nine pints of skilly (a gruel made from a mix of flour, salt and water). Such black-market trading provided a means of securing little luxuries otherwise denied to the prisoner, an opportunity to improve their condition in defiance of official stipulations. Importantly, however, convict black economies did not operate on a level playing field. As the assumed name 'Timothy Greedy' implies, some convicts were able profit at the expense of others. Before the ration ever reached the ganged convict it went through many hands. Convict butchers, cooks and overseers ensured that invariably the best cuts were siphoned off and the flour adulterated, if not by the contractor, then by the convict bakers themselves. Martin Cash reported that at Port Arthur a great quantity of the flour was purloined by those employed in the bakehouse, either for their own use, or to be issued as bribes to overseers.[55] The convicts who toiled in the gangs did not have such easy access to the stores and had instead to put up with the consequences of such corruption. Their diet was almost certainly more meagre than that stipulated in the official ration tables.

In the eyes of the convict administration food was a tool which could be used to discipline convicts by rewarding the good and punishing the wicked. For most convicts their best defence was to see the ration as a 'wage' earned through hard work, rather than an indulgence bestowed

[52] M.L., Tas Papers 325 Richmond Benchbook, 5 June 1833.

[53] M.L., Tas Papers 325 Richmond Benchbook, 15 August 1833.

[54] Miller, L. (1846) *Notes of an Exile to Van Diemen's Land*, McKinstry, Fredonia, 264–265.

[55] Cash, M. (1940) *Martin Cash, the Bushranger of Van Diemen's Land in 1843–4*, Walch, Hobart, 57–58.

by kind-hearted masters or other officials. The difference in viewpoint ensured that the level of the ration was a source of constant negotiation between masters and their assigned servants in the private sector and administrators and their convict charges in the public. One of the reasons for this was that, once in the convict's hand, food could also be used to barter (or gamble) for other articles such as pipes, tobacco, alcohol, sex, clothing and fishing hooks and lines. These were activities which enabled escape from the routine of daily convict life, or perhaps even the means to slip beyond the bounds of a penal station or road gang with the hope of securing a passage on an American or French whaler bound for liberty. It is perhaps not surprising that offences which involve the theft or illicit consumption of food are often encountered in benchbook proceedings. In convict Australia ration politics was serious business.

An Antipodean Carceral Archipelago

The landscape of punishment and production that emerged in Eastern Australia in the wake of the Bigge Report does not fit easily with the traditional view of the evolution of Western criminal justice systems. As Braithwaite has pointed out, these have been dominated by accounts of the rise of the prison, a process that commenced with the creation of bridewells and houses of correction in the sixteenth-century and culminated with the construction of the nineteenth-century penitentiaries that owed much to the philosopher Jeremey Bentham's design for a panopticon.[56]

Famously, transportation to Australia was opposed by Bentham, who saw a resumption of the overseas export of criminals as antithetical to the principles of his plans for an architectural surveillance machine. Convict Australia's lack of reliance on walls has encouraged the view that the founding of the Australian 'Thief Colony' marked an anachronistic turn in the history of British criminal justice. This was, it might be argued, something of an aberration subsequently corrected through the construction of London's Millbank and Dublin's Richmond gaol. It was these institutions, and the many penitentiaries that followed, that put British and

[56] Braithwaite, J. (2001) Crime in a Convict Republic, *The Modern Law Review*, 64(1), 11–14.

Irish correctional policy back on a Benthamite track.[57] The visual contrast between the bloodied, splayed prisoner bound to the triangles and the forbidding walls of the prison serves to reinforce the point. The first was a colonial exception to the metropolitan rule, a reminder of penal transportation's links to the plantation world of the Atlantic and the terrifying early modern displays of state power publicly enacted through the mutilation of the body of the offender. By contrast, the second was a pointer to the growth of institutional forms of power that were to increasingly shaped lived experience. In Michel Foucault's words, Bentham's design for a panopticon formed a blueprint—not just for a new form of prison—'but also for a hospital, for a school, for a workshop'. It was in short a template 'for all institutions'.[58] Foucault did not see these as constituting discreet edifices, but as interlocking disciplinary devices that acted in concert to shape a new form of citizenship. He saw Bentham's mill for grinding rogues honest as a first institutional step in the construction of a societal wide 'carceral archipelago'.[59]

Despite Foucault's fascination with Bentham's panopticon, the phrase 'carceral archipelago' did not reference a prison, but was instead a linguistic borrowing from Solzhenitsyn's account of the operation of the Soviet gulag. Like the sprawl of labour camps that Solzhenitsyn described, the penal stations, houses of correction and road and chain gangs that developed in Eastern Australia were connected one to another.[60] The roads that convicts were marched along, the brigs that carried them between penal stations, and the watchhouses and local lockups in which they were temporarily housed, formed a vast institutional network. The critical point here, is that the lack of reliance on one single surveillance institution necessitated the rapid development of other tools for monitoring the bodies of criminals on the move. There are synergies here with the way trains were used in the Soviet gulag and later Russian Federation to connect a distributed system of incarceration. Indeed, a case can be made that the operation of convict management in Australia outstripped

[57] Heany, H. (1974) Ireland's Penitentiary 1820–1831: An Experiment That Failed, *Studia Hibernica*, 14, 28–39.

[58] Foucault, *Discipline and Punish*, 196–209.

[59] Foucault, *Discipline and Punish*, 293–308.

[60] Moran, D., Piacentini, L. and Pallot, J. (2011) Disciplined, Mobility and Carceral Geography: Prisoner Transport in Russia, *Transactions of the Institute of British Geographers*, New Series, 37(3), 446–460.

anything implemented by way of prison surveillance in pre-twentieth century Britain. Recent work has also shown that it was far less bloody than previously imagined, or at least rapidly transitioned post-Bigge into a less bloody form of state control. This does not make the systems of labour management that evolved in Eastern Australia after 1822 any less chilling.[61]

Flogging was a brutal form of punishment. It could take over an hour to administer a hundred strokes of the lash, the standard form of punishment for an absconder from a penal station. Such an ordeal would render an individual unconscious, reducing them to a limp, bloody mess.[62] Yet, the use of the lash declined rapidly after the establishment of a network of penal stations and female factories. As can be seen from Fig. 3.2, the peak year of flogging in Van Diemen's Land coincided with the tabling of the first volume of the Bigge report.[63]

Violence is a weapon of the weak. As the colonial state established the means to confine the disorderly, it resorted less to public displays of force. While the rate of execution in the Australian colonies was much higher than Britain, it reduced after 1830. As the colonial state acquired the means to subject an ever-greater proportion of the convict population to secondary transportation, it reduced its former reliance on the use of the death penalty. In New South Wales in 1828, for example, many forms of simple larceny were made non-capital. The decline in the colonial execution rate was accompanied by a change in the way that hangings were conducted. In the first decade of the nineteenth-century prisoners were not only executed in public, but their remains were gibbeted. Such practices were rare after the tabling of Bigge's extensive recommendations. They were in fact abolished in New South Wales in

[61] Maxwell-Stewart, H. (2020) Western Australia and Transportation in the British Empire 1615–1939, in Gregory J. and Marshall, L. eds. *The Carceral Colony: Studies in Western Australian History*, 34, 5–22.

[62] Maxwell-Stewart, *Closing Hell's Gates*, 77–90.

[63] Edmonds, P. and Maxwell-Stewart, H. (2016) 'The Whip Is a Very Contagious Kind of Thing': Flogging and Humanitarian Reform in Penal Australia, *Journal of Colonialism and Colonial History*, 17, 1.

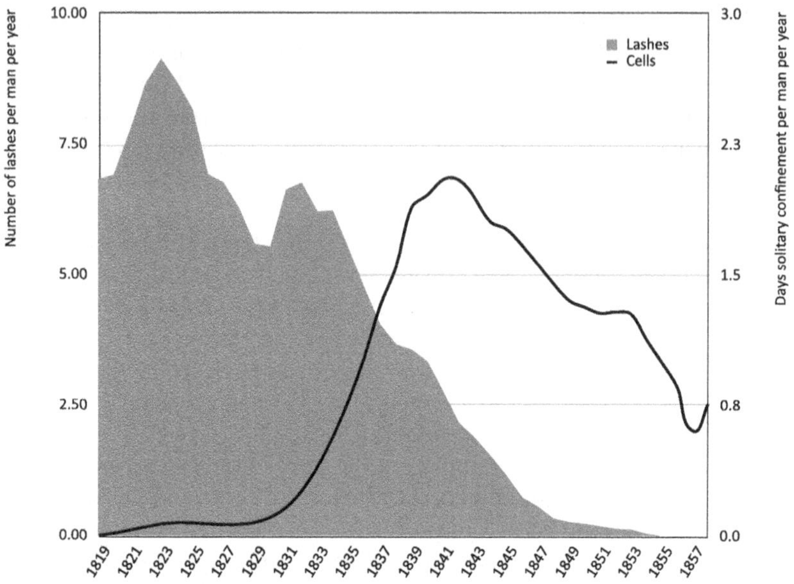

Fig. 3.2 Reconstructed rates of flogging and solitary confinement, Van Diemen's Land 1817–1860 (five-year moving average) (*Sources* T.A., Con 31, 32 and 33)

1837.[64] The last public gibbetting in Britain was 1832, although prisoners were gibbetted within the walls of Millbank until 1842.[65] Rather than lagging behind metropolitan reforms, Australian practice kept pace and on occasion pre-empted changes in the operation of criminal justice in Britain and Ireland.

Even before they were landed on the 'fatal shore' the transported were subjected to an array of sophisticated measures of control. The convict vessel was more than a transoceanic paddy wagon. While every transport ship operated as a place of confinement, each also contained a schoolroom and a hospital. It is easy to forget the extent to which the ship could also functioned as a workspace. Divided into watches and divisions, convicts

[64] Anderson, S. (2020) *A History of Capital Punishment in the Australian Colonies, 1788 to 1900*, Palgrave Macmillan, London, 19–54.

[65] Maxwell-Stewart, Western Australia and Transportation in the British Empire, 5–22.

were put to work scrubbing deck, washing clothes, airing bedding and sewing, as well as performing that most prison-like of tasks—picking oakum.[66] The convict vessel was a collection of institutions contained within one wooden hull—a floating system of prison management that umbilically-linked metropolitan and colonial places of incarceration. Its key task was to discipline convict bodies while on the move. The process of converting the 'idle poor' into penal labourers commenced before they had been disgorged into the charge of a colonial administration.[67]

As well as its human cargo, the transport vessel conveyed much by way of paperwork to Australia. This included the indent, the legal document that transferred labour rights in the sentence of convicts to the colonial administration. It also carried British and Irish hulk and goal reports. These documents formed the nucleus of an archive designed to manage the operation of an increasingly complex colonial penal system. After 1816, all convicts were interrogated before they were disembarked. As part of this 'rite of passage' each was informed that the colonial administration already knew much about their circumstances and that any lies detected as part of the interrogation process would result in punishment. Colonial officials credited such checks and balances with ensuring that the information elicited from convict charges was broadly correct. Subsequent cross-tabulations of the details coughed-up by convicts support this assessment.[68] As well as a record of next of kin, place of birth, literacy, age, conviction history and workplace skills, a detailed physical description of each convict was committed to file.

Manipulation of prisoner's liberational desires was crucial to convict management. Following the process of interrogation and description each was informed that progress through the various levels of the transportation system would rely on future conduct. The wicked would sink into the dark underworld of the crime class yard, road party, chain gang and penal station, while those that conformed would rise to a ticket-of-leave

66 Kippen, R. and Maxwell-Stewart, H. (2015) Sickness and Death on Convict Voyages to Australia, in Baskerville P. and Inwood, K. eds. *Lives in Transition: Longitudinal Research in Historical Perspective*, McGill-Queens UP, Toronto, 43–70.

67 Shepherd, J. and Maxwell-Stewart, H. (2021) Rites of Passage: The Voyage to Convict Australia and the Creation of the Penal Labourer, *Australian Historical Studies*, 52 (4), 470-90.

68 Maxwell-Stewart, H. (2016) The State, Convicts and Longitudinal Analysis, *Australian Historical Studies*, 47(3), 419–423.

and early release. This was a reiteration of the message that collaboration would be rewarded and resistance punished which had been instilled in convict charges in British and Irish institutions and during the long sea passage. It is not particularly surprising that those promoted to positions as deck captains, constables, schoolteachers, hospital assistants and barbers on-board convict vessels were more likely to have received favourable reports in the hulks. The reward for good service in one institution was promotion in the next. By contrast those selected to bring stores up from the hold and clean water closets were likely to have received unfavourable reports. Just as it held sway at sea, the opinion of the surgeon superintendent influenced outcomes on land. His recommendation was sufficient to secure a convict a favourable sinecure, while a bad report could condemn a man to a road gang or woman to the factory. It is not surprising that those who occupied positions of authority on a convict vessel were more likely to be recruited into the ranks of the colonial police.[69]

The maintenance of colonial order relied on the co-opted services of convict men and women. Overseers, flagellators, watchmen, clerks, matrons, hospital attendants, schoolteachers and convict constables played a crucial role in ensuring that the dictates of the administration were translated into effective action at ground level. As the connection between service on the vessel to Australia and police recruitment reveals, a great deal of care appears to have been taken in the selection of these minor officials. Former soldiers, for example, were sought after for service in the police. Indeed, analysis of British hulk records reveals that convicts with previous military service were more likely to be transported to the Australian colonies, while those with construction skills were disproportionately sent to work in the naval dockyards in Gibraltar and Bermuda.[70] Such selection underscores the demand in the Australian penal colonies for police recruits. By 1828 there was one policeman for every 96 persons in New South Wales—a measure of the levels of state control exerted on life in Eastern Australia.[71]

Like the convict police, gang overseers and sub-overseers had a strong incentive to enforce work effort as 'good behaviour' accelerated their

[69] Shepherd and Maxwell-Stewart, 'Rites of Passage'.

[70] Maxwell-Stewart, H. (2022) Bentham, Convict Transportation and the Great Confinement Thesis, in Schofield, P. and Causer, T. eds. ***Bentham and Australia: Convicts, Utility and Empire***, University College London Press, London.

[71] Evans, Creating an Object of 'Real Terror', 59.

progress to freedom. On the other hand, failure to perform risked a return to the gang. In May 1834 overseer John Chapman was sentenced to six months hard labour on Notman's road party after Convict Superintendent Ronald Gunn observed the chain gang under his charge idling under the pretence that it was raining.[72] Similarly, in October 1838 George Kent was dismissed from his post as sub-overseer after the police magistrate witnessed men in his charge being 'lazy' and idle.[73] Watchmen too could feel the force of the law for any perceived lapse. On 10 July 1834, three Launceston Chain Gang watchmen were prosecuted, one for neglect and the other two for failing to have their swords with them while on duty. All three were sentenced to be broken back into the chain gang for two weeks.[74]

The fear of demotion was balanced by the liberal financial rewards provided to informers. Those like Adam Beveridge's cook who reported two runaways he had seen sheltering in the eastern hut on Beveridge's Tamar estate were handsomely rewarded. The going rate was £2 per absconder—a sum that would be lodged in the informer's bank account.[75] By contrast those that ran forfeited any accumulated funds, these being used to subsidise the reward paid to those who helped to resecure the convict department's lost property.

Marriage, sex and reproduction were also controlled. The increase in respectable arrivals created a demand for domestic servants—especially female servants. The well-credentialed family in Australia was expected to run a liberally serviced household. As James Dixon advised, while one servant was necessary for a small family in England 'two or three' were required in Van Diemen's Land'.[76] The peculiarities of colonial Australia meant that the majority of domestic servants had to be supplied from the ranks of the transported. Female labour was in particularly short supply. Because of gender imbalances the services of women who arrived free were hard to retain, the opportunity of social elevation through marriage

[72] M.L., Tas Papers 277 Launceston Benchbook, 14 May and 4 June 1834.

[73] M.L., Tas Papers 292 Oatlands Benchbook, 10 October 1838.

[74] M.L., Tas Papers 277 Launceston Benchbook, 10 July 1834.

[75] M.L., Tas Papers 277 Launceston Benchbook, 16 July 1834.

[76] Dixon, J. (1839) *The Condition and Capabilities of Van Diemen's Land as a Place of Emigration Being the Practical Experience of Nearly Ten Years Residence*, Smith, Elder and Co., London, 54.

prompting many to leave their employment.[77] In 1830 there were 1.8 free men to every free woman in Van Diemen's Land and 6.8 male convicts to every female convict.[78] As unfree workers, a contract could be more effectively imposed upon convict women.[79] In order to increase the supply of bonded labour the state reversed its pre-Bigge policy of encouraging marriage. While nearly 45 percent of female convicts still under sentence in Van Diemen's Land were married in 1822, the proportion dropped to a little over 7 percent in the decade 1832–1842.[80]

Disciplinary devices were also created to criminalise convict attempts to form de facto unions while under sentence. Convict servants who fell pregnant were sent to the house of correction. After giving birth mothers were permitted to wean their children. Thereafter they were separated—the convict being shifted to a separate yard to undergo a period of six months punishment.[81] This mostly consisted of labour at the washtubs servicing the laundry requirements of the state and nearby private households. Suitably chastised female convicts were redeployed into assigned service, whereas their children were sent to what were euphemistically known as orphan schools. The factory was much more than a disciplinary institution—it was an ancillary device designed to facilitate the servicing of colonial middleclass households.[82]

[77] Prinsep, A. (1833) *The Journal of a Voyage from Calcutta to Van Diemen's Land Comprising a Description of That Colony During Six Months Residence*, Smith Elder and Co., London, 113; Widowson, H. (1829) *Present State of Van Diemen's Land Comprising an Account of Its Agricultural Capabilities with Observations on the Present State of Farming* etc. etc. *Pursued in That Colony and Other Important Matters Connected with Emigration*, S. Robinson et al., London, 60–61.

[78] Forsyth, W.D. (1970) *Governor Arthur's Convict System: Van Diemen's Land 1824–36*, Sydney University Press, Sydney, 205.

[79] Their supply was restricted to married settlers. Widowson, *Present State of Van Diemen's Land*, 60–61.

[80] Reid, K. (2007) *Gender, Crime and Empire: Convicts, Settlers and the State in Early Colonial Australia*, Manchester University Press, Manchester, 138.

[81] Kippen, R. (2005) 'And the Mortality Frightful' Infant and Child Mortality in the Convict Nurseries of Van Diemen's Land, International Workshop organized by the IUSSP Scientific Committee on Historical Demography, the Ecole des Hautes Etudes en Science Sociales, and the Institut National d'Etudes Démographiques, Paris.

[82] Frost, L. (2012) *Abandoned Women: Scottish Convicts Exiled Beyond the Seas*, Allen and Unwin, Sydney, 33–45.

Rather than being the products of a backward-looking regime, many of these colonial innovations were later incorporated into metropolitan systems of control.[83] This included the use of identifiers to ease the task of tracking information that referenced the same convict across multiple record series. The voluminous conduct records informed the prison license system introduced in Britain in 1857.[84] Many other legal structures created to regulate Antipodean convict lives were subsequently adopted by British and Irish penal managers. The ticket-of-leave, for example, pre-empted parole, and the mark system was incorporated into British prisons from 1861 following what was seen as its successful Australian implementation.[85]

In contrast to the penitentiary, the management of convict labour in Australia was not confined to discreet institutions. This was a system of criminal management that linked country estates, urban businesses and private houses with lumber camps, remote road parties, houses of correction, lockups and penal stations. It was a landscape of surveillance that could be applied to urban as well as rural areas. Because there was no single institutional wall enclosing Australia's penal inmates, the colonial version of carceral archipelago consisted of, not one, but a host of institutional environments whose collective disciplinary practices enabled the distribution of power through-out the social body. Curfews, high levels of policing and personal identification systems, including passes and an associated paperwork bureaucracy, made it possible to operate a form of panoptic surveillance that went far beyond anything envisaged by Bentham. This was a system that placed the eyes of a gaoler on street corners, roads, public houses and other nodes of communication, rather than constraining the gaze of the state to fixed points at the centre of expensive and restrictive buildings. This was a system of state control that had the ability to peer into bank accounts and under beds. It policed the

[83] Maxwell-Stewart, The State, Convicts and Longitudinal Analysis, 414–417; Roberts, D. (2017) Colonial Gulag: The Populating of the Port Macquarie Penal Settlement, 1821–1832, *History Australia*, 14(4), 588–606.

[84] Forsythe, W. (1987) *The Reform of Prisoners 1830–1900*, Croom Helm, London, 73; Chartrand, V. (2014). Penal and Colonial Politics Over Life: Women and Penal Release Schemes in NSW, Australia, *Settler Colonial Studies*, 4(3), 305–320.

[85] Winter, S. (2016) Coerced Labour in Western Australia During the Nineteenth-Century, *Australasian Historical Archaeology*, 34, 6; Millett, P. (2007) The Distribution of an Offensive Population: Classification and Convicts in Fremantle Prison, 1850–1865, *Studies in Western Australian History*, 25, 51.

sex lives and leisure practices of prisoners, as well as daily work routines. While the inhabitants of the pre-Bigge Rocks resisted colonial attempts to number and order their lives, by the 1820s numbers were everywhere. They were stencilled on clothing aiding the identification of public works convicts, used to link the records of the convict department, manage the careful measurement of commissariat stores, and serially order applications to marry. Indeed, record keeping penetrated so many aspects of everyday colonial life that it anticipated the closed-circuit television camera of a more modern age.

This was a formidable machine of labour control and enforcement. An important part of this book is explaining the way in which these societal chains were loosened, enabling Australia to develop by the second half of the nineteenth-century into a comparatively open and democratic society. In order to explore that process it is necessary to look in greater detail at the functioning of the magistrates' bench—the institution that pinned the colonial carceral archipelago together. It was the bench that heard disciplinary matters, adjudicated labour disputes, weighed up the merits of convict complaints, held masters to account and generated the lines of ink that populated the conduct records that sought to hold every convict in place.

CHAPTER 4

Battling the Bench

A distinction often made between the plight of convicts and other unfree workers is that in the Australian colonies, masters were not permitted by law to punish their charges. In his 1811 account of New South Wales, for example, D.D. Mann referred to specific prohibitions on free persons striking convicts.[1] Rather than directly administering punishments, private individuals had to bring a complaint to a magistrates' bench. Any breach of these regulations could result in a ban on future access to government labour. While this might appear to offer the unfree protection from the caprice of private sector masters, it also meant that all charges brought against a convict were documented. In the case of Van Diemen's Land the conduct records, which include a summary of every charge, case outcome, and sentence brought against a convict survive in their entirety. This chapter starts by examining the record of convict prosecution and sentencing in that colony before moving on to take a look at the ways in which the magistrates bench operated both there and in New South Wales. It argues, that despite appearances, the bench offered convicts few protections. Instead, the operation of the law in Eastern Australia

[1] Mann D. (1811) *The Present Picture of New South Wales*, John Booth, London, 23–24.

H. Maxwell-Stewart and M. Quinlan, *Unfree Workers*, Palgrave Studies in Economic History,
https://doi.org/10.1007/978-981-16-7558-4_4

provided substantial support to employers. The chapter ends by looking at the impact court decisions had on convict life course outcomes. It argues that variations in prosecution and sentencing pattern have shaped Australia's past in profound and surprising ways.

The Black Books and the Hierarchy of Labour Exploitation

As in other unfree labour systems, there was no single state of unfreedom in convict Eastern Australia. Individual experience of penal servitude varied according to sex, age and skill as well as time and place. The work experience of those convicts who had completed apprenticeships in the building trade or as cabinet makers and blacksmiths was likely to differ from that of the unskilled. The number of unfree workers engaged at a particular location could also make a difference. Overseers regulated work on large estates, providing social distance between convict and master absent on smaller properties. A large workforce also enabled skill specialisation, while in smaller enterprises unfree workers were expected to do a variety of different tasks. Work might be physically demanding on a newly acquired property where land needed to be cleared, but less challenging on an established farm. Any task that involved high inputs of physical labour and low levels of skill was likely to be managed through the use of negative incentives, including the threat of physical punishments and the withdrawal of rations. On the other hand, tasks that required specialised skills and smaller number of workers equipped with expensive tools or charged with the management of livestock or other capital assets were more likely to be managed through the use of incentives.[2] The situation is a little more complicated for female convicts, who will form a major focus of this book. While they were rarely deployed in groups, especially in the private sector, the domestic work that the vast majority were tasked with performing brought them into direct contact with their master and his family. They were constantly under view although much of the work that they performed was likely to be managed by the use of incentives

[2] Fenoaltea, S. (1981) Slavery and Supervision in Comparative Perspective: A Modal, *Journal of Economic History*, 44(3), 673–643; Maxwell-Stewart, H. (1997) Convict Workers, 'Penal Labour' and Sarah Island: Life at Macquarie Harbour, 1822–1834, in Duffield, I. and Bradley, J. eds. *Representing Convicts: New Perspectives on Convict Forced Labour Migration*, Leicester University Press, London, 143–145.

simply because it was in the household—a place where there were many opportunities for a disgruntled worker to wreak havoc.

Such variation in workplace conditions was not unusual in unfree societies. Slave working conditions differed, even within the bounds of a plantation. Domestic servants, sugar boilers, carters and other skilled hands were more likely to be rewarded at work compared to those who laboured in gangs. The experience of field hands tasked with cropping sugar cane, a brutal job, differed from those who cultivated coffee, which differed again from those who worked in mixed agriculture.[3] The work that some slaves undertook was sufficiently lucrative for their owners to provide them with incentives, including cash payments. Maritime slaves in Bermuda, for example, were rewarded with a share of the profits of a voyage—payments that recognised their commercial value as skilled seaman. They were also permitted to trade on their own behalf, selling private property in overseas ports. Such incentivisation ensured that slave sailors shared the same commercial interests as their master. There was an added advantage in that accumulation of shore-based assets, alongside family ties, dis-incentivised flight.[4]

A feature of labour exploitation in the Australian colonies was that more coercive tasks tended to be reserved for punishment labour. In the plantation world work was often organised according to colour and place of birth. African born slaves were more likely to be engaged in field work. Conversely, those who worked in more skilled jobs as artisans, drivers, stockkeepers and servants were more likely to be creoles and have lighter skin.[5] In Australia, the division of tasks depended largely on conviction history. Those convicts who were brought before the colonial courts while under sentence were less likely to be provided with incentives and were

[3] Dunn, R. (2007) The Demographic Contrast Between Slave Life in Jamaica and Virginia, 1760–1865, *Proceedings of the American Philosophical Society*, 151(1), 43–60; Geggus, D. (1993) Sugar and Coffee Cultivation in Saint Domingue and the shaping of the Slave Labor Force, in Berlin, I. and Morgan, P. eds. *Cultivation and Culture*, 73–100; Craton, M. (1978) Hobbesian or Panglossian? The Two Extremes of Slave Conditions in the British Caribbean, 1783–1834, *William and Mary Quarterly*, 3rd Ser., 35, 324–356; Neal, *The Rule of the Law in a Penal Colony*, 34–35.

[4] Jarvis, M. (2002) Maritime Masters and Seafaring Slaves in Bermuda, 1680–1783, *William and Mary Quarterly*, 59(3), 585–622.

[5] Dunn, R. (1993) Sugar Production and Slave Women in Jamaica in Berlin I. and Morgan, P. eds. *Cultivation and Culture: Labour and the Shaping of Slave Life in the Americas*, University Press of Virginia, Charlottesville, 49–72.

disproportionately deployed in ganged work supervised by overseers. This division helped to reinforce the ideological underpinnings of transportation. Those who transgressed the law made fitting beasts of burden. In short, this was a system that sought to draw equivalence between levels of work intensity and criminality.

The fact was, however, that the majority of charges brought against convicts were work-related. Therefore, incapacity to perform a task became a moral failing in its own right. The same was true of any attempt to protest against the conditions under which the convict served. In short, those that downed tools risked merely confirming their degraded status as fit subjects of labour exploitation. The power of 'convictism' was not just that it was an effective labour extraction device, but that it could also be used to disempower dissent. Those that protested against terms under which they served risked reinforcing their status as criminals, and therefore fit subjects of punishment.[6]

In the language of the convict administration, it was the undeserving who would sink down through the various levels of the post-Bigge convict system. However, analysis of punishment rates reveals a more complicated picture. A problem with any work-based punishment system is that individual experience is likely to be governed by the extent to which their labour could be put to productive use. Convicts who possessed human capital were less likely to be punished in the colonies than those that lacked the capacity to generate profits for master and state.

One way of masking this deficiency was to equate low skill with criminality. Both nineteenth-century observers and subsequent historians have labelled unskilled convicts as 'urban ne'er-do-wells'.[7] According to the New South Wales settler, Lieutenant Breton, a London pickpocket was a 'worthless good-for-nothing blackguard'.[8] Urban convicts were described by other observers of Australian settler society as the 'most depraved'— 'having been brought up in ignorance' living off the proceeds of 'habitual

[6] Gilchrist, C. (2006) The "Crime" of Precocious Sexuality: Young Male Convicts and the Politics of Separation, *Journal of Australian Colonial History*, 8, 57–58.

[7] Robson, L. (1965) *Convict Settlers of Australia*, Melbourne University Press, Melbourne, 157–158.

[8] Breton, W. (1835) *Excursions in New South Wales, Western Australia and Van Diemen's Land During the Years 1830, 1831, 1832 and 1833*, Richard Bentley, London, 279.

crime'.[9] The stereotype was convenient in masking the profits masters derived from convict labour while simultaneously propagating a view of convicts as quintessentially useless examples of the idle poor. It of course also helped to justify the use of the lash, solitary confinement and other coercive punishments employed as labour extraction tools.

Even these measures could not disguise the extent to which those who lacked bargaining power fell through the cracks of the post-Bigge penal order. Willem Pockbaas who arrived in Van Diemen's Land from the Cape colony on board the *William Glen Anderson* in 1831 was sent to Port Arthur as he was not fit for work elsewhere having been previously mauled by a lion. Transported for cattle theft, this 50-year-old Khoi cripple had no prospect of being assigned. Because he was not capable of turning a profit, he was dispatched to the invalid party that toiled on the remote Tasman Peninsula.[10] There he was joined by others who were impaired by physical disabilities that prevented them from earning more than their keep. The young also gravitated to these remote outposts of hard labour. Juvenile convicts had first been sent to Macquarie Harbour penal station by Lieutenant-Governor Arthur in 1827. While there was always plenty of work for adolescent female convicts, they could be employed as scullery maids or turn their hand in other ways to servicing the houses of the colonial élite, adolescent males were less useful. They lacked both skills and strength. Worse, most were transported for seven years, the minimum sentence that a convict could be ordered to serve. This meant that, any master who took on a prisoner lad risked losing out in the deal as there was no guarantee that they would receive a return on the investment in rations by the time their adolescent charge was eligible for a ticket-of-leave.[11]

In the case of Van Diemen's Land, the Conduct Records can be used to reconstruct magistrates' bench activity over time, providing a record of the rates at which convicts were arraigned and the overall punishment load. On average a male convict received a total of 24 lashes and

[9] Therry, R. (1863) *Reminiscences of Thirty Years Residence in New South Wales and Victoria*, London, 18.

[10] Willem Pockbass, per *William Glen Anderson*, Police No. 773, T.A., Con 18-1-21, Con 27-1-5 and Con 31-1-35.

[11] Maxwell-Stewart, H. (2008) *Closing Hell's Gates: The Death of a Penal Station*, Allen and Unwin, Sydney, 230.

Table 4.1 Distribution of punishments for male and female convicts arriving in Tasmania 1803–1853

	Female (total)	*Mean per convict*	*Male (total)*	*Mean per convict*
Strokes lash	25	0.0	1,435,775	24.3
Days solitary	278,237	20.9	548,881	9.3
Days hard labour	3,606,776	270.4	16,045,600	272.0

Sources T.A., Con 31, 32, 33, 40 and 41

spent 9 days in solitary and toiled at hard labour for 272 days (see Table 4.1). Only one female convict appears to have been sentenced to be flogged in Van Diemen's Land, although others were sentenced to beating in New South Wales and on Norfolk Island. On 15 March 1806 Elizabeth Murphy was charged with writing 'or causing' to be written a letter to Francis Dring, a fellow convict, 'contain[in]g the most infamous Language & accusing him of a most heinous Crime'. For this offence she was ordered by Lieutenant-Governor Collins to be tied by her hands to a cart drawn by the gaol gang, stripped and given 25 lashes.[12] While the practice of flogging women ceased in the first decade of the nineteenth-century, female convicts served on average the same number of days hard labour as men and spent over twice as long in a solitary cell (21 days compared to nine). This considerable punishment load did not fall evenly across the rank and file of prisoners.

There were marked seasonal trends in the distribution of court cases and resultant punishments. Male convicts were significantly more likely to be prosecuted in the summer compared to winter. This may reflect increased work intensity during the harvest, but it was also a product of the greater number of hours men were expected to work in summer when the days were longer. Such seasonal trends in prosecution were much less noticeable in the case of female convicts. Since they mostly worked as indoor servants, their hours of labour were dictated by the needs of the household to which they were assigned—rather than daylight. Their daily routines were not as markedly affected by the vagaries of the weather. Rain could completely halt the work of a gang, for example, but did not impact on the operation of a kitchen. Longer working days and constant

[12] Elizabeth Murphy per *Glatton*, NSW and *Sophia* VDL, Police No. 10, T.A., Con 40-1-7.

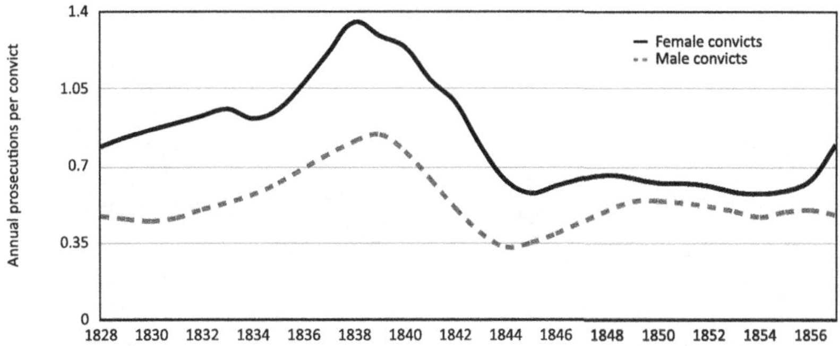

Fig. 4.1 Annual prosecution rates for male and female convicts in Van Diemen's Land (three-year moving average) (*Sources* T.A., Con 31, 32, 33, 40 and 41)

supervision might also explain why the rate at which female convicts were prosecuted was considerably greater than male (see Fig. 4.1). Accommodation within the walls of the big house may have brought some material comforts, but it meant in return that most convict women were never far from the beck and call of master and mistress nor from their disciplinary gaze.

As Fig. 4.1 also reveals, there were marked fluctuations from year to year in the rate at which male and female convicts were prosecuted in Van Diemen's Land. These prosecution rates were not driven by changes in the underlying propensity of transported convicts to commit criminal acts. There is no evidence that the convict workforce in 1839 was disproportionately composed of a certain type of offender compared to 1843 when prosecution rates were much lower. There were, however, big changes in the cost of maintaining a convict in those two years.

It is possible to calculate the monetary cost of the ration using the price of its basic components.[13] While the remuneration of convicts in private service was fixed by the ration scale set by government, the cost to employers varied. When the price of goods was low, employers could make handsome profits from convict labour. At other times, rising prices for meat and flour reduced the difference between the monetary value

[13] Meredith, D. and Oxley D. [2005] Contracting Convicts: The Convict Labour Market in Van Diemen's Land 1840–1857, *Australian Economic History Review*, 45(1), 66.

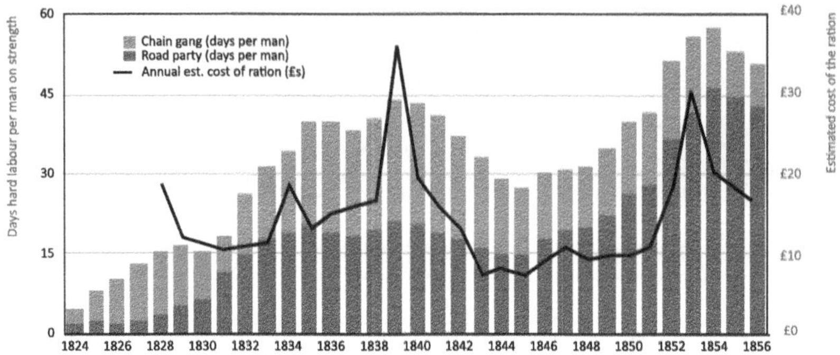

Fig. 4.2 Number of days hard labour performed by male convict and the cost of the ration (*Sources* T.A., Con 31, 32 and 33 and Meredith, D. and Oxley D. (2005) Contracting Convicts: The Convict Labour Market in Van Diemen's Land 1840–1857, *Australian Economic History Review*, 45(1), 45–72)

of the ration and a free wage. At such moments some masters, and the contractors that supplied goods to the commissariat, might have been tempted to save money by adulterating flour or substituting inferior cuts of meat. On occasions employers wrote to magistrates to test the extent to which official stipulations could be watered down in the face of rising prices. Charles Cowper sought the permission of the Goulburn bench in August 1839 to dilute the rations supplied to his assigned servants, complaining wheat flour had reached famine prices.[14] Such market effects had a direct bearing on rates of prosecution, punishment patterns and the distribution of convict labour between the public and private sector. They were also a common trigger for convict protest. To provide an illustration, the annual rationing bill for a male convict in Van Diemen's Land was 4.8 times more costly in 1839 compared to 1843 (see Fig. 4.2). This posed masters with a dilemma. Unlike free workers, convicts could not be hired and fired in the conventional sense. The master, however, did have the option of resorting to the magistrates' bench.

[14] M.L., 2482/1 CY Reel 954 Goulburn Benchbook, 1821–1849, 12 August 1839.

The Operation of the Bench

Many masters appear to have used the bench to dispense with the services of those convicts who were 'unprofitable', were worn out, or were no longer required for other reasons. One common seasonal practice was to return workers to government in autumn after the harvest and shearing were over. Surgeon and farmer J.W. Hudspeth returned nine servants on 16 April and 4 May 1835 while Oatlands Police Magistrate Thomas Anstey returned three servants on 27 February 1837.[15] These cases reveal the extent to which the bench acted as a labour bureau as well as a court, a practice that involved the collusion of leading citizens and officials. This may help explain why bench and police office letter books never commented on such returns or their timing. There appears to have been a pervasive view that masters (or at least well-connected masters) had a right to dispense with assigned servants as and when they saw fit.[16]

Incompetent or uncooperative workers were also returned on a regular basis. Alice MacArthur was described by her master as 'useless to him'.[17] In September 1836 Major Newman, a settler at the Black Brush, Van Diemen's Land, described George Brown and John Kelly as 'perfectly useless on a farm'.[18] The terms 'useless' or 'no longer required' can commonly be found in bench proceedings, although occasionally other wording was employed by those who resorted to the bench to turn servants over. Mr. Lamprill of Old Beach said of Ellen Walker that she 'does not suit as a servant.'[19] Such convicts were usually returned to the services of government. While they were not normally subjected to punishment, they were likely to be placed in the 'assignable class' at the female factory or in a 'hiring gang' where the watchful eye of a matron or overseer increased prosecution risk.

A system which rewarded ability was always likely to prove costly to those who were impaired. The issue of how to deal with convicts with disabilities proved a constant problem for convict administrators. This

[15] M.L., Tas Papers 290, Oatlands Benchbook, 16 April, 4 May 1835 and 27 February 1837.

[16] See for example M.L., 289 New Norfolk Police Office Letterbook April to October 1838.

[17] M.L., Tas Papers 326, Richmond Benchbook, 11, 29 October 1838.

[18] M.L., Tas Papers 2, Richmond and Brighton Benchbook, 28 September 1836.

[19] M.L., Tas Papers 2, Richmond and Brighton Benchbook, 14 February 1837.

included those who were injured in the course of work. On 13 May 1835 Kimberly, a farmer in Bagdad, Van Diemen's Land, returned John Taylor on the grounds that he was unable to work due to a bad leg. Three weeks later J. Bailey returned Richard Hill as he was ruptured and therefore 'unable to do the work required of him on the farm.' Both were sent to the Invalid Party at Green Point.[20] Employers could also dispense with older, less capable or worn-out workers by laying charges against them and then seeking replacements. Another reason for returning workers was they had formed 'bad connections' or were associating with persons of bad character. This was the fate that befell William Titley, a servant of Green Ponds innkeeper Robert Stodart, who was sent the Hobart Barracks in July 1835.[21]

On the other hand, charges might be used to extend a sentence. In March 1838 Samuel Newton preferred a complaint that his master, Woodward, had falsely charged him with pilfering potatoes in order to get his sentence extended for a year. It was unusual for a convict who had been awarded a substantial sentence extension to be returned to the service of their existing master. The case, however, was immediately dismissed and Newton was charged with laying a false complaint and awarded 50 lashes.[22] It was possible to use the bench to manipulate sentencing arrangements. Convicts who wished to apply for an indulgence, such as a ticket-of-leave which provided the ability to work for a wage, or permission to marry, were required to demonstrate that they had steered clear of the courts for a suitable length of time—usually a year. The need to keep a clean sheet provided the master with considerable power. A strategically placed charge might extend the service of a valued worker.

Using a charge to dismiss an assigned servant guaranteed the supply of another. Thus, it made sense to bring strategic charges against unskilled and other less profitable workers in the hope that the next man or woman would prove more capable. Such practices did not escape the attention of the Quakers Backhouse and Walker who wrote an extensive report on the operation of convict labour in Van Diemen's Land. They confirmed that complaints were often made of settlers 'bringing frivolous charges

[20] M.L., Tas Papers 2, Richmond and Brighton Benchbook, 13 May and 6 June 1835.

[21] M.L., Tas Papers 2, Richmond and Brighton Benchbook, 1 July 1835.

[22] M.L., Tas Papers 326, Richmond Benchbook, 9 March 1838.

against men who are not very efficient servants, and of some magistrates for listening to expressions of desire that such may be committed to road-parties; and for acting upon such suggestions rather than upon the merits of the respective cases.'[23]

A bench had a range of sentencing options at its disposal. If it found in a master's favour, it could admonish a convict or give them a warning. It might also sentence a prisoner to a short stint in the public stocks. In urban areas a male convict might be sentenced to undergo a few days hard labour on the treadmill. While the use of flogging declined over time, lashes were relatively cheap to administer. Both male and female convicts could be sentenced to a solitary cell. In the case of all of these punishments, an assigned servant could be back working for their master or mistress within a few days. A magistrate could, however, order a convict to be sent to a road party, chain gang or female house of correction. A bench of more than one justice of the peace could also order a sentence extension of up to three years and could recommend service in a penal station. As Fig. 4.2 reveals, magistrates altered sentencing strategies to suit the interests of employers. When rationing costs rose relative to free wages, the rate at which male convicts were sentenced to road parties and chain gangs increased. In effect, this pushed rationing costs back onto government, enabling employers to reduce the number of prisoner-servants they maintained and hire free workers to fill the gap, switching back when economic circumstances suited.

The point illustrates the extensive ways in which the management of free and unfree workers intersected in the Australian colonies. Former convicts continued to live with the effects of penal transportation long after they had gained their freedom. Competition between the two sectors reduced wage rates and impacted on the legislation governing waged workers and free apprentices. The first master and servant laws enacted in New South Wales in 1828 and in Van Diemen's Land in 1837 empowered a single part-time magistrate to adjudicate free labour disputes in contrast to British and Irish practice. Both laws tried to extend the power the bench exercised over convicts to other categories of workers. The 1828 New South Wales law survived until 1840. The 1837 Van Diemen's Land law, however, failed to gain royal assent and was disallowed in 1839. Glenelg, the Secretary of State for the Colonies, informed

[23] British Parliamentary Papers, XLII (1837–1838), Copy of Despatch, Note (G) Testimonials by Messrs. Backhouse and Walker, 25.

Lieutenant-Governor Sir John Franklin that a perceived problem with the legislation was the imbalance between the penalties outlined for servants and those for masters. In his words: 'This law also fails in the essential conditions of reciprocity as the offences of Masters against their Apprentices and Servants are very inadequately punishable.'[24] The 1828 New South Wales law was equally lopsided but slipped through at a time of perceived crisis—such intercolonial inconsistencies in labour law were not uncommon.[25]

These lopsided laws were designed to subordinate free workers, particularly former convicts transitioning to life post-sentence via tickets of leave. While the imbalance of power that characterised the regulation and treatment of convict workers was worse, in broad terms the difference was one of degree not kind. Subordination of workers in both the free and the unfree sector of the colonial economy was the key objective. In order to achieve this, it was necessary to ensure that the penalties for labour infractions were severe and the means of redress open to disgruntled workers limited. Court records are replete with cases attesting to this. To cite but one example, in October 1839 large landholder Daniel Stanfield prosecuted Richard Jones, William Carson and William Parker for absence and refusal to work. Ticket-of-leave holders Jones and Carson were imprisoned for two months hard labour and had their tickets suspended while Parker, who was free, received one month with hard labour—hardly a trifling penalty for a day's dissent.[26]

There were few checks and balances. Magistrates were prohibited from trying their own servants. Even here, however, there were means of getting round the prohibition. In 1838 Robert Wales defended himself from this criticism arguing he tried John Alexander, not as his servant, but because the man had assaulted a constable.[27] Part-time magistrates on occasion played musical chairs, trying each other's servants. On 26 May 1837 farmer W. Brodribb prosecuted William Pickering for general

[24] Davidson, A. (1975) An Analytical and Comprehensive History of the Master and Servant Legislation in Tasmania, Masters of Law thesis, University of Tasmania, 52.

[25] Quinlan, M. (2004) Australia 1788–1902: A Working Man's Paradise? in Hay, D. and Craven, P. eds. *Masters, Servants, and Magistrates in Britain and the Empire, 1562–1955*, University of North Carolina Press, 219–250.

[26] M.L., Tas Papers 270, Hobart Benchbook, 29 October 1839.

[27] M.L., Tas Papers 33, Morven records, Tasman Peninsular Correspondence and Case extracts, Wales to CPM Hobart, 27 September 1838.

idleness. One of the presiding magistrates, Benjamin Berthon, then immediately stepped down from the bench to level the same charge against one of his own servants.[28]

The close ties, if not outright overlap of employers and magistrates, manifested in other ways. A magistrate visiting John Bingle's Invermein Upper Hunter Valley estate tried three of Bingle's assigned servants for neglect while staying as a guest. While the case caused some consternation, the Hobart *Colonial Times* argued that it provided proof that practices in New South Wales differed little to those in Van Diemen's Land.[29] More broadly the deviation in practices from rules highlights the limits of imperial oversight. One of Glenelg's issues with the 1837 Master and Servant Act was the imprecise ways in which it defined an offence. This reflected the manner in which the law was applied to convicts and free alike, and colonial imperatives to secure workplace deference and control insubordination in a labour market that was often more favourable to workers than in Britain and Ireland.

Prior to the mid-1830s benches frequently flouted the due process of the law, although Governor Bourke attempted to overhaul their operation amidst protest from those adversely affected. The only constraint on magisterial abuses in Van Diemen's Land, however, was the occasional rebuke for imposing penalties that exceeded those legally prescribed. Richmond magistrate James Gordon was admonished in December 1831 for the number of lashes he had awarded, while another justice of the peace who had ordered a female convict to be confined in the stocks was similarly admonished in January 1832.[30]

Not all magistrates lacked humanity. In June 1832 the Goulburn Bench resolved not to proceed with a complaint against Charles Bennett on account of the state of his slop clothing, noting that the required allocation had not been received by the No. 38 Road Party for some time.[31] However, such instances were rare and even as transportation wound down in New South Wales employers were not above writing to benches decrying the failure to punish insubordinate servants. In August 1840

[28] M.L., Tas Papers 2, Richmond and Brighton Benchbook, 26 May 1837.

[29] *Colonial Times*, 18 February 1834.

[30] M.L., Tas Papers 265, Hobart Police Office Letterbook Correspondence, 27 December 1831 and 25 January 1832.

[31] M.L., 2482/1 CY Reel 954 Goulburn Benchbook, 1821–1849, 5 June 1832.

William Campbell wrote to Goulburn Police Magistrate George Stewart complaining of two recent cases where charges had been dismissed. He railed that John Ashworth, charged with disobedience, had returned to his workplace 'boasting to his fellow servants of having triumphed over his overseer at the Bench.'[32]

On occasion the colonial press criticised the arbitrary and oppressive rulings of some benches. In May 1841 the conservative *Cornwall Chronicle* in a piece entitled 'Gaol Tyranny and Magisterial Despotism' deplored the case of one person imprisoned for 70 consecutive days for insolence. It also alleged that two convicts, Philip Keating and John Lane, had been 'thrown into the George Town black hole – for it does not deserve the name of gaol – where they were confined for sixty days and fed on bread and water during that time, and were then turned out of the place, without any change whatsoever having been preferred against them, or knowing for what they were incarcerated.'[33] The criticism caused a flurry of correspondence at the George Town Police Office with acting police magistrate George Stephen Davies indicating that the men had been apprehended on suspicion of involvement in conveying smuggled gin but, as an appended note observed, his response did not address the allegation that they had been placed on bread and water without charge.[34]

Courts gave masters a degree of discretion in shaping the punishment inflicted to best meet their needs. Suspected ringleaders could be singled out for exemplary prosecution in the hope this might cower others, while more valued workers might be spared. Masters might also withdraw charges on a promise by workers that they would mend their ways or intercede with the court to reduce the punishment where a convict expressed contrition.[35] Court proceedings and other records suggest that employers frequently used the threat of charges in an effort to secure compliance.

Courts, especially lower or magistrates' courts, played a pivotal role in efforts to subordinate convict workers. Prosecutions for various forms of dissent or uncooperative behaviour dominated court proceedings. Less

[32] M.L., 2482/1 CY Reel 954 Goulburn Benchbook, 1821–1849, 27 August 1840.

[33] *Cornwall Chronicle*, 1 May 1841.

[34] M.L., Tas Papers 261, George Town Magistrates Letterbook Correspondence Dated 6, 23 May, and 2 June 1841.

[35] See for example M.L., Tas Papers 290, Oatlands Benchbook, 16 November 1836.

than 1 percent of the charges brought against serving convicts in Van Diemen's Land were for assault and less than 8 percent were for offences against property (see Table 9.1). The balance was made up of prosecutions for public order offences and breaches of the rules and regulations of the convict system, the majority of which relate to the work processes.

In some regional centres, multiple cases were tried every sitting day, work-related charges accounting for almost all cases brought before the bench. The magistrates tasked with prosecuting these charges generally lacked legal training and had limited knowledge of the laws they ruled on. They themselves were frequently employers of convict labour and were usually close acquaintances of the masters and mistresses whose convicts they tried.

Many convicts were tried for being insolent (an offence unknown under master and servant law) to masters, overseers and other officials. On 19 October 1818 five workers convicted of insolence to the inspector of public works in Hobart received 50 lashes and were ordered to work in their own time for three months.[36] In October 1833 the charge of being insolent to Macquarie River farmer Adam Robertson earned two assigned servants six hours in the stocks.[37] On 27 August 1835 Richard Cushion received four months hard labour for being repeatedly insolent to the overseer of his Green Point employer Joseph Steel, while Mary Robertson was admonished for being insolent to her master two days later.[38] On 12 April 1837 Sarah Campbell received a month at the wash tubs at the female factory for being 'impudent' to her mistress in the morning of the previous day.[39] In February 1838 Robert Taylor was convicted of 'specific insolence' to his Richmond district master William Mansfield, the latter listing a litany of incidents including that Taylor had the temerity to complain about the state of the clothes he had been supplied with.[40] A

[36] We are indebted to David Roberts for this information. CO 201-134, 334, 19 October 1818.

[37] M.L., Tas Papers 256, Campbell Town Prisoner Records and Sentences, 12 October 1833.

[38] M.L., Tas Papers 2, Richmond and Brighton Benchbook, 27, 29 August 1835.

[39] M.L., Tas Papers 2, Richmond and Brighton Benchbook, 12 April 1837.

[40] M.L., Tas Papers 326, Richmond Benchbook, 10 February 1838.

month later, Henry Brown received a similar sentence for extreme insolence to his master.[41] Insolence charges were also used to target protest leaders or those who were more outspoken than others. James McDonald received 20 lashes for insolence in October 1834 immediately after he and other workers in his gang had been prosecuted for neglect.[42]

Insolence could also lead to a more serious charge of using threatening language which warranted a severe penalty. Convicts who overtly threatened the status quo could also be charged with insubordination, although this was more typically associated with physical assault or threats to strike a master or other superior. On 3 June 1833 the Richmond Bench sentenced James Lloyd to Port Arthur for a year for threatening to strike his master William Nicholls Junior, while gardener James Phillips received six months in a chain gang for a similar offence against Alexander Goldie, agent for Sir James Owen's Orielton estate.[43]

Evidence arising from insolence cases reinforces the lopsided nature of the judicial apparatus put in place to reinforce the authority of masters. When reprimanding Thomas Turner for not moving some bullocks, Michael Fenton told him 'you are very negligent and [I] can swear you don't like to do anything.' Turner retorted 'yes I dare say you will swear anything.'[44] The power of the master's word in court was not to be underestimated. In most cases convicts offered no defence to the charges proffered against them, conscious of the lopsided nature of the law and the risk of being slapped with a counter charge of contempt. When a defence was mounted, it seldom seems to have carried much weight. Charged with absence and disobedience by Sussex farmer William Henry Glover, Thomas Wright stated that the delay in returning to his master's property had been occasioned by a fatal accident. On the voyage by schooner to Hobart a man had been lost overboard and had unfortunately drowned. The resultant search had delayed the assigned servant's return. Despite this defence Wright still received a three-month stint in the Richmond Chain Gang.[45] Questioning the court or other authority figures risked retribution. Denying he had tried to abscond William Henderson

[41] M.L., Tas Papers 326, Richmond Benchbook, 8 March 1838.

[42] M.L., Tas Papers 277, Launceston Benchbook, 17 October 1834.

[43] M.L., Tas Papers 325, Richmond Benchbook, 3 June 1833.

[44] M.L., Tas Papers 238, New Norfolk Benchbook, 2 January 1840.

[45] M.L., Tas Papers 323, Richmond Benchbook, 8 October 1832.

told the court that Mr. Jones 'had a spite' with regard to him. For his pains in speaking out Henderson was rewarded with a six-month hard labour sentence to Notman's road party, a notorious punishment gang.[46] It cannot have escaped the attention of convicts that mounting a defence generally did more harm than good.

Prosecuting Masters and Mistresses

As British subjects, convicts did have notional rights in law, although these were heavily circumscribed by their status as convicted felons. They could lodge allegations of ill-treatment, including physical assault by masters and overseers, or complain about the quality or quantity of the rations, clothing and or bedding supplied to them. Those in public works, female factories and penal stations could complain to the superintendent, who, in the case of penal stations was also empowered as a magistrate. Those assigned into private service could lodge a complaint with the closest bench. Visiting magistrates were also instructed to make routine calls to road parties, chain gangs and probation stations. However, the convicts who used these mechanisms to lodge complainants rarely met with success. Charges brought by serving prisoners were routinely dismissed as false or frivolous, language which was seldom used to describe the outcome of cases brought by masters.

It is not surprising that convict servants infrequently brought charges against masters for threatening or abusing them. The rare exceptions to this were disproportionately brought by female convicts, although these too were invariably dismissed. In December 1836 Isabella Dixon swore that following a dispute over wearing a bonnet when going for a Sunday walk with her master, New Norfolk Innkeeper Neils Basstian, he had attempted to strike her with his fist. When she stepped back to avoid the blow she claimed that he called her a 'damned stinking strumpet.'[47]

In the majority of cases, however, the benchbook did not even record the substance of complaints brought by convicts. On occasions the subsequent counter charges brought against the complainant reveal something of the wider context. On 8 November 1834, for example, Thomas Allsop received 50 lashes from the Campbelltown bench in New South Wales for

[46] M.L., Tas Papers 277, Launceston Benchbook, 2 June 1834.

[47] M.L., Tas Papers 285, New Norfolk Police Office Letterbook, 27 December 1836.

making a 'false and frivolous complaint against his master for giving bad bread, [and] refusing to work for two days'.[48] Similarly, four servants of Charles Harrison were punished for lodging a frivolous complaint and spending a night in Hobart before proceeding to court.[49] Ticket-of-leave holders were less likely to make complaints, but when they did the outcome differed little. George Bagshaw had his ticket suspended for six weeks and was discharged to the Campbell Town working party in Van Diemen's Land for 'lodging a grievous complaint against his master.'[50]

Some convicts sought to bring complaints to other officials, although this could also prove a risky strategy. On 5 February 1830 Macquarie Harbour inmate Hugh Holland was charged with 'falsely reporting' to the settlement surgeon, Dr. Garrett, that he was 'tyrannically and oppressively treated by his Overseer'. The court punished him for not bringing the matter to the attention of the 'Commandant or Superintendent' as specified in the settlement rules.[51]

To lodge a formal complaint those in assigned service had to first ask for permission to leave their place of employment. This provided masters with a check against would-be complainants and a means of prosecuting those who sought to approach a bench without seeking prior permission. Convicts who fronted up to a bench without a pass risked severe punishment. John Tomkins was charged on 21 February 1835 with: 'Preferring a frivolous and groundless complaint against Mr. Walker and Insolence in the Presence of the Magistrate & quitting his master[']s house without first asking for a pass'. Just to make sure that the charge stuck, he was also accused of 'carrying away a quantity of tea, sugar and bread that had been issued out to him as rations'. As punishment he was sentenced to a chain gang for three months, a sentence that was altered on review by the lieutenant-governor to a stint at Port Arthur penal station.[52] Another difficulty could be the distance to the requisite court—to be fair a problem for employers too. For example, even in the smaller and

[48] For this and similar cases heard before this Bench see M.L., 2482/6 CY Reel 954 Campbelltown Benchbook, 23, 27 October and 8 November 1834, 3 April 1835.

[49] M.L., Tas Papers 270, Hobart Benchbook, 12 September 1839.

[50] M.L., Tas Papers 256, Campbell Town Prisoner Records and Sentences 27, 29 August 1836.

[51] Hugh Holland, per *Medina*, Police No. 666, T.A., Con 31-1-19.

[52] John Tompkins, per *Royal George*, Police No. 521, T.A., Con 31-1-43.

more densely settled colony of Van Diemen's Land an assigned servant of John Foster at Cape Portland had to travel 80 miles to lodge a complaint of ill-usage before the George Town Bench.[53] Those who took clothing and rations with them for the journey risked further punishment as John Tomkins found to his cost.

There were occasional victories. Mr. Walpole, a settler on the Prosser River in Van Diemen's Land charged two assigned servants with leaving their service without a pass in September 1832. The prosecution was dismissed, however, when it became apparent there had been serious deficiencies in the provision of the men's meat and other rations.[54] Even such rare successes could prove pyrrhic. In early 1834 all the servants of New Norfolk farmer Maria Ramus were withdrawn following a complaint made by William Pale. In the words of the police magistrate Edward Dumaresq, he was not surprised at this outcome given 'the many and various complaints I have heard of the manner in which they have been treated.' Despite the success of this action, Pale was nevertheless ordered to a road party for two months for using 'bad language' to his mistress.[55] Convicts who lodged complaints risked other forms of retribution. An assigned servant named Carlow who unsuccessfully charged his master Hugh McGuinness with assault on 26 March 1833 found himself facing a charge of neglect and insolence by his master just six days later.[56]

The sanctions awarded to masters on the rare occasions that complaints were upheld were mild compared to the risks associated with successful counter-prosecution faced by convict complainants. In March 1838 when James Saunders complained of being assaulted by his Muddy Plains employer (a Mr. Robinson), the bench merely recommended that he be returned to the Crown. No sanction or criticism of Robinson was entered into the court record.[57] When convictions did occur, they usually resulted in the employer being fined or having their assigned servants withdrawn. In February 1833 when Thomas Wilkinson pled guilty to assaulting and beating his servant James Quinn he was fined five shillings

[53] M.L., Tas Papers 261, George Town Magistrates Letterbook, 16 July 1841.

[54] M.L., Tas Papers 323, Richmond Benchbook, 27 September 1832.

[55] M.L., Tas Papers 284, New Norfolk Police Office Letterbook Dumaresq to CPM, 1 February 1834.

[56] M.L., Tas Papers 323, Richmond Benchbook, 26 March and 2 April 1833.

[57] M.L., Tas Papers 326, Richmond Benchbook, 24 March 1838.

plus two shillings and sixpence costs.[58] In December 1838 Sydney draper and mercer David Jones (founder of a retailing empire) was fined 40 shillings after striking two assigned females he alleged were quarrelling and neglecting their work.[59] In April 1841 Lake Bathurst landholder John Cottington was charged with assaulting a group of convict shearers and shooting one after they requested a glass of grog. The Berrima Assizes dismissed the case on the grounds that Cottington was a respectable and peaceful man.[60]

Collaboration, Obedience and Punishment in the Surveillance State

While convicts were managed in ways that were designed to encourage informing and other acts of collaboration, attempts to calculate the number who sided with their penal managers is fraught with difficulty. While a host of petty officials were recruited from the ranks of the prisoners, it is unclear whether those selected to perform the roles of flagellator, watchman, matron, overseer and constable had much choice in the matter. William Gates claimed that convicts were compelled under threat of punishment to act as special constables in pursuit of bushrangers for example.[61] Analysis of selection processes demonstrates that prisoners recruited to the colonial police were disproportionately composed of those with former military service, further evidence that selection, as opposed to volunteering, played an important role in the enlistment process.[62] Rates of recruitment are a crude gauge of collaboration for other reasons too. Many of those who had acted in some formal capacity subsequently engaged in an act of collective protest, just as many protestors were later elevated to petty office. Just because a convict worked for part of their sentence as a paid official, did not mean that their compliance was bought or that collaboration was a fixed state of affairs.

[58] M.L., Tas Papers 323, Richmond Benchbook, 18 February 1833.

[59] *Monitor*, 14 December 1838.

[60] *Sydney Morning Herald*, 19 April 1841.

[61] Gates, W. (1961) *Recollections of Life in Van Diemen's Land/by William Gates, One of the Canadian Patriots. Ed. with an Intro., Notes and Commentary by G. Mackaness*, Ford, Sydney, 22.

[62] Maxwell-Stewart, H. (1999) The Rise and Fall of John Longworth: Work and Punishment in Early Port Arthur, *Tasmanian Historical Studies*, 6(2), 98.

These caveats aside, it was relatively common for convicts to serve in some form of official capacity. In the case of the police, levels of recruitment can be measured since these positions were advertised in the *Government Gazette*. In all, 4013 male convicts, or 6.2 percent of the 64,816 disembarked in Van Diemen's Land, served as a constable while under sentence in that colony.[63] While there are no equivalent appointment lists for other positions, we estimate that around one in ten male convicts occupied a position of authority at some point over the course of their sentence. Rates of recruitment amongst female convicts were considerably less, reflecting the smaller number of positions open to women.

It is also possible to estimate degrees of obedience by examining the proportion of convicts who were never prosecuted while under sentence. Once more, some words of caution are warranted. A convict with skills that were in demand might engage in acts of protest, but never appear in court. There is a great deal of evidence that private sector employers were reluctant to risk losing skilled men and women, and as result sought to negotiate with their charges rather than resort to the courts. As we have seen, rates of prosecution also varied according to labour market conditions. Finally, some convicts died early in their sentence before they had the opportunity to accumulate colonial prosecutions. These caveats aside, some 14 percent of convicts transported to Van Diemen's Land have no charges listed on their conduct records, indicating that they were sufficiently compliant to escape prosecution.

By comparison, 17 percent of male convicts and just under 23 percent of female convicts were gazetted as runaways on at least one occasion.[64] The rates of prosecution for work related offences were also far greater than the proportion of convicts employed as petty officials or those who were sufficiently obedient to escape court action. Over 332,000 individual prosecutions for workplace related offences were brought between 1816 and 1860 in Van Diemen's Land alone. In all just over 79 percent of male convicts and 66 percent of female convicts were prosecuted for a work-related offence on at least one occasion. While it is impossible to know how many of these charges resulted from actions that were consciously designed to disrupt the process of labour, or otherwise attempt to agitate

[63] *Hobart Town Gazette*, all issues 1817–1860.

[64] *Hobart Town Gazette*, all issues 1817–1860.

for or affect an amelioration of conditions, the evidence suggests that acts of non-compliance considerably outnumber acts of collaboration and that far more convicts chose not to follow orders than were obedient.

These acts of non-compliance had consequences. The range of sanctions applied by colonial courts complicate any attempt to calculate the burden of punishment. To overcome this problem, we created a standardised punishment index by treating each sentence to 7 days in solitary as the equivalent of 25 lashes, or 180 days hard labour or 90 days hard labour in chains. The use of such an index enables an evaluation of the severity of punishments awarded by magistrates' benches in Van Diemen's Land. This reveals that insubordination and absconding were treated with greater severity than thefts (see Fig. 4.3). Perhaps surprisingly, threats of violence were likely to attract sanctions that were just as severe as those meted out for aggravated assault. This might be because threats brought against masters and superiors were more likely to result in a court

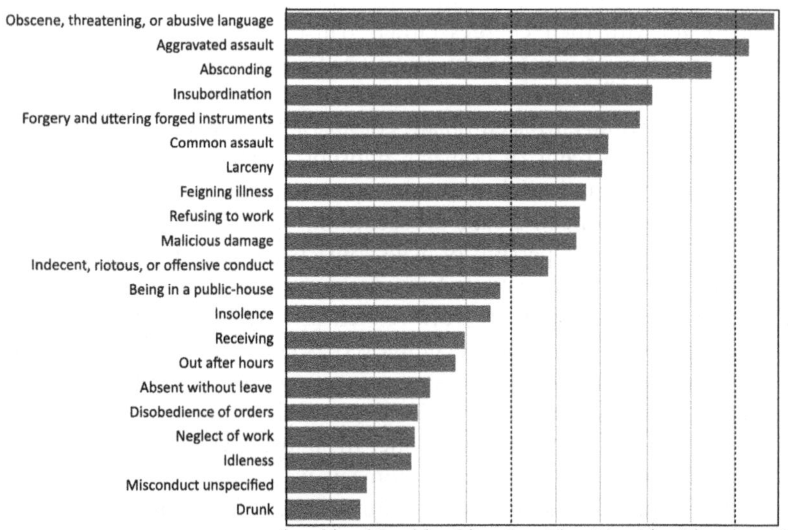

Fig. 4.3 Mean punishments by charge awarded by benches in Van Diemen's Land (*Sources* T.A., Con 31, 32, 33, 40 and 41.Punishment index: 7 days solitary = 1; 25 lashes = 1; 180 days hard labour = 1; 90 days hard labour in chains = 1 For example, a sentence to 7 days solitary followed by 90 days hard labour out of irons is scored at 1.5)

appearance than words issued in anger against those who did not occupy positions of authority. Figure 4.3 also reveals that colonial lower courts sentenced those who refused to work, feigned illness, or were offensive or riotous to punishments that were as severe as those dealt out for common assaults and larcenies. The courts drew a distinction, however, between malingering and idleness. The later, was less severely punished as were charges of disobedience of orders and neglect of duty.

The degree to which convicts were at risk of punishment varied by decade of arrival, length of sentence, age and skill. We used a regression model to explore the extent to which these factors influenced the levels of punishment awarded to male convicts in Van Diemen's Land (see Fig. 4.4). This uses the same punishment index employed in Fig. 4.3, enabling days in cells, lashes and hard labour performed in and out of irons to be plotted on the same scale. The model confirms that convicts

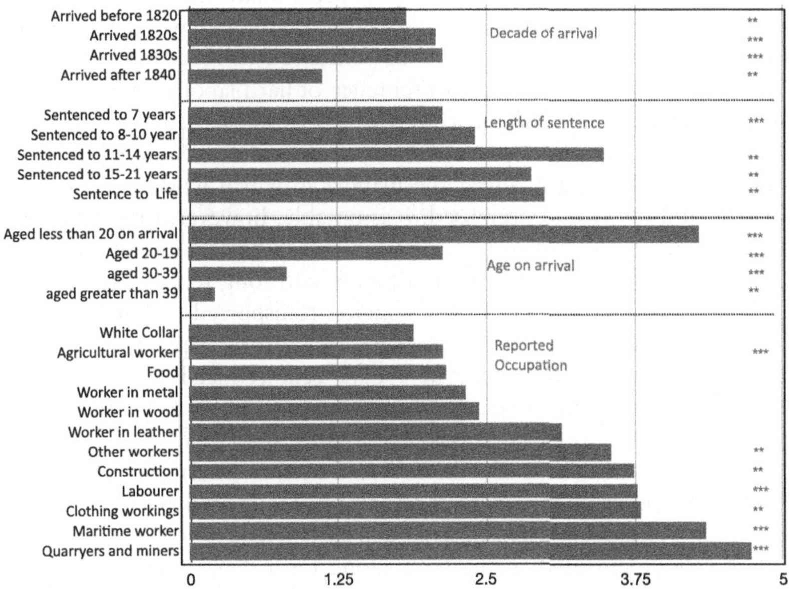

Fig. 4.4 Regression estimates for punishments associated with decade of arrival, sentence, age and occupation (male convicts only) (*Sources* T.A., Con 31, 32, and 33 four % sample, 20,489 individual punishments.*** = significant at 1 percent level, ** = 5 percent, * = 1 percent. Ordinary Least Square Regression)

who arrived after 1840 were at less risk of punishment than those that arrived in earlier decades. It also confirms that convicts serving shorter sentences were less likely to be punished. This relationship was not liner, however. Those sentenced to between 11 and 14 years transportation were at greater risk of punishment in the colonies than those sentenced to 15 years and more. There were also marked differences in the distribution of punishments awarded to convicts of different ages. Those who arrived as teenagers experienced double the punishment load of convicts who were in their twenties. These in turn were punished twice as severely as those who were aged 30 or greater on arrival. This is revealing, for while younger convicts might have given masters more trouble, they are also likely to have been less useful since they had fewer opportunities to acquire work skills.

The model confirms that skill did indeed have a bearing on levels of punishment. Accounting for period of arrival, age and sentence length, white collar workers were less likely to accumulate a record of punishment than other workers. Agricultural labourers and workers in wood and metal were also less likely to be sentenced to serve time in a solitary cell, be flogged or undergo a sentence of hard labour. Other workers whose skills were in less demand were at risk of substantially greater levels of punishment. This was particularly true of maritime workers, quarriers and miners. This might reflect the manner in which work in vessels and quarries and mines was organised. It is notable, however, that these were industries with a long history of collective work protest in Britain.

The uneven distribution of punishment had long term consequences. Linked life course data for female convicts transported to Van Diemen's Land provides evidence that exposure to sensory deprivation punishments, especially confinement in a dark cell, reduced life expectancy. These results cannot be explained by other events likely to be markers for poor health, such as elevated conviction rates, poor levels of literacy and engagement in sex work. Furthermore, the risks associated with sensory deprivation punishments were long-lasting. Compared to women with no history of solitary punishment, female convicts who were placed in a dark cell experienced medium and long-term deteriorations in health that were sufficiently severe to cut their lives short. What is particularly concerning is that the mean number of days solitary confinement women were exposed to was double that of men (20.9 days compared to 9.3). This particular form of state punishment impacted unevenly across the sexes.

Women were affected by punishment in other ways too. While it is unlikely that a direct pathway linked sensory deprivation with decreased fertility, a history of such punishments was nevertheless associated with a decline in colonial births. The relationship can be explained by the ways in which female convict sexual and familial relationships were policed. This constituted a form of economic birth control designed to benefit settler élites at the cost of family formation for convicts and former convicts. As well as leaving a long-term mark on the demographic profile of the colony, this may have also contributed to other health outcomes. There is a well-established link between infertility and mental health—not being able to have children can have psychiatric impacts.[65] Female convicts who failed to raise a colonial family were also more likely to experience financial and other hardships in later life. Lack of a supporting kin, and the resultant income insecurity in old age, may have heightened the risk of arrest and institutionalisation. The disadvantages associated with aging without the support of family may have also contributed to the shortened life expectancy observed for women exposed to sensory deprivation while under sentence.

A sentence to penal transportation was no trivial thing. The convicts sent to New South Wales and Van Diemen's Land were regimented disciplined and accounted for in ways that pre-empted later social controls. They were also subjected to high levels of state sanctioned violence. The punishments and conditions of work they experienced continued to shape their lives long after they became free, impacting on colonial family formation and life expectancy. These were significant insults. In the second half of this book we document the ways in which convicts resisted by combining to protest against those forms of punishment and labour exploitation they considered unjust.

[65] Doyle, D. and Carballedo, A. (2014) Infertility and Mental Health, *Advances in Psychiatric Treatment*, 20(5), 297–303.

PART II

Excarceration—Patterns of Resistance and Collective Action

CHAPTER 5

Shipboard Mutinies

There was only one successful mutiny on a convict vessel bound from Britain or Ireland to Australia. The *Lady Shore* was seized in 1797 by disaffected members of its crew and New South Wales Corps guard. While threats and rumours of mutiny are said to have been commonplace, these have been attributed to a 'combination of overreaction by the crew especially ship officers, boasting by convicts, and the intelligence—accurate or exaggerated—offered by informants'.[1] As a result, the degree to which the security measures on Australian-bound convict vessels were tested remains to be fully assessed.

While the notices placed in colonial newspapers have ensured a high degree of visibility for convict absconders on land, their would-be maritime counterparts accused of plotting to seize transport vessels have remained more difficult to identify. While a few were executed at sea, the majority of those accused of conspiring to mutiny on the passage to Australia were sent to coercive locations on arrival. From the 1820s small numbers of convicts were dispatched direct to penal stations on the recommendation of the surgeon superintendent as a result of their alleged conduct at sea. Those considered less culpable were merely detailed to

[1] Brooke, A. and Brandon, D. (2005) *Bound for Botany Bay: British Convict Voyages to Australia*, National Archives (UK), Kew, 142.

H. Maxwell-Stewart and M. Quinlan, *Unfree Workers*, Palgrave Studies in Economic History,
https://doi.org/10.1007/978-981-16-7558-4_5

chain gangs. Owen Griffiths was sent to Port Arthur on arrival, for example, for 'Gross insubordination on board the prison ship "Katherine Stewart Forbes" in [the] month of April last to wit on the 4th, 5th, & 6th & conspiring to take that vessel & induce others to join in the same.'[2] In similar fashion Alexander Kaye was sent on arrival in Sydney to Newcastle Penal Settlement for 12 months after being involved in a conspiracy to seize the *Atlas* in 1819.[3] While inquiries were sometimes held when the vessel docked in Hobart or Sydney, trials were rare. One reason for this was that there was considerable doubt about the authority of colonial courts to try convicts for an offence committed on the high seas.[4]

While the journals kept by the surgeon superintendents on the voyage to Australia can be revealing, they are often restricted to medical matters. It was after all in a surgeon's interest to downplay any disciplinary issues that might have occurred on the long voyage. Each was held accountable for the condition the convicts on disembarkation, a bonus of £50 contingent on attending faithfully to their duties.[5] While it has been argued that the threat of mutiny was inflated by the manner in which some convicts sought to lay false charges in the hope of receiving rewards that would ameliorate their own conditions, the evidence suggests that surgeons were wary about putting vessels into lockdown on the basis of unsubstantiated hearsay.

In line with current medical opinion most surgeon superintendents believed in miasma theory—in short that disease was spread by the smell of corrupt or fetid matter. They placed great weight on the degree to which fresh air should be circulated through the prison. Regular airing kept smells down and helped to ensure that confined spaces did not become damp. It was for this reason that the decks were often dry scrubbed—water being thought of as an agent that promoted atmospheric

[2] James May, per *Katherine Stewart Forbes*, Police No. 981; T.A., Con 31-1-30; James Smith, per *Katherine Stewart Forbes*, Police No. 1525, Con 31-1-39; Owen Griffiths, per *Katherine Stewart Forbes*, Police No. 833, Con 31-1-16.

[3] McKenzie, K. (2106) *Imperial Underworld: An Escaped Convict and the Transformation of the British Colonial Order*, Cambridge University Press, Cambridge, 33.

[4] *Cornwall Chronicle*, 10 September 1842.

[5] Bateson, C. (1959) *The Convict Ships*, Brown, Son and Ferguson, Glasgow, 21.

deterioration. Surgeon superintendents also placed much store in exercise. This they thought was crucial to the maintenance of their convict charges. Security threats inevitably compromised carefully orchestrated hygiene regimes and were therefore especially unwelcome. Rather than taking convict informers at face value, it is apparent that many surgeons were sceptical about tales of plots said to have been hatched. Joseph Steret on board the *Bardaster* went as far as to dish out 48 lashes to one of his convict charges 'for stating that there was a Mutiny on board' when the surgeon's own investigations failed to find supporting evidence of such a conspiracy.[6]

Colonial officials themselves often found it difficult to get to the bottom of what had occurred at sea. As the magistrates Josiah Spode and Peter Mulgrave concluded of an investigation they conducted into an alleged plot to seize the *Strathfieldsay* in 1831:

> We have the Honor to state that we have been on board that vessel and after a minute investigation of all the circumstances connected with the supposed offence we can only come to the conclusion that much turbulence and insubordination existed during part of the voyage amongst a portion of the convicts but the proof of anything like a conspiracy to seize the *Strathfieldsay* rests solely upon the unsupported testimony of one convict whose statement however had the salutary effect of inducing a degree of caution on the part of the officers in charge that must have frustrated a very mischievous attempt on the part of the prisoners.[7]

On the *Eleanor*, a vessel that conveyed many of the 1830 Swing rioters to Sydney, the guard reacted to a sudden rush towards the prison door firing and killing two convicts and wounding two more. At the subsequent inquest considerable doubt arose as to whether there had been an attempt to seize the vessel. Several witnesses argued that the prisoners had surged towards the door in order to acquire biscuits distributed from a bag.[8] Similar ambiguity surrounded a reported mutiny on the *Chapman* in 1817. Although seven convicts had been killed in a reported attempt

[6] See conduct record for Thomas Johnson, per *Bardaster*, Police No. 906, T.A., Con 31-1-25.

[7] J. Spode and P.A. Mulgrave to Colonial Secretary, T.A., CSO1/559/12359.

[8] *Australian*, 5 August 1831 and *Hobart Town Courier*, 20 August 1831.

to seize the vessel, others alleged that panicked soldiers had fired through the grating into the prison, ignoring convict cries for mercy.[9]

Amongst the charges and counter charges filed in relation to convict voyages it is difficult to know what does and does not count as an attempted mutiny. There is a wider point to be made here. As E.P. Thompson noted in relation to the study of violence, quantitative analysis can yield misleading results.[10] The incidence of violence may be less important than the effect that terror is calculated to produce. At the risk of stating the obvious, acts that are statistically rare often have impacts that are far greater than other more common occurrences. Attempts to innumerate reports of mutinous proceedings on transport vessels are no exception. The dangers that emanated from a transport vessel's prison did not necessarily have to be commonplace to be threatening.

The taking of a vessel was by definition a collective exercise. It could not be undertaken by a small number of individuals—something more than honour amongst thieves was required to set mutiny in motion. In this sense the very notion that convicts might seize a transport vessel was liberational because it threatened the state's ability to physically exile convicts and to strip them of identity. Mutinous proceedings could have effects that were as contagious as any below-deck infection. As Atkinson eloquently put it: 'when any single convict stood up for shared principle it was as if he declared (looking about him), "I *rebel* — therefore we *exist*"'.[11]

Rediker points out in relation to slavery that the ship was a factory in the sense that it produced a commodity for the market. At the start of the voyage it loaded a multi-ethnic collection of people. By the time the vessel had arrived in the New World those that had survived had been converted into slaves.[12] As argued in Chapter 3, convict voyages played a critical role in the process of converting the idle poor into docile labourers. The surgeon James Mercer reported the routine adhered to aboard the *Albion* convict vessel in 1823. The 200 prisoners were subjected to a system of regimentation from the moment they were delivered on board. At first

[9] Quinlan, *Origins of Worker Mobilisation*, 105.

[10] Thompson, E. (1975) Folklore, Anthropology, and Social History, *Indian Historical Review*, 3(1), 255. See also Rediker, M. (1987) *Between the Devil and the Deep Blue Sea*, Cambridge University Press, Cambridge, 215.

[11] Atkinson, 'Four Patterns of Convict Protest', 50.

[12] Rediker, M. (2007) *The Slave Ship: A Human History*, Viking, London, 9–10.

light fifty were bathed in seawater ensuring that every man got a cold dunking once every four days. At six bells all bedding was passed up on deck to be aired and stowed in the nettings. At 8 o'clock breakfast was served, following which two messes were selected in rotation to clean the prison. Depending on the weather the decks were either washed and scrubbed or dry scraped with holy stones. The surfaces were also sprinkled with lime. At 7 bells all prisoners were sent below to prepare for dinner. After they had been fed each mess was mustered on the quarter-deck where the surgeon ensured that every man drank his allotted draft of anti-scorbutic. At half past ten on Sundays and Thursdays the prisoners were inspected to make sure that they were shaved clean. Clothes were washed Tuesday and Friday. At other times the seamen and mechanics amongst the convicts were employed in tasks about the vessel and the rest in picking oakum—that is pulling apart strands of old rope.[13]

With the exception of the private cabins reserved for officers and full-paying passengers, a ship was public space.[14] It was well suited to the introduction of industrial discipline. On every vessel the convicts were divided into messes of six, each under the charge of a mess captain chosen from amongst their ranks. The latter was made responsible for all utensils that were issued as well as leading each mess in its daily round of chores. The surgeon also appointed other trustees who were responsible for the supervision of several messes. These were generally referred to as boatswains or deck constables on male vessels and mess or deck matrons on female vessels. Those who performed their allotted duties could expect a favourable note to be entered on their colonial conduct record. While Mercer reported that the convicts on the *Albion* were allowed time in the afternoon for 'merryment and some manly exercise', the surgeon sought to extend his control over that too. Alongside the singing, dancing, leapfrog and sparring matches he instigated the formation of a society for the 'suppression of vices' Mercer installed the Bristol shoemaker and pick-pocket Joseph Sloggett as president, a man whom he described as 'a saint with only one leg'. Sloggett had other more earthly qualities however. He had been transported thirteen years earlier and had spent four years on

[13] Surgeon's Journal for the *Albion*, N.A., ADM101/1/8.

[14] Denning, G. (1992) *Mr Bligh's Bad Language: Passion, Power and Theatre on the Bounty*, Cambridge University Press, Cambridge, 18–34.

board the hulks. He knew what was expected of him and was happy to aid Mercer in the policing of petty crimes and other backsliding tendencies.[15]

While the rituals of daily life on a convict vessel were crucial to maintaining hygiene, they had an important ancillary function in that they prepared convicts for the experience of forced labour in the Australian penal colonies. Like a factory town, the convict vessel was organised so that every aspect of life, including domestic routines and leisure, could contribute to the wider goal of preparing the convict for colonial servitude.[16] The ship, in this sense, was an institution—or perhaps more accurately, a floating collection of institutions. Each vessel contained a prison, a hospital and a schoolroom—spaces where convicts were regimented in preparation for their disembarkation in Australia.[17] That convict vessels were multi-functional increased their symbolic value. As well as resisting the process of being exiled, mutineers also conspired to carry an engine of the state off into the wild blue yonder. To put it another way, prisoners do not normally steal the gaols in which they are incarcerated.

Convict mutineers threatened to unpack themselves in other ways too. Navigational skills were crucial to the success of the enterprise. While convicts might threaten to slit the throats of all on board, they were only truly dangerous when they transcended their status as prisoners. David Bracewell, described by the surgeon on the 1826 voyage of the *Layton* as 'mutinous' and 'a very bad fellow' was especially threatening because of his trade—he was a seaman.[18] Much the same could be said of the boatman Charles Ecclestone charged with 'using mutinous language to a sentinel'. The words he uttered had more bite since they were issued by one familiar with his environment to a landlubber, who though equipped with a Brown Bess, was otherwise literally all at sea.[19] As Alan Atkinson

[15] Surgeon's Journal for the *Albion*, N.A., ADM101/1/8.

[16] Robbins, W. (2005) Spatial Escape and the Hyde Park Barracks, *Journal of Australian Colonial History*, 7, 83.

[17] Damousi, J. (2007) *Depraved and Disorderly: Female Convicts, Sexuality and Gender in Colonial Australia*, Cambridge University Press, Cambridge, 15–16.

[18] David Bracewell, per *Layton*, Police No. 972, T.A., Con 23-1-1 and Con 31-1-1.

[19] Charles Ecclestone per *Layton* (2), Police No. 470, T.A., Con 31-1-11 and Con 18-1-13.

has noted, it is surely no coincidence that the only attempted mutiny on the First Fleet was led by two former sailors.[20]

On board the *Argyle* in 1831 suspicion fell on two convicts, George Scantlebury and William Philip, who were found in possession of a notebook while on deck exercising. When questioned, the men admitted to marking the ship's passage—a habit that they had formed long ago, both men being accustomed to the sea.[21] While recommendations attesting to both men's former good behaviour had been lodged with the ship's officers prior to departure, these only served to intensify suspicions. The 22-year-old Scantlebury was recommended for his good service in the navy under the command of a Captain James, while two former employers of the 51-year-old Philip wrote to appraise his new penal masters of his good character. Before being convicted and sentenced to life for maliciously setting fire to his own vessel, he had been employed in the coasting and foreign trade for 25 years.[22] During that time he had 'carried away no mast, lost no cable nor anchor'. As a Mr. Osborne wrote from Philip's hometown of Padstow, Cornwall: 'He is a good sailor an able mariner and a person I verily believe is deserving of encouragement'.[23] In this case the two men's collective knowledge of the sea confirmed their guilt just as securely as it gave the lie to the notion that the transported were members of the idle poor who chose not to work, living instead by crime and crime alone.

As it turns out there is a sting in this particular tale. As punishment for plotting the progress of the vessel, William Philips was sent on disembarkation in Hobart Town to Macquarie Harbour penal station. There he gave clandestine lessons in navigation to the construction crew of the *Frederick*, the last vessel to be built at the site. By these means he managed to even the score with the state. The *Frederick* was successfully seized by ten convicts in January 1834 and sailed to Chile.[24]

[20] Atkinson, A. (1998) *The Europeans in Australia: Vol. 1*, Oxford University Press, Oxford, 113.

[21] Petition to His Excellency Lieutenant Colonel George Arthur Esquire Governor of Van Diemen's Land And Its Dependencies &c &c T.A., CSO1/539/11703.

[22] William Philip, per *Argyle*, Police No. 730, T.A., Con 18-1-3 and Con 31-1-35.

[23] R.W. Avery, 1 February 1831 and A. Osborne 15 December 1830, T.A., CSO1/539/11703.

[24] Maxwell-Stewart, *Closing Hell's Gates*, 265.

As the surgeon superintendent on the *Katherine Stewart Forbes* pointed out, securing those accused of mutiny during the passage to Australia was not necessarily the end of the matter. He reported how he had discovered that a 'numerous gang' amongst the convicts had plotted in the hulks to seize the vessel and carry her to the United States of America. His subsequent investigations had uncovered a second plan to take a boat immediately after the vessel arrived in port in order to get ashore previous 'to a description of their persons being taken'.[25] This demonstrated both an alarming degree of familiarity with the procedure for processing convicts and the failure of the punishments inflicted on board the vessel to stamp out self-liberational desires.

It seems likely that some plans to seize vessels were originated in conversations that occurred prior to departure. The papers forwarded from the hulks regularly identified those amongst the convicts thought to be potential threats. In some cases prisoners had already disclosed their hand. At least twenty of the convicts embarked on board the *Coromandel* in 1838 had already been charged with mutiny. The disturbance was serious enough for the Secretary of State to order that they all be sent road parties and penal stations upon disembarkation in Van Diemen's Land.[26]

Most plots were hatched amongst a small core, usually members of the same mess. Some shared pre-voyage experiences. Four of the eleven conspirators on the *Isabella* in 1842 had been convicted in courts in Lancaster and another three had been courts martialled in Halifax, Nova Scotia. Convicts convicted in Canada also featured in the plot to take the *Sarah* in 1837. Of the eleven ringleaders three had been convicted in Montreal and a fourth at Three Rivers, Lower Canada.[27] By the time they had embarked on the *Sarah*, these four had already shared the experience of being shipped as prisoners across the Atlantic.

In order to put a plot into action the initial core of conspirators had to be expanded. It would need more than one mess to take a convict

[25] Patrick McTernan to Colonial Secretary 16 July 1832, T.A., CSO1/605/13784.

[26] T.A. Con 31-1-3, 248 and 250; Con 31-1-8, 49; Con 31-1-12, 116 and 139; Con 31-1-17, 20–21 and 23; Con 31-1-25, 1, 278 and 280–283; Con 31-1-32, 48 and 50 and Con 31-1-36, 54.

[27] Andre, Kellershire, Police No. 558, Con 31-1-25; Francois Xavier Leclair, Police No. 1053, Con 31-1-25; George Rollard, Police No. 1218, Con 31-1-37 and Jean Baptiste Gauthier, Police No. 1247, Con 31-1-6.

vessel. Beyond sheer numbers, specialists also needed to be recruited. These included navigators and those in positions or trust who might have access to such items as keys and arms. This was always dangerous. If those approached refused to participate they might give the game away. The conspiracy to take the *Navarino* was hatched by six Ulstermen (three Catholics and three Protestants). It was betrayed by a 45-year-old Catholic labourer from Limerick.[28] Provincial allegiances were strong in Ireland.

Some mutineers attempted to bind others to the plot through the use of oaths and other devices. William Chapman reported that while he was lying in his berth on the *Argyle* he was asked by Frampton, one his neighbours, 'if you had a ship what would you do?' He was then asked to sign a piece of paper, an attempt to secure his allegiance to the enterprise. Chapman had cold feet from the start. According to his later testimony, he asked Frampton what would happen to the soldiers and sailors only to be told they would be heaved over the side of the vessel. To which he replied 'we must never see our country again if anything of that happens'. Frampton then said 'Damn and bugger the country, can't we live as well in another'. This appears to have had little appeal to Chapman.[29] A former poacher who had been transported for stealing a faggot of wood and a pickaxe, he had left a wife and a child behind in Dorchester.[30] The information that he provided to the surgeon-superintendent secured a favourable recommendation, useful for securing future indulgences including a possible assisted passage for his family. The wives and children of deserving convicts were sometimes permitted to travel to the Australian colonies to be reunited with their husbands.[31] A perpetual problem that convict mutineers faced was that their self-liberational desires provided escapist opportunities for informers.

Richard Jones, transported on the *Isabella Watson* in 1842, drew on his considerable experience of conspiratorial movements in an attempt to control loose tongues. A clerk by training, Jones had been the secretary of the Dublin Ribbon Society, an anti-protestant republican organisation

[28] State Library New South Wales, Tas Papers 304, 29–60 and D5.

[29] *Colonial Times*, 7 September 1831.

[30] William Chapman, per *Argyle*, Police No. 1240, T.A., Con 31-1-7.

[31] McIntyre, P. (2011) *Free Passage: The Reunion of Irish Convicts and Their Families in Australia 1788–1852*, Irish Academic Press, Dublin, 51–68.

that also operated as a quasi-benefit society. As well as corresponding with other Ribbonmen, the Dublin police thought that he had been party to an 1836 attempt to blow up a statue of William III. According to Garvin, Jones was instrumental in attempting to link the Dublin society to other Ribbon groups in northern Leinster and Ulster.[32] The majority of his co-mutineers on the *Isabella Watson* came from precisely this region. Four were from County Cavan, two from Longford and one from Meath. All the conspirators gave their religion as Catholic. Ribbon societies used a system of passwords, oaths and secret signs to organise members. According to the farm labourer James Byrne, Jones approached him on 15 May to ask him if he 'would be one of the party'. He then took a book out of his pocket, probably the catechism used at Ribbon meetings, in order to bind Byrne to the plan. The oath may have been effective at keeping some quiet. Francis Gafney confessed that he too had been asked to join the conspiracy, but on the advice of his brother and another prisoner had shunned the plotters. Although he refused to join the plot, he did not turn informer.[33]

Planning was evident in other conspiracies. The convicts onboard the *Atlas* managed to obtain some form of poison when the vessel pulled into Rio de Janeiro to resupply. Convicts were sometimes employed as servants and this appears to have provide an opportunity to adulterate the military rations. It was only after a sizeable proportion of the guard had become mysteriously ill that the Irish prisoners rose up on 3 March 1802 in an attempt to seize the vessel. A mutiny in the same year on board the *Hercules* was only supressed after 14 convicts were killed in an attempt to take the vessel.[34]

Radicalism on convict vessels was not limited to prisoners. Part of the crew on the *Prince Regent* mutinied on 17 December 1830. For the rest of the voyage they were put in irons—joining the convicts.[35] Whereas the surgeon and ship's officers could force the free to inhabit spaces normally reserved for the unfree, this only served to strengthen the similarities between crew and convict. Sailors too could be flogged and placed in

[32] Garvin, T. (1982) Defenders, Ribbonmen and Others: Underground Political Networks in Pre-Famine Ireland, *Past and Present*, 96, 133–155.

[33] SLNSW, Dixson Library, Add 537.

[34] Ramsey Silver, L. (2002) *Australia's Irish Rebellion: The Battle for Vinegar Hill*, Watermark Press, Sydney, 89.

[35] T.A., Papers Concerning the *Prince Regent*, CSO1/442/9841.

the solitary confinement box that was secured to the deck of many transport vessels. The diet that convicts were fed was based on naval rations and every surgeon charged with maintaining discipline during the voyage was naval trained. While the industrial landscape of the ship was used to regulate the lives of convict passengers, this was also true of the men who were employed to sail it. They too worked to ship time. While they did not come on board with their feet shackled in irons, the vessels that they served on were nevertheless coercive institutions.[36]

When James McTernan on the *Sarah* uncovered a plot to seize the vessel he discovered to his alarm that at least one member of the crew was implicated. As he informed the colonial secretary on arrival in Hobart Town: 'I found Wilson, one of the sailors, so unequivocally involved, not only as an abettor, but as one whom by his … promise, their chief reliance rested as well for information as for aid by conveying arms to the mutineers'.[37] This was McTernan's tenth voyage as a surgeon superintendent and he had already had at least one other run-in with would-be mutineers. On the *Ocean* sailing to New South Wales in 1823 he had placed five ringleaders he thought were determined to possess the vessel in irons. Rather than selecting a military guard to watch over the miscreants, he picked twelve 'good' convicts to watch them at night.[38] This may have reflected a desire to keep security in-house. Despite the explicit instructions provided to officers on transport vessels, relations between surgeons, masters and military officers were often strained by voyage end.[39] Indeed it is noticeable that the only successful mutiny on a convict vessel—the seizure of the *Lady Shore* in 1797—was engineered by the military detachment. The event, however, illustrated how blurred the line between convict, seaman and soldier could become.

[36] Linebaugh, P. and Rediker, M. (2000) *The Many-Headed Hydra: Sailors, Slaves, Commoners and the Hidden History of the Revolutionary Atlantic*, Beacon, Boston, 143–173.

[37] James McTernan to Colonial Secretary, T.A., CSO 5/19/398.

[38] Brooke and Brandon, *Bound for Botany Bay*, 146.

[39] British Parliamentary Papers (1972) Instructions to Surgeons Superintendent on Board Convict Ships Proceeding to New South Wales or Van Diemen's Land, 1832, in *Correspondence and Papers Relating to Convict Transportation 1810–41*, vol. 6, Irish University Press, Shannon, 253–258.

The detachment of New South Wales Corps detailed to act as guard on this vessel contained a large number of 'recruits' from the Savoy military prison. Deserters were routinely transported as convicts while Britain was at peace. When at war, however, both military and civilian convicts were pressed into service.[40] Amongst these unwilling recruits were several who had been enlisted from gaol as well as a number of prisoners of war including a helmsman and pilot from the captured French corvette *La Bonne Citoyenne*. The convicts they were charged with guarding consisted of 66 women and one man, the latter being the 'notorious' adventurer and swindler Major Semple Lisle. Lisle later wrote an account of the affair in which he explicitly linked the troubles encountered during the voyage to the display of radicalism that those on board witnessed while anchored at Spithead. As he described it, the 'British fleet laying close to us, was then in a state of open rebellion'.[41] The Spithead mutiny broke out on 16 April 1797 when sixteen ships of the line refused to weigh anchor when ordered to join the blockade of Brest. The dispute lasted until 15 May when the government conceded to the bulk of the mutineers' demands.[42] By then the *Lady Shore* had set sail. Lisle alleged that it was a somewhat hurried departure spurred on by a desire to distance the convict vessel from the 'mutiny then raging on board His Majesty's ships, by which we were surrounded'.[43]

To the casual observer the *Lady Shore* may well have appeared to represent a distortion of the proper state of affairs on a transport vessel. After all, when she hastily set sail Lisle, a member of the officer class, was numbered amongst the felons whilst several former convicts could be counted amongst the ranks of the soldiers. While the voyage was hardly typical it did serve to illustrate the fine line that separated convict, soldier and sailor. As far as the Naval Board was concerned, however, the female convicts below decks were far from innocent bystanders. It was widely

[40] Maxwell-Stewart, H. (2010) Convict Transportation from Britain and Ireland, 1615–1870, *History Compass*, 8, 9.

[41] Semple, L. (1800) *The Life of Major J. G. Semple Lisle Containing a Faithful Narrative of His Alternate Vicissitudes of Splendour and Misfortune*, Stewart, London, 181.

[42] Rodger, N. (2004) *Command of the Ocean: A Naval History of Britain, 1649–1815*, Norton, New York, 446–453.

[43] Semple, L. *The Life of Major J. G. Semple Lisle*, 182.

thought that the affair was sexually charged and that social and physical intercourse between convicts and guard had led to the loss of the vessel. After the taking of the *Lady Shore* military detachments ceased to be placed on female transports because the risk that the guard would fraternize with their charges was considered too great.[44]

Damousi has argued that 'mutiny and disorder came to carry different meanings for male and female convicts'. As she puts it: 'For women, notions of disorder were conceived in sexual terms and a particular form of surveillance was undertaken accordingly'.[45] While this is true there is a danger of overlooking the threat that female convicts posed to security. Attempted mutinies were certainly not restricted to male vessels. When James Hall attempted to crack down on what he referred to as 'prostitution' amongst the female convicts on the *Brothers* in 1824 he claimed that 'Six women conspired to murder me ... and did actually form a mutiny of an alarming nature, in which I was knocked down in the prison, beaten and kicked'. He alleged that the revolt had been instigated by James Thompson Meach, the chief mate, who had offered the women a bottle of rum in return for dispensing with Hall. While Meach was subsequently cleared of instigating mutiny, the incident confirmed that sexual relations on female transports were policed for more than ideological reasons.[46]

For all the attempts to spatially and socially separate convicts from crew and soldiers, conspiracies continued to be uncovered that involved those located both within and outside the ship's prison. A problem was that, while those who sailed and guarded the ship might technically be free, the circumstances they faced were close enough to those experienced by convicts to highlight the coercive nature of both forecastle and the barrack room. If this applied to sailors it was especially the case for soldiers. As the rank and file pressed from the Savoy prison into service with the New South Wales Corps understood, to be shipped as a soldier to Botany Bay was to receive a sentence of exile—it was de facto transportation. The military units that replaced the New South Wales Corps did a tour of duty that routinely encompassed first service in the Australian colonies and then British India. Rankers were often away for seven years, the length of the minimum sentence to transportation. Indeed, some

[44] Bateson, *Convict Ships*, 26.

[45] Damousi, *Depraved and Disorderly*, 19.

[46] Bateson, *Convict Ships*, 225–226.

soldiers deliberately offended in order to get court martialled reasoning that a sentence to transportation was preferable to the privations of barrack life.[47]

As Colonel Breton, who commanded a regiment in New South Wales, argued in his evidence to a British Parliamentary Inquiry: 'demoralization was … produced amongst the troops by their intercourse with the prison population, which could not be prevented, because many of the men found their father brothers and other relatives, amongst the convicts'.[48] Even where there were no kinship ties there were plenty of convicts who had served time in the forces. On board the *Somersetshire* bound for Hobart in 1841 a plot was uncovered that involved both convicts and guards. One of the convict ringleaders subsequently clapped in irons was William McCauley, a groom from County Fermanagh who had previously served nine years in the Enniskillen Dragoons. McCauley and his co-accused, Arthur Hewiett and John Winkfield, managed to persuade three privates and a bugler of the 99th regiment to join the conspiracy. It was subsequently alleged that their plan was to kill the officers and set any remaining loyalists adrift in the ship's boats. The mutineers intended to then sail the vessel to South America, by far and away the most popular destination for would-be convict mutineers. So serious was the threat that the ship put into Cape Town so that a court martial could be assembled. The four soldiers were put on trial for 'conspiracy to take forcible possession of the ship and do forcible injury to the officers on board', although one of them subsequently turned Queen's evidence. Of the remaining three, John Agnew was sentenced to be shot by firing squad and Walter Chisolm and John Kelly transported for life.[49]

[47] Hilton, P. (2010) "Branded D on the Left Side": A Longitudinal Study of Military Convicts Transported to Van Diemen's Land, Ph.D. thesis, University of Tasmania, 216–219.

[48] Molesworth, W. (1967) *Report from the Select Committee of the House of Commons on Transportation Together with a Letter from the Archbishop of Dublin on the same Subject and Notes by Sir Wiiliam Molesworth, BART Chairman of the Committee 1838*, Wakefield, Adelaide, 16.

[49] *Colonial Times*, 31 May 1842; *Launceston Examiner*, 4 June 1842. Although he spent ten days in the condemned cell Agnew's sentence was commuted to life imprisonment. Incarcerated for nine months on Robben Island Agnew was eventually forwarded to Van Diemen's Land on the *John Renwick* in 1843, Walter Chisolm and John Kelly arrived the previous year on the Surrey. D.L., Add 537, p. 239 and M.L., D 5.

After a plot to take the *Isabella Watson* was uncovered it emerged that the conspirators included at least one soldier. While relieving himself at the heads, private Barney Macanally told two prisoners that there were some amongst the guard who would not participate in any attempt to put down a mutiny. Instead, they would as he put it 'make their water on the pistols and flintlocks so that they would not go off'. Later in the voyage another Irish soldier ordered to stand guard over the conspirators was ironed after he was seen making Ribbonman signals to one of his prisoners.[50]

Following three attempts to seize vessels between April and August 1842 Franklin, the Lieutenant Governor of Van Diemen's Land, requested that navy ships be selected as convict transports in the future. As the *Launceston Examiner* put it, 'There are many two-deckers cruising, about the British Channel which might be advantageously spared for this duty'. Such measure would increase discipline and remove the added danger of 'the too frequent insubordination of sailors in the merchant service'.[51]

The voyage to Australia was designed to be an informative experience, part and parcel of the process of turning the convicted into penal labourers. Despite the isolation and the daily regime of deck scrubbing, washing and oakum picking, that process was contested. If the four months spent at sea was deigned to atomise convicts then the surgeon superintendents failed in their duties. Whereas it is difficult to count mutiny attempts they were certainly not infrequent. A survey of voyages to Van Diemen's Land reveals that concerns about a plot to seize the vessel were raised on approximately one voyage in ten. Convicts were routinely punished for mutinous actions in the hulks and during the voyage itself. Plots hatched amongst small groups of conspirators had to be transmitted to a wider circle of confederates to be put into action. While convicts outnumbered crew and military detachments, transport vessels doubled as prisons the seaborne inmates were always under surveillance, especially when on deck. Attempts to recruit beyond the initial core usually led to betrayal despite the use of oaths, signed agreements and other devices. The main reason for this was that informers stood to gain

[50] John A. McDonald extract from the log of the *Isabella Watson*, 2 May–20 July 1842, SLNSW, ML, MSS 1808/Box 1.

[51] *Launceston Examiner*, 23 September 1842.

considerable advantages. Despite the high level of betrayal, ships' officers and colonial officials continued to be wary of the threat of mutiny.

The conspirators were drawn from a wide variety of backgrounds. Some were transported for explicitly political offences whereas others were illiterate labours convicted of property crimes. They came from both rural and urban areas and from the length and breadth of the British Isles. Some had been sentenced in other parts of the British Empire, and this was especially the case with soldiers. Both former soldiers and sailors featured prominently amongst those identified as ringleaders. Not all of those who participated in plots to take transport vessels were convicts. Throughout the transportation era, ships officers and colonial officials were surprised by the extent to which the 'dreams of mutiny' hatched in prisons below deck spread into those quarters of the ship occupied by the guard and crew. It was former sailors who had been pressed into service with the New South Wales Corps who played the lead in the capture of the *Lady Shore* in 1797. That mutineers had almost certainly acted in partnership with the female convicts was not lost on the government who henceforth removed military detachments from female convict vessels. The fact was that 'those lads' who 'contrived a plan', to quote from the convict ballad the *Cyprus Brig*, were not necessarily lads nor necessarily lagged.

The experience of radicalism at sea had implications for convict management on land. Whereas the state attempted to use the process of transportation as a means of producing docile bodies, the convicted had other ideas. Although all bar one attempt to seize a transport vessel failed, the prisoners disgorged onto the shores of the Australian colonies were certainly not done with attempts at self-liberation.

CHAPTER 6

Issuing Demands and Threats and Striking Deals

In February 1822 James Straiter was charged with 'exciting his master's servants to combine, for the purpose of obliging him to raise their wages and increase their rations'. As well as advocating a collective approach to labour negotiation Straiter had personally fronted up to his master, the powerful landowner Charles McArthur, threatening that any failure to concede to the men's demands would result in retaliatory action. McArthur was left in no doubt that his flock was at risk. He had Straiter arraigned for 'violently resisting' his orders' and 'setting at defiance all those in authority on the establishment'.[1]

It emerged in court that unrest had been simmering on Charles McArthur's property for some months. His convict workforce had unsuccessfully lodged a complaint about the quality of their rations. Giving evidence Charles' brother, Hannibal Macarthur, said that Straiter had told him that he well knew the value of sheep and the wool on their backs. The militant assigned servant also implied that he could calculate the cost of rations, and therefore, the overall benefits that accrued from hiring convict labour over free. He was in no doubt that the Macarthurs could afford the monetary payments and other claims demanded by their assigned servants. While the case ended up in court, it was evident

[1] *Sydney Gazette*, 1 March 1822.

H. Maxwell-Stewart and M. Quinlan, *Unfree Workers*, Palgrave Studies in Economic History,
https://doi.org/10.1007/978-981-16-7558-4_6

that the Macarthurs had already made significant concessions to their convict workers. It emerged, for example, that Straiter had been promised £15 wages per annum, plus other significant performance bonuses. The episode provides clear evidence that convicts engaged in both wage and effort bargaining, although it also illustrated the ways in which the Macarthurs had attempted to claw back the value of the conceded concessions through exorbitant charges made for goods purchased at the estate store.[2]

This chapter will describe the ways in which convicts negotiated with private sector masters and public administrators in an attempt to lay down ground rules for the manner in which work would be rewarded. This included both monetary payments and appropriate levels of in-kind incentives for the completion of certain tasks. A minimum ration standard was a particular sticking point. Here both quantity and quality were issues. Convicts campaigned against the adulteration of flour—the substitution of corn or barley for wheat was a common complaint. They also combined to resist attempts to pass off inferior or rancid cuts of meat as part of the daily ration. In addition, they negotiated over the length of the working day and access to time off at weekends and on public holidays. As well as arguing over what constituted base-line payment levels, convicts also combined to push for improvements in working conditions. Much of this agitation was conducted verbally. Where such demands were not met, it was common to issue threats leaving masters and convict managers in little doubt about the consequences of not listening to their unfree workers. Some also attempted to escalate matters by appealing to higher authority. This usually took the form of a petition, although on occasion convicts attempted to use the law to gain redress.

Wage Bargaining

Although the payment of wages to convicts was proscribed in 1824 the practice continued to be widespread. In 1835 a Campbell Town shopkeeper admitted that his two convict shopmen were in receipt of wages when he prosecuted them for stealing liquor.[3] Occasionally

[2] *Sydney Gazette*, 1 March 1822.

[3] Dillon, M. (2008) Convict Labour and Colonial Society in the Campbell Town Police District, 1820–1839, PhD thesis, University of Tasmania, 135.

the non-payment of promised monetary bonuses to convicts triggered strike action. In November 1839 Michael Riley and Robert Harvey asked Hobart tailor, Michael Fitzgerald, for money and indicated they would not work unless this was forthcoming. Fitzgerald refused, initially charging both with insubordination, but altered this to misconduct in trying to extort money from him. For their pains Riley received 36 lashes and Harvey was sent to a chain gang for six months.[4]

While the payment of convicts was technically prohibited, many successfully negotiated for monetary incentives. This was particularly true of those who possessed skills that were hard to replace or at times of the year when masters needed every hand on deck. Both the harvest and shearing presented significant opportunities for rural convicts to flex their muscle in an attempt to secure better conditions. As a report from Yass published in the Sydney *Monitor* in January 1840 put it:

> Convicts assigned to private service have made up their minds to do what quantity of work they please. Ten shillings per acre to cut wheat, was offered by one or two gentlemen, as an indulgence and encouragement to work well that sum was exclusive of their rations and slops and two glasses of rum daily; they however refused to exert themselves, unless they had fifteen shillings per acre, which of course was given to them. Assignees well knowing it was only time lost to take them to Court, and even when convicted, the punishment is considered by these rascals to be so lenient, that they come home laughing in their sleeves at the trouble they have given their masters.[5]

The supply of cash and other incentives to convicts as an inducement to labour, especially outside of government hours, remained widespread. As a result, despite extraordinarily high levels of policing, it proved impossible to stop convicts from spending monies and other perks gained through workplace bargaining on alcohol, gambling and other leisure pursuits. This was the case even in highly restricted environments such as penal stations and female factories. The monetisation of the ration opened up opportunities for effort bargaining, black market trading and other activities which effectively derailed administrative plans at every level of the convict system.

[4] M.L., Tas Papers 270, Hobart Benchbook, 4 November 1839.

[5] *Monitor*, 13 January 1840.

In the end the colonial administration abandoned the attempt to run a cashless unfree labour system. Following the publication of the Molesworth Report, a second attempt was made to regulate the convict labour market. This was organised around passholder contracts signed by the would-be employer of convict labour and the colonial administration. The new system was introduced in Van Diemen's Land in 1840 and was intended to circumvent the possibility of convicts striking individual deals. In practice, however, this remained hard to achieve. A minimum convict wage was set at £9 per year for a male passholder and £7 for a female, although the master still had to provide rations, accommodation and bedding. There was considerable room for convicts to bargain for increases in the in-kind component of this remuneration package, even if their wage was fixed. Another aspect of the scheme that was widely criticised was that each convict had the right to refuse a contract extension. The maximum amount of time that a passholder could be signed up for was a year. This provided further room to bargain for better conditions, although this provision was removed in 1847 when the passholder system was tightened-up.[6] Even after this, however, there is plenty of evidence that the tightened regulations failed to check convict bargaining.

In May 1846, for example, a Kangaroo Point employer named Hecksher prosecuted three convict sawyers for neglect after they refused work in pursuit of a claim for higher wages. The prosecution was dismissed, however, when it was revealed that Hecksher had already agreed to pay the men for each 100 feet sawn or around £1 per week—a sum which was well in excess of the £9 per year specified in the passholder contract he had signed with government.[7] In short, once employers agreed to wages beyond those enforceable, as many appeared to have done because the specified rates were so far below market rates, they lost the capacity to refer disputed wages to the courts. As with the assignment system, regulations designed to control the supply of cash to convicts were difficult to administer, if for no other reason than they limited the master's options as well as those of their unfree charges.

[6] Meredith and Oxley, 'Contracting Convicts', 48–49.

[7] *Colonial Times*, 15 May 1846.

Incentive Bargaining

The supply of non-monetary rewards also provided opportunities for convicts to bargain for more favourable conditions. Goods received as perks typically included clothing, shoes, hats and bonnets or extra rations like tea, sugar, alcohol and tobacco. In November 1829, 13 convicts on Webber's Tocal Estate near Paterson in the Hunter Valley were prosecuted for refusing to work unless 'they received the usual indulgence allowed in harvest time', in this case a dietary supplement of sugar or milk.[8] In other cases, bargaining disputes over additional rations or other rewards are implied or ambiguously alluded to in newspaper reports. In December 1826 the *Sydney Gazette* related that a Windsor landholder had prosecuted several workers from a group that had refused work. The grievance that triggered the protest appears to have been a failure to increase the bonus payment of sugar offered as an incentive to bring in the harvest.[9] Claims for additional rations, alcohol and tobacco during harvest or shearing were common. While the difficulties encountered in directly bargaining over wages might have been a factor in the creation of these practices, they reflected centuries old customs in rural work. Indeed, such convict 'customary practices' carried over to the organisation of free work. In-kind payments continued to be made to reapers and shearers as seasonal performance bonuses long after the ending of the convict era.[10]

While often fragmentary, court records contain substantial evidence of bargaining over the terms and conditions of employment by convicts and considerable use of collective sanctions to reinforce these claims. On 24 November 1835 several New Norfolk brickmakers demanded extra rations before they would burn a kiln of bricks. They agreed to return to work, but three days later again struck. It was this second action that resulted in the matter being brought before the courts, although even then they escaped punishment, being ordered instead to return to work. The failure to impose sanctions may have been indicative of their scarce skills. Whether their action was part a push for additional rations

[8] Walsh, B. (2007) Heartbreak and Hope, Deference and Defiance on the Yimmang: Tocal's Convicts 1822–1840, PhD thesis, University of Newcastle, 235–236.

[9] *Sydney Gazette*, 13 December 1826.

[10] See Quinlan, M. (2018) *The Origins of Worker Mobilisation: Australia 1788–1850*, Routledge, New York; Quinlan, M. (2020) *Contesting Inequality and Worker Mobilisation: Australia 1851–1880*, Routledge, New York.

customary in some other activities (like harvest work) or a response to the inadequacy of those supplied (common in public works gangs) is unclear.[11]

What is clear, however, is that demands for additional rations were often made and frequently conceded to. Sometimes individual workers attempted to bargain for in-kind remuneration. James Harkins was sentenced to three days solitary on bread and water in October 1836 for refusing to work unless supplied with extra rations.[12] As the case illustrates, demands for extra food were likely to result in court sentences that placed workers on punishment diets in the same way as time was frequently added onto the sentences of recaptured absconders.

Many employers provided alcohol as an incentive, because they knew that this could be an effective inducement to labour. This was despite the fact that the practice was specifically forbidden. This was particularly the case when the weather was inclement. Rain could bring labour on the public works to a standstill and convicts assigned to outdoor work in the private sector would often refuse to work in wet conditions unless an incentive was provided. The provision of such inducements was sometimes recorded in diaries or revealed in court proceedings. Mrs. Bailey of Broadmarsh prosecuted three servants for indecent language, one having called her a 'bloody old whore'. It emerged in court that all three were rather the worse for wear having been provided with 'a little extra to drink' as an inducement to toil on a wet Sunday. The implication was that a considerable amount of alcohol had been provided to get the men to work in foul weather on their day off. One of the workers was admonished after her intercession while the other two were ordered to a road gang for six months with a recommendation that they should not be returned to her service.[13] The case highlights the extent to which the issue of alcohol was regarded as a regular practice and the capacity of employers to shape sentencing on the basis of past behaviour—something many workers undoubtedly knew from direct experience or word of mouth.

Convict workers attempted to re-establish customary practices for workers in Britain and, on occasion, argue for new customary expectations

[11] M.L., Tas Papers 237, New Norfolk Benchbook, 24 November 1835.

[12] M.L., Tas Papers 290, Oatlands Benchbook, 29 October 1836.

[13] M.L., Tas Papers 2, Richmond and Brighton Benchbook, 25 May 1837.

in relation to particular work practices. There is an irony here, in that the introduction of waged work in Britain and Ireland was accompanied by a sustained attack on workers' rights to traditional perks and perquisites.[14] Attempts to deny a wage to convicts in the Australian colonies meant that those whose services were in demand were in a position to argue for an Antipodean reimplementation of those perks and other similar rights. Again, much of the evidence comes from court cases. In April 1829, for example, a Mr. Parker was forced to withdraw charges of stealing maize brought against two Port Macquarie convicts after it emerged that he had told them they might have a cob or so for planting and feeding pigs.[15] The right to gather wheat and barley that had not been cut by harvest gangs was a traditional perk provided to rural workers in Britain and Ireland, although as we have seen, access to such gleanings became less common as wages replaced in-kind payments.

Demands for a daily quantity of grog when washing sheep, an essential pre-shearing task that required men to work in creeks or water-filled pits, had become a well-established norm by the 1820s. Refusal by some landholders to provide alcohol during sheep-washing caused frequent disputes. Those who struck work and were prosecuted are likely to have been symptomatic of wider bargaining, evidence of which can also be found in diaries and individual prosecutions. In January 1835 Oatlands landholder William Foord prosecuted Edward Smith for 'gross insubordination in threatening his master's life and using violent and abusive language.' Foord had paid a visit to his men while they were sheep-washing. Smith had used the appearance of his master to demand a quart of wine. When this was refused, he called Foord a 'bloody scoundrel' shouting that 'every man and every mother cries shame on you for treating your servants as you do'. He then refused to work, threatening to knock Foord's block off with an axe. The court extended his sentence by three years and ordered him to be sent to Port Arthur.[16]

Conceding to demands to increase incentives could trigger escalating demands. Matthew Mitchell, for example, charged two of his assigned servants with 'mutinous and disrespectful conduct' after they refused a

[14] Emsley, C. (1987) *Crime and society in England 1750–1900*, Longman, London, 103–124.

[15] AONSW., Reel 2723 Port Macquarie Benchbook, 30 April 1829.

[16] M.L., Tas Papers 290, Oatlands Benchbook, 2 January 1835.

bottle of rum on Christmas Eve as 'it was not enough.'[17] Such disputes reinforce the way in which employers attempted to cloak incentives in the language of paternalism. Such 'indulgences', especially those distributed on festive occasions, were gifts supplied out of the kindness of the employer's heart. Convicts, on the other hand, argued that payments in-kind were earned through labour and constituted a right, rather than a perk. Court cases provide evidence of how such differing interpretations could give rise to workplace disputes.

Oatlands district landholder, Peter Roberts, charged four convict sheep washers with insubordination in December 1841. In court he stated that, while he had promised the men spirits, they had demanded additional tea and sugar. When these were provided, they had bargained for an even greater supply of spirits. This is an unusual case in that it yields details of prolonged negotiations and effort bargaining over a period of time. The case is also atypical in that the charge was ultimately dismissed, although the men were reprimanded for using improper language in the presence of their master.[18] Punishing all those performing essential tasks, like sheep washing, would have inflicted harm on the employer and convicts exploited this. Most masters recognised that while brutal punishments might suppress the immediate threat of dissent, they often did so at a cost. Masters and overseers needed a degree of cooperation from their convicts. When six convicts 'neglected their duty' on James Meehan's property in January 1826 he chose to make an example of three. James and his son Thomas gave evidence that the men had done very little work, with some sleeping in the fields during working hours. Nonetheless, he interceded to have the sentence of 25 lashes suspended.[19] Meehan had bemoaned the lacklustre performance of his convict workforce since giving evidence to the Bigge Report, but it was the height of summer, and he needed the cooperation of his men. It was not uncommon for masters to bring retrospective complaints, conceding to convict demands in order to get work accomplished before attempting to use the courts to wind these back when the need to complete important seasonal tasks had passed.

[17] AONSW., Port Macquarie Benchbook, 29 December 1831.

[18] M.L., Tas Papers 291, Oatlands Benchbook, 24, 27 December 1841.

[19] AONSW., CY366 Liverpool Benchbook, 28 January 1826.

Bargaining for Access to Time

Working in their 'own' time was another significant way convicts could supplement their income. This practice had originally been permitted in the early days of the colonies to boost self-sufficiency, but was later prohibited. Even prior to prohibition, disputes arose as colonial authorities manipulated the task-work regime. In 1817 sawyers at Pennant Hills, north-west of Sydney went on strike in protest over rations and increased workloads that diminished the capacity to work on their own account. For organising this action, the two ringleaders received 100 lashes each.[20] In March 1818 five sawyers working at the Hobart sawpits were charged with neglect, their overseer stating they had barely completed half their allotted task-work before walking off the job. Several claimed they had attended a funeral while another (Owen Swift) said he stopped to move timber that might otherwise have been stolen. One funeral attendee (George Thatcher) was acquitted, while the other four had their allotted task-work doubled for the following week.[21]

In both New South Wales and Van Diemen's Land the abolition of wage payments to convicts in 1824 was associated with systematic attempts to extract greater effort from convict labour, especially through the expansion of the gang system and shifting assignment practices in favour of large rural employers. Following his appointment as Lieutenant-Governor in Van Diemen's Land, George Arthur relied on a relatively small number of colonial officials to implement the necessary bureaucratic apparatus to administer these changes. In August 1825, John Lakeland, Superintendent of Convicts responded to an enquiry from the colonial secretary regarding the prosecution of a sawyer at the Hobart lumber-yard who had attested that he could complete his weekly task-load of 500 square feet in just two days. While insisting that sawyers were regularly mustered like other convicts, Lakeland confirmed that those that reached their allotted task of 750–800 square feet per week were given time off in lieu.[22] What the sawyers did in the remaining time was not explained, but presumably many continued to work on their own account. Efforts to earn money through such means even occurred in remote settlements like

[20] Robbins, W. (2001) The Management of Convict Labour Employed by the New South Wales Government 1788–1830, UNSW PhD thesis, 34–37.

[21] M.L., Tas Papers 196, Hobart Benchbook, 24 March 1818.

[22] T.A., CSO1/1/305 7319, correspondence Lakeland to Montagu 29 August 1829.

Macquarie Harbour. On 4 October 1825 Leslie Ferguson, a convict who worked in the lumberyard at that settlement was charged with 'making & selling a box contrary to orders.'[23] Presumably this too was an article made in his 'own time.'

Covert practices enabling convicts to work for wages on their own behalf seem to have flourished at least for some categories of work where employers could use it as an incentive. As they were prohibited, these practices only come to attention as a result of disputes that was severe enough to breach the code of silence that favoured both parties. Francis Forbes, for example, permitted his boatmen to work one week in four for their own benefit and paid them the going rate for free-labour (12–14 shillings). However, in January 1833 a dispute arose over the number of loads provided and Forbes charged his men with disobedience and insolence. Elijah Williams, adjudged the chief instigator and spokesmen for this group of unfree workers, received 10 days on the treadmill while the others were reprimanded.[24]

Some enterprising employers sought to act as agents, lending out their assigned workers or raking off a percentage of the earnings their convicts derived from extra work.[25] Margaret Wilson, charged with absence from Burrows' household, told the court that 'her mistress was in the habit of allowing her to employ herself in the manner she liked, away from her house, and that she was obliged to pay a sort of weekly rent for this indulgence.' Wilson could not call supporting witnesses and this, together with her 'impudent manner', earned her three months in the third class at the female factory. However, on the following Wednesday two of Burrows' male servants went before the bench claiming that Burrows 'allowed them to work for any person who chose to employ them, upon their paying a certain weekly stipend to their master for this indulgence, and that he refused to give them any clothes, although they paid him what they earned.' The Bench ordered Burrows to give the men their due and to return them to the government. For its part, the *Monitor* argued these revelations should cause the Bench to re-visit Wilson's punishment.[26]

[23] Leslie Fergusson, per *Minerva*, Police No. 38, T.A., Con 31-1-13.

[24] AONSW., Reel 2682, Liverpool Benchbook, 28 January 1833.

[25] *Monitor*, 31 March 1832.

[26] *Monitor*, 31 March 1832.

For convicts, working on their own account offered an opportunity to earn money, but there was also an incentive to minimise effort in government or assigned service in order to maximise private income. Amongst assigned servants, especially those with trade skills, masters preferred a task-work regime that guaranteed a minimum output and some tolerated their servants working on their own account after allotted work quotas had been met. Again, these practices only tended to come to light when a dispute arose. In January 1831, for example, an assigned journeyman tailor charged his O'Connell Street master, David Smith, with taking a coat that he claimed was his own property as it had been made after completing his agreed task.[27]

In gangs, while both temporal and task-work controls applied, convicts still tried to secure income through 'outside' activities. A group on the Jericho Road Party were prosecuted in January 1840 for working for themselves in government hours.[28] Some also exploited government materials. Several members of the Oatlands Assignable Party were charged with making buckets for their own use with government materials, while three members of the New Norfolk Engineering Department were charged with cutting stone in the government quarry and selling it for their own benefit.[29] Employers, or their overseers, were also prosecuted for engaging prisoners. Patrick Dunn, overseer to Carlton landholder Joseph Steel overseer, was fined £10 (plus £4 and 6 shillings costs) for employing three Green Point Invalid Party members for upwards of one hour without having any lawful reason for doing so.[30]

In May 1835 three members of the Ross Public Works Party were found guilty of working on their own account, aided by their overseer who was dismissed and sent to Port Arthur. All three were punished together with two of Mrs. Abbott's servants who 'trafficked' the goods produced. Their conviction was considerably assisted by another gang-member who gave evidence for the Crown, thereby escaping punishment

[27] *Sydney Gazette*, 11 January 1831.

[28] M.L., Tas Papers 291, Oatlands Benchbook, 10 January 1840.

[29] M.L., Tas Papers 291, Oatlands Benchbook, 17 March 1841; Tas Papers 238, New Norfolk Benchbook, 27 March 1840.

[30] M.L., Tas Papers 2, Richmond and Brighton Benchbook, 11 December 1835.

for his involvement.[31] In December 1839 two blacksmiths in Oatlands received four days solitary for working on their own account and four other gang members were convicted on neglect and gross misconduct for 'working for an individual in the township' carting timber.[32] Eighteen months later a member of the same gang was charged with a similar offence, while the overseer was convicted of allowing men in the wood cart to saw timber for private individuals, indicating others were involved and that the practice was organised. Both received a six-month extended sentence.[33]

While the post-Bigge Report changes were designed to peg the remuneration of convicts to the public sector ration, this proved difficult to implement in practice. Regulating the hours of work was an associated problem. Government convicts were expected to work during daylight that is twelve hours in summer and eight in winter, but not on Saturday afternoon or Sunday. They were also granted two holidays a year, Christmas Day and Good Friday.[34] Such a labour regime did not always suit the private sector. Harvest work had to be completed no matter what the day of the week for example. To do otherwise was to risk losing a crop to the vagaries of the weather. The landowner, William Archer, prosecuted one of his assigned men, William Rogers, for disobedience. As his overseer, James Parsons, elaborated to the bench:

> Yesterday afternoon at three minutes to four o'clock this man with some others came home, out of the field where he had been at work — I asked him what he came home for—he said it was sundown — I told him to go and put some Hay in the carts for the bullocks — he said 'I'll be damned if I do — it is sundown'.[35]

The difficulty that Archer and his overseer faced was that when the clock reached four Rogers was technically within his rights. Since work in the government sector was regulated by the rising and setting of the sun, this applied to the private sector too. This is why the charge was careful to

[31] M.L., Tas Papers 256, Campbell Town Prisoner Records and Sentences, 30 May 1835.

[32] M.L., Tas Papers 291, Oatlands Benchbook, 19 December 1839.

[33] M.L., Tas Papers 291, Oatlands Benchbook, 25 August 1841.

[34] Chief Police Magistrate Matthew Forster, T.A., POL 481, Tasmanian Archive.

[35] T.A., Longford Benchbook, 2 July 1836, LC362-1-3.

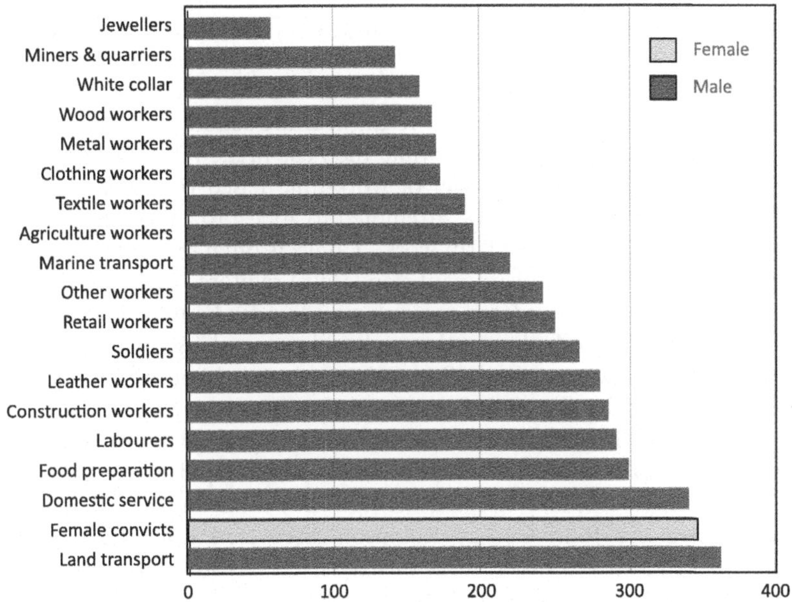

Fig. 6.1 Insolence (charges per 1000 convicts) (*Sources* T.A., Con 31, 32, 33, 40, and 41. Note grooms and coachman classied as 'Land transport' workers)

specify that there were three minutes of the working day left. Whatever the actual time that the dispute took place, however, Rogers could be tried for insolence—an offence for which he was awarded 50 lashes.[36] If a convict spoke inappropriately to their master or mistress they could be punished no matter how legitimate the issue they were attempting to raise.

The effects of this are illustrated in Fig. 6.1. Those convicts whose work brought them into greater contact with class superiors were more likely to be charged with insolence than others. Prosecutions for speaking back were disproportionately brought against grooms and coachman, domestic servants and cooks. As female convicts in assigned service were

[36] William Rogers, per *York* (2), Police No. 833, T.A., Con 31-1-37.

almost exclusively employed as servants, they too faced a disproportionate risk of being charged with speaking inappropriately to masters and mistresses. By contrast, robust conversations with overseers and other lower managers were less likely to result in court action.

As Bruce Hindmarsh argues, while the post-Bigge reforms attempted to enforce a standardised model of work-time based on the regulation of government labour, masters 'attempted to appeal to a more traditional model of the obligations of farm work'. Convicts often resisted this imposition, pointing to the government standard to reinforce their case. When William Johnston was ordered to work on a Sunday he told his master 'I have worked six bloody days in the week without working on a Sunday … you may go and bugger yourself'.[37] Others pretended not to hear instructions delivered after the end of working hours. Three convicts assigned to David Lord in Brighton (Van Diemen's Land) greeted their overseer's requests to move some bullocks after sunset with 'stupid silence'.[38]

Assigned servants also asserted the right not to labour on public holidays as overseer John George Robinson discovered when he tried to rouse W.E. Lawrence's men from their quarters. As Robinson related to the Longford bench, 'Yesterday morning I desired all the men to set to work'. They all duly responded except for James Harris and John Collins, who not only refused, but persuaded three others to return to the hut. When Robinson spoke to Collins 'he answered very insolently "What am I to come out for? This is Good Friday and I don't intend to work."' Robinson conceded that 'if these men had asked me in a proper manner' a half-day holiday would have been granted. While Harris was charged with 'refusing to work and inducing the rest of the men not to do anything', he was found guilty of 'disorderly conduct' while Collins was convicted for being insolent. Both were sentenced to a form of protracted Lent in the Longford watch-house dark cell, where they were imprisoned for a week on a diet of bread and water.[39]

[37] Hindmarsh, 'Yoked to the Plough', 203.

[38] M.L., Tas Papers 323, Richmond Benchbook, 14 February 1833.

[39] John Collins, per Red Rover, Police No. 1200, T.A., Con 31-1-7; James Harris, per Surry, Police No. 982, Con 31-1-19 and T.A., Longford Benchbook, 2 April 1836, LC362/3.

Ration Bargaining

As well as fighting to maintain control over their own time, convicts also sought to maintain ration standards. Assigned servants would refuse to accept Kangaroo *in lieu* of beef or mutton. While masters saw no difference between the two, meat was meat, convicts were unwilling to accept anything which in their eyes cost an employer little or nothing. In short, if the ration was not purchased or sourced from the master's paddocks it was not a ration.[40] In similar fashion John McCartney refused to accept a sheep's head and pluck, or offal as part of his ration, although such items were not uncommon in nineteenth-century plebeian diets.[41] Rising costs might also trigger protests when masters attempted to substitute cheaper items. When the price of tea in Hobart reached ten shillings a pound in 1825, James Sutherland attempted to substitute 'coffee' made from roasted wheat much to the disgust of his assigned servants who promptly rejected it.[42]

The supply of short rations, inferior cuts or items that were not fresh could trigger disruptions in the normal deferential dialectic that governed master-servant relations. At 5 p.m. on 31 July 1839 seven prisoners came to the house of William Nichols Junior to ask for supper. Nichols told them to return to their hut as they had been issued with rations. Clearly affronted by imposing on his family and somewhat intimidated, he called a constable and had the men charged with misconduct and duly punished. Four were flogged and the ringleader was sent to one of the newly constructed probation stations.[43] The scale of punishment revealed the extent of the affront. The message that had been delivered to Nichols was nevertheless clear. If the daily provisions provided by the 'big house' fell short of worker expectations, convicts would refuse to tug forelock and play the dutiful servant.

Allegations of shortfalls in the quantity or quality of rations were also a common trigger for protests amongst public sector convicts. This was the

[40] Copy of Despatch from Lieutenant-Governor Sir *John Franklin* to Lord *Glenelg* relative to the present system of Convict Discipline in *Van Diemen's Land*. Note G Testimonials by Messrs. Backhouse and Walker, British Parliamentary Papers, XLII(1837–8), 32.

[41] 23 November 1836, T.A., LC 362/3.

[42] As quoted in Hindmarsh, B., 'Yoked to the Plough', 165.

[43] M.L., Tas Papers 270, Hobart Benchbook, 1 August 1839.

case even in penal stations. Thomas Lempriere, the commissariat officer at Maria Island penal station on the east coast of Van Diemen's Land, reported that one morning after breakfast a delegation of convicts from No. 4 hut came to the store to complain about the quality of the ration. Their spokesperson, George Lacey, said 'the meat stunk and had done so for the last 3 days past'. Lempriere reported that he smelt each piece declaring it as 'sweet as possible'. The commandant also found the meat fit for consumption, whereupon the deputation marched up to his quarters and dumped the suspect ration on his doorstep. They were ordered back to collect it, but as soon as they got to the bridge over the creek they threw the meat into the water and walked off.[44]

Refusals to eat rations were fairly common. Usually these occurred as a result of disputes over the content and quality of items supplied. On occasion, however, such rejections accompanied withdrawals of labour. Since the ration was widely perceived as a wage, those who withdrew labour also engaged in hunger strikes to underscore their discontent. This was a rejection of both work practices and the sub-standard way in which work was remunerated. As the enquiry into conditions at James Mudie's Hunter Valley property found, men might 'lay down their meat' as well as their tools.[45]

Forming Combinations and Sharing Information

Bargaining or collective action in pursuit of rewards and in defence of working conditions was not confined to men. Female factories, like other government labour depots, were places where information about working conditions and norms were exchanged. Both male and female convicts often arrived at a property forewarned of local conditions, or at the very least, with an understanding of the norms that prevailed in similar workplaces. On at least two occasions convict women in factories organised a combination amongst domestic servants. In May 1839 the *Cornwall Chronicle* lamented that Launceston Female Factory inmates had combined to standardise demands for the quality of dresses supplied by

[44] Lempriere, T. (1954) *The Penal Settlements of Early Van Diemen's Land*, Royal Society of Tasmania, Launceston, 27–51.

[45] Roberts, D. (2017) Masters, Magistrates and the Management of Complaint: The 1833 Convict Revolt at Castle Forbes and the Failure of Local Governance, *Journal of Australian Colonial History*, 19, 70.

masters to domestic servants. The paper complained that having obtained such goods, the women ensured they were returned to the factory for misconduct where the incentives they had acquired were distributed amongst inmates according to a pre-arranged agreement.[46] Three years earlier the *Sydney Monitor* reported a similar combination at the Parramatta Female Factory. In this case when a 'refractory female servant who was under examination for refusing to work', admitted that she 'was acting in conformity with a compact entered into in the Factory'.[47] The walls of government institutions do not appear to have been very effective in preventing communication between the unfree. In May 1831 the Superintendent of Convicts in Launceston wrote to the Superintendent of the George Town Female Factory urging him to take action to prevent the women there from using the post to send letters to men in Launceston. He claimed that this was a practice that occurred on an almost weekly basis.[48]

New assigned servants were also briefed about working standards. In February 1833 Sussex farmer W.H. Glover prosecuted his domestic servant Sarah Smith for improper conduct 'in endeavouring to persuade her fellow servant to neglect her work.' Smith did not deny the charge. As she told the court: 'I tried to persuade Ann Griffiths who was a new servant last Sunday week not to clean rooms on a Sunday as it was bringing new rules into the house.' Some of the conversation was overheard and when Griffith was confronted by Mrs. Glover, she related what she had been told.[49] Tellingly, Smith herself had only been with the Glovers four months, a stay cut short by the bench who returned her to the factory to undergo hard labour for a month.

Other convicts banded together to protect their interests in the same way that would-be mutineers attempted to bind others to their plans. In August 1835 sub overseer Daniel Newman was charged with forming a combination with Robert Heath Hall and William Sarjent. The three men had taken a 'Solemn Oath binding themselves jointly to support the other'. Newman was sent to Port Arthur to be worked at his trade, while

[46] *Cornwall Chronicle*, 11 May 1839.

[47] *Sydney Monitor*, 19 December 1836.

[48] M.L., Tas Papers 278, Launceston Convict Superintendent Letterbook, correspondence 23 May 1831.

[49] M.L., Tas Papers 323, Richmond Benchbook, 19 February 1833.

the other two were dispatched to a road party for twelve months.[50] On 19 October 1818 at least six convicts were tried 'for conspiring with others to raise the price of work'.[51] Similar charges were laid against another group of convicts in October 1820.[52]

On other occasions convicts combined to resist punishments. Benjamin Gibbs, who also took part in the October 1818 conspiracy to raise wages, had previously been charged with 'Aiding and abetting Letitia Goodman to break a Padlock off an Iron Collar' which had been placed round her neck for punishment. For this he was awarded 200 lashes.[53] The punishment of hair-cutting was loathed by women in female factories. When informed she would have her cut by Hobart Factory Superintendent Joshua Drabble on 20 April 1827, Ann Wilson reacted violently, smashing windows until restrained and confined in a room from which she later escaped with the connivance of other inmates.[54] Hair-cutting sparked a number of strikes and riots, like one at the Parramatta Female Factory in March 1833.[55] The counter-productive nature of such punishments helps explain why they were relatively uncommon. Many prisoners were also punished for assisting escapes. In September 1833 two members of Notman's Road Gang were charged with aiding and abetting the escape of nine others. While one was acquitted the other was consigned to 60 days hard labour.[56] In October 1839 three members of the New Norfolk Assignable Party were similarly charged with being 'privy to the absconding of a man named Collins from the works yesterday without

[50] Daniel Newman, per Caledonia, Police No. 94, T.A., Con 31-1-29; William Sarjent, per *Bengal Merchant*, Police No. 914, Con 31-1-38 and Robert Heath Hall, per *Asia* (IV), Police No. 783, Con 31-1-19.

[51] Joseph Peck, per *Indefatigable*, Police No. 4, T.A., Con 31-1-34; Marier Tickner, per *Indefatigable*, Police No. 5, Con 31-1-42; James Dagger, per *Ruby*, Police No. 8, Con 31-1-9; Joseph Hoare, per *Pilot*, Police No. 62, Con 31-1-18; William Bradley, per *Kangaroo*, Police No. 37, Con 31-1-1; Benjamin Gibbs, per *Union*, Police No. 3, Con 31-1-13.

[52] William Jackman, per *Lady Castlereagh*, Police No. 40, T.A., Con 31-1-23.

[53] Benjamin Gibbs, per *Union*, Police No. 3, T.A., Con 31-1-13.

[54] Correspondence Drabble to Lakeland 1 May 1827, T.A., CSO1/1/2450.

[55] Hendriksen, G. Liston, C. and Cowley, T. (2008) *Women Transported: Life in Australia's Convict Female Factories*, NSW Parramatta Heritage Centre/University of Western Sydney, 15–24.

[56] Launceston Benchbook, 14 September 1833, T.A., LC346-1-15.

giving notice to the overseer'. They both received three days solitary confinement.[57]

A great many convicts were also prosecuted for obstructing attempts to charge and punish others. In March 1832 Margaret Gordon was sentenced to 14 days in the cells and to be placed in the crime class for six months for 'Refusing to go to the House of Correction as ordered & endeavouring to persuade the rest of the Females not to proceed in the Van.'[58] Mary Ann Smith and Jane Walker took the keys off Alice Lakeland, the overseer of the Ross Female Factory, locking her in a cell.[59] Others refused to go into solitary cells or give evidence in court when called upon to do so.[60] Many were also punished for refusing to assist masters, overseers and constables in the course of their duty. Jane Hill refused to get a light when called upon to do so by the chief constable, thereby hindering his attempts to search her master George Hutton's house.[61]

Another way in which prisoners combined was to inflict retribution on those who provided information to masters or government officials. James Edwards was punished at Port Arthur for 'upbraiding his overseer' for reporting him to the settlement office. The offence earned Edwards a one-month stint in the settlement chain gang.[62] In similar fashion, Alfred Caesar Joy was award 50 lashes and placed in a chain gang for six months in October 1826 for 'Using threatening language to & upbraiding Peter Aylward' and threatening to 'burn him' after the later provided evidence that led to the prosecution of several convicts.[63] Flagellators, particularly those who had plied their trade in penal stations, risked serious retaliatory action. William Hopper was sent to the chain gang for three months in 1827 for 'Assaulting & upbraiding John Flinn with cutting the men's flesh at Macquarie Harbour & endeavouring to incite the prisoners in the

[57] M.L., Tas Papers 238, New Norfolk Benchbook, 24 October 1839.

[58] Margaret Gordon, per Henry, Police No. 54, T.A., Con 40-1-3.

[59] Jane Walker, per *Cadet*, Police No. 708; Mary Ann Smith, per *Tory*, Police No. 817, T.A., Con 41-1-18, 17 April 1851. Alice Lakeland and her husband were appointed overseers at Ross (a joint husband & wife appointment) on 7 February 1851, see Blue Book for 1851 CSO50/2.

[60] Fanny Jarvis, per *Westmorland*, Police No. 142, T.A., Con 40-1-6.

[61] Jane Hill, per *Tory*, Police No. 727, T.A., Con 41-1-18, 22 April 1852.

[62] James Edwards, per *Bussorah Merchant*, Police No. 250, T.A., Con 31-1-9.

[63] Alfred Caesar Joy, per *Juliana*, Police No. 122, T.A., Con 31-1-23.

P[rison] B[arracks] to ill use him.'[64] Convicts who gave information that led to the apprehension of runaways could also find themselves the target of retaliation. William Barker was sent to Notman's road party for six months when he was found guilty of threatening James Hawkins after the latter had apprehended an absconder.[65] In similar fashion Eliza Churchill was intimidated by Catherine Owens and Ellen Scott after she made a statement to an April 1842 Board of Enquiry into Prison Discipline in return for a pardon.[66]

Just as employers categorised some workers as lazy or troublemakers, so too convicts categorised gang overseers and employers in terms of their treatment of the workers assigned to them. Such understandings seldom reached public records, but did so frequently enough to indicate the practice was not uncommon. A convict might, for example, tell an employer he was well-known as a tyrant or as a bad master. In February 1840 Fenton Forest landholder and political notable, Captain Michael Fenton, prosecuted three servants on loan for the harvest for 'making false reports prejudicial to the character of their master to a man named John Hall with intent to induce him to refuse going to that service.' Hall testified that Charles Day, James Stevens and William Tucker told him Fenton's farm was 'a very bad place.'[67] The son of a former Sligo High Sheriff who had pursued a military career before emigrating, Fenton regularly appeared before the bench to prosecute his servants. He was also a strong defender of the convict regime having been appointed to the Legislative Council in 1840.[68] The three convicts who dared to besmirch his reputation received three months hard labour in chains and were returned to the Crown for misconduct.

James Smith who had previously served time at Port Arthur penal station for plotting a conspiracy on board the *Katherine Stewart Forbes* on route to Van Diemen's Land was subsequently tried for 'Refusing to work and telling his master [Mr Mills] on 2 occasions that he would sooner be

[64] William Hopper, per *Phoenix*, Police No. 420, T.A., Con 31-1-18.

[65] William Barker, per *Asia* 3, Police No. 1011, T.A., Con 31-1-1, 21 May 1833.

[66] Frost, L. (2001) Eliza Churchill Tells ..., in Frost, L. and Maxwell-Stewart, H. eds. *Chain Letters: Narrating Convict Lives*, Melbourne University Press, Melbourne, 79–90.

[67] M.L., Tas Papers 238, New Norfolk Benchbook, 4 February 1840.

[68] Robson, L. (1966) Fenton, Michael (1789–1874), *Australian Dictionary of Biography*, Melbourne University Press, Melbourne, 371.

in a chain gang than in private service.' A three-month stint in irons did little to change his mind. Returned to Mills he was again charged with 'Having exhibited a spirit of great insubordination'. This time he was sent to the Grass Tree Hill Road Party and ordered not to be returned.[69] Such threats were not uncommon. Thomas McCormick was tried in February 1832 with 'Insubordination, disobedience of orders, [and] threatening his master's life'. For this he was sentenced to two months imprisonment and hard labour and ordered to be returned to Government, 'his master being apprehensive' of his wellbeing as a consequence 'of the threats of this man'.[70]

Diaries provide evidence of the shock of masters and mistresses when they discovered they too were judged and that such assessments were being used as a means of establishing work norms. James Cubbiston Sutherland, a Van Diemen's Land magistrate, recorded an October 1824 exchange with one of his assigned servants.

> I said I thought there was an abundance of time after 3 o'clock to wash his 3 shirts — He then complained that other settlers allowed every Saturday afternoon (Mr Reid and others) to their men — but that I was different and he plainly saw the more he did for me the more unreasonable I was.[71]

The entry serves to illustrate master frustrations at convict attempts to use information about other work practices to establish hours and conditions of service. While a record of prosecution was used to justify labour exploitation, the most onerous tasks being reserved for recidivists labouring on short rations, convicts advocated a reverse system of values. Those masters who did not provide their convict servants with appropriate levels of remuneration were the subject of below decks disapprobation in female factories, government gangs, sly grog shops and police station watch-houses. The circulated details of local employment practices informed convict attempts to bargain for better conditions. The very fact that fresh arrivals were interrogated prior to disembarkation, reveals the extent to which the convict administration recognised that

[69] James Smith, per *Katherine Stewart Forbes*, Police No. 1525, T.A., Con 31-1-39.

[70] Thomas McCormick, per *Bussorah Merchant*, Police No. 1037, T.A., Con 31-1-6.

[71] Diary of James Cubbiston Sutherland, 23 October 1824, T.A., NS 61/1.

lower order exchanges of information posed a threat to authority. If new arrivals were provided with the opportunity to talk to old-hands they would learn which were the best trades to claim—confounding public and private sector attempts to profit from convict labour as opposed to inflicting punishment through work in accordance with the principles of criminal justice.

While any form of verbal repost laid a convict open to a charge, language could form an effective means of helping to reshape labour practices. Individual and collective challenges to those in authority were common. This could include ribald songs and doggerel or critical statements made within a master's or overseer's hearing.[72] Five women were charged at Ross Female Factory on 9 April 1851 with 'causing a great disturbance and using improper language'.[73] The charge followed the prosecution of another five for not washing clothes entrusted to their care in the proper manner.[74] One of the women, Mary Fogerty, was further charged with upbraiding the wards woman, presumably for reporting the names of those involved.[75]

Though often combined with other charges, prosecution for insolence was commonplace. Boot-closer William Rosnell had his existing sentence of transportation extended 18 months in February 1837 for telling his master, the Hobart shoemaker Charles Flegg, that 'he would be damned if he would work' unless paid.[76] In March 1833 the *Sydney Herald* reported that Ann Fogerty and Elizabeth Maria 'were placed laughing and giggling at the bar, on charge of keeping their master's

[72] Frost, L. (1999) "Singing and Dancing and Making a Noise": Spaces for Women, *University of Tasmania Occasional Paper* 52, 1–20.

[73] Mary Conroy, per *Kinnear*, Police No. 930, T.A., Con 41-1-19; Margaret Casey, per *Cadet*, Police No. 961, Con 41-1-21; Mary Robertson, per *Baretto Junior*, Police No. 543, Con 41-1-27; Elizabeth Bartley, per *St Vincent*, Police No. 1018, Con 41-1-25.

[74] Mary Ann Robertson, per *Cadet*, Police No. 488, Con 41-1-21; Mary Ann Robinson, per *Elizabeth and Henry*, Police No. 407, T.A., Con 41-1-11; Mary Johnson, per *Earl Grey*, Police No. 379, Con 41-1-26; Jane Williams, per *Earl Grey*, Police No. 854, Con 41-1-26; Elizabeth Anderson, per *Elizabeth and Henry*, Police No. 231, Con 41-1-17.

[75] Mary Fogerty, per *Lord Auckland*, Police No. 407, T.A., Con 41-1-20.

[76] William Rosnell, per Circassian, Police No. 857, 21 February 1837, T.A., Con 31-1-37 and *Elliston's Hobart Town Almanack and Ross's Van Diemen's Land Annual* 1837.

house in an uproar the previous night, by milling in the kitchen, and when ordered to become calm, with giving their master a volley of abuse of the choicest selection.'[77] Three convicts on David Lord's Brighton property in Van Diemen's Land involved in a running dispute about the appropriate hours of labour, kept up such a racket at night singing and cursing and swearing that they kept the whole house awake.[78] Some convicts also spoke out in court after being sentenced—an action which invariably invited a rapid repost. In June 1854 groom Thomas Hartley received a sentence of 14 days solitary confinement after which he was ordered to be returned to his Battery Point master, J.H. Cox. Hearing the latter, Hartley announced that he would never serve Cox again, at which point he was charged with insolence to the presiding magistrate and sentenced to two months hard labour.[79] Thomas Davis went one stage further. When a sentence of 75 lashes was passed upon him for absconding from Port Arthur, he produced a stone that he had concealed in his jacket and threw it at the commandant. He was sentenced to an additional 100 lashes for this offence. Undeterred he absconded again the following month. This time when he was apprehended and tried, he threatened to shoot the magistrate, Captain Mahon. For this he was sentenced to two years imprisonment and hard labour.[80]

This oppositional ideology is perhaps best summed up by a description of a convict tattoo committed to file as part of the pre-disembarkation examination process. When Thomas Green arrived on the *Enchantress* in 1833 his right arm was inscribed with the phrase 'May the Sun never rise on the Palace of the Tyrant nor set on the Cottage of the Slave'.[81] It was an appropriate dictum for a place where the unfree argued that the limits of the working day were set by the passage of the sun. Green's tattoo also summed up the essence of a counter ideology that sought to disarm the language of 'convictism' by associating naked labour exploitation with the injustice of slavery.

[77] *Sydney Herald*, 28 March 1833.

[78] M.L., Tas Papers 323, Richmond Benchbook, 14 February 1833.

[79] T.A., LC247-1-25, Hobart Benchbook, 17 June 1854.

[80] Thomas Davis, per *Argyle*, Police Number, 693, T.A. Con 31-1-10.

[81] Thomas Green, per *Enchantress*, Police No. 917, T.A. Con 18-1-6.

Petitions and Complaints

The confrontation over the appropriate time to wash shirts that Sutherland recorded in his diary appears to have not ended up in court. One suspects that this was common, and that bench proceedings are representative of a minority of workplace negotiations that went wrong, rather than the majority where convicts struck deals with masters, mistresses, overseers or other labour managers. Where negotiations were unsuccessful, convicts resorted on occasion to appeals to higher authority. In 1817 the women transported on the *Canada* petitioned for monetary compensation due to the privations they had endured during the voyage. They were particularly exercised over the shortage of water.[82] Many petitions were triggered by the removal or reduction of additional incentives, particularly sugar, tea or tobacco. Such withdrawals resulted in the drawing up of memorials from a group of convicts working on the government farm at Emu Plains and at Bathurst in 1822, and coal miners on the Tasman Peninsula in 1840.[83]

On occasion convict letter writers bypassed the regular chain of command. Such letters often contained multiple signatures and were usually despatched without the knowledge of local managers. Their interception could trigger savage punishments. On 29 November 1827 four Macquarie Harbour convicts were awarded 50 lashes for 'causing a letter of an improper purport to be written' and affixing their names to this. Thomas Lawton, a member of the settlement boat crew, was also tried with conveying the missive on board the Brig *Prince Leopold* while Richard Biggs, who had been employed in the settlement schoolroom, was identified as the author. Biggs was awarded 75 lashes and Lawton 100 in addition to a six-month stint in irons.[84] While the stakes were high, such clandestine petition writers were occasionally successful. In the

[82] AONSW., CSO, Petition from Female Convicts Arrived per Canada for Remuneration for Beef Rations which they Agreed to Forgo on the Voyage on Account of Shortage of Water.

[83] Records Office NSW CSO petition of prisoners of Bathurst re tea and sugar ration Reel 6065 4/1798 P165.

[84] Henry Williams, per *Surrey*, Police No. 132 T.A., Con 31-1-45; John Knight, per *Recovery* (NSW) *Woodlark* (VDL) Police No. 178, Con 31-1-27; Charles Lewis, per *Commodore* Hayes, Police No. 264, Con 31-1-27; Thomas Cummings, per *Maria*, Police No. 322, Con 31-1-6; Thomas Lawton, per *Dromedary* (NSW) and *Anne* (VDL), Police No. 88, Con 31-1-27; Richard Biggs, per *Morely*, Police No. 606, Con 31-1-1.

same year a smuggled petition managed to make its way from Macquarie Harbour to Britain. This plea for a review of colonial sentencing practices was addressed to Joseph Hume, the parliamentary member for Aberdeen. Hume had a reputation for speaking out on colonial matters and was sometimes referred to as the 'post-box for colonial complaints'.[85] He took the matter seriously, writing directly to Lieutenant-Governor Arthur demanding a review of all sentences to secondary punishment in Van Diemen's Land.[86]

It was more common, however, to bring a complaint of ill-treatment, poor rations, clothing or accommodation before a local bench or convict superintendent. Many convicts lived in tents or rough huts that afforded little protection from the elements, especially in winter. An assigned servant charged Hugh McGuiness with not supplying sufficient bedding and complained of 'not being lodged in a weather tight hut'. The complaint, however, was dismissed.[87] Despite his age William Peebles received 25 lashes for disobedience and disorderly conduct when the eighteen year-old brought his sleeping cloaks into his master's kitchen and piled up wood in the fire at midnight on a June winter evening. When challenged by his master, William Wilson, he described his bed 'as not fit for a dog.'[88]

Such complaints were often collective, both because the ill-treatment was often generalised to a workplace and because collective complaints were more likely to be believed. There was both safety-in-numbers as well as a greater chance of gaining redress. In August 1821 five servants on George Salter's farm south of Hobart complained at the poor quality of the meat supplied and that their master had removed a sieve they used after grinding their grain.[89] The complaint was upheld, and the men were returned to government. Similarly, in May 1827 the Sydney

[85] *HRA*, III, VIII, n. 683, pp. 971–973 and Eddy, J. (1969) *Britain and the Australian Colonies 1818–1831: The Techniques of Government*, Oxford University Press, Oxford, 48 and 57–59.

[86] Joseph Clark, Thomas Bird and James Cock to Joseph Hume Esq., May 1828, *HRA*, III, VIII, pp. 618–621; Chief Justice to Lieutenant-Governor, 12 September 1829 and Clark, Bird and Cock to House of Commons, May 1828, *HRA*, III, VIII, pp. 616 and 620.

[87] M.L., Tas Papers 323, Richmond Benchbook, 22 January 1833.

[88] M.L., Tas Papers 325, Richmond Benchbook, 24 June 1833.

[89] T.A., LC247-1-1 Hobart Benchbook, 18 August 1821.

bench described an example of the pork supplied by D.D. Mathews to his servants as 'scarcely fit for dogs, much-less human beings'. Rejecting Mathews' argument that servants should accept the good with the bad, the bench ordered the removal of his men.[90] In the same month 17 members of Laragay's road gang at Longbottom succeeded in petitioning over the amount and quality of their rations after being charged with refusing to work.[91] In December 1833 the overseer at J.D. Rowe's Berrima district estate was ordered to obtain meat from Mr. Riley by 3 p.m. that day after a complaint lodged by four servants.[92] In August 1838 five assigned convicts at Lachlan McAllister's Clifton farm successfully lodged a complaint of ill-treatment which resulted in the men being removed and returned to the government. McAllister was so outraged he wrote a letter of complaint to the Colonial Secretary.[93] Rates of success were highest where the object of the complaint was other convicts, rather than free individuals and especially free individuals of standing. In October 1840, 12 convicts in the Hyde Park Barracks complained of a deficiency in their rations. An investigation discovered that some of the cooks were holding back articles and offering these for sale on the black market.[94]

More typically, however, complaints were dismissed as frivolous. This was the Bathurst bench's response to a charge of ill-treatment brought by 18 men of the Western Road Party in 1827. While these complainants escaped with a reprimand, in many instances the workers involved were punished. In September 1834 the Hobart Bench dismissed William Nest, Thomas Miller and Robert Alexander's claim of receiving insufficient bread from their master and then ordered them to receive 25 lashes each 'for preferring a frivolous charge.'[95] A month later the New Norfolk bench was equally unsympathetic when four servants of W. Bannon complained that maize was being mixed with wheat flour in their bread.[96] Even when a complaint was upheld convict petitioners might still find

[90] *Sydney Gazette*, 28 May 1827.

[91] *Sydney Gazette*, 1 June 1827.

[92] AONSW., Reel 664, Berrima Benchbook, 27 December 1833.

[93] *The Colonist*, 28 August 1838.

[94] *Sydney Gazette*, 20 October 1840.

[95] *Colonial Times*, 2 September 1834 and 9 September 1834.

[96] T.A., LC375-1-1, New Norfolk Benchbook, 27 October 1834.

themselves on the receiving end of judicially sanctioned thrashing. In May 1831 the Maitland bench ordered an unnamed employer to provide slops, but also ordered the convicts involved to receive 50 lashes for the insolent way in which they made their complaint.[97]

As outlined in chapter four, some masters refused to grant servants permission to lodge a complaint, or tried to pre-empt the complaint by bringing charges of their own. When several servants of Northern Midlands' settler Robert Hepburn tried to lodge a complaint of harsh treatment, they were sentenced to seven days solitary for coming to the Police Office without permission.[98] In rural districts in particular, cases were held by magistrates who were the neighbours and social acquaintances of the landholders that convict complainants sought to gain redress from. It was a brave justice of the peace who broke class ranks in order to highlight irregular practices on the estate of a neighbour. To do so was to risk the opprobrium of the regional ruling élite. As a result, some convicts sought redress in lower courts situated in towns and cities, far away from their designated district of employment. In August 1831 four servants assigned to Mr. Jenkins at Eagle Vale went before the Sydney magistrates, claiming their mistress had refused to give them rations. They were ordered, however, to be 'returned to Campbelltown to be dealt with' locally.[99]

In sum, taking a complaint before the local bench was commonly a fruitless and risky option. Surviving evidence indicates the vast majority were summarily dismissed and in many instances the workers themselves were punished for absconding, absence or making a frivolous complaint. Some groups tried to lodge their complaint before authorities like the Governor, Superintendent of Convicts or a court in Hobart or Sydney hoping to get a more even-handed hearing. Complaints of judicial bias—itself a dangerous act—made little difference, and invariably they were ordered to lodge their case before the appropriate local authority. Even when claims succeeded magistrates usually only ordered the master to rectify the deficiency. In the case of repeated or blatant transgressions, the

[97] *Monitor*, 18 May 1831.

[98] T.A., LC83-1-6, Campbell Town Benchbook, 4 April 1842.

[99] *Sydney Herald*, 29 August 1831.

Table 6.1 Outcome (%) in cases where convicts were prosecuted for bringing false charges against masters, mistresses and other convict managers

	Male	*Female*
Dismissed or acquitted	19.2	1.4
Returned to crown	7.7	8.5
Solitary confinement	19.2	22.5
Hard labour	46.2	64.8
Flogged	7.7	
Iron collar or head shaved		4.2
Total	100.0	100.0

Source T.A., Con 31, 32, 33, 40, and 41

complaining convicts might be returned to government or transferred to another master.[100] Given the cost of free labour this was a considerable sanction for the master, but represented little by way of compensation for the convict. This helps explain why aggrieved convicts mostly turned to other remedial action.

John Hirst argued that convict rights before the law would have been 'thrown into peril' if the colonial state had ever felt threatened.[101] The evidence of this book suggests that those rights were always more apparent than real. Our comprehensive survey of magistrates benchbooks in New South Wales and Van Diemen's land uncovered remarkably few cases where convicts successfully prosecuted masters and mistresses. The few that we did find were invariably for cases bought against small scale farmers or shopkeepers who lacked social standing. Magistrates appear to have been very reluctant to publicly shame large landholders by finding in favour of their servants. By contrast, male and female convicts in Van Diemen's Land were charged on 747 occasions with bringing 'false', 'frivolous', 'foolish', 'ridiculous' or 'vexatious' charges against masters, overseers and other convict managers. As Table 6.1 reveals, just over a quarter of male convicts so charged escaped punishment, other than being returned to crown service for reassignment elsewhere. This might be described as a pyrrhic victory, suggesting that a significant number of counter action brought against complaining convict were little more than face-saving device designed to save the court the embarrassment of finding against the master. Charges brought against female convicts for

[100] See for example T.A., LC375-1-2 New Norfolk Benchbook, 14 November 1838.

[101] Hirst, J. (2008) *Freedom on the Fatal Shore*, Black Inc, Melbourne, 125.

bringing frivolous charges were significantly less likely to result in a mere reprimand, however. As Table 6.1 highlights, however, in the case of both sexes a convict who brought a charge against a superior risked a sentence to hard labour or a dark cell.

Conclusion

While we suspect that the majority of demands made by convicts and associated appeals to authority went un-recorded, we have been able to plot those we encountered in a survey of surviving benchbooks and digitised newspapers. These are detailed in Table 6.2. In all, we find evidence of 53 cases where two or more convicts are recorded as issuing workplace demands and a further 83 where such demands were backed up by the issue of threats. Convict petitions are rarely referred to in the sources that we have used. We could find evidence of only eight that were specifically focussed on working conditions. We suspect, however, that a more detailed search of the Colonial Secretary's correspondence files for New South Wales and Van Diemen's Land will yield many more examples. We did find substantially more evidence for court actions lodged by convicts. Groups of convicts took their master or mistress to court on at least 107 occasions, although we have detailed elsewhere the success rate for these actions was low and the majority resulted in counter prosecutions.

Suppressing complaints or harshly punishing dissent was not costless for employers because it could aggravate relations and induce an ongoing withdrawal of cooperation. This chapter started with a labour dispute amongst the Macarthur's assigned servants, and it is perhaps appropriate to return to the same property by way of a conclusion. The bench sought to resolve James Straiter's mutinous conduct and the dangerous precedent it set by attempting to set an example. For having the temerity to confront the Macarthurs he was sentenced to receive a staggering 500 lashes. After this ordeal was completed the bench ordered him to serve one month's solitary confinement on bread and water, and then to serve the remainder of his sentence at the Port Macquarie penal settlement. This unspeakably horrendous and almost certainly illegal punishment was awarded out of fear. It was an attempt to drown out convict protest with blood, lack of light and social exile. It also gave the lie to the *Monitor*'s claim that the punishment that magistrates meted out to those who engaged in labour negotiations were 'so lenient', that assigned servants would 'come home

Table 6.2 Summary of charges brought against convicts for issuing demands or appealing to authority

	1788–1700	*1801–1810*	*1810–1820*	*1821–1830*	*1831–1840*	*1841–1850*	*1851–1860*	*Total*
Issuing of demands								
Made demands			3	9	28	11	2	53
Threats		1	1	13	53	13	2	83
Sub total		1	4	22	81	24	4	133
Appeals to authority								
Petition			2	4	2			8
Court action		1		14	44	8	3	70
Sub total		1	2	18	46	8	3	78
Combined total		2	6	40	125	32	7	212

laughing in their sleeves at the trouble they have given their masters'.[102] The truth was, however, that the more trouble the bench meted out, the more masters encountered in return.

In April 1826 Alexander Archibald received 50 lashes for absconding when he tried to lodge a complaint in Sydney against Hannibal Macarthur for ill-treatment and being supplied with poor rations. On the same day Macarthur brought three other servants before the Berrima bench on charges of insolence and neglect. One of these, John Middleton, had his sentence upgraded to 100 lashes for contempt, stating that he did not wish to return to his master.[103] Archibald and another servant, Thomas Evans, were subsequently charged with neglect in May and August.[104] The court records make it clear that ongoing resentment resulted in a string of retaliatory actions including calculated go-slows notwithstanding the harsh punishments meted out by the local bench. Like other landowners, the Macarthurs' options were restricted. Some workers could be easily sacrificed but others had skills difficult to replace. While Archibald was sentenced to a three-months on an iron gang for neglect, Evans was only admonished—a recognition of his skill in managing sheep. In the next chapter we describe the ways in which failure to listen to the claims, complaints and grievances of convicts could result in a further reduction in work effort through go-slows and strikes.

[102] *Monitor*, 13 January 1840.

[103] AONSW., Berrima Benchbook, 3, 29 April 1826; *The Australian*, 15 April 1826.

[104] AONSW., Berrima Benchbook, 29 May and 17 August 1826.

CHAPTER 7

Go-Slows, Strikes and Effort Bargaining

In July 1833 around 60 men employed in Notman's road party quit their work to march in a body into Launceston to lodge a complaint about their treatment. Two magistrates and an assistant colonial surgeon were duly despatched to investigate the men's claims which were found 'groundless'. The men were ordered back to work, but were not otherwise punished. The following Wednesday at least eleven downed tools and refused to work while another two were flogged for absconding. Yet, as it turned out, this was a mere taster of what was to come. On Thursday morning a messenger arrived in Launceston with the news that the whole gang was in 'a complete state of mutiny'.[1] In all 33 prisoners were charged with insubordination. Of these, all bar one was sentenced to receive 100 lashes. The exception, a man named James Clarke, was awarded 150 strokes. This was an illegal punishment, although one that could be justified by breaking the charge into two component sections, one punished with the legal maximum of 100 lashes and the other with 50.

[1] *Launceston Advertiser*, 5 September 1833.

H. Maxwell-Stewart and M. Quinlan, *Unfree Workers*, Palgrave Studies in Economic History, https://doi.org/10.1007/978-981-16-7558-4_7

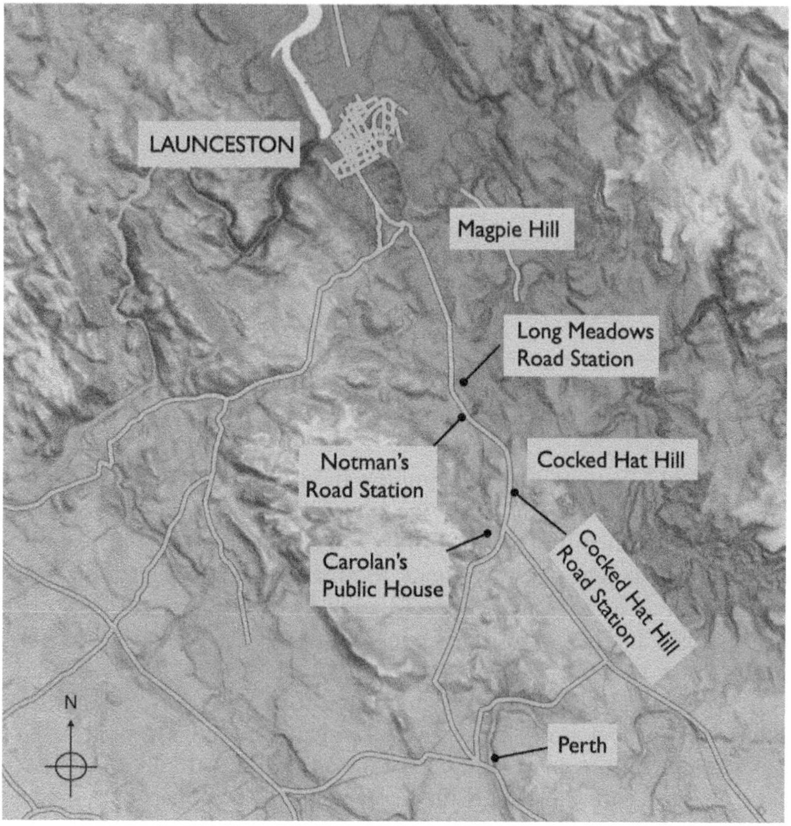

Map 7.1 Location Map Notman's Road Party

Notman's gang was a punishment detail which in the years from 1831 to 34 was charged with constructing a new line of road between Perth and Launceston. The gang started out from the foot of Magpie Hill cutting a line passed Kerry Lodge and to the west of the Cocked Hat Hill and the back of Carolan's public-house (see Map 7.1).[2] This road party had a reputation for being composed of 'rogues doubly and trebly convicted', men who were as 'unprofitable, in way of labor, as they are villains in

[2] *Launceston Advertiser*, 25 July 1833.

disposition and habit'.[3] Yet, while some convicts were sent to Notman's gang following convictions in the Quarter Sessions, many others were absconders or had been dispatched there by magistrates after participating in work place disputes. The bar for admission into this punishment detail was not high. James Jeal was sent to Notman's gang after being found not guilty of obtaining money by false pretences, 'there being a deficiency of legal proof'.[4] Legal proof was not needed, however, to condemn a convict to a road gang. Thomas Brophy was sent to the same location after he was found to be in possession of a new hat for which he could give no satisfactory account.[5]

The extra 50 lashes singled out Clarke as the ringleader of the 31 July 1833 mutiny. While no benchbook survives to shed further light on the strike, Clarke's conduct record reveals that this was not the first such action he had participated in. A plasterer and slater in his mid-20s, he had been sent to Notman's road gang for insubordinate and mutinous conduct towards his master on 27 December 1832. He had previously been punished for leaving his work and getting drunk on Good Friday and, on another occasion, a Sunday.[6] The timing of these prosecutions are revealing. Clarke had a previous history of agitating for time off from labour on public holidays and the Sabbath.

The scale of the punishment inflicted on Clarke and his fellow strikers attracted a good deal of comment. Justifying the level of force sanctioned by magistrates Kenworthy and Davis, 'An Inhabitant' wrote to the *Launceston Advertiser* to advise that 'the next morning, the whole gang turned out to their work at the usual hour, and have continued to attend to their duty ever since'. In his opinion 'this state of things never would have been brought about ... by a less severe measure'.[7] Certainly, the extraordinary levels of punishment meted out reveal the extent to which this mass protest rattled the sensibilities of the regional convict managers.

This chapter examines effort bargaining, deliberate neglect and go-slows and convict strikes. It will look at the form these actions took and

[3] *Launceston Advertiser*, 5 September 1833.

[4] *Tasmanian*, 31 August 1832.

[5] *Tasmanian*, 35 May 1833.

[6] James Clarke, per *Asia* (3), Police No. 810, T.A., Con 31-1-6.

[7] *Launceston Advertiser*, 5 September 1833.

the issues which sufficiently excited convicts to dampen labour participation or to withdraw from it altogether. It also looks at the ways in which the collective withdrawal of labour played out across private and public sector workplaces and the different ways in which convict men and women responded to what they saw as an attack on their rights.

Go-Slows and Effort Bargaining

Go-slows and effort bargaining need to be seen in the context of the structures of management control. The difficulty here is that it can be hard to separate the products of intense workplace discipline from reactions to the use of coercion to coax labour from unwilling bodies. While losing tools, for example, might be read as a form of dissent, as both accidental and deliberate losses could attract severe punishment, caution should be exercised. Ganged convicts were strictly monitored, increasing the chances that loss or damage to equipment and other acts associated with failing to maintain output would be detected. For example, two convicts in Notman's gang received a two-month extension of their sentence for losing their tools at Long Meadows in 1834.[8] Such a loss might reflect an attempt at workplace sabotage, or merely the close supervision which characterised this particular gang which operated as a form of de facto penal station in the interlude between the winding down of Macquarie Harbour and the scaling up of Port Arthur. One of the few ways of throwing light on isolated episodes like this is to analyse them in the context of other prosecutions.

Output restriction and the slowing of work took many different forms. Literally tens of thousands of cases of neglect and idleness, many collective, went before the courts. Analysis of the Tasmania conduct records reveals that over 37,000 charges of neglect of duty and 14,000 prosecutions for idleness were lodged in that colony alone.[9] It is clear from court records that many prosecutions were brought only after repeated instructions to increase the pace of work had been ignored. In March 1839 the overseer of the New Norfolk Assignable Party remonstrated with three men for idling. He only put them on a charge, however, after

[8] M.L., Tas Papers 277, Launceston Benchbook, 4 October 1834.

[9] Total count of T.A., Con 40 and 41, four percent sample on Con 31, 32 and 33.

he returned sometime later and found them still standing idle.[10] In early February 1834 three groups of men attached to the Launceston chain gang tasked with working in the gravel pits were charged with neglect over four days. Their overseer, Samuel Smith, told the court that the second group had been neglecting their work for a week while Gillespie, another overseer, stated that others had refused to assist when two carts became dangerously entangled. The men gave a variety of reasons for not working, including illness and near-sightedness—pleas which the court rejected. They were all sentenced to receive 25 lashes or an additional month's hard labour. Over the same period two other groups of Launceston public works convicts numbering ten men in total were convicted of neglect.[11]

While mass-prosecutions were not the norm, charges were often preferred against groups of convicts numbering between two and ten. Many such cases were recorded as 'continued idleness,' 'repeated idleness,' 'continued neglect' 'general laziness' or other terms that implied prosecution for multiple events committed over a period of time. Charges of idleness or neglect were especially common in places of secondary punishment and the wording of some implies a concern that those prosecuted were consciously or unconsciously encouraging practices that would result in a decline in output. Thus, William Robertson and Robert Veitch were charged at Macquarie Harbour penal station with 'neglect of duty and setting a bad example' to their gang on 16 August 1828.[12]

The imposition of task-work by colonial authorities was one way in which administrators sought to combat coordinated output restrictions, specifying minimum acceptable levels of work. On occasion a failure to achieve the allotted task load was specified in charges. Six Macquarie Harbour convicts were prosecuted for not accomplishing their weekly task-work on 18 October 1828, while Thomas Hemming and Samuel Smith were charged with failing to provide a proper quantity of nails five days later.[13] On 17 April 1830 another two Macquarie Harbour nail

[10] M.L., Tas Papers 238, New Norfolk Benchbook, 14 March 1839.

[11] M.L., Tas Papers 277, Launceston Benchbook, 4, 5, 7 February 1834.

[12] William Robertson, per *Elizabeth and Henrietta*, Police No. 232, T.A., Con 31-1-34; Robert Veitch, per *Chapman*, Police No. 35, Con 31-1-42.

[13] Thomas Hemming, per *Malabar*, Police No. 360, T.A., Con 31-1-18; Samuel Smith, per *Princess Charlotte*, Police No. 636, Con 31-1-38.

makers were prosecuted for 'attempting to impose on the engineer storekeeper', claiming that a higher number of nails had been supplied than he could count out.[14]

Go-slows were prosecuted across a huge range of different working environments. Jericho Inn-keeper Daniel O'Conner prosecuted three servants for idleness and neglect when tasked with digging potatoes. He found two of the men lying down while the other acted as a look-out.[15] Two farm servants of T.G. Tabart received six months hard labour for 'incorrigible idleness'. Gilbert Robertson found his bullocks standing idle when his servants were meant to be ploughing. They responded insolently when he remonstrated with them. Edward Bryant complained that his servants had ploughed little more than six acres in four days.[16] William Nicholls prosecuted two female servants (both transported on the *Westmoreland*) for 'gross neglect of duty' alleging nurserymaid Anne Wilson had failed to keep the children's bed dry.[17]

In February 1834 two convicts were reprimanded for cutting only half the reeds they were tasked with gathering—the men claimed that a high-tide had inhibited their efforts.[18] An almost identical case occurred nine months later, the overseer complaining that two to three times as much should have been loaded on a cart in the course of a day.[19] Later that same year another 12 men were charged with completing insufficient work on a drain they were digging from the Launceston Female Factory to the river.[20] In October 1834 overseer Edward Spencer complained that the men he had tasked with nailing a fence had done nothing all afternoon.[21] In the Newcastle coalmines in New South Wales and the equivalent operation on the Tasman Peninsula, Van Diemen's Land, output was measured by the number of skip or wagon-loads. Both the number of skips and the

[14] Thomas Singleton Hawley, per *Richmond*, Police No. 402, T.A., Con 31-1-18; James Chetter, per *Caledonia*, Police No. 491, Con 31-1-6.

[15] M.L., Tas Papers 290, Oatlands Benchbook, 17 November 1836.

[16] M.L., Tas Papers 323, Richmond Benchbook, 7 September 1832; M.L., Tas Papers 238 New Norfolk Benchbook, 24 September 1839.

[17] M.L., Tas Papers 292, Oatlands Benchbook, 8 June 1838.

[18] M.L., Tas Papers 277, Launceston Benchbook, 10 February.

[19] M.L., Tas Papers 277, Launceston Benchbook, 12 November 1834.

[20] M.L., Tas Papers 277, Launceston Benchbook, 21 June 1834.

[21] M.L., Tas Papers 277, Launceston Benchbook, 10 October 1834.

degree to which they should be filled were common sources of dispute. British miners organised checkweighmen to safeguard workers' interests against management assessments of outputs. There was a particular incentive to do this as miners were paid according to the number of skips filled. For convict coalminers there was no opportunity for lodge or union organisation. Disputes, however, still occurred. In August 1835 John Dowling received one month's hard labour for claiming that he had brought 16 skips to the surface, although his overseer insisted the correct number was 15.[22]

Restricting output was particularly widespread in gangs. In 1835 two Oatlands public works convicts were reprimanded for sitting down in a quarry while another two received a similar reprimand for 'idleness and gossiping.'[23] In April 1836 several convicts working in the New Norfolk stone quarry were convicted of neglect of work, their superintendent arguing their slow labour caused the carters to wait to pick up sufficient stone.[24] Charges of failing to break enough stone were so common in road gangs that prosecutions were weekly events.[25] Two members of the Malcolm's Hut Party were placed in solitary confinement for breaking nine feet of stone, when required to break sixteen feet.[26] Those charged with filling wheelbarrows also limited their effort, as did those wheeling the barrows.[27] Overseer Jeremiah Wilson prosecuted several men who resisted fully filling their barrows. One of these, Moses Barr, argued that the barrow he was tasked with filling was oversized. Since it did not conform to the regular standard, he refused to fill it for Wilson 'or anybody else'. For his 'disobedience and insolence' he was sentenced to 25 lashes.[28] On another gang, overseer Edward Price charged two men with taking 20 minutes to fill their carts with earth—considerably longer

[22] M.L., Tas Papers 33, Tasman Peninsula correspondence 31 August 1835, 31 July 1838. Tuffin, R. (2008) Where the Vicissitudes of Day and Night Are Not Known: Convict Coal Mining in Van Diemen's Land, 1822–1848, *Tasmanian Historical Studies*, 13, 35–61.

[23] M.L., Tas Papers 290, Oatlands Benchbook, 31 January 1835 and 3 July 1837.

[24] M.L., Tas Papers 237, New Norfolk Benchbook, 26 April 1836.

[25] See for example M.L., Tas Papers 292, Oatlands Benchbook, 3 August 1837.

[26] M.L., Tas Papers 326, Richmond Benchbook, 17 April 1839.

[27] See of example M.L., Tas Papers 292, Oatlands Benchbook, 3 May and 25 July 1838.

[28] M.L., Tas Papers 292, Oatlands Benchbook, 22 November 1837.

than others. He argued that the two had formed the habit of only half filling their shovels.[29]

This case highlighted the extent to which go-slows needed to be coordinated if they were to achieve their objectives. They worked best where the whole gang slowed. Overseers and other managers often rewarded those who exceeded quotas in an attempt to break up such collective agreements. Attempts to speed up production by chastising individuals often precipitated wider disputes. A group of four convicts received terms of solitary confinement for issuing threats after overseer James Glenn remonstrated with them for being idle and gossiping.[30] In March 1824 six members of the Orphan School clearing gang convicted of neglect were ordered to be denied all indulgences until they made up 'their back work.'[31] Go-slows also occurred in response to perceived ill-treatment. In November 1836 two members of the Longford Road Party, Thomas Arnold and Barnaby Wilford, were flogged for putting scarcely anything in their barrows. When confronted they said that they had deliberately reduced each load in protest over the quality of their rations. This explanation earned them an additional dose of 10 lashes each for insolence.[32]

Several members of Samuel Smith's gang were convicted of pilfering stones from adjoining piles and adding them to their own in June 1834. Another six workers in the same gang prosecuted for a similar offence in August denied the charge, claiming they had only picked up a few loose broken stones.[33] Such actions might be seen as opportunistic, rather than solidaristic. When exercised at scale, however, they had the potential to undermine the organisation of work outputs. Once some piles were depleted and others 'enhanced', measuring and managing worker effort was seriously undermined. This accounts for the heavy sentences such cases attracted. All the convicts in Smith's gang charged with this offence were awarded six weeks in chains. Revealingly, the bench split up the participants sending them to different punishment

[29] M.L., Tas Papers 291, Oatlands Benchbook, 3 December 1841.

[30] M.L., Tas Papers 291, Oatlands Benchbook, 6 January 1842.

[31] AONSW., Liverpool Benchbook, 29 March 1824.

[32] T.A., LC362-1-3 Longford Benchbook, 2 November 1836.

[33] For this and other cases see M.L., Tas Papers 277, Launceston Benchbook, 2, 13 June and 30 August 1834.

gangs—a clear indication that the action was perceived as a coordinated attempt to hinder production. The deliberate scattering of activists between different punishment locations was a common tactic designed to quell the 'distemper' of collectivism.

Convicts resorted to many different tactics to slow production. Prosecuting William Judge for disobedience in February 1834, Launceston Chain Gang overseer Samuel Smith testified he had noted of late it had become the practice of a number of the men to visit the privy four or five times during the day.[34] Other tactics included varying the pace of work. Such coordinated go-slows could be difficult to detect. In January 1837 five members of the Oatlands public works gang were sentenced to hard labour in a road party for 'general neglect and irregularity' in their work.[35] Other practices included lifting picks letting them drop without applying force or, as another exasperated overseer complained, convicts might lean on their 'arms and lift up their hammers' but 'it would be a long while before it would fall again.'[36] Targeted delays in one activity could have cascading effects, wrecking carefully planned work cycles. In February 1841 an overseer lamented that, as three prisoners were late leaving the barracks, the entire gang was delayed by 20 minutes.[37]

Such struggles could turn into a game of cat and mouse, as convicts increased and decreased work intensity depending on whether or not they were under the watchful eye of an overseer or master. In April 1834 Lieutenant Kenworthy, placed in charge of the Engineering Department in Launceston, explained his decision to prosecute the convict William Anderson for neglect of duty. Anderson, who had been sentenced to receive 50 lashes, was a watchman who had been placed in temporary charge of a gang. When Kenworthy had approached from an 'unexpected direction', he found that the men under Anderson's charge were not at work. As he told Ronald Campbell Gunn, the Superintendent of the Launceston Prison Barracks, this practice had occurred repeatedly. After the lieutenant had reproved and forgiven the men on a number of occasions, he decided to prosecute. In his words, 'under these circumstances

[34] For this and similar cases see M.L., Tas Papers 277, Launceston Benchbook, 4 February and 8 May 1834.

[35] M.L., Tas Papers 290, Oatlands Benchbook, 18 January 1837.

[36] M.L., Tas Papers 292, Oatlands Benchbook, 7 March 1838.

[37] M.L., Tas Papers 291, Oatlands Benchbook, 26 February 1841.

I consider in passing so severe a sentence that unless the overseers were compelled to look after their gangs no work would be done at all.'[38] The gang also experienced the wrath of the bench. Ten received an additional month's hard labour, six got 25 lashes and three were awarded 30 strokes for idling and smoking. Just two were let off with a reprimand.[39]

Gang members who did not participate in such organised actions might find themselves the subject of threats and assaults by others.[40] John Jones, a tailor who had been transported for stripping stockings from a disinterred body, was first assigned to Lightfoot's tailoring establishment in Hobart. From there he was sent to Notman's road party after he was charged with 'insolence and threatening to take his masters life'. In December 1832 he was twice flogged along with fellow members of his gang for neglect of duty. The following May he turned approver, providing 'evidence before the police magistrate against two prisoners'. This necessitated his rapid removal to the Launceston Penitentiary in order to ensure his safety. From there he was elevated to position of messenger to the chain gang and then to a billet in the post office before finally being appointed a constable.[41] His trajectory through the convict establishment's many 'Chinese boxes', to borrow David Neal's phrase, illustrates the rewards and potential pitfalls of collaboration.[42]

Promoted convicts faced another set of dilemmas. Overseers, sub-overseers and watchman could find themselves in a particularly invidious position. On the one hand, adherence to the routines imposed by managers might render them the target of convict retaliation, while a failure to maintain the pace of output could lead to the loss of a billet and its associated incentives. These usually included better clothes, sleeping quarters, food and tobacco. David Smith, for example, was punished for allowing a group of workers under his charge to rest for half an hour after

[38] M.L., Tas Papers 278, Launceston Convict Superintendent Letterbook, 1 May 1834, Gunn to Spode.

[39] M.L., Tas Papers 277, Launceston Benchbook, 17 April 1834.

[40] M.L., Tas Papers 292, Oatlands Benchbook, 9 November 1838.

[41] John Jones, per *Argyle*, Police No. 520, Con 31-1-24.

[42] Neal, David. (1987) Free Society, Penal Colony, Slave Society, Prison? *Historical Studies,* 22, 89, 512.

working hard in the earlier part of the day. For this he was sentenced to seven days solitary confinement.[43]

In late June 1840 Oatlands chain gang overseer Patrick Jenkins gave evidence that one worker refused to work until he had eaten his bread, another was punished for telling Jenkins he would 'rather go to hell' than be dictated to by his overseer, while a third said he could not work effectively with Jenkins constantly barking orders at him. All three were sentenced by the visiting magistrate to receive two days solitary for neglect and insolence. Two other members of the gang received longer terms of solitary confinement for speaking back after being ordered to put their pipes away. Two weeks later matters escalated when another two convicts were charged with insubordination and assaulting Jenkins. Tellingly, another four received periods in solitary confinement for failing to come to the overseer's assistance.[44] As the incident indicates, go-slows could rapidly escalate into open defiance and strikes followed by targeted violence.

Go-slows were by no means confined to road parties. Arthur McCann complained to the Berrima bench that he had ordered some men to move logs, but when he returned several hours later, he found that what had been done could have been accomplished in five minutes.[45] Charles Hewitt complained to his sawyers that their week's work was deficient by 70 feet. When they refused to make up the deficiency in the following week, he charged them, and the bench duly sentenced them to receive 50 lashes each.[46] William Bowman failed, however, to secure a conviction when he complained he had sent his assigned convicts to the cedar grounds on three occasions, but that on each they had returned with nothing.[47]

[43] M.L., Tas Papers 277, Launceston Benchbook, 11 February 1834.

[44] M.L., Tas Papers 291, Oatlands Benchbook, 24, 26 June and 8 July 1840.

[45] AONSW., Berrima Benchbook, 28 October 1833.

[46] AONSW., Berrima Benchbook, Sutton Forest Petty Sessions, 17 March 1834.

[47] AONSW., Berrima Benchbook, 29 April 1834.

Women also engaged in organised output restriction. Fyans, the Commandant at Moreton Bay penal station complained that 'a considerable number' pretended to be ill on a daily basis.[48] The allotted task-load for a group of women engaged in spinning at the Hobart Female Factory was specified in terms of the weight of yarn completed each day. In October 1823, a total of 20 women were charged with wetting their yarn 'with intent to defraud by increasing its weight.' They were sentenced to seven days solitary confinement. The four ringleaders—Elizabeth Boucher, Mary Ann Kelly, Ellen Stewart and Margaret Morgan—also received three months in the factory's Crime Class Yard.[49] This was a coordinated and planned action.

Refusing to Work and Collective Insubordination

Many charges for refusing to work appear to be connected to wider disputes about working hours. Margaret Smith was charged on 31 August 1835, for example, with 'Insolence to her master on Sunday 30th Aug. & refusing to do her work'. The protest earned her a one-month stint at the Cascades Female Factory wash tubs.[50] Ann Wilks plainly stated the issue to her master. She was sentenced in January 1838 to one month in the solitary working cells for 'Misconduct in refusing to stay at her place unless she had a Day given her every week'.[51] Likewise, Mary Coyle was punished while in the hiring depot for refusing to engage in hired service on passholder wages 'until she was allowed all Sundays to herself' (emphasis in the original).[52]

When Bridget Callaghan and Agnes McDevott refused to work for John Dyer in Launceston, they were sentenced on 14 September 1849 to two months' hard labour.[53] On 28 July 1830, Bridget Hobbs and Sophia Fitzpatrick were both sentenced to serve a year in the female house of correction for, 'Aggravated insolence & abuse' to their mistress', Mrs.

48 O'Connor, Power and Punishment, 133.

49 Hendriksen et al., Women Transported, 55.

50 Margaret Smith, per *Edward*, Police No. 257, T.A., Con 40-1-9.

51 Ann Wilks, per *New Grove*, Police No. 270, T.A., Con 40-1-9.

52 Mary Coyle, per *Emma Eugenia*, Police No. 492, T.A., Con 40-1-2.

53 Bridget Callaghan, per *Kinnear*, Police No. 928, T.A., Con 41-1-19 and Agnus McDevott, per *Navarino*, Police No. 280, Con 40-1-4.

Oakes. When brought before the New Norfolk bench they were further charged with 'gross insolence to the Magistrate'. For this affront the local justice of the peace, Robert Officer, ordered them to serve the first two weeks of their stint in the factory in the dark cells on a restricted diet of bread and water. Held in the local watchhouse until an escort could be arranged to take them to the house of correction, the two women refused to set out on a Saturday. This was a day when public works' convicts had the afternoon to themselves. For resisting attempts to move them out of government hours the Principal Superintendent of Convicts in Hobart extended their sentence to the dark cells by an additional three days.[54]

Sometimes convicts refused to do specific duties. Sarah Connen and Elizabeth Kenny refused to clean the yard at the Ross Female Factory when ordered to do so in May 1849.[55] Washing appears to have been particularly detested. On 18 October 1837 at least 19 women confined in the Launceston Female Factory were charged with 'Disorderly conduct in refusing to attend religious instructions in chapel' and also with refusing their dinner. This episode occurred before the practice of recording religious affiliation on female convict records commenced. While it is possible that some of these women were Catholics, Mary Roberts had been born in the Channel Islands and Mary Davis in Kinsale, County Cork, it is unlikely doctrinal matters motived all 19. The temporary hunger strike that followed suggests that this was a dispute over work, attendance at chapel being seen as a government duty imposed on the convict's day off. Refusal to consume the government ration was probably designed to reinforce this point.[56] Other protests at female factories also occurred

[54] Bridget Hobbs, per *Borneo*, Police No. 118, T.A., Con 40-1-5; Sophia Fitzpatrick per *Harmony*, Police No. 67.

[55] Sarah Connen, per *Elizabeth and Henry*, Police No. 804, T.A., Con 41-1-11 and Elizabeth Kenny, per *Emma Eugina* 4, Police No. 287, Con 41-1-9.

[56] Amelia Taylor, per *Arab*, Police Number, 121, T.A., Con 40-1-10; Mary Donally, per *Edward*, Police No. 164, Con 40-1-3; Sarah Cashel, per *Edward*, Police No. 248, Con 40-1-1; Mary Gillard, per *Edward*, Police No. 149, Con 40-1-3; Jane Howard, per *Edward*, Police No. 227, Con 40-1-5; Christina Johnson, per *Edward*, Police No. 112, Con 40-1-5; Ellen Wilson, per *Edward*, Police No. 252, Con 40-1-9; Charity Stevens, per *Eliza*, Police No. 170, Con 40-1-9; Grace Grant, per *Frances Charlotte*, Police No. 130, Con 40-1-3; Mary Watson per *Frances Charlotte*, Police No. 230, Con 40-1-9; Ann Smith, per *Hydery*, Police No. 220, Con 40–1-9; Margaret Connor, per *Jane*, Police No. 221, Con 40-1-1; Maria Wright, per *Jane*, Police No. 227, Con 40-1-9; Mary Smith, per *Mary III*, Police No. 214, Con 40-1-9; Emma Bolton, per *New Grove*, Police No. 307, Con 40-1-1; Ann Wilks, per *New Grove*, Police No. 270, Con 40-1-9; Mary Roberts, per

on weekends, suggesting that orders to work on Saturday afternoon or Sunday were seen as a violation of inmate rights. On Monday 6 May 1839, 47 women were charged at the Cascade Female Factory with 'Insubordination' on the previous Saturday in 'forcibly violently & in a turbulent manner resisting Mr. Hutchinson & with openly refusing to obey his commands'.[57]

Other convicts struck over wages. Jemima Bagott, described as a plain cook, was sentenced to six months' in the Crime Class at the Female Factory in 1837 for telling her master that she would not work unless she received £15 per year.[58] Emma Waddington and Elizabeth Archer refused to work for the Fentons in June 1844 for £9 per year as stipulated under the newly introduced passholder system.[59] In similar fashion Margaret O'Brien refused to work for the £10 per year contract imposed upon her in 1845, while John Mullins refused to extend his contract to work for Cowens, unless his passholder wage was increased.[60] Other convicts in hiring depots and assignable gangs refused to sign-up for contracts on the grounds that the wages were inadequate.[61]

Some employers became exasperated with their assigned convicts returning them to Government. This was the case with Sydney dressmaker Miss Wyle who charged two of her female servants with disobedience and insolence in February 1835 requesting that they be dismissed from her service.[62] Likewise, however, many convicts refused to serve in particular households. This was a common form of protest amongst women. The refusal often occurred just after a convict had received a punishment and

Westmorland, Police No. 163, Con 40-1-8; Elizabeth Baker, per *William Bryan*, Police No. 273, Con 40-1-1; Susan Kirby, colonial conviction, Parramatta, Police No. 105, Con 40-1-5.

[57] See for example Mary Smith, per *Atwick*, Police No. 329, T.A., Con 40-1-10.

[58] Jemima Bagott, per *Edward*, Police No. 298, T.A., Con 40-1-1.

[59] Elizabeth Archer per *Rajah*, Police No. 138, T.A., Con 40-1-2 and Emma Waddington, per *Navarino*, Police No. 396, Con 40-1-10.

[60] Margaret O'Brien, per *Hope*, Police No. 555, T.A., Con 40-1-2 and John Mullins per *David Clarke*, Police No. 3026, Con 33-1-13, 18 October 1848.

[61] See Mary Ann Quinlan, per *Hope*, Police No. 11, T.A., Con 40-1-8, 24 September 1845; Mary Ann McIntosh, per *Woodbridge*, Police No. 74, T.A., Con 40-1-6; Jane Shachan, per *Tasmania*, Police No. 653, Con 41-1-4, 12 June 1846; John Wickes, per *Enchantress*, Police No. 1567, Con 31-1-6, 5 September 1846.

[62] *Sydney Monitor*, 18 February 1835.

Table 7.1 Female convict charged with refusing to comply with orders

	*N*º	%
Refusing to work	856	64.2
Refusing to proceed to or remain in employment	237	17.8
Refusal to proceed to a female factory or to receive punishment	43	3.2
Refusal to go to church	29	2.2
Refusing to obey the orders of her husband	30	2.3
Other refusals to comply with authority	136	10.4
Total	1333	100.0

Sources T.A., Con 40 and 41 series

might be read as a means of extracting compensatory justice. In October 1832 Mary Williams and Ellen Robins refused to return to William Ashburner's residence at Carrick as ordered when they were released from solitary confinement at the Norfolk Plains watch-house.[63] Catherine Gale was charged on 13 February 1837 with, 'Refusing to remain in her service after having suffered her sentence to Solit[ar]y. Conf[inemen]t'. Gale, who had only recently arrived in the colony, had been charged by her master on a Monday for being absent without leave. The timing of the charge suggests that this was one of many occasions where convicts were prosecuted for quitting their work on a Sunday. Many assigned servants fought protracted battles with masters in an attempt to secure the Sabbath as a day that was free from labour. Gale lost round one of this battle when she was ordered to a dark cell for two days on bread and water. She used the punishment as a means, however, of pressing her point— refusing to work for a master who treated their servants in such a manner.[64]

No master high or low was exempt from this kind of labour withdrawal. Mary Ann Farmer had the temerity to refuse to remain in her service at government house, Hobart Town. For this she was sent to the factory for six months with orders to be worked in the separate treatment cells for two of these.[65] As can be seen from Table 7.1, 237 women were prosecuted in Van Diemen's Land for quitting a master's service or

[63] Mary Williams, per *Mellish*, Police No. 157, T.A., Con 40-1-9; Elin Robins, per *Eliza*, Police No. 76, Con 40-1-7.

[64] Catherine Gale, per *Westmoreland*, Police No. 177, T.A., Con 40-1-4.

[65] Mary Ann Farmer, per *Naverino*, Police No. 184, T.A., Con 40-1-4.

refusing to enter service with a particular household when ordered to do so. This represented 18 percent of all prosecutions of female convicts for refusal to follow orders.

Some punishments provoked strong reactions which were reinforced by withdrawals of labour. Two members of Benjamin Scammell's 'notorious gang', Joseph Lane and Michael Sullivan, were charged with using threatening language to their overseer and refusing to work. Both men had recently been double ironed. As the *Australian* reported, Lane 'threatened to settle his overseer as soon as the time should arrive when he would be free from those unpleasant appendages to his legs'. While Sullivan 'sat down on his shovel, and threatened impotently' that he 'would be hanged if he remained any longer in that gang'. Both men were ordered to receive 25 lashes.[66]

Other cases provide evidence that strikes only occurred when other attempts at bargaining had failed to effect a change in management practices. This in itself is a reminder that a count of collective action pieced together from court records will result in an underestimate of actual levels of protest. In February 1828, for example, testimony provided at the trial of four convicts for refusing to break up a paddock revealed that this action was part of a running series of disputes over work intensity. When the four were brought before the court their spokesman, Thomas Williams, told the magistrate it was not their intention to do their master any good—a remark that earned him 75 lashes.[67] The threat to do a master 'no good' was a recurring phrase found in many bench proceedings.

Where convicts were collectively charged for neglecting their duty, the most common defence was that they had been doing their best, but that levels of output had been hindered by illness or the provision of inadequate clothing, rations or tools.[68] Lack of adequate footwear was a common complaint. In January 1842, for example, three members of the Oatlands Chain Gang received terms of solitary confinement after refusing to work in protest at the state of their shoes.[69] In January 1827 three convicts assigned to Dr. Douglas refused to travel to a remote

[66] The *Australian*, 19 July 1826.

[67] AONSW., Cawdor Benchbook, 18 February 1828.

[68] See for example M.L., Tas Papers 277, Launceston Benchbook, 26 June 1834.

[69] M.L., Tas Papers 291, Oatlands Benchbook, 19 January 1842.

station unless supplied with new clothing, and in January 1837 servants assigned to J. E. Manning refused to work until supplied with fresh slops.[70] These cases are typical of literally hundreds of rations, clothing and accommodation-related convict strikes found in surviving records. In almost all cases these defences made little difference. This helps explain why many convicts charged with neglect of work offered no defence.

Claims of inability to work through ill-health were a recurring source of both individual and collective withdrawals of labour. In April 1824 two assigned servants, Anne Osborne and Mary Murphy, were charged by Major Henry Antill with repeated disobedience. Osborne told the bench she had neither the health nor strength for kitchen work. Both were placed in solitary confinement when they refused point blank to return to their service.[71] It was common in such cases for workers to be referred to a medical examination—although this rarely proved sympathetic. In October 1835 eight members of the New Norfolk public works gang refused to work on the grounds of sickness but, when a doctor deemed them fit the ringleader, James Isaacs, was sentenced to receive 25 lashes. Over the next eight weeks four further groups (including several from the original eight) were convicted of neglecting work and feigning sickness—an indication of a wider and more prolonged struggle.[72]

In August 1841 overseer Francis Goodwin testified he had brought three gang-members who claimed to be too sick to work before the surgeon twice. On both occasions they were pronounced fit to work and the man identified as the ringleader was given a month extended sentence of hard labour and removed from the district.[73] When groups of convicts were brought before the courts for idleness it was common for a number to claim they had injuries which were responsible for slowing their rate of labour participation.[74] Suspected malingerers were routinely referred to the local bench where they were charged with neglect, disobedience, refusal to work or feigning sickness. Three members of the No. 41 Road

[70] AONSW., Cawdor Benchbook, 15 January 1827 and Yass Benchbook, 12 January 1836.

[71] AONSW., Liverpool Benchbook, 28 April 1824.

[72] M.L., Tas Papers 237, New Norfolk Benchbook, 24, 31 October, 14 November and 5, 19 December 1835.

[73] M.L., Tas Papers 291, Oatlands Benchbook, 13 August 1841.

[74] See for example M.L., Tas Papers 277, Launceston Benchbook, 14 May and 13 June 1834.

Party in New South Wales, received seven days solitary confinement in May 1831 when they were charged with malingering, while two out of a group from the No. 5 Road Party charged with feigning sickness in July 1834 received 50 lashes.[75] On occasion evidence presented indicated workers had justification for refusing to work. Eight months earlier six members of the same gang were charged with malingering, although most had just returned to work from the hospital. Their request for blankets to shield them from the cold and aid their recovery (it was midwinter), received short shrift from the overseer. They were duly brought before the Picton bench which sentenced all six to solitary confinement for periods ranging from 10 to 14 days.[76] In general, however, the nature of the available evidence makes it impossible to distinguish genuine claims of sickness from acts of malingering. The incidence of collective charges of feigning sickness suggests, however, that this was a common form of go-slow tactic.

Go-slows and collective cases of neglect often overlapped or merged with strike action. In April 1834 overseer Richard Hughes charged seven men with neglect and idleness and another five with refusing work or absence over a two-day period.[77] Efforts to combat go-slows could erupt into strikes especially where there had been a disruption of accepted work practices. Overseer Robert Jackson refused two men time to boil some water, telling one he would have to stop them idling, and telling other workers to stop lying down. This rapidly escalated into an outright refusal to work—a withdrawal of labour designed to reinforce the right to take a tea break. Eight of those involved in the incident were charged with insubordination. The man who sparked the protest received a 12-month sentence extension while the other seven were awarded 75 lashes each.[78]

Strikes or other forms of non-participation also occurred in relation to other health-related issues. The state of the weather was a common complaint. The precise point at which the weather might become sufficiently inclement to call off work was an arbitrary matter. Convicts who

[75] AONSW., Picton Benchbook, 12 May 1831 and Berrima Benchbook, 7 July 1834.

[76] AONSW., Picton Benchbook, 6 & 9 August 1830.

[77] M.L., Tas Papers 277, Launceston Benchbook, 3, 4 April 1834.

[78] M.L., Tas Papers 277, Launceston Benchbook, 8 November 1834.

made the call ahead of an overseer were likely to be prosecuted for stopping work on the 'pretence' it was raining.[79] In November 1829 a gang of Port Macquarie convicts charged with refusing to till cabbages claimed the surgeon told them they did need to work when it rained.[80] The same month James Whitehead, George Smith and Jem Gregory received 25 lashes for refusing to work at Busby's Bore near Sydney during a deluge.[81] In November 1830 seven members of a road party lent to assist Sydney region landholder Dr. Wardell with the harvest, refused an order to remove sheep on a Saturday due to rain and pleas of illness. Four of these men were ordered to receive 25 lashes due to their involvement in an earlier strike, and the remainder seven lashes.[82] This was one area where convict protests appear to have met with some degree of success. Returns for the Bridgewater chain gang in Van Diemen's Land, for example, reveal that they were not expected to labour in inclement weather.[83] In some penal stations, punishment labour was reorganised so it could be performed under shelter. At Macquarie Harbour the chain gang was tasked with grinding flour under cover of the sifting house and at Port Arthur stone breaking was organised under cover in a yard at the back of the penitentiary. By contrast, convicts who laboured outside out of irons were exempt from work when the weather was bad.[84]

The poor quality of rations received was also a common trigger for go-slows and strikes. The Cascades and Parramatta female factories were the sites of repeated strikes in response to reductions in the quantity and quality of food. In 1839 a total of 50 inmates refused work at the Cascades and violently resisted the efforts of their superintendent to restrain them.[85] In August 1825 six men assigned to Alfred Elyard's Cawdor district estate received 25 lashes each for refusing to work because they had no rations.[86] On 23 May 1826, eight members of the Western Road Party near Bathurst were charged with absence

[79] See for example M.L., Tas Papers 277, Launceston Benchbook, 14 May 1834.

[80] AONSW., Port Macquarie Benchbook, 11 November 1829.

[81] *Australian*, 20 November 1829.

[82] *Sydney Gazette*, 20 November 1830.

[83] Bridgewater Station Report: T.A., CSO 1/552/12078.

[84] Maxwell-Stewart, *Closing Hell's Gates*.

[85] Hendriksen, *Women Transported*, 62.

[86] The precise date is illegible but prior to September 1825. M.L., Cawdor Benchbook.

and disobedience. Four were sentenced to receive 50 lashes each while another three were severely reprimanded on account of their previous good conduct. The ringleader, David Jilks, who was also charged with insolence, was sentenced to serve six months in irons in another gang. The evidence given to court suggests the men left the gang for a number of hours to secure food from a nearby estate where a sheep was slaughtered. This followed complaint about their rations and a refusal to work.[87] Fifteen months later 18 members of the same gang, including four of those prosecuted in May 1826, lodged a complaint against their overseer George Williams. Once more they singled out the quality of the rations and the ill-treatment they had received. They complained that the meat that they were supplied with was largely composed of bone, that their huts were unfit because they were constructed from inferior materials and that Williams had behaved oppressively, continually bringing them before the Bathurst bench to be flogged. One of the men, James O'Neil, also argued that Williams was a proved perjurer. Williams' superior testified he was perfectly satisfied with the regular returns on rations provided to him by the overseer. This attestation to correct paperwork, and Williams own denials, were enough for the bench to dismiss the complaint as 'frivolous', and the men were reprimanded and returned to their gang.[88]

Enough cases reached court to indicate that bargaining over allowances in terms of extra rations (especially tea, sugar and tobacco or grog during harvests) was widespread. On 7 January 1833 three convicts at William Suttor's farm refused work after he stopped supplying them with tea and sugar. The men were tried the same day and the ringleader, John Smith, was sentenced to an iron-gang while his compatriots, Hough and Mead, received 25 lashes.[89] While some things like sugar were not stipulated in government rations, they were regularly supplied as an indulgence to reward good behaviour or as an additional incentive at harvest time. Some convicts viewed the supply of sugar as a requisite and attempts to withdraw such indulgences as a sanction, or after the harvest had been completed, often sparked retaliatory withdrawals of labour.

On other occasions ganged convicts stopped work, claiming they had met their allotted quota while their overseers denied that they had been

[87] AONSW., Bathurst Benchbook, 23 May 1826.

[88] AONSW., Bathurst Benchbook, 29 August 1827.

[89] AONSW., Bathurst Benchbook, 7–8 January 1833.

engaged in task-work and ordered them to continue until sunset.[90] One exasperated chain gang overseer complained that, although he told the prisoners to abide by government hours, a group left off at 5 p.m. and did not return for an hour. It being February, this was long before lack of light brought an official end to the day.[91] Three servants of Yass district landholder James Rose received 100 lashes each in July 1835 for refusing to start work before their breakfast cakes were ready, this being their second court appearance in a week.[92]

Conflict over the appropriate time to start work often hinged around the provision of breakfast. In June 1834 twelve members of a Launceston gang refused to fall in for breakfast despite repeated remonstrations from their overseer to do so. Four of these men had their terms of hard labour extended by 30 days and the rest were awarded 20 lashes each.[93] In September 1835 Broadmarsh farmer William Stanfield prosecuted four servants for neglect in not getting up till after six o'clock on Monday morning and only then when he called them to do so. Two received three months hard labour while the others were admonished.[94] Similarly, in November 1838 a Richmond shopkeeper prosecuted two workers for getting up late.[95] Defining the hours of work was a recurring theme in these disputes. A central question was the extent to which the hours of government labour defined the start and finish time of the private sector working day. When asked to rise at 6 a.m. in June 1833, George Allen told Carlton farmer Hugh Maginnes that this was contrary to government regulations. This earned him a four-month sentence to hard labour with a recommendation that he should not be returned to the property. Convicts who argued about working conditions toe to toe with masters and mistresses were generally ejected from properties in an effort to prevent the spread of dissent to other workers.[96] When "old James Stynes" was ordered by his master to rise at 5.45 a.m. he replied "do you

[90] See for example M.L., Tas Papers 277, Launceston Benchbook, 19 February 1834.

[91] M.L., Tas Papers 277, Launceston Benchbook, 21 February 1834.

[92] AONSW., Reel 682, Yass Benchbook, 21, 28 July 1835.

[93] M.L., Tas Papers 277, Launceston Benchbook, 5 June 1834.

[94] M.L., Tas Papers 2, Richmond and Brighton Benchbook, 23 September 1835.

[95] M.L., Tas Papers 326, Richmond Benchbook, 19 November 1838.

[96] M.L., Tas Papers 325, Richmond Benchbook, 24 June 1833.

think I'd get up before daylight, I won't do it"—an outburst that earned him a three months' stint in the Richmond Chain Gang.[97]

In October 1832 a dispute arose in Sussex farmer Thomas Austin's kitchen when two servants refused to go to their work until they had finished breakfast. Austin testified that the men had been provided sufficient time to eat although it emerged in court that, while they had been supplied with beef, the weekly bread ration had run out. Both men were sentenced to 30 days hard labour.[98] David Lord's overseer John Morley found three servants playing at jumping over a post-and-rail fence they were supposed to be erecting. They told him they had not had breakfast and would not commence work until this was supplied. Morley reported in court that the men told him 'that if they were to be kept on govt· rations, they would show me govt. work and that if I did not know govt. rules they would let me know them'.[99] Morley took the men before the bench charging them with disobedience, neglect and gross insolence with one receiving three months hard labour and the other two 10 days.

Short breaks were also sought during work-time. In March 1826, 17 members of the Liverpool Orphan School gang received 25 lashes for lying down during working hours.[100] In November 1834 four members of the Launceston Public Works Gang were prosecuted after they returned to the gang late and asked to sit down. When permission was refused, they sat down anyway.[101] In July 1826 a group of Scammell's gang discovered sharing a bottle of rum in their hut, were punished for refusing to cease when ordered to do so by their overseer.[102] Many strikes were triggered by disagreements over what constituted a reasonable workload. On 9 December 1835 a landholder prosecuted two workers for coming back from their work before seven o'clock in order to fill a water cask—something he claimed they had no right to do.

Job tasks or the allocation of particular work was another source of disputation. In December 1833 Gilbert Robertson charged three assigned servants with insubordination for refusing to cook for men in the huts

[97] M.L., Tas Papers 325, Richmond Benchbook, 11 October 1833.

[98] M.L., Tas Papers 323, Richmond Benchbook, 6 November 1832.

[99] M.L., Tas Papers 323, Richmond Benchbook, 14 February 1833.

[100] AONSW., Liverpool Benchbook, 15 March 1826.

[101] M.L., Tas Papers 277, Launceston Benchbook, 4 November 1834.

[102] *Australian,* 26 July 1826.

after the regular cook fell ill. The men claimed they had not refused, but had instead told Robertson that they did not know how to go about the task. The bench was unimpressed, while two were admonished, the third received 36 lashes. On the same day Robertson prosecuted another servant James Coleman for telling his mistress he would only make shoes for men on the farm.[103] Another frequent point of contestation revolved around the tasks convicts could be expected to perform, often entailing customary lines of demarcation. In July 1828 the Port Macquarie boat-crew refused to carry luggage brought ashore, asserting they were seamen not labourers. They were sentenced to seven days in a chain gang. Similarly in April 1831 the same crew refused to assist in unloading lime, one of a series of strikes they engaged in.[104]

Strikes and other actions brought before courts often represented pressure points of contestation, part of an ongoing effort-bargaining struggle or the result of a change in circumstances like the introduction of a new overseer. On 1 September 1825, for example, members of a clearing gang near Camden refused work, telling their overseer Edward Farley that they had completed their allotted tasks. When Farley ordered them to resume work, gang-member James Hartley told him he was a bigger tyrant even than Burke, the then Governor of New South Wales. Another gang-member Peter Miller told Farley he would not burn the top of trees as ordered even for 'Mr. Macarthur'—a reference to the most powerful landholding family in the district. Nine members of the gang were tried before the Cawdor bench, six getting 25 lashes and the three ringleaders 50.[105]

Private sector masters also prosecuted convicts for refusing to work outside government hours, on a Sunday or to work before breakfast or another meal had been served. In July 1833 Joseph Perkins received 25 lashes for refusing feed the pigs at David Lord's Pittwater Estate on Sunday afternoon after the worker who normally did the task had left the property to see a doctor. Three other workers were reprimanded for refusing to aid Lord's overseer John Morley's efforts to take Perkins for punishment.[106] James Woolley was sentenced to one month's hard

103 M.L., Tas Papers 325, Richmond Benchbook, 6 December 1833.

104 AONSW., Port Macquarie Benchbook, 23 July 1828 and 27 April 1831.

105 AONSW., Cawdor Benchbook, 3 September 1825.

106 M.L., Tas Papers 325, Richmond Benchbook, 16 July 1833.

labour for repeatedly refusing to cut a 'little fire wood' for his mistress on Sunday morning, while William Wayland received three days solitary for refusing to fetch a load of turnips on a Sunday morning for his Broadmarsh master.[107] Those who gave explicit reasons for not engaging in the work process could find themselves in even more trouble. When William Alexis told Dr Hall and his wife that he would not work in the garden all week and then cook dinner on Sunday, he received 12 months in chains for 'gross disobedience' and 'habitual insolence.'[108] The latter part of the charge suggests that this tussle had a protracted history.

As many convicts pointed out, Sunday labour ate into time workers used for their own activities. When Thomas Wilkinson ordered two servants to unyoke bullocks being used to pull a log for their firewood it provoked an angry exchange. Joseph Pilgrim told him that working through the weekend gave him no time to wash his shirt, which he had not been able to clean for a fortnight. For this outburst Pilgrim had his sentence to transportation extended six months and was ordered to be imprisoned at hard labour for three of these. His compatriot, David Robinson (also transported on the *Lord William Bentwick*), received a 12 month extended sentence and six months in the Richmond Chain Gang.[109]

Workers also refused to work on Christmas Day, New Year and Good Friday. Desailly charged four servants with repeatedly refusing to work all day on 1 January 1833, although in this case the Clarence Plains bench merely admonished them.[110] In March 1827 eight members of a Liverpool district gang were charged after refusing to work, stating they thought it was a holiday. As a punishment they were ordered to work three Saturday afternoons.[111] On 27 December 1836 magistrate Benjamin Berthon charged five of his workers with insubordination for refusing to work on Christmas day. Again, these workers were severely admonished, rather than punished.[112]

[107] M.L., Tas Papers 2, Richmond and Brighton Benchbook, 11 August and 23 September 1835.

[108] M.L., Tas Papers 2, Richmond and Brighton Benchbook, 6 March 1837.

[109] M.L., Tas Papers 325, Richmond Benchbook, 23 September 1833.

[110] M.L., Tas Papers 323, Richmond Benchbook, Clarence Plains 2 January 1833.

[111] *Sydney Gazette*, 13 March 1827.

[112] M.L., Tas Papers 290, Oatlands Benchbook, 27 December 1836.

Conclusion

Prosecutions for neglect of duty and refusing to work merely confirmed in the minds of convict managers that criminals were by nature work-shy. As such, punishing the recalcitrant for not pulling their weight could be construed as a virtue. Just as it was common for those with vested interests in the slave trade to argue that the rigorous management of the plantation helped to rescue benighted Africans from the barbarism of the dark continent of their birth, so the beneficiaries of convict labour argued that providing thieves with a work ethic constituted a wider societal good.[113] Yet, the inefficiency of the lash as a tool of labour management lay at the heart of economic critiques of all unfree labour systems. As Adam Smith argued 'Work done by slaves … is in the end the dearest of any. A person who can acquire no property, can have no other interest but to eat as much and labour as little as possible'.[114] In short, it was not just criminals that refused to work with alacrity in the absence of positive inducements to do otherwise. Like slaves and other unfree workers, transported convicts resisted the circumstances of their labour exploitation in a concerted effort to improve the safety and general conditions of work as well as levels of remuneration. In short, our analysis reveals that they were adept at organising in an attempt to lose their chains by downing their tools, no matter the number of lashes that rained down on their backs as a consequence, or the thickness of the walls of the dark cells within which they were incarcerated.

Court records drawn from the collective action database provide some indication of the immense scale of resistance although case numbers do not equate to instances of collective action as each event could trigger multiple court actions while some workers were charged with multiple offences at the same trial. Between 1788 and 1860 we have evidence of 6721 court actions in relation to 796 instances of collective neglecting of duty, 334 instances of collective insolence or abuse associated with management demands to increase work intensity and 1756 cases where convicts were charged with collectively refusing to work. This activity is summarised in Table 7.2.

These figures demonstrate the scale of labour withdrawals by convicts but are still under-counts for other reasons. Female convicts, for example,

[113] Green, *A Fistful of Shells*, 265.

[114] Smith, A. (1776), *Wealth of Nations*, 387.

Table 7.2 Instances of convict collective go-slows, workplace insolence and strikes 1788–1860

	1788–00	*1801–10*	*1811–20*	*1821–30*	*1831–40*	*1841–50*	*1851–60*	*Total*
Go-slows etc	10	6	4	161	529	76	10	796
Insolence	2	1	1	48	220	69	3	344
Strikes	8	8	20	283	946	381	110	1756
Total	20	15	25	492	1695	526	123	3422

were more likely to be charged with work-related offences compared to their male counterparts, but much less likely to be charged in groups. This reflects the ways in which convict women were dispersed in small numbers across many households, rather than any comparative lack of militancy. Outside of factories and hiring depots, it was uncommon for more than two or three women to be assigned to the same household. While it was difficult for convict women in the private sector to withdraw labour *en mass*, they demonstrated their militancy through other actions. As detailed in Table 7.1 convict women in Van Diemen's Land were frequently prosecuted for refusing to return to, or remain in, the service to which they had been assigned, effectively passing judgment on the employment practices of particular households. While a similar number of charges were brought against men, there were many more convict men than women in assigned or passholder service at any particular point in time. In relative terms female convicts were four times more likely to be charged with taking this form of action compared to their male counterparts.

Agricultural labourers, skilled artisans and food preparation workers were also less likely to be brought to court for downing tools compared to other transported workers. By contrast, former soldiers, miners and quarrymen were disproportionately charged with refusing to work. These men had already been subjected to high levels of industrial discipline before they were transported to Van Diemen's Land and this prior experience of collectivisation is likely to have informed their propensity to participate in colonial strike action (see Fig. 7.1). In general terms, however, those unfree workers disproportionately charged with refusing to work were less likely to possess skills that were in colonial demand. They were

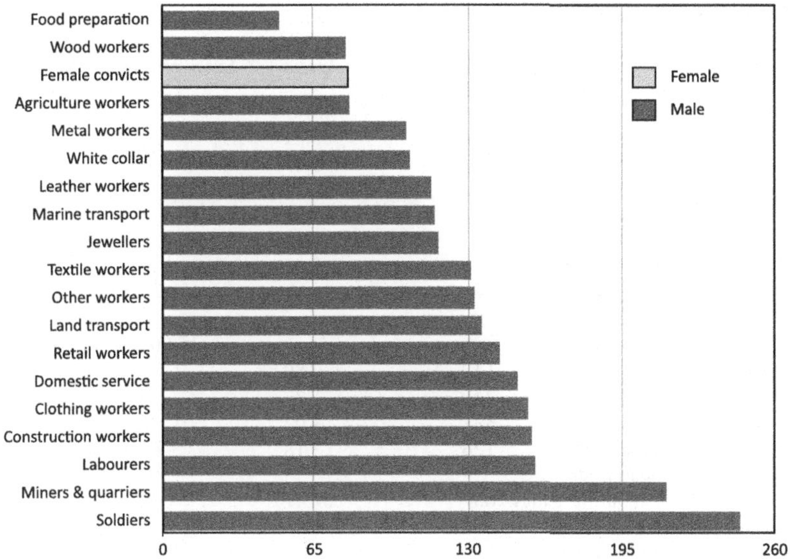

Fig. 7.1 Refusing to Work (charges per 1000 convict workers) (*Source* T.A., Con 31, 32, 33, 40 & 41)

therefore at greater risk of demotion to a punishment gang, penal station or factory. Levels of colonial militancy reflected management practices. Wherever large bodies of workers were subjected to collective regimentation, prosecution rates for refusing to work increased. Examination of strike action across public and private sector employment reinforces the point. While assigned, ticket of leave and passholder convicts account for 46 percent of all strike actions, on average 65 percent of male and female convicts were engaged in private sector work at any given point. By contrast the 35 percent of convicts in government employment were responsible for half of all strike actions (see Table 7.3).

Convict workplace protests were focused on a relatively small range of issues. Transported unfree workers were most likely to take action against managers who attempted to force them to work on Saturday afternoons, Sundays or public holidays. An indication of the double standard in the manner in which colonial workplace regulations were implemented was that convicts who attempted to privately sell their labour on a Sunday could be charged with 'Sabbath breaking', an offence for which masters

Table 7.3 Strike action by sector of employment

Sector	*Type of work*	*Number of strikes*	*Percent*	*Sector percent*	*Percent of convicts*
Private	Rural workers	627	35.71		
	Cooks & servants	90	5.13		
	Bootmakers	22	1.25		
	Tailors	20	1.14		
	Retail workers	19	1.08		
	Other private sector workers	37	2.11		
				46.00	65.00
Public	Brickmakers	14	0.80		
	Sawyers	24	1.37		
	Seamen	53	3.02		
	Miners & quarrymen	126	7.18		
	Labouring gangs	657	37.41		
	Other public sector workers	15	0.85		
				50.00	35.00
Unknown		52	2.96		
Total		1756	100.00	100.00	100.00

Sources Benchbooks and selected newspapers. T.A., CSO1/700/15332; CSO1/741/16030; CSO1/746/61110; CSO1/893/18969; CSO5/1/130/3087; CSO5/1/30; CSO 49/7/1838

appear to have been exempt.[115] Convicts also took exception to orders to work outside of public sector hours, unless adequate compensation was forthcoming in the form of incentives or bonus payments. Other common issues that triggered collective action included being forced to work outside in inclement weather, or without adequate clothing (especially footwear) or rations. After the reintroduction of officially sanctioned convict wages in Van Diemen's Land under the passholder system, convicts also regularly struck over wages.

Go-slows, strikes and other forms or workplace action tended to congregate—one such action being followed by another. Where work intensity increased because new land was being broken in or convicts

[115] See for example James Watkins per *Coromandel*, Police No. 206, T.A., Con 31-1-45 and Thomas Peffrey per *Lord Hunbgerford*, Police No. 206 Con 31-1-34, 31 October 1826.

were ordered to cut the line of a road through difficult country, the rate of prosecution for work related protests could increase dramatically. A change in management could also lead to a serious deterioration in labour relations.[116] The same was true of attempts to cut back on rights that convicts saw as customary, such as the reduction in the time allowed for meal breaks.

To return to the example that this chapter opened with, it is possible to plot the number prosecutions brought against convicts working under the charge of Robert Notman on the road between Launceston and Perth in the early 1830s. While, the benchbooks for the Launceston Police District are missing for this period, the police charge book survives. Using this, musters, newspaper summaries of court proceedings and absconding notices placed in the *Hobart Town Gazette,* a total of 262 convicts who worked in this punishment detail can be identified. Reference to their conduct records enables a reconstruction of prosecutions in the period from 1 January 1831 to 31 December 1833. In this period there were 60 collective prosecutions in this gang for neglect of duty, idleness, feigning sickness or otherwise reducing work effort. In the same period groups of convicts were charged with refusing to work or insubordination on 16 occasions. Figure 7.2. plots these events by date and the number of convicts prosecuted on each occasion.

This reconstruction gives the lie to 'the claim that the 3350 lashes inflicted on backs of the participants in the July 1833 mutiny quelled the rebellious spirit of Notman's charges. The gang did not meekly submit as a result of this show of visceral force. There were another nine strike actions in this road party in the remaining months of 1833 and on a further 16 occasions convicts were collectively punished for not applying themselves at work.[117]

Notman's running battle with his charges spilled over into the following year. On 7 March 1834 no fewer than 18 members of this road gang were charged with neglect and less than a month later on 2 April 1834 another overseer to the same gang, Richard Cloak, charged a further 20 with the same offence. One of these men earned an additional penalty of 28 days solitary on bread and water for gross insolence in the

[116] Roberts, D. (2017) Masters, Magistrates and the Management of Complaint: The 1833 Convict Revolt at Castle Forbes and the Failure of Local Governance, *Journal of Australian Colonial History,* 19, 61.

[117] Launceston Charge Book, T.A., POL 451-1-4.

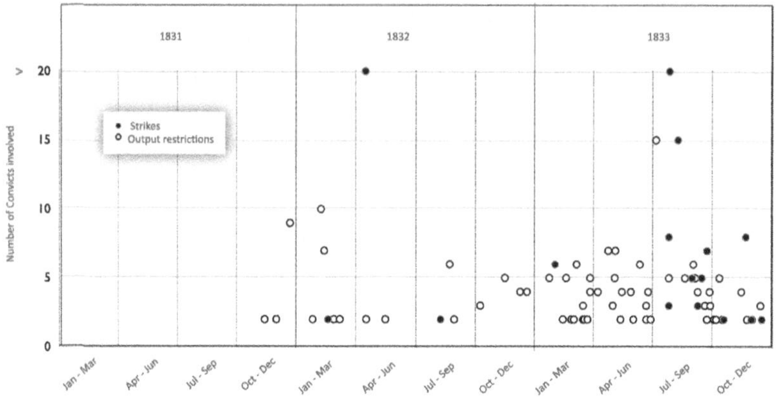

Fig. 7.2 Collective prosecutions for neglect of work, idleness, refusing to work and insubordination Notman's road party 1831–33 (*Source* T.A., Con 31, 32, 33, 40 & 41, POL 451, Launceston Charge Book)

hearing of the magistrate. Shutting people up was critical to the majesty of the judicial apparatus. On 9 April, Cloak returned to court to prefer charges of neglect against 36 men. Of these 23 were flogged, another seven reprimanded and six had their terms of hard labour on the gang extended.[118] Things did not improve. Samuel Smith prosecuted another 20 strong group in late July and hauled the same number of men before the bench in early August 1834. The second group pleaded in court that they could not break the amount of stone required in the allotted time, although this was dismissed as one of 'many frivolous excuses' put up in their defence.[119]

Figure 7.2 also reveals that Notman's charges had previously locked horns with their superintendent. A cluster of collective charges were brought against members of this gang in late 1831 and the first half of 1832, culminating with the prosecution of 46 convicts on 17 June 1832 for 'Disobedience of orders in refusing to go to work'. All were punished by being placed on reduced rations for six weeks. Like all road parties, turnover in the gang was high. Many convicts were sent to be disciplined by 'Bobby' Notman for a few months, before being returned

[118] M.L., Tas Papers 277, Launceston Benchbook, 7 March and 2, 9 April 1834.

[119] M.L., Tas Papers 277, Launceston Benchbook, 29 July and 8 August 1834.

suitably chastised to their assigned service. Despite constantly changing gang membership, every one of the 16 collective prosecutions for refusing to work or insubordination in the period 1832–3 shared at least one participant with another such action. These links are visualised in Fig. 7.3. The same was true of the 60 collective output restrictions. Many convicts were involved in multiple such actions, William Parradise, a 20-year-old labourer from Rochester in Kent, participated in 10 such disputes over this two year period and Joseph Sibley, James Jeal and William Johnson six each. In short, common experience linked these events into a connected chain of protests.

There also appears to have been co-ordinated action between subsections of this road party. It was common practice for the men at any particular station to be divided into different parties, each detailed with the performance of a particular task. Billeted men would be charged with preparing meals or mending tools, while the individual gangs would be sent to work on different sections of the road, or would be charged with other menial tasks such as crushing aggregate. At Notman's road party a group of men worked in irons in a chain gang and were housed in a barracks, sometimes referred to as a penitentiary. They were also placed on an inferior diet. By contrast, non-ironed members of the gang were accommodated in huts. An examination of the charges for 30 July 1833,

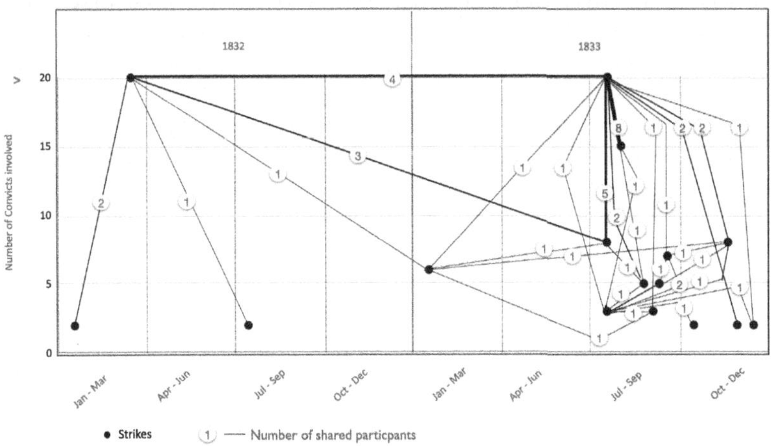

Fig. 7.3 Participation across multiple strike actions, Notman's road party 1832–33

the day before the large-scale mutiny, reveals that a total of sixteen individuals were charged with work-related offences. Eight were prosecuted for disobedience of orders and refusing to work. They were given terms of between one and two months 'hard labour and imprisonment'. Three other gang members were sentenced to 10 days solitary for 'refusing to work'. In the charge sheet the names of this group are bracketed together suggesting that this was a different protest. Finally, five members of the chain gang were charged with 'idleness and neglect of work', four were flogged and one reprimanded.[120]

Thus, three parties of men were prosecuted on the same day for either withdrawing their labour altogether or restricting output suggesting co-ordinated action. This was no doubt triggered by the dismissal of the complaint brought by the 60 convicts from Notman's party who had recently marched into town to air their grievances.[121]

In the absence of benchbooks it is difficult to isolate the issues that lay at the heart of this protracted battle between convicts and their managers on the muddy line of road that led out of Launceston. The men in Notman's gang were said, however, to be infested with lice—largely because they were supplied with insufficient clothing.[122] Food also appears to have been an issue. Those protesters who were not flogged were placed on reduced rations, a punishment that may have escalated rather than diminished the rate of protest. As Fig. 7.2 shows, there was a clear alignment between the timing of output restrictions and strikes. Yet, the convicts under Notman's charge were just as frequently prosecuted for voting with their feet. A reconstruction of absconding records reveals that they left this coercive working environment in droves. This second form of labour withdrawal is the subject of the next chapter which, in the absence of words, uses actions to give a voice to Australia's long forgotten convict protesters.

[120] Launceston Charge Book, T.A., POL 451-1-4, 30 July 1833.

[121] *Launceston Advertiser*, 5 September 1833.

[122] *Independent*, 28 February 1833.

CHAPTER 8

Absenteeism, Absconding and Escape

When Theophilus Lightfoot, a tailor and draper who had a business in Elizabeth Street, Hobart Town, ordered his assigned servants to bed at 10.00 o'clock at night James Alison retorted, 'you shall not hunt me like a b[lood]y slave'. He then threatened his master with 'by Heaven's, a blow'. The *Tasmanian* reported: 'This Mr Lightfoot's "kind and forgiving temper" could not endure. The "knight of the thimble" was accordingly ordered by the bench to leave off tailoring for the amusing change of pickaxe and shovel exercise, at Mr. Notman's road party, for six months'.[1] This was not the first time that Lightfoot had charged Alison. Five months earlier on 3 April 1832 the young Shropshire tailor had been sentenced to a month's hard labour in a road party for being absent from Lightfoot's premises for an hour and a half without leave.[2]

Lightfoot's shop in Elizabeth Street was composed of 'four commodious rooms'. Anyone who passed through the ground floor of this retail establishment would enter a yard at the back of the building. On the other side of this was a workshop 'capable of accommodating four and twenty men'. Attached to this was 'a large and dry' room, 'fitted

[1] *Tasmanian*, 7 September 1832.

[2] James Alison, per *Red Rover*, Police No. 421, T.A., Con 18-1-2; Con 27-1-5 and Con 31-1-2.

H. Maxwell-Stewart and M. Quinlan, *Unfree Workers*, Palgrave Studies in Economic History,
https://doi.org/10.1007/978-981-16-7558-4_8

up with bed-berths, and a kitchen or men's cook-house'.[3] In December 1832 at least ten other convicts shared this establishment with Alison. Like him six of these were skilled tailors. Two more were errand boys, useful for making deliveries around town and manning the shop. Finally, the premises also accommodated two female assigned servants. Elizabeth Denny, a laundry maid from County Cork, cleaned and serviced the shop and the private rooms reserved for Lightfoot and his family, while Elizabeth Wilson, a needlewoman from York, is likely to have worked alongside the male tailors in the workshop.[4]

A return completed two years later reported that Lightfoot also employed three free tailors. As he put it in a letter to the paper, however, he preferred to employ convicts. In part this was because those who were not shackled by a sentence refused to sign up for the piece rates he offered. In November 1833 a strike was organised by the newly formed Hobart Journeyman Tailors' Benefit Society. This seems to have been a well-organised combination, which met at J. Priest's licensed establishment also located in Elizabeth Street—it was a common practice for unions to meet in public houses at this time. From there a letter was circulated amongst Lightfoot's workers, free and unfree, calling upon them to 'stick up for their rights privileges, and higher wages, and no longer to allow masters to make a property out of the sweat of their brow'. Lightfoot broke the action with the assistance of the Board of Assignment, laying off the free and replacing them with the unfree.[5] The episode provides an object lesson in the manner in which the private sector deployment of convict labour enabled masters, to not only benefit from the exploitation of convicts, but to use them to beat down the wages of free workers.

[3] *Colonial Times*, 26 June 1832. See also Read, R. (2020) Convict Assignment and Prosecution Risk in Van Diemen's Land 1830–35, Ph.D. Thesis, University of Tasmania, 170.

[4] 1830 Convict Muster Van Diemen's Land, N.A. (UK), HO10/47; 1832 Convict Muster Van Diemen's Land HO10/48; 1833 Convict Muster Van Diemen's Land, HO10/49; 1835 Convict Muster Van Diemen's Land HO10/50; Elizabeth Denny, per *Hydery*, Police No. 141, T.A., Con 27-2-1; Con 40-1-3; Elizabeth Wilson, per *Hydery*, Police No. 209, Con 27-2-1; Con 40-1-9.

[5] *Hobart Town Courier*, 14 March 1834.

Between January 1828 and January 1836 at least 36 convicts worked and slept at Lightfoot's Elizabeth Street tailoring establishment. A reconstruction of their conduct records reveals that Lightfoot's business had been threatened by strike action on a previous occasion. On 15 September 1829 five of his convict tailors were prosecuted for refusing to work on a Monday. That all five were merely reprimanded suggests that this earlier strike may have achieved some of its objectives.[6] Absenteeism presented Lightfoot with a more significant problem, however. Over this eight-year time period, his convicts were charged with being absent, absconding or attempting to escape from the colony on 66 occasions. The loss in work hours was considerable. As well as time lost through walking off the job, Lightfoot went short-handed while his convict men and woman sat in the stocks; languished in solitary cells, road parties and chain gangs; or trod out the boards in the treadwheel yard of the penitentiary.

In his pioneering assessment of convict protest Alan Atkinson didn't include the withdrawal of labour through absenteeism or running away, mainly because magistrates' benchbooks rarely recorded the issues that motivated convicts to leave their workplace.[7] As David Roberts argued these might vary from a desire to affect a permanent escape to a temporary leave of absence designed to gain relief from the monotony of convict life.[8] While the former might be characterised by the illegal movement of convicts from outlying rural to urban areas, there are plenty of examples of prisoners who attempted to quit the colony altogether. Work by Ian Duffield, for example, emphasised the prevalence of piratical attempts at escape by seizing vessels.[9] Regardless of the difference in scale between temporary absence by convicts and attempted escape such actions were once viewed as unconnected to working conditions and apolitical—a view that has recently begun to undergo significant change.[10]

[6] George Humbleton, per *Woodford*, Police No. 869, T.A., Con 31-1-22; John Mason, per *William Miles*, Police No. 644, Con 31-1-29; Richard Rowe, per *York*, Police No. 571, Con 31-1-34; Samuel Southall, per *Layton*, Police No. 820, Con 31-1-39 and William Wood, per *Lady Harewood*, Police No. 935, con 31-1-45.

[7] Atkinson, Four Patterns of Convict Protest, 36.

[8] Roberts, D. (2005) A "Change of Place", Illegal Movement on the Bathurst Frontier, 1822–1825, *Journal of Australian Colonial History*, 7, 97.

[9] Duffield, Cutting Out and Taking Liberties, 197–227.

[10] Connell, R. and Irving, T. (1980) *Class Structure in Australian History, Documents, Narrative and Argument*, Melbourne University Press, Melbourne, 50. See also Irving,

As we have already seen in the case of Lightfoot's tailoring business, absconding and absenteeism were costly for employers of convict labour. We argue that no analysis of convict labour withdrawals would be complete without incorporating time lost through the taking of 'French leave', to use a colonial colloquialism. One reason for this is the sheer scale of prosecutions. Charges of being absent without leave and absconding dominate the list of offences itemised in conduct records. In Van Diemen's Land alone, 23,469 women were charged with being absent and 5373 with absconding while men were charged with being absent 61,525 times and absconding on 19,200 occasions.[11] In all, 26 percent of prosecutions brought against convicts were for movement-related offences. In short, convicts were much more likely to be charged with stealing themselves than they were other items of property.

Such acts could result in severe penalties. More convicts were sent to penal stations for absconding, for example, than any other offence. We would further argue that an analysis of the timing of temporary and extended absences and a detailed reading of associated press reporting and court prosecutions can do much to identify the motives that induced convicts to walk off the job in such large numbers. As well as piecing together convict motives, an aim of this chapter will be to enumerate the rate of collective absconding, as well as to connect such acts to other forms of protest. We will do this first through an analysis of temporary withdrawals of labour before moving on to explore other attempts by convicts to leave their place of work on a more permanent basis.

Absenteeism

As we have already seen, much of the struggle between convicts and their managers revolved around the hours of work. Claims over the start and finish of the working day and the right to recreational breaks and holidays lay at the heart of many disputes. Yet, even outside of government

T. (2018) Review of Michael Quinlan, The Origins of Worker Mobilisation: Australia 1788–1850, Routledge, London, 2017, *Economic and Labour Relations Review*, 29(2), 263–268.

[11] Based on a complete count of all bench summaries in Con 40 and 41, Conduct Records for female convicts, and a four percent systematic longitudinal sample of Con 31, 32 and 33, Conduct Records for male convicts.

Table 8.1 Days on which convicts were prosecuted for being out after hours or absent

Day of the week	*Male %*	*Female %*
Sunday	39.8	36.3
Monday	13.7	18.9
Tuesday	8.0	11.3
Wednesday	7.2	9.6
Thursday	7.6	8.4
Friday	11.2	7.8
Saturday	12.4	7.7
Total	100.0	100.0

Sources Con 31, 32, 33, 40 and 41. $N = 835$

hours convict access to their 'own time' was constrained. An examination of charges for 'being absent' or 'out after hours' reveals the extent to which prisoners who attempted to access recreational pursuits or seek waged work in 'their own time', were prosecuted. Such prosecutions were common events. Analysis of the day of the week in which convicts were arrested for being absent reveals that over a third of all arrests occurred on a Sunday—a day, when at least in theory, convicts were exempt from labour (see Table 8.1).

As this record of prosecution reveals, convicts were expected to spend their leisure hours confined to their designated quarters, with the exception of the Sunday obligatory trip to church. While William Cordeaux granted four servants a half-holiday for St. Patrick's Day in March 1825, it was on condition they stayed on the farm. All four were sentenced to be flogged when discovered in a public house.[12] Accordingly, many assigned convicts attempted to socialise without leaving their place of employment, congregating in workspaces such as kitchens or in stock huts. Such activities also led to prosecutions, especially where drinking, socialising with the opposite sex and gambling were involved. On 20 December 1838 three female servants assigned to Radcliff were admonished for being in the loft with Mr. Woodward's male servants the previous night. Two of the male servants were convicted of misconduct and abusive language against Woodward's overseer who discovered this party of clandestine revellers, one receiving six months hard labour in chains and the other 25

[12] AONSW., Liverpool Benchbook, 19 March 1825.

lashes.[13] Emma Hely and Jane Prior received terms in the Hobart Female Factory after being charged by Cahill, their employer, with being absent from their bedroom and engaging in 'immoral behaviour'. Another assigned servant, Robert Wood, received three months hard labour for the same offence and was removed from the district.[14] Gambling or playing cards, common working-class recreations, were also proscribed. Seven of Alexander Goldie's servants at Orielton were prosecuted after their overseer found them playing cards in their hut.[15]

Many assigned convict workers faced a conundrum. They could either take recreational leave on their employer's estate or property and risk punishment there for misconduct, or risk being charged with absence. This tension is illustrated by a sequence of incidents on the Minto estate of George Howe in June 1834. On 9 June Howe prosecuted a group of his assigned servants for being drunk and disorderly on the Sabbath. A fortnight later he charged another group (including some involved in the original prosecution) with neglect and absence. A month later one of these men, Patrick Murphy, was charged with leaving his employer's farm to make a frivolous complaint against his overseer, for which the magistrate ordered his sentence to be extended and returned him to the Crown.[16] This sequence highlights the manner in which collective action often involved multiple issues, and a sequence of different events that could playout over weeks or even months. A similar pattern of deteriorating relations occurred on William Edward Riley's estate in February 1834 when six workers were prosecuted in the space of three days.[17]

Some servants travelled considerable distances away from the property they were assigned to in order to socialise. The desire to escape their employer's premises temporarily even extended to those working for publicans. William Courtney and James Johnson were prosecuted by Pontville innkeeper, James Burnipp, for absenting themselves on Sunday

[13] M.L., Tas Papers 326, Richmond Benchbook, 20 December 1838.

[14] M.L., Tas Papers 291, Oatlands Benchbook, 30 November 1841.

[15] M.L., Tas Papers 326, Richmond Benchbook, 25 April and 2 May 1839.

[16] AONSW., 2482/6 CY Reel 954, Campbelltown Benchbook, 9, 23 June and 26 July 1834.

[17] AONSW., 2482/6 CY Reel 954, Campbelltown Benchbook, 8, 9, 10 February and 8 March 1834.

afternoon and returning drunk.[18] Leaving their place of employment often meant a trip into town. McCogle prosecuted two of his assignees for repeated disobedience and staying in the township on Saturday night contrary to instructions. Both were sentenced to seven days solitary. He returned another two to government service the following day who were probably also involved in the same extended absence.[19] Many convicts sent to urban centres on their mater's business overstayed their pass, taking advantage of the absence from the constraints of life on a rural estate.

While it is easy to dismiss such absences as merely attempts to slope off for a drink, a smoke or a sexual encounter, this rather misses the point. In convict Australia the exercise of leisure could in itself form a political act. It was precisely because 'private time' was so heavily policed that charges of being absent were frequent. Susannah Cook was sent to the crime class in the female factory in January 1831 for, 'Leaving her Master's premises at improper times by getting out of her Bedroom window'. Yet, the 'improper time'—that is late at night—was the convict's time in the sense that it was outside of the hours of labour. Although the sun had long since gone down marking the end of the working day, Cook was still technically held captive in her master's house.[20]

As detailed in Chapters 6 And 7, private sector masters battled to keep their assigned servants at work over the weekend. This was particularly so during periods of peak labour demand such as harvest. While some employers tolerated temporary absences where these did not cut too deeply into their pockets, others were less prepared to engage in tacit bargaining over both the amount of leisure time due to their assigned servants and the range of activities they were free to pursue in their 'time off'. Five servants of Pittwater farmer David Lord charged with being absent on Sunday 14 October 1832, although all five were reprimanded for the absence rather than being formally punished. In 1836, Nicholls, an Oatlands-district employer, complained his servants had absented themselves on Sunday, notwithstanding repeated warnings.[21] In New South Wales, Thomas Meehan prosecuted three of his farm servants for absence

[18] M.L., Tas Papers 2, Richmond and Brighton Benchbook, 6 July 1835.

[19] M.L., Tas Papers 292, Oatlands Benchbook, 4 February 1839.

[20] Susannah Cook, per *Providence*, Police No. 81, T.A., Con 40-1-3.

[21] M.L., Tas Papers 290, Oatlands Benchbook, 3 April 1836.

on Sunday. Each was awarded 25 lashes. Despite the relatively severe punishment meted out by the bench, Meehan found himself back in court a week later when the same men and two others absented themselves again. When he demanded to know why they had left, several of them spoke to him in an impertinent manner.[22]

Demands for time-off during customary celebrations like Christmas and Boxing Day were particularly common. Four of Charles Throsby's servants were sentenced to the treadmill for being absent on Boxing Day 1825.[23] On 27 December 1830, George Harpur prosecuted 12 convicts – ten of his own assigned servants and two lent from the No. 41 Road Party to help with the harvest—for absenting themselves on Christmas Day. This despite the fact that this was a recognised holiday for public sector convicts—as the two loaned men are likely to have pointed out to their assigned co-workers. While benches often showed leniency for offences that occurred during traditional festive occasions, this was not always the case. In prosecuting Harpur's assigned servants, the Picton magistrates were persuaded that the extra rations of tobacco and beer they had been provided constituted adequate compensation for the loss of free time. The bench ordered 75 lashes to be inflicted on four of the absentees and 50 lashes each on the remainder.[24] Other employers moderated penalties inflicted on festive revellers. Captain Dumas merely reprimanded his servants who were absent on Christmas Day and Boxing 1832, as did John Leake when three of his servants were discovered to be absent from his Rosedale estate on Christmas Eve 1833.[25]

Where time off was granted, it was often as an inducement to labour—or a recognition of effort expended during shearing or harvest or other periods of work intensity. Like other incentives, however, such indulgences could be clawed back. Indeed, control over access to leisure had the advantage that the master did not have to seek the backing of a magistrate—what was in their largesse to give, could just as easily be taken away.

[22] In the second case two were sentenced to four months in a chain gang, two to 36 lashes and one to 25 lashes. M.L., Liverpool Benchbook, 29 April and 6 May 1826.

[23] AONSW., Liverpool Benchbook, 31 December 1825.

[24] AONSW., Picton Benchbook, 27 December 1830.

[25] M.L., Tas Papers 323, Richmond Benchbook, 27 December 1832; Tas Papers 256, Campbell Town Prisoner Records and Sentences, 26 December 1833.

An assigned servant who was not in favour was almost certain to be prosecuted if they left the property without leave while valued men and women were more likely to be given the benefit of the doubt.

It is possible that masters who were magistrates felt obliged to lead by example, cracking down on convict access to leisure time. As part of a regional élite, it was important for them to be seen to set and maintain standards. The various members of the Archer family, who were large estate holders and magistrates in northern Van Diemen's Land, frequently prosecuted their servants for being absent. Rather than suppressing dissent, however, this appears to have escalated workplace tension. In June 1840 Thomas Archer brought seven of his servants, including Mary Law and Elizabeth Goodyer, before the Longford bench charged with absence on Saturday night, refusing to work and gross insolence. The nature of this compound charge suggests that the attempt to call his assigned servants to account for their collective temporary absence triggered a further withdrawal of labour as well as angry words. All seven were duly convicted and punished, with Law having her sentence in solitary confinement extended for misconduct in talking to the prisoner in the neighbouring cell.[26]

It is impossible to know precisely how many prosecutions for being absent relate to events that happened outside of the government working day, and might be seen as part of a struggle over access to 'free time'. More than half, however, involved arrests in public houses or because the convict was out 'after hours'. This, in conjunction with the marked skew towards Sunday prosecutions, reveals the extent to which the post-Bigge reforms were aimed at wresting back control of convict private time. The majority of these cases were brought by the police, rather than private sector masters. Indeed, the reason why there was one policeman for every 89 colonists, both free and unfree, was the substantial investment in manpower required to extend surveillance beyond the walls of the master's residence and the confines of the penitentiary and factory.[27] It was the extraordinarily high levels of policing that provided the colonial state with the ability to peer into smoke-filled bars and control access to the theatre, skittle grounds, billiard halls and the races. The police were

[26] T.A., LC362-1-4, Longford Magistrates Court Benchbook, 22, 25 and 29 June 1840.

[27] Petrow, Policing in a Penal Colony, 375.

particularly proactive when it came to the surveillance of brothels and 'disorderly houses'.

Many female convicts challenged the validity of the powers assumed by masters and mistresses. William Sorell, the son of a former Lieutenant-Governor of Van Diemen's Land, went in pursuit of his assigned servant, Mary Ann Laing, when she left his property on a Sunday. Sorell found Laing at 7.00 p.m. in Thomas Ikin's house in Davey Street and ordered her back home in his dual capacity as master and magistrate. She refused on good grounds. Not only was it her day off, but magistrates did not have the authority to try their own servants. She could nevertheless be tried for contempt. She was sentenced by the principal superintendent of convicts to three months hard labour in the factory followed by five days in solitary confinement. For good measure, he ordered that she be assigned 'up the Country' after the completion of her sentence.[28]

Masters had little say in prosecutions brought by the police, but could intercede on behalf of their servants when they were brought to court. This helps explain why many of those charged with being absent received the equivalent of a 'slap on the wrist'. In all 23 percent of such charges brought against male convicts resulted in an acquittal or reprimand. By contrast only one percent of men charged with absconding were let off with a reprieve. The courts were much less lenient when it came to the prosecution of absenteeism amongst female convicts. Only 11 percent of such charges resulted in acquittals or reprimands, less than half that of their male counterparts. This is a stark reminder—if a reminder was needed—of the imbalance in the way the sexes were policed. To provide an example of the coercive measures used to curb female convict attempts at socialisation, in September 1849 Sarah Neilson was arrested for being found in a public house sitting with a man who had his 'arm round her neck'.[29] For this 'crime' she was given three months hard labour with instructions to be deployed in the interior far away from the attractions of Hobart.

Many prosecutions for being absent were collective. In August 1826 a group of servants assigned to two Windsor district employers, McDougall and Smith, received 12 lashes each for being absent and found in a local

[28] Mary Ann Laing, per *Borneo*, Police No. 78, T.A., Con 40-1-5.

[29] Sarah Neilson, per *Woodbridge*, Police No. 123, T.A., Con 40-1-8.

pub.[30] In August 1836 Selina Turner and Thomas Hart were prosecuted by their employer for being out after hours. They were found talking in the street after 9 p.m., an offence for which both were sentenced to 48 hours solitary on bread and water. Two weeks later two members of the Oatlands public works gang were sentenced to six days solitary after they were found in bed with Captain Pedder's female servants on a Saturday night.[31] Richmond landholder, John H. Butcher, prosecuted three servants for being absent all Saturday night and Sunday morning possum-hunting without permission, while the servants of Oatlands landholder, Thomas Anstey, were charged after being found in a public house on Friday night.[32]

As some of these examples illustrate, assigned servants from several properties took leave on occasions to socialise away from their places of employment. On 11 June 1832 Sarah Jacobs was sentenced to be placed in the cells for six days and thereafter to be sent to the crime class at the factory for 'Absenting herself remaining out the whole night & found at the Dolphin public house at 10 o'clock in the Morning.' Sarah Bree's conduct record reveals that she was also charged with the same offence. The clerk who wrote up the entry made a revealing slip. He started to write 'them[selves]' and then crossed this out, inserting the word 'herself'. The purpose of the conduct record was to individualise each transgression. Anyone perusing the record of either woman would have little sense that the two had sat in company, Bree having slipped away from Lieutenant Simmonds' residence in Murray Street and Jacobs from Edgar Luttrell's house in Battery Point.[33] No doubt employment conditions in these two households were a topic of conversation as the two women drank in company in the confines of the Dolphin across town in Campbell Street[34] Since individual employers prosecuted their own employees the records undoubtedly understate the number of convicts

[30] *Australian*, 30 August 1826. See also M.L., Tas Papers 2, Richmond and Brighton Benchbook, 24 August 1835.

[31] M.L., Tas Papers 290, Oatlands Benchbook, 15, 29 August 1836.

[32] M.L., Tas Papers 326, Richmond Benchbooks, 6 June 1839; Tas Papers 291, Oatlands Benchbook, 25 September 1841.

[33] Sarah Jacobs, per *Mermaid*, Police No. 49, Con 40-1-5 and Sarah Bree, per *Eliza*, Police No. 158, T.A., Con 40-1-1. Melville, Henry (1832) *The Van Diemen's Land Almanack*.

[34] *Colonial Times*, 1 October 1830.

from different properties who socialised together. That convict workers were able to link up in this manner suggests some level of tacit coordination and provides further evidence of the networks via which information about different employment practices circulated.

As Table 7.1 illustrates, the Australian 'long weekend' has a distinguished history. Several witnesses to the Molesworth Committee noted that convict 'mechanics' were notorious for their habit of taking an extra leisure day, usually Monday, 'to spend what they receive in wages'.[35] George Binsom told his master that shoemakers did not work the first day of the week.[36] It was precisely this type of activity that the walls of Hyde Park Barracks and other public sector institutions were designed to prevent. Despite brick walls and associated curfews, clocks, gatekeepers, watchmen, policemen and an elaborate system of rewards and fines, such absenteeism persisted. Analysis of conduct records and benchbooks reveals that this was a practice that was certainly not limited to skilled male convicts. While most arrests for absenteeism for both sexes occurred on a Sunday, the next most common day of arrest was a Monday.

The policing of convict leisure was certainly not limited to the private sector. In February 1827 several members of Benjamin Scammell's road-party in New South Wales were flogged for being absent on Saturday afternoon and Sunday.[37] The Berrima bench ordered three members of the Argyle Bridge gang to receive 25 lashes for being absent on Sunday 26 January 1834. The punishment appears to have had little effect as seven members of the same party were charged with being absent on Sunday 16 February.[38] Such prosecutions for collective weekend absences from public sector gangs were commonplace across both colonies. Five members of a Hobart road party were punished after they were found to be absent from their huts at 7 p.m. on Saturday 21 July 1827.[39] Likewise, five convicts belonging to the Oatlands public works were prosecuted for

[35] Minutes of Evidence, Rev. W. Ullathorne, 8 February 1838, *British Parliamentary Papers,* XXII, (1837–8), 18 and E. Parry, 26 February 1838, 46; see also Thompson, E.P. (1967) Time, Work-Discipline, and Industrial Capitalism, *Past and Present*, 38, 73.

[36] M.L., Tas Papers 292, Oatlands Benchbook, 21, 22 May 1838.

[37] AONSW., Liverpool Benchbook, 21 February and 16 March 1826.

[38] AONSW., 2482/6 CY Reel 954, Campbelltown Benchbook, 20 January 1834; AONSW Reel 664, Berrima Benchbook, 27 January and 17 February 1834.

[39] M.L., Tas Papers 268, Hobart Benchbook, 24 July 1827; Tas Papers 323, Richmond Benchbook, 15 October 1832; Tas Papers 277, Launceston Benchbook, 4 October 1834.

being out of their barracks after hours on Saturday night on 30 May 1835, as were three members of the Bagdad Road Party who received three months hard labour for being absent and in the *Crown Inn* on Sunday afternoon in June 1836.[40] In May 1825, Edward Walsh, overseer of the Cowpastures Road Party, tried a number of his gang for absence, complaining that several had incited the other gang members to take leave without permission. In February 1834 nine members of the Argyle Bridge gang were charged with various periods of absence the previous Sunday.[41] Some in public works also refused to go to chapel on Sunday.[42]

Absconding

As well as short-term absences convict managers also struggled to keep their workers from absenting themselves on a more permanent basis. This despite the lengths that the Australian colonial administration went to track down its lost property and the scale of the punishments it meted out to those who were apprehended. The pursuit of escaped convicts was international in its scale. Descriptions of prisoners thought to have clandestinely left the colonies were routinely forwarded to London where they were printed in the *Police Gazette,* also known as the *Hue and Cry*. This periodical was first issued under the name the *Quarterly Pursuit* by the Bow Street Police Office in 1772. By the 1830s over 160,000 copies were printed each year and circulated to mayors and principal officers of every city and town in the British Isles, justices of the peace, keepers of jails and houses of correction, the metropolitan police, the War Office, Horse Patrol, police offices as well as the commanding officers of military regiments. Copies were also circulated outside of the British Isles to each colony and further afield.[43] Partially as a result of such trans-imperial surveillance exercises, runaway Australian convicts were apprehended in

[40] M.L., Tas Papers 290, Oatlands Benchbook, 1 June 1835; M.L., Tas Papers 2, Richmond and Brighton Benchbook, 17 June 1836.

[41] AONSW., Reel 664, Berrima Benchbook, 17 February 1834.

[42] For some examples see M.L., Tas Papers 291, Oatlands Benchbook, 29 October 1840.

[43] See for example *Colonial Times*, 8 February 1831, The *Courier*, 20 January 1843.

Valparaiso, Mauritius, Bombay, Calcutta and Rio de Janeiro—testimony to the reach of the 'open air panopticon'.[44]

Within the colony itself pecuniary rewards and fines played an important role in the state's attempts to clamp down on the illicit movements of convicts. A reward of £2 was regularly provided for the capture of runaways. As this could only be claimed if the absconder had been advertised in the *Government Gazette*—these otherwise dull official circulars gained a surprising wide circulation.[45] The provision of bank accounts for prisoners provided the colonial administration with further means to impose financial checks and balances aimed at reducing clandestine movements. Recaptured convicts risked forfeiting their savings. Monies taken from the accounts of apprehended absconders were used to reimburse the state by covering the costs of rewards paid out to their capturers.

As well as absconders, would-be employers were at risk too. The standard fine for harbouring runaways was £10 (although more could be levied in cases considered severe). Half of this sum was provided to informers.[46] This had a double advantage of encouraging convicts to 'dob' on other prisoners, while simultaneously depositing money into the informant's bank account thereby providing them with a disincentive to put into effect any self-liberation plans of their own. Yet, despite repeated reframing of the legislation criminalising the employment of convict absconders, harbouring remained a problem. In 1826, for example, the *Colonial Times* reported that magistrates were agitating for a further legislation due to the ease with which convicts could be induced to neglect their work and abscond.[47]

There were considerable advantages to employing convicts who were illegally at large. The settler William Bryan was accused of harbouring a convict who he had employed for three years to round up cattle.[48] In 1842 a Mr. Drummin was fined £15 for hiring two absconders to split timber at 'a very low wage'.[49] It is likely that at times runaways formed

[44] Maxwell-Stewart, *Closing Hell's Gates*, 54.

[45] Roberts, 'A Change of Place', 112.

[46] *Hobart Town Gazette and Van Diemen's Land Advertiser*, 5 March 1824.

[47] *Colonial Times*, 26 May 1826.

[48] McKay, The Assignment System of Convict Labour, 138–40.

[49] *Colonial Times*, 11 October 1842.

something of a cheap labour reserve. In return for harbouring absconders, some employers offered wages far below the market rate. Labour shortages also provided opportunities for absconders. British, French and American merchant vessels and whalers were regular visitors to colonial ports. Deaths at sea and desertions often meant that these ships were short crewed by the time they berthed. Matthew Forster, the Chief Police Magistrate in Van Diemen's Land warned that absconders from road parties in the interior were attracted to town with a view of getting on board such vessels. In order to further such plans he claimed that runaways attired themselves 'in the garb of sailors'. A mode of disguise which in his opinion necessitated restrictions in the free movement of legitimate mariners, since if Jack Tars were allowed 'to perambulate the town at all hours without passes' there was nothing to prevent convicts who were similarly 'habited' mingling with them in order to effect their escape.[50] These concerns were warranted. As can be seen from Fig. 8.1, convicts with maritime skills were twice as likely to be advertised as absconders compared to those who had worked as farm labourers.

The elaborate measures put in place to police the movements of prisoners also restricted the movement of the free. Theoretically, no worker—free or unfree—was permitted to remove themself from their place of employment without giving notice and obtaining the prior permission of a magistrate. While convicts could only legitimately travel if they carried a pass issued by their employer and counter signed by a magistrate, such a system made little sense unless free workers carried papers too.[51] While competition with convict workers reduced colonial wage rates, free workers found their ability to bargain with employers was further restricted by the rules that governed the movement of labour in the penal colonies.

Visiting vessels were routinely searched prior to departure, a form of surveillance that could have implications for ship's officers. The master of the *Essex* was fined £10 and costs after he unwittingly hired a runaway from the Campbell Town Road Party. In his defence the master claimed that he had been shown a certificate of discharge from the ship *Ebro* recently arrived from London. The fraud was only detected when the ship was searched by the police prior to clearing port. By chance one of the

[50] *The Colonist*, 31 December 1833.

[51] *Hobart Town Gazette and Van Diemen's Land Advertiser*, 5 March 1824.

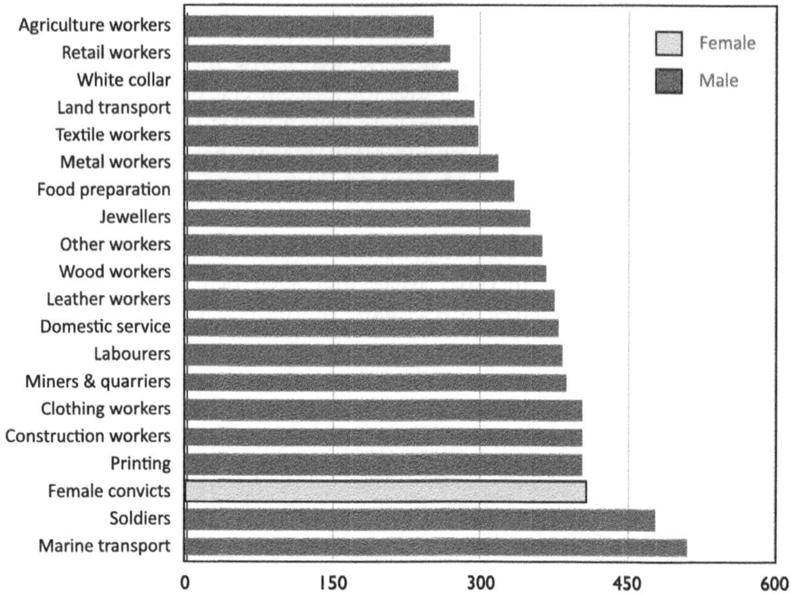

Fig. 8.1 Absconding (attempts per 1000 convicts) (*Sources* T.A., Con 18, 19, 23, 33 and 41 and Hobart Town Gazette 1824–60)

constables recognised the absconder and arrested him—no doubt keen to pocket the reward.[52]

As it turns out, however, there were also financial incentives for would-be convict absconders. Several masters complained that when assigned servants ran they took their clothes with them. As a settler from the Cross Marsh bemoaned, it cost 30 shillings to buy slops for a convict servant who when kitted out might 'on some frivolous pretext' abscond from his service, 'carrying all his good clothes along with him.' By the time a servant was apprehended and returned to his or her master, anything of value was likely to have been sold or exchanged.[53] For this reason it was not uncommon for absconders to be tried with stealing the clothes that they ran in, a charge that substantially upped the ante increasing the severity of the sanctions that could be applied by a sentencing magistrate.

[52] *Cornwall Chronicle*, 28 October 1840.

[53] *Hobart Town Courier*, 22 November 1828.

Table 8.2 Mean punishments for male convicts charged with absconding, being absent and all other offences (1816–1860)

	Mean lashes	*Mean days cells*	*Mean days roads*	*Mean days chains*	*Mean days treadwheel*	*Mean fine (shillings)*
Absconding	55.6	17.0	242.1	293.8	13.2	5.0
Absent	32.1	6.4	98.0	97.7	9.3	8.2
Other Offence	35.5	6.0	134.5	163.2	10.9	18.5

Sources Con 31, 32, 33. N = 13,268 (four percent systematic sample of male charges)

Ironically, even the state's primary anti-absconding weapons proved to have monetary value. In 1828 an alarmed principal superintendent of convicts wrote to the colonial secretary to report that a prisoner in a chain gang could secure 'half a dozen' certificates of freedom 'in a few days for about 20 or thirty shillings each.' The difficulties in prosecuting free individuals for loss of paperwork made it difficult to stamp out such trafficking. The best the state could do was to issue periodic lists of missing certificates and issue duplicates on payment of a fee of five shillings.[54] This was only partially effective as counterfeit passes were also in circulation. In June 1834 the Berrima bench charged William Smith and William Sheedy with absconding and possessing false papers.[55]

Worse was to come. It became apparent that some absconders struck deals with their captors, living on credit in remote stock huts until half of the £2 reward had been spent. Absconder and clandestine landlord would then walk to the nearest police office where the escapee would be cashed in having effectively already spent a substantial proportion of the money the state had invested in their recapture.[56]

The punishments awarded to absconders underscore the extent to which the offence was perceived as a major threat. Nearly a quarter of all male convicts convicted of absconding were flogged, averaging over 55 lashes per beating (see Tables 8.2 and 8.3)—significantly more than the mean number of strokes meted out to those prosecuted for

[54] T.A., John Lakeland, 28 January 1828, CSO1-1-199, 4745, 240–244.

[55] AONSW., Reel 664, Berrima Benchbook, 13 June 1834.

[56] Dillon, M. (2008) Convict Labour and Colonial Society in the Campbell Town Police District 1820–1839, Ph.D. Thesis, University of Tasmania, 110 and 140–141.

Table 8.3 Punishments awarded for absconding, being absent and other offences, Van Diemen's land, 1816–1860 by sex

	Acquitted or admonished	*Cells*	*Flogged*	*Hard labour*	*Hard labour in chains*	*Sentence extended*	*Other*	*Total*
Male								
Absconding	0.9	6.8	15.0	27.5	33.6	14.7	1.6	100.0
Absent	21.3	24.0	11.5	23.8	8.5	0.0	10.9	100.0
All other	14.3	25.0	12.1	21.0	11.8	1.2	14.5	100.0
Female								
Absconding	1.5	12.2	–	62.6	–	23.5	0.2	100.0
Absent	11.1	32.3	–	55.8	–	0.1	0.7	100.0
All other	16.0	25.7	–	46.0	–	1.7	10.6	100.0

Sources Con 31, 32, 33, 40 and 41. *N* = 97,612 charges (total count of all female, plus a four percent systematic sample of male charges)

other offences. Over a third (36 percent) were sentenced to serve in irons, a sanction applied to under 10 percent of other offenders. The average amount of time apprehended absconders were ordered to serve in fetters was also far in excess of that for non-movement related offences—294 days compared to 163. Many of those sentenced to hard labour in and out of chains were removed to penal stations while female convicts charged with absconding were routinely removed to female factories.

If absconders gambled on cutting their sentences, state sentencing strategies were aimed at raising the stakes. Apprehended absconders were at significantly greater risk of having their sentences extended. While a comparatively rare sanction, a bench consisting of at least two magistrates was empowered to recommend an extension of a sentence of up to three years. Nearly 15 percent of male absconders had their terms of service lengthened compared to just one percent of those charged with other offences. At over 23 percent the rate was even higher for female convicts. The message was emphatic—clandestine attempts to shorten sentences to transportation were likely to increase, rather than decrease, the amount of time served. Absconding was treated more seriously than strike action and all but the most serious attacks on overseers. It was also prosecuted more seriously than most acts of theft. The lengths the state went to in order to keep convicts in place reveal much about the worth of convict labour and the wider political economy of labour extraction. In the following section we use newspaper, court, conduct records and absconding notices to explore the factors that drove, or enticed, male and female convicts away from their place of employment in such large numbers.

Interpreting Movement Offences

While convicts ran from a wide range of locations including private assignment, the rate of desertion amongst ticket-of-leave holders was low, see Table 8.4. Although in any given year about a quarter of male convicts held tickets, only 2.3 percent of advertised runaways were ticket-of-leave men. Women who were in receipt of tickets were even less likely to be gazetted as runaways. If pull factors were primarily responsible for enticing convicts to elope, higher rates of absconding might be expected amongst this group of workers who had more autonomy than other private and public sector convicts. By contrast male convicts in road parties were three times more likely to abscond than might be expected given the mean number deployed to these locations at any given point in time. As Brand observed, increases in the severity of punishment was an important impetus for absconding.[57] Indeed, fluctuations in the number

Table 8.4 Breakdown of locations from which convicts absconded and mean annual distribution of male and female prisoners, Van Diemen's land 1824–1860

	Male absconders (%)	*All male (%)*	*Female absconders (%)*	*All female (%)*
Ticket-of-leave	2.3	25	0.3	24
Assigned or Passholder	33.3	34	93.6	56
Public works	20.1	15	3.3	2
Road gang or Female factory	34.6	11	2.8	18
Chain gang	6.2	6		
Penal station	3.6	9		
	100.0	100.0	100.0	100.0

Sources *Hobart Town Gazette* 1824–60

[57] Brand, I. (1990) *The Convict Probation System; Van Diemen's Land, 1839–1854*, Blubber Head Press, Hobart, 62.

of convicts undergoing punishment on the public works explains 46 percent of the variation in male absconding rates over time. This is not in itself surprising. Road gangs were employed in labour intensive tasks designed to extract punishment through increased levels of physical exertion. Convicts reacted by voting with their feet—a strong indication that much convict absconding was motivated by push factors. Table 8.4 also reveals the extent to which leg irons, penal stations and the walls of the female factory were able to put a break on the practice of absconding. These measures were effective at keeping convicts at work, but this was a success achieved at a considerable price. These were expensive institutions to construct and maintain.

Some apprehended convict workers linked their decision to abscond to working conditions. Harsh treatment, poor rations and clothing were common complaints when absconders were recaptured. Edward Holloway and Andrew Phenn who were sentenced to 50 lashes for absconding from the Sandy Bay road gang with a number of others in 1835 told the Bench they had left due to the privations in the rations supplied by their overseer. On this occasion the evidence of mistreatment was so compelling that the bench determined to investigate the matter further.[58]

Some court cases reveal that absconding followed the failure of an earlier protest, including complaining to a master or a strike. At other times both actions were almost coincident. In March 1834 for instance, seven convicts belonging to the Bridgewater gang were charged with defacing their irons with intent to escape while three others were convicted of refusing work.[59] On 6 December 1844 James Dickie, Charles Gordon and John Porter were each charged with insubordination with others in endeavouring to create a riot and also breaking out of confinement at night from the Hamilton Farm to which they were assigned.[60]

The reconstruction of go-slows, strikes and other output restrictions in Notman's road party outlined in the previous chapter can be used to illustrate the point. Not only did this gang experience multiple labour disputes

[58] *Colonial Times*, 15 September 1835.

[59] *Colonial Times*, 11 March 1834.

[60] James Dickie, Police No. 6706, T.A., Con 33/28; Charles Gordon, Police No. 10706, Con 33/45 and John Porter, Police No. 12883, Con 33/54.

in the early 1830s, but it also had the highest rate of convict absconding in Van Diemen's Land in these years. Furthermore, the dates on which convicts absconded from the gang cluster around those on which gang members were prosecuted for restricting labour participation or withholding it altogether (see Fig. 8.3). Indeed, this visualisation reveals that increases in absconding, especially collective absconding, followed in the wake of prosecutions for neglect of duty and malingering. In short, their appears to be a strong relationship between different forms of output restriction and labour withdrawal, suggesting that escape and other forms of protest had their roots in a similar set of grievances.

Some absconders from Notman's gang moved considerable distances before lodging complaints about their treatment. On 27 March 1832 John Smith and George Moore were tried in Hobart by the Chief Police Magistrate and the Principal Superintendent of convicts for absconding from Notman's Road Party and making a 'false complaint' against Notman and William Lyttleton. In his capacity as Launceston Police Magistrate, Lyttleton had presided over 63 percent of the 940 prosecutions brought against convicts labouring in Notman's gang in the period 1831–3.

As with so many appeals to higher authority, this attempt to travel 190 kilometres in order to bring allegations of mistreatment to the attention of colonial administrators achieved little. Smith and Moore were sentenced to hard labour for two years. When they declared that if sent back, they would immediately abscond again, they were despatched to the remote penal settlement at Macquarie Harbour.[61] In similar fashion an additional six months was added to Alexander Low, Edward Read and William Bickerstaffs' sentence for absconding from Notman's Gang 'by command of the Lt· Gov. for having made false complaints before John Leake and James England Esq. when apprehended as runaways'.[62]

On several occasions convicts in Notman's Party expressed their desire to abscond. Telegraphing an escape attempt made little sense if the intent of the would-be absconder was to slip the shackles of the state and secure an early release. It has a great deal of logic, however, if the act

[61] John Smith, per *Bussorah Merchant*, Police No. 1103, T.A., Con 31-1-39; George Moore, per *Sir Charles Forbes*, Police No. 782, Con 31-1-30.

[62] Alexander Low, per *Morley*, Police No. 245, T.A., Con 31-1-27; Edward Read per *Strathfieldsay*, Police No. 751, Con 31-1-37; and William Bickerstaff, per Georgiana (2), Police No. 1807, Con 31-1-5.

of absconding was designed as a form of labour withdrawal—this was a pointed and blunt form of protest 'if you continue to treat me like this I will leave'. In March 1833 Joseph Turner and Thomas Collins were removed to a penal settlement for three years for repeatedly absconding from Notman's Road Party and 'threatening to abscond again'. In June of the same year another three convicts in the same gang were clapped in irons for a month for threatening to run away.[63] As a form of protest this has much in common with refusals by assigned convicts to remain in a particular service or to return there after being punished for refusing to work on a Sunday or after masters had attempted to exercise excessive control over their time off.

There are other ways in which it is possible to determine the factors that might have induced convicts to leave a place of employment. Male convicts were more likely to abscond in summer. The harvest was a time of intense work activity for rural convicts, and this may have prompted some to withdraw their labour. There is some evidence to support such an interpretation. On occasion government convicts lent to farmers to assist with the harvest absconded before they turned up at the property to which they had been allocated. This was the case with a group of about 40 sent from the Hyde Park Barracks to Bathurst in early 1841 who took advantage of the ending of transportation to New South Wales to slip away. Although at least 16 were apprehended by September, others managed to remain at large for some time.[64]

Absconding patterns for convicts in Van Diemen's Land, however, reveal similar trends for convicts whose work routines were less likely to be impacted upon by the seasonal demands of the harvest. Male convicts assigned to urban businesses and those in public works gangs also ran at higher rates during the summer for example. This might reflect weather conditions, running in winter was a less attractive option. December peaks in absconding were also associated with a withdrawal of labour at Christmas and New Year. Yet, it appears to have been the hours of available daylight that most impacted on male runaway patterns. As the length of the working day was fixed by the rising and setting of the sun, work intensity increased dramatically for outdoor workers in the summer months (see Fig. 8.4). Our data shows that the male convicts acted

[63] Launceston Police Charge Book, T.A., POL 451–4, 16 March and 5 June 1833.

[64] *NSW Government Gazette*, 24 August and 10 September 1841.

Table 8.5 Rates at which male and female convicts absconded in different sized groups

Size of absconding party	*Male*	*Female*
Ran on own	62.8	95.7
Ran with one other	17.8	3.4
Two other	8.4	0.3
Three other	4.9	0.1
Four other	2.5	0.1
In a group of five or more	3.6	0.4
	100.0	100.0

Source 22,683 runaway notices, *Hobart Town Gazette*, 1824–60

accordingly, withdrawing labour in larger numbers. Indoor work was less impacted by these seasonal fluctuations. While female assigned-servants and passholder labourers were more likely to take 'French leave' over the December festive season, runaway patterns were influenced less by the length of the working day. Indeed, lack of sunlight and cold weather increased the intensity of their working day, as grates had to be cleaned and lit and candles and oil lamps serviced.

Many men and women chose to run in company. In August 1839 Eliza Lemon and Catherine Connor were arrested by a constable in Windmill Street Sydney, after their mistress Mrs Catherine Stephens reported they had left her premises with their clothing. Lemon got a month and was ordered to be returned to service while Connor was only reprimanded after the intercession of her mistress—this being her first offence.[65] This differentiation was common. Convicts might abscond together, but previous conduct and skills could significantly impact on the severity of punishments meted out if and when they were apprehended. Mary Smith received three months hard labour in a factory for absconding from her Oatlands employer Jonathon Barlow, while her compatriot Agnes Boys was remanded so her character (that is, prior conduct record) could be examined.[66]

In general, however, male convicts were much more likely to abscond in company with another runaway than female (see Table 8.5). A third of all escape attempts that involved a male runaway were collective compared to under five percent for female. Where convict women did run in

[65] *Monitor*, 28 August 1839.

[66] T.A., LC390-1-2 Oatlands Magistrates Court Benchbook 2 December 1847.

company it was most likely to be from the confines of female houses of correction. One of the earliest reported incidents occurred in 1813 when Elizabeth Darts, Mary Lucas and Mary Fearns were reported as absconding from the Parramatta Female Factory on 12 August. They were soon followed by four other inmates in September (Ann Alar, Jane Hurst, Mary Irwin and Catherine Flynn) who were still at large four months later.[67] Most instances of collective absconding involved between two and four women, though larger escapes did occur. Liz Griffiths, Priscilla Jones, Sarah Ellis, Ann Clarke, Sarah Wells (alias Longhurst), Judith Deylesby and Charlotte Hopkins absconded in late February 1816 and were not apprehended until August of that year.[68]

There were instances of collective absconding from most if not all female factories in New South Wales and Van Diemen's Land. Some factories were particularly prone to the practice. Overcrowding in the Hobart Town Factory facilitated escapes. In December 1825 nine women tried to abscond, one of 18 instances of individual or collective absconding between 1824 and 1828 from this institution.[69] In June 1826 Sarah Wilson, Anne Riley and Elizabeth Slater were tried by the Launceston Magistrates Court for absconding from the George Town Female Factory. The escape followed the removal of women from the Hobart Factory to George Town in June 1826 after at least 20 had participated in a riot.[70] Collective attempts to break out of female factories frequently followed in the wake of other forms of protest in similar fashion to the pattern of absconding from Notman's Road Party. In April 1828 Sarah Wilson, Mary Sample and Catherine Taylor were charged with breaking down their cells in a bid to escape following their prosecution for sabotaging spinning wheels the previous evening.[71]

As Table 8.5 reveals, even where convicts absconded in company it was most likely to be in small groups. Limiting the numbers involved in individual absconding attempts made sense, as this enhanced the overall prospect of success. A large body of runaways was likely to result in the

[67] *Sydney Gazette*, 21 August, 2 October and 25 December 1813.

[68] *Sydney Gazette*, 2 March, 18 May and 17 August 1816.

[69] Hendriksen et al. *Women Transported*, 56 citing *Hobart Town Gazette*, 10 December 1825.

[70] T.A., LC346-1-1, Launceston Magistrates Court Benchbook, 9 November 1826.

[71] Hendriksen et al. *Women Transported*, 55.

swearing-in of special constables and the mobilisation of field police and even military detachments. On occasions, however, absconding attempts were planned by larger groups. A party of 21 convicts ran from Deloraine Probation Station in October 1845 after a failed gang strike and another group of 16 left Notman's Road Party in November 1833.[72] Serial absconding in small groups from the same location over a few days or several weeks was a more common practice, however. Emma Barfoot, Mary Rafferty and Mary Taylor, for example, were reported as having absconded from the Parramatta Factory on 10 June 1820. They were followed a week later by Ann Hillyer, Elizabeth Cowen, Mary England and Catherine Lowrie, while Mary O'Hara and Mary Salmon absconded on 24 June. Between 16 and 30 December of the same year another three groups totalling 10 women absconded from the same location.[73] Serial absconding not only minimised the visibility of runaway groups, but stretched the government resources that could be devoted to their apprehension notwithstanding the substantial rewards on offer.[74] Other female factories in New South Wales including Bathurst and Port Macquarie experienced collective serial absconding of this nature.[75]

Convicts were also more likely to abscond in company from gangs. While most prisoners who escaped from private service ran on their own, the rate of collective absconding increased with the severity of the labour extraction process. On average each attempt to escape from a penal station involved the gazetting of more than two prisoners (Fig. 8.2). The actual rate is likely to have been greater, since some runaways were apprehended before the Government Gazette went to press. This was particularly the case for those encumbered with leg irons. A heavy emphasis on ganging not only triggered higher running rates, but resulted in increased collective withdrawal of labour.

For convicts absconding had much to commend itself when compared to other forms of protest such as strikes, verbal confrontations and collective reductions in work intensity. All forms of protest were likely to attract

[72] *Hobart Town Gazette*, 15 November 1833; Dunning, T. and Maxwell-Stewart, H. (2002) Mutiny at Deloraine, Ganging and Convict Resistance in 1840s Van Diemen's Land, *Labour History*, 82, 35–47.

[73] *Sydney Gazette*, 16, 23 and 30 December 1820.

[74] *Sydney Gazette*, 10, 17 and 24 June 1820.

[75] See for example *New South Wales Government Gazette*, 4 December 1833, 7 October 1835 and 16 December 1835.

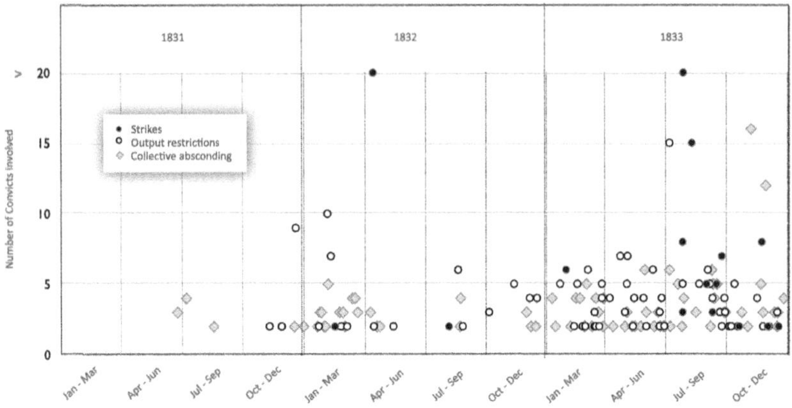

Fig. 8.2 Absconding, absenteeism, output restrictions and strikes in Notman's Road Party (*Source* T.A., Con 31, 32, 33, 40 and 41, POL 451, Launceston Charge Book)

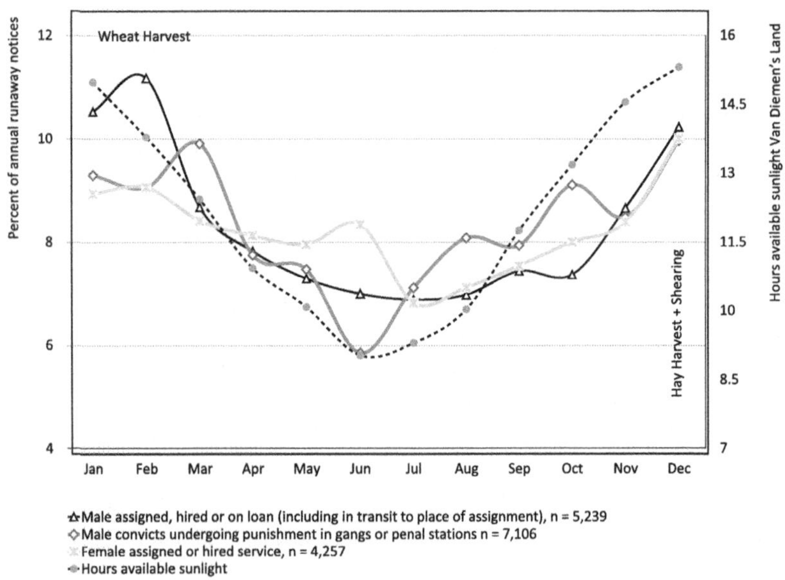

Fig. 8.3 Annual absconding patterns in Van Diemen's Land 1824–1860 (*Source* Hobart Town Gazette 1824–60)

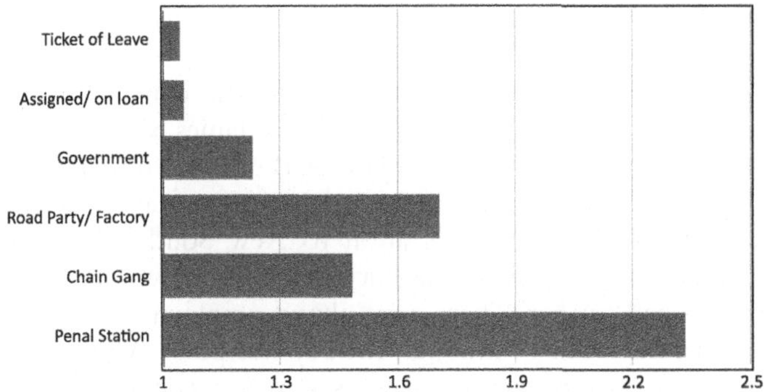

Fig. 8.4 Mean number of convicts involved in each escape by location (*Source* Hobart Town Gazette 1824–60)

severe punishments, but most had the additional drawback that the chastised convict was returned to their former coercive work environment. This opened up the possibility of further retributive treatment and other sanctions such as the withdrawal of indulgences. By contrast a successful absconder always had the opportunity to 'melt' into the ranks of the free lower orders, escaping such retribution.

In practice, most absconders were quickly apprehended, so quickly in the case of Bexley farmer J. Chandler's female servants that their apprehension was recorded before an absconding notice was even published.[76] Absconding from rural estates, especially those located far from conurbations, presented considerable challenges for all assigned servants, but this was particularly true for women. Few women remained at large for more than a week or two. This highlights the challenges facing absconding women, especially in rural areas. It was difficult for them, for example, to secure service in another household without a recommendation from their former employer. Women, especially unescorted women, were more visible in a society with a profound gender-imbalance. This is not to say that all female absconders were apprehended quickly. Trudy Cowley has uncovered evidence of long-term escapees aided by former shipmates

[76] *New South Wales Government Gazette*, 30 December 1835.

and contacts in the wider community. It is likely that similar networks operated in New South Wales.[77]

By contrast a considerable proportion of male convicts managed to evade recapture for lengthy periods. In 1839 James Shalvey was apprehended in Sydney and sentenced to Port Arthur for two years after being absent for 12 months during which time he had managed to slip across the Bass Strait.[78] Once transportation to New South Wales ended in 1840 and demand for labour in Port Philip increased the chances of arrest diminished further. There were always employment opportunities for itinerant male workers although the pay was poor. While the punishments inflicted on recaptured runaways were considerable, the tales of those that eluded recapture provided inspiration for others, particularly those that were already engaged in disputes with masters or local administrators. In short, the more coercive the working environment, the more likely convicts were to risk slipping the shackles of a sentence by walking off the job.

Conclusion

Access to unfree labour enabled Theophilus Lightfoot to reduce the rates he paid his free workers. Competition between the free and the unfree also enabled him to dictate other conditions of work. Free tailors complained that he kept them cross-legged 12–14 hours a day in his workshop.[79] Indeed, his Elizabeth Street sweat shop was perhaps the perfect illustration of the ways in which penal transportation enabled the exploitation of both the free and the unfree. While the convict tailors Lightfoot engaged were unpaid and hamstrung by the coercive nature of the rules and regulations that enabled the colonial state to minutely police their lives, they knew that at the end of the day they would have to be fed no matter what. Ironically, this is a certainty that was not shared by their free counterparts. This gave his unfree workers a degree of latitude. While the post-Bigge Report legal constraints imposed upon convict labour were designed to keep them unpaid and locked in place, Lightfoot and other

[77] Cowley, T. (2005) *A Drift of 'Derwent Ducks': Lives of the 200 Female Irish Convicts Transported on the Australasia from Dublin to Hobart in 1849*, Research Tasmania, New Town.

[78] *Hobart Town Courier*, 11 January 1839.

[79] *Hobart Town Courier*, 31 March 1834.

private sector masters found that the margins of these regulations were constantly tested. Nowhere was this more evident than in the battle to delineate the daily and weekly limits of a sentence to transportation.

In the years from 1828 to 1835 Lightfoot's assigned servants were charged on 95 occasions. The vast majority of these prosecutions were for movement offences. His convicts were brought before the court for being absent on 60 occasions and for absconding on a further six. In December 1830 all seven of his assigned tailors were arraigned for failing to attend the muster at church. Four were charged with the same offence in May 1832 and a further two were prosecuted with not attending church muster in June 1832 after 'repeated warning'. The wording on the charge suggests that this was something of a running battle. The tailor William Peckitt was sent to Notman's Road Party for six months after he swapped Sunday service at Mr. Connolly's chapel for the attractions of a sly grog shop.[80] Others walked out of Lightfoot's shop on a Sunday, not returning until Monday morning or when they were apprehended in the Dallas Arms, the home of the messenger of the Principal Superintendent of the Prison Barracks, or attempting to walk out with his neighbour's female assigned servants.[81] Even Lightfoot's convict errand boys gave him trouble. He took two to court for being absent on New Year's Eve 1832.[82] While keeping his convict charges in place presented Lightfoot with a constant challenge, these absences were not random. Convicts were most likely to be charged with being absent after the end of the public sector hours of labour. Despite the restricted size of his Elizabeth Street establishment, by 1835 he had resorted to employing an overseer in an attempt to increase the number of eyes that could be invested in the weekly task of keeping his charges in place.

As the *Tasmanian* put it, a general issue faced by Lightfoot and other employers of skilled unfree labour was that convict mechanics 'claim to themselves all the rights and privileges of free men, and quote the hours of labour and the wages paid to similar persons in London and elsewhere in the mother country, unmindful that they are expiating the crimes which

80 *Tasmanian*, 16 November 1832.

81 James Shackleton, per *Isabella*, Police No. 1747, T.A. Con 31-1-40; James Mayhen, per *Dromedary*, Police No. 188, Con 31-1-29; William Peckett, per *Layton*, Police No. 446, Con 31-1-34.

82 Thomas Mason, per *Elizabeth*, Police No. 939, T.A., Con 31-1-11; Joseph Read, per *England*, Police No. 918, Con 31-1-37.

sent them out'. As the paper continued, it was precisely this species of convict worker who cluttered up the courtroom 'on the Monday morning habited in their Sunday garments, charged with every species of Sabbath breaking'.[83] Technically, however, it was not the convict who broke the Sabbath, but the masters who sought to encroach on the free time of their charges.

As our analysis has shown, absenteeism was particularly widespread. Far from being limited to mechanics, the tactic was employed by male and female assigned convicts across the private sector. It formed the principal means by which convict workers attempted to exert rights over free time and as such was a work-related protest, rather than a work centred action. Convicts did not use this tactic to walk off the job but rather attempted to walk away with their own time. That it was a tactic that convicts employed in defence of the right to Saturday afternoon and Sunday off, rather than a wider attempt to ameliorate the conditions of work, does not mean that it was either trivial or apolitical in nature. These battles for the weekend intensified at particular times of the year, notably Christmas, New Year and Easter.

Absenteeism was also used to claim time off on a Monday, in similar fashion to the campaign by skilled workers in Britain to claim a 'Saint Monday' holiday—a day free of labour required in order to recover from the excesses of Sunday night. Such actions were motivated by convict desires to ensure that the sentence imposed upon them by British and Irish courts had daily limits. These were forms of protest that were designed to loosen the shackles imposed upon them by limiting the power of sentence to command all of their time. The state and private sector masters, on the other hand, sought to restrict the time convicts could spend socialising, especially with prisoners employed in other establishments. Control over free time was also important in order to stop convicts selling their labour and gaining access to cash.

Absconding was another significant form of convict protest, although it was generally targeted at a different range of issues. Rather than an attempt to gain access to free time, withdrawal of labour through running was usually triggered by the same issues that provoked go-slows and strike actions. This included, the quality and quantity of the rations supplied, the state of clothing and footwear and other terms and conditions of work.

[83] The *Tasmanian*, 15 June 1832.

There was a marked annual variation in the rate of running, particularly amongst male convicts. This might be driven by a number of factors, including the weather. The increased hours of labour in summer, however, are likely to have been important. A detailed reconstruction of collective actions in Notman's Road Party in the early 1830s reveals that rates of absconding, particularly collective absconding, increased in line with other collective prosecutions for neglect of duty, refusing to work and insubordination suggesting a common set of causes.

Unlike benchbooks, our principal source of information for most other forms of protest, a complete series of government gazette notices documenting attempts to run survive. These started to make a regular appearance in New South Wales in 1814 (although many reports appear well before this date). They were not systematically included in the *Hobart Town Gazette*, however, until 1824. Comparisons with prosecutions for absconding recorded in conduct records suggest that newspaper notices underestimate the prevalence of the practice, mainly because some convicts were quickly apprehended. These caveats aside, however, we have used the gazettes to estimate the number of occasions two or more convicts were advertised as running from the same location on the same day. As can be seen from Table 8.6, convicts engaged in this form of action in impressive levels. Male and female convicts ran in company on at least 6470 occasions, a form of action that led to 20,038 individual withdrawals of labour although some of these convicts absconded in company on more than one occasion.

Absconding was an important form of action if for no other reason than the enormous challenges and costs it posed for private employers and government. It also had implications for the wider community in that policing runaways required all sections of society to carry papers. Absconding was disruptive to the administration of labour and was expensive both in terms of time and the resources devoted to apprehending and prosecuting runaways. Notwithstanding very harsh penalties it proved impossible to stamp out. For private employers absconding represented a loss of assigned labour which could prove especially costly where the worker's skills were in short supply or seasonal demand for labour was at its peak. There was also a contradictory tension in that some employers were only too happy to engage workers without inquiring too closely into whether they were free or were on the run. Attempts to penalise employers who engaged absconding convicts seem to have had at best a limited deterrent effect.

Table 8.6 Numbers involved in collective absconding in New South Wales and Van Diemen's Land

	1788–1800	*1801–1810*	*1810–1820*	*1821–1830*	*1831–1840*	*1841–1850*	*1851–1860*	*Total*
Group absconding	3	38	146	2001	2740	1214	328	6470
Numbers involved	28	104	400	5533	8421	4459	1094	20,038

Sources *Hobart Town Gazette*, 1824–60; *Sydney Gazette and New South Wales* Advertiser, 1803–1832; *New South Wales Government Gazette*, 1840–50

While convict women ran at a greater rate than convict men, they were less likely to leave their place of employment in partnership with others. In part this reflects the conditions of employment in the private sector. As we have seen in the previous chapter, small numbers made it difficult for female convicts to collectivise in the same way as male unfree workers. Even amongst male workers, collective absconding was less prevalent amongst assigned servants. By contrast, male convicts ran in disproportionate numbers from road parties—an indication of the degree to which push factors in the form of increased levels of coercion and labour intensity drove absconding rates. They were also more likely to run in company from these locations. The walls of female factories, leg irons and the remote locations in which penal stations were located were all effective at cutting down rates of absconding. These, however, were costly and expensive institutions to maintain. In this sense, high levels of absconding achieved at least victory of sorts by cutting into profit levels.

While absconding and absenteeism were motivated by different factors, both constituted significant forms of action. In terms of levels of prosecution, they took up more court time than any other form of charge brought against convict workers. Convicts in this sense voted with their feet in a concerted campaign to control access to free time, enforce limits to the working day and to highlight what they perceived to be abuses of government rules and regulations. While walking out was the most prevalent form of convict action, it was not the only way to get back at employers and overseers. The next chapter explores the means by which convicts resorted to retaliatory action jeopardising the livelihood and on occasion, well-being, of those who attempted to overly profit from their crimes or use the law to otherwise gag the mouths of protesters.

CHAPTER 9

Compensatory Retribution

Early in 1834 Charles Vaughan Waldron, a former officer in the 39th regiment, disciplined two of his female assigned servants—Sarah McGregor and Mary Maloney. Both were sent to the factory before being returned to Waldron's Illawarra property, south of Sydney. Soon after he again found reason to fault their work. In particular, he remonstrated with Maloney for failing to clean the veranda. In return she begun to abuse him, calling him a 'b[loo]dy old soldier' and cursing his entire family. Waldron ordered the recalcitrant servant into the kitchen where he threatened to take her before the bench again. At this point McGregor intervened, demanding to go with her friend if Maloney was taken before a magistrate. Waldron refused, as on this occasion he had not found her at fault. Both women then set upon their master beating him on the head and neck at which point his wife, Jemima Waldron, called on four assigned male servants to assist her husband. They all refused to obey.

Seeing this, Waldron's twelve-year old son rushed to his father's defence, hitting Maloney in the face. On observing the bruising to her husband's head, Jemima Waldron shouted 'you wretched women what have you done to my husband?' to which Maloney replied by pulling up her clothes and saying she would stick the old soldier with a carving knife. Charles Waldron composed himself sufficiently to write a letter calling for assistance before complaining of a dry tongue and shaking head. When

H. Maxwell-Stewart and M. Quinlan, *Unfree Workers*, Palgrave Studies in Economic History,
https://doi.org/10.1007/978-981-16-7558-4_9

she came to his aid, Jemima noticed that the whole of his right side appeared to be paralysed.[1] The Waldrons' neighbours attempted to detain McGregor and Maloney until the police arrived. Resisting attempts to restrain them, the two women stripped and danced naked in the courtyard of the house. As the *Sydney Herald* put it, the whole episode illustrated how the factory instilled a spirit of insubordination amongst those sent there to be supposedly disciplined.[2] Waldron died shortly afterwards and his two former assigned servants were put on trial for murder.

This chapter examines the ways in which convicts in New South Wales and Van Diemen's Land sought to extract compensatory retribution from masters, mistresses and convict managers who failed to respond to other forms of action. It will start by examining attacks on property and livestock, before moving on to explore ways in which some convicts used fists, boots and improvised weapons to openly confront managers. This will include action taken against other prisoners who provided information to the managers of convict labour that aided the prosecution or otherwise contributed to the breakup of other forms of collective action. Finally, it will examine theft—an act not usually categorised as a form of resistance. While it is impossible to establish the degree to which the many prosecutions for the destruction of property, physical assaults and the appropriation of articles were politically motivated, as we shall see, some such actions were explicitly linked to wider grievances. The timing of others strongly suggests that they were connected to the same issues that prompted convicts to combine in order to restrict output or withdraw labour altogether. In short, when other forms of action failed to address a problem, some convicts took matters into their own hands, forcibly extracting compensation.

Destruction of Property

Some forms of sabotage were more likely to be carried out by individuals rather than groups. This included mistreating animals or breaking tools or machinery. Edward Stewart, for example, was sentenced to 50 lashes for damaging a steam engine owned by the Australian Agricultural

[1] *Australian*, 24 February 1834.

[2] *Sydney Herald*, 23 January 1834.

Company in November 1837.[3] In the absence of further context, it is difficult to know whether these acts were planned. Some actions certainly appear to have arisen spontaneously in the course of a dispute. Mary Ann Furze was prosecuted for 'neglect of duty, using threatening language to the Dispenser of medicine and destroying the fresh water kept for Hospital use' on 9 September 1824. It sounds as though the tipping of the water butt was an angry response committed on the spur of the moment. At the time Furze was employed as a nurse on Small Island, a tiny rock in the middle of Macquarie Harbour which housed the penal settlement hospital. As there was no water on this island or neighbouring Sarah Island, this moment of protest required the despatch of a water detail to the mainland to undo.[4]

While sabotage of this nature might be blamed on the work of a few disgruntled individuals, 'whose aim was to settle a personal score rather than to right a public wrong', masters often claimed that the chief obstacle to effective prosecution was that the few were protected by the many.[5] Despite the fact that individuals were more likely to be prosecuted for the destruction of property, such acts were often collective in the sense that they were connected to a wider landscape of dissent. As Peter Murdoch replied when asked if it was common for convict servants to injure cattle 'out of revenge', 'I think it depends very much how the men are fed and treated'.[6] Where they failed to gain the willing cooperation of assigned servants, masters risked damage to their property through careless or wilful negligence.

Motive for some acts can be deduced through the wording on charges or the sequence of prosecutions. On 29 November 1822 Macquarie Harbour convict timber-getter John Vickers was charged with 'destroying some of the working tools at Gordon River & endeavouring to persuade some of his fellow prisoners not to work.' Eleven days later another four convicts were charged with 'breaking a saw wilfully'. The four were also charged with neglect of duty, suggesting that the action was viewed as

[3] AONSW., Newcastle Benchbook, 21 November 1837.

[4] Mary Ann Furze, per *Princes Charlotte*, Police No. 12, T.A., Con 40-1-3.

[5] Hobsbawm, E. and George, R. (1985) *Captain Swing*, Penguin Books, Harmondsworth, 171.

[6] Minutes of Evidence; Peter Murdoch, 22 March 1838, *British Parliamentary Papers*, XXII (1837–8), 123.

a collective attempt to restrict output.[7] Similar actions occurred on rural estates, in mines and other workplaces. In February 1837 James Austin and Robert South were charged with destroying property on Captain Jonathon Coghill's Camden estate. Although only South was charged with wilfully doing so, Austin was subsequently prosecuted for losing his master's property six weeks later.[8] At the Tasman Peninsula coal mines groups of convicts were repeatedly charged with 'carelessly destroying' coal skips by allowing them to fall down a shaft or otherwise damaging them.[9] These were expensive pieces of equipment that might take days to replace. A well-timed action could considerably impede production, providing downtime for many workers.

Some actions involving the destruction of property were explicitly collaborative. Four Macquarie Harbour convicts were charged, for example, with 'damaging a pine log whilst sawing it' on 4 February 1828.[10] Other actions took more time and were planned. In January 1832 the *Sydney Herald* reported that Thomas Tindall received 50 lashes and John Pigot, and Michael Fox 25 lashes each for 'doing everything contrary to their master's orders, planting cuttings of vines upside down, and building one side of a house eighteen inches higher than the other, and divers other frolics'.[11] Just over a year later the same newspaper reported that servants of a Williams' River settler had killed five valuable rams, pulled up and destroyed most of his tobacco crop and 'threatened to assassinate their master at the first convenient opportunity.'[12] There is evidence of collective sabotage across a wide range of other occupations, including tradesmen. Shoemaker Thomas Burgoyne was sent to the hulk chain gang for 12 months for 'Wilfully and maliciously destroying a pair of lasts', the property of his master Thomas Parker 'and declaring at the same

[7] John Vickers, per *Lady Ridley*, Police No. 13, T.A., Con 31-1-42.

[8] AONSW., 2482/6 CY Reel 954 Campbelltown Benchbook, 11 February and 20 March 1837.

[9] M.L., Coal Mines Benchbook, A584-1-1, 30 April 1839; 25 September 1839 and 18 March 1841.

[10] James Carr, per *Castle Forbes*, Police No. 254, T.A., Con 31-1-6; James Daniels, per *Albion*, Police No. 317, Con 31-1-9; John Salmon, per *Commodore Hayes*, Police No. 550, Con 31-1-38; Richard Copperwaite, per *Princess Charlotte*, Police No. 654, Con 31-1-6.

[11] *Sydney Herald*, 2 January 1832.

[12] *Sydney Herald*, 14 February 1833.

time he would never do another stroke of work' for his master.[13] Like the destruction of coal skips, lack of shoes could bring an effective stop to labour and it is perhaps not surprising that they were a common target. George Collier was charged with burning the shoes he had been supplied with and general neglect by his master.[14] In June 1835 Point Puer boy, John Smith was convicted of wilfully destroying the shoes he was making and inciting his fellows into 'improper conduct' stating they would be better off in Port Arthur. Smith got his wish, being removed across the bay to that settlement after first serving five days solitary confinement.[15]

Sabotage, a favoured and costly form of payback, drew on a long tradition of such acts in Britain and Ireland. Incendiarism and the maiming of livestock could be particularly effective in that they were actions that could be planned in ways designed to conceal the identity of the perpetrator. While both were capital offences, it was notoriously difficult to detect and prosecute those responsible—especially where the action had the tacit support of other workers.[16] This is reflected in the wording of charges brought against assigned servants. At least two of Michael Lackey's men were charged with 'General misconduct & suspicion of cutting out the Tongue of a mare their masters property'. While in the absence of evidence the men escaped punishment, they were nevertheless returned to government and assigned out of the district.[17]

The ease of starting a fire—pipe smoking was almost universal amongst assigned workers—and the frequency of accidental blazes, many were occasioned by Summer-lightning strikes, made this a popular form of retaliatory action. The failure of co-workers to speak out considerably hindered attempts at prosecution. While it only took one individual to set light to a wheat stack, this does not mean that the act was not collectively planned. On 5 September 1831 Joseph Archer's wheat stacks burst into flames not long after the prisoners had knocked-off work at his Burlington property in northern Van Diemen's Land. Archer's overseer, John Tait, immediately ran to the two huts nearest the fire to rouse the men into

[13] Thomas Burgoyne, per *Lord Hungerford*, Police No. 467, T.A., Con 31-1-1.

[14] M.L., Tas Papers 323, Richmond Benchbook, 6 November 1832.

[15] M.L., Tas Papers 33, Tasman Peninsula correspondence, 17 June 1835.

[16] Thompson, E. (1975) The Crime of Anonymity, in Hay D. et al. eds. *Albion's Fatal Tree; Crime and Society in Eighteenth Century England*, Allen Lane, London, 255–344.

[17] Frederick Ansell, per *England*, Police No. 506, T.A., Con 31-1-2, 28 August 1838.

action. There he encountered the prisoner George Stewart. The latter was leaning against the wall of his hut calmly smoking a pipe. He was in full view of the blaze and when Tait approached him he said, 'in a very careless manner', 'Oh dear, what is the matter'. Although Stewart had been refused a new issue of clothing the day before and William Thomas, who lived with him, had had his incentive allowance stopped a fortnight before the fire, no evidence could be found to link the two men with the destruction of the stacks.[18]

This was not the first time that Archer stacks had mysteriously burst into flames. He had written to John Burnett, the colonial secretary, on 25 October 1829 to inform him that the previous 'afternoon some one or more of my convict servants have set fire to a stack of oats and barley belonging to me containing about 500 bushels'.[19] As he informed Burnett in a subsequent letter, some of the men in his employ had 'exhibited for a length of time a degree of insolent and improper conduct'. As punishment he had suspended the additional allowances supplied to four of his assigned servants just prior to the fire.[20]

Joseph Archer estimated the damage resulting from the 1831 fire at £500 and strongly suspected that his assigned servants had 'culpably suppress'd' the extent of the information they knew. He petitioned the governor for the replacement of all the men employed at Burlington, but the colonial secretary was unwilling to comply.[21] Archer, one of the largest landowners in the colony, was far from powerless. He could use the withdrawal of extra rations and other incentives as a form of workplace coercion or charge a convict at the house of one of his fellow magistrates. Yet, as he lacked the ability to monitor every one of his assigned servants' day and night, he remained vulnerable to attacks on his property.

His frustration was shared by other masters. On 27 November 1831 a fire erupted in wheat stacks belonging to D. Ballantyne, government inspector of stock at New Norfolk. Again, incendiarism was suspected and an investigation undertaken, but as with most other such cases there

[18] Examination of John Tait, T.A., CSO 1-547-11913.

[19] Joseph Archer to Colonial Secretary John Burnett, 25 October 1829, T.A., CSO 1-428-9632.

[20] Joseph Archer to Colonial Secretary John Burnett, 2 November 1829, T.A., CSO 1-428-9632.

[21] The information and Complaint of Joseph Archer to John Burnett Esq., 28 January 1832. T.A., CSO 1-547-11913.

is no evidence anyone was brought to trial for the matter.[22] In April 1837 the *Australian* reported that a stack containing over 600 bushels of wheat, besides a quantity of barley and oats belonging to a Wollombi farmer named Merton had been destroyed by fire. Several servants 'who had been lately punished and were heard to threaten their master' were placed 'in custody on suspicion of being concerned in the crime.'[23] In 1838 a number of Lachlan McAlister's Clifton Farm servants tried to lodge a formal complaint of ill-treatment which, like so many others, was dismissed by the local bench. Shortly thereafter wheat stacks at the farm were burned, but notwithstanding the offer of substantial reward (£50 to a free man or a conditional pardon to a convict) the culprits escaped detection.[24] In 1832 several convicts set fire to a haystack of their master Edward Gough's Verulam property near Launceston before absconding. While they were apprehended and prosecuted for arson, they escaped conviction as the only evidence was the dying testimony of one of those involved.[25]

As Bruce Hindmarsh has observed, the alacrity or lack thereof with which servants helped masters extinguish fires (whether resulting from natural events or design) was a persistent issue.[26] The enthusiasm with which assigned convicts set about the task of dousing a blaze was likely to be in inverse proportions to levels of indulgences received. Where the latter were turned off, or did not meet convict expectations, master might expect little by way of support. In July 1825, for example, six convicts on Dr. Elyard's Stonequarry farm received 25 lashes when they refused to work because they had no rations. In August 1826 three convicts on the same farm were also prosecuted for refusing to work until they had been supplied with back rations of tea and sugar and a 21 lb slab of meat. As in many disputes, a growing estrangement between master and servants is evident in this series of actions. In April 1826 Elyard's barn, which was full of wheat gathered in the recent harvest, burned down. As the *Sydney Gazette* reported, his assigned servants gave 'but little assistance' fighting

22 M.L., Tas Papers 265, Hobart Police Office Letterbook correspondence 30 November and 1 December 1831.

23 *Australian*, 28 April 1837.

24 *Monitor*, 8 August 1838; *The Colonist*, 18 and 25 August 1838.

25 *Launceston Advertiser*, 22 February 1832.

26 Hindmarsh, 'Yoked to the Plough', 139–143.

the blaze. A suspicious Elyard charged four men with incendiarism. They were acquitted for want of evidence, but nevertheless returned to the Crown.[27] Elyard's workers made their views clear during the August 1826 trial over the second ration strike. Samuel Wood told his master he did not 'want anything to do [with] you, or with your bullocks or will I stay on your farm much longer.'[28]

Fearful of payback it was common to request the removal of servants suspected of involvement in incendiarism, as Joseph Archer did following the loss of his Burlington stacks. Even where this occurred, however, it did not necessarily eliminate the problem. The *Hobart Town Courier* urged that men sentenced by magistrates for misconduct to road or chain gangs should be kept as far as away from their master's farm as possible as they might abscond, and even worse, induce others to do so, in order to attack the property of their former employer.[29] In April 1833, the magistrate William Bryan lost a large quantity of stacked grain and a barn containing about two thousand bushels of threshed wheat to a fire which was supposed to have been the work of an incendiary.[30] In September of that year Thomas Mullin, a convict in Notman's Road Party, was charged with lighting the fire. As it turns out, this man and Bryan had prior history. Mullin had been sentenced to Notman's Gang for four months for refusing to work for Bryan when ordered to do so on New Year's Day 1833. His former master appears to have been concerned about the prospect that Mullin—a soldier who had been transported for desertion—might seek to extract revenge. A note that he should not be returned to Bryan's Glenore property was inserted into Mullin's conduct record. In the event this turned out to be an ineffectual precaution. Mullin absconded from his gang on 6 February and succeeded in remaining at large until 13 May. As the administration belatedly realised, this provided him with ample opportunity to slip across country in order to ensure that Bryan paid a high price for forcing his men to work on a day they regarded as a holiday.[31]

[27] *Sydney Gazette*, 10 May 1826.

[28] AONSW., Cawdor Benchbook, 7 and 20 August 1826.

[29] *Hobart Town Courier*, 6 June 1834.

[30] The *Colonist*, 23 April 1833.

[31] Thomas Mullin, per *Bengal Merchant*, Police No. 664, T.A., Con 31-1-29.

Sabotage by workers in convict gangs or under close supervision was more difficult to effect, at least if workers wanted to escape detection. Some did not, however. Jericho Chain Gang inmates Edward Eason and John Mills were sentenced to 12 months hard labour in January 1841 for gross misconduct in setting fire to a hut and obstructing efforts to extinguish it—a blatant and very public act of retaliation.[32]

Some acts which resulted in the destruction of government property were explicitly linked to other forms of protest. This was especially the case with absconding and absenteeism. In December 1829 eight convicts in the Port Macquarie Barracks were charged with conspiracy in failing to provide information in relation to a broken window that had been used to affect a temporary absence from the building by other convicts.[33] Fires might be lit to distract attention when making an escape, but more typically incarcerated prisoners would combine to break their chains or prison cell walls to facilitate escape.

While leg irons were highly effective in curbing runaway rates, they did so at some price. Workers encumbered with several pound of iron rivetted to their legs were slower to move to and from work. This is a good example of the ways in which convict resistance increased the costs associated with managing labour, while simultaneously cutting the rate of output. Yet, although leg irons put a dent in absconding, they did not entirely eliminate the problem. Samuel Dudley and Thomas Smith, for example, were sentenced to serve two months additional hard labour in May 1841 for 'having their irons altered so as to remove them at pleasure.'[34] Rivets could be sawn through, or irons could be distorted by smashing them against a hard surface 'ovalling' them so that they could be twisted off a prisoner's ankle. They were also prone to metal fatigue. To guard against this the blacksmith would cut a notch in each basel every time they were fitted—a means of identifying irons that had passed their use-by-date.[35]

Walls were another expensive way of curbing rates of absconding. A gaol was built at Notman's Road Party in order to try and reduce the

[32] M.L., Tas Papers 291, Oatlands Benchbook, 4 January 1841.

[33] AONSW., Reel 2723 Port Macquarie Benchbook, 28 December 1829.

[34] M.L., Tas Papers 291, Oatlands Benchbook, 10 May 1841.

[35] Leppard Quinn, C. (2007) Why Leg Irons Were Not Emancipated: The Role of Convict Leg Irons in Van Diemen's Land and New South Wales, 1788–1853, BA Honours thesis, School of History and Classics, University of Tasmania.

rate at which convicts ran from that location. That this was used to house the chain gang was in itself admission that irons alone were insufficient to hold in place those determined to run. Almost as soon as this structure was completed it was put to the test. Nine prisoners successfully broke out of the building in September 1833, a further 12 were charged with insubordination and attempting to break through the wall in December of the same year and Robert Eustace and John Collins each received 20 lashes in August 1834 after they set fire to the building in order to effect their escape.[36] In November 1839 two prisoners in the Spring Hills Road Party were charged with having 'implements of escape and destruction' in their cell, one of whom, Robert Eccles, was removed to Port Arthur.[37] Such escape attempts often required a degree of collective action and organisation such as when eight prisoners in the Launceston Penitentiary cut their blankets into strips in August 1834 to construct a rope.[38]

Others were prosecuted for destroying the implements of punishment. Charles Wellings was sent to the Oatlands Chain Gang for a year in October 1828 after he burned all the Cat O' Nine Tails entrusted to his charge as flagellator.[39] Equipment was always vulnerable to acts of sabotage. On 2 September 1829 Macquarie Harbour convict Robert Greenfield was charged with 'wilfully impeding the work of one of the Mills by miss-screwing part of the machinery.'[40] The mill in question was designed to be used by the chain gang who were tasked with grinding the settlement's grain. While only one individual was prosecuted, many are likely to have benefitted from the halt to production caused by this 'mishap'.

Convicts also sabotaged production by damaging themselves. Thomas Joyce and Thomas Porter were sentenced to serve six months hard labour in chains when they were thought to have deliberately scalded themselves while stationed at the coal mines on the Tasman Peninsula.[41] Morgan Edwards, a convict who had first been sent to Macquarie Harbour for suspicion of having committed a burglary and then spirited

[36] M.L., Tas Papers 277, Launceston Benchbook, 21 August 1834.

[37] M.L., Tas Papers 291, Oatlands Benchbook, 21, 25 November 1839.

[38] M.L., Tas Papers 277, Launceston Benchbook, 25 August 1834.

[39] Charles Wellings, per *Commodore Hayes*, Police No. 527, T.A., Con 31-1-45.

[40] Robert Greenfield, per *Countess Harcourt*, Police No. 234, T.A., Con 31-1-14.

[41] M.L. Coal Mines Benchbook, AF584, 25 November 1839.

away to Moreton Bay after being found not guilty of murdering an overseer, cut off his own fingers to avoid ganged labour.[42] In November 1822 James Mason was punished for a similar offence at Macquarie Harbour. He was sentenced to receive 50 lashes for 'Disabling himself by cutting off two of his fingers in order to deprive the Government of his labour'.[43] The wording of the charge is telling. It reveals that this act of self-mutilation was treated as an attack on property because the government possessed rights in Mason's labour for the duration of the seven-year sentence passed upon him by the Somerset Assizes in Taunton for highway robbery.[44]

Assaults

As well as self-inflicted injuries convicts were also prosecuted for attacking others. Despite the emphasis that penal administrators and masters placed on the criminal and vicious nature of their convict charges, prosecutions for assault were something of a rarity. As Table 9.1 shows, less than 2 percent of all charges brought against male and female convicts serving in Van Diemen's Land were for crimes of violence. Indeed, the record of assaults committed by convicts pales into insignificance when put alongside the record of state-sanctioned violence inflicted on the bodies of prisoners as punishment for breaking regulations. Based on punishment rates in Van Diemen's Land we estimate that somewhere in the vicinity of

Table 9.1 Nature of charges laid against male and female convicts in Van Diemen's land

	Female	*Male*
Offences against the person	1.2	1.5
Offences against property	5.1	7.6
Offences against the currency	0.1	0.2
Offences against good order	32.2	25.9
Offences against regulations	61.4	64.8
Total	100.0	100.0

Source Total count Con 40 and 41 (N = 84,344 charges), 4 percent sample Con 31, 32, and 33 (18,806 charges)

[42] O'Connor, 'Power and Punishment', 24–26.

[43] James Mason, per *Dromedary*, Police No. 185, T.A., Con 31-1-29.

[44] *Bath Chronicle and Weekly Gazette*, 8 April 1819.

Table 9.2 Identity of victims of convict assaults (percentage)

	All female	*Male assigned*	*Male gangs*	*Male penal station*
Masters and mistresses	12	24		
Spouse	4			
Master' child	11	4		
Other free managers	6	6	2	3
Constable, overseer, etc.	37	26	65	43
Other convicts	30	40	33	54
Total	100	100	100	100

Source Con 31, 32, 33, 40, and 41. $N = 430$

3 million strokes of the lash fell across convict backs and 1.5 million days were spent in solitary confinement in the period 1788–1860.

Table 9.2 provides a breakdown of the minority of assault charges that specified the social status of the victim of convict violence. Constables, watchmen, overseers, flagellators, matrons and other prisoners who served as petty officials were a common target. In all, 37 percent of assaults by female convicts were directed at other prisoners that occupied these roles. They were also the target of nearly two thirds of all assaults for which male convicts in road parties and chain gangs were prosecuted and 43 percent of all such acts committed in the confines of penal stations. Attacks on masters, mistresses and other free officials were less common, but certainly not infrequent. A quarter of all assault charges brought against male assigned servants where the victim was specified were for attacks on employers, while a further 6 percent targeted magistrates and other free officials. Female convicts were just as likely to be charged with assaulting the children of their masters and mistresses as they were for violent acts directed against the adult members of the household to which they had been assigned. This in itself is a reminder of the multiple ways in which masters and mistresses were vulnerable to compensatory actions by disgruntled assigned servants, as Harriet Smith reminded her master, Lieutenant James Corbett. When he threatened to send her back to the factory for insolence, she told him she could easily poison him and his family.[45] There were other more subtle ways in which female assigned

[45] Harriet Smith, per *Mellish*, Police No. 175, T.A., Con 40-1-9, 27 April 1831.

servants could exact revenge. Maria Wood, a house maid and servant of all work from Dublin, taught obscene songs to the daughter of her master, the Oatlands police magistrate Thomas Anstey.[46]

As Wood's actions demonstrate, while any outright assault was likely to result in a heavy punishment, there were other ways of signalling dissatisfaction. When David Lord's overseer John Morley, confronted three assigned servants over their lack of work intensity, one of them, a man named James Sims, felled a tree '12 yards long' which fell across his path. The shaken Morley claimed in court that he was not given the 'least notice' and could easily have been killed. When he asked why he had not been given any warning, Simms 'insolently' reported that he 'had enough to do to mind his work', without also minding out for his overseer. Incensed, Morley threw a stick at the man. Simms picked this up and raising it over the overseer's head told him that he wished that the felled tree had knocked his 'bloody brains out'.[47] Actually, Sims had form for cutting down far bigger things than trees. He had been transported for life for destroying the bishop's palace during the 1831 Bristol riots.

A problem that masters commonly encountered was the reluctance of other assigned servants to intervene in workplace conflicts, as Waldron found out to his cost. In October 1833 Daniel Stanfield prosecuted Robert Fox with disobedience of orders in refusing to come to his assistance when he was attacked by another of his assigned servants, George Harwood. In the subsequent court case this attack was described as a 'most violent and outrageous assault and battery'. When confronted over the lack of assistance he had rendered his master, Fox left Stanfield in little doubt as to where his sympathies lay. In addition to being charged with failing to render assistance to his master, he was also prosecuted with using 'threatening language' to Stanfield. It is perhaps not surprising that as well as being awarded 50 lashes, the bench recommended that he be assigned 'in some other district'.[48]

Such assaults were often indicative of accumulated frustration and anger or a breakdown in relations. In November 1820 three of P.G.

[46] Maria Wood, per *Sir Charles Forbes*, Police No. 91, T.A., Con 40-1-9, 31 October 1831.

[47] M.L., Tas Papers 323, Richmond Benchbook, 14 February 1833 and James Simms, Per Katherine Stewart Forbes, Police No. 1516, T.A., Con 31-1-39.

[48] Robert Fox, per *Andromeda*, Police No. 306, T.A., Con 31-1-13 and George Harwood, per *Asia* (2), Police No. 263, Con 31-1-19, 19 October 1833.

Hogan's assigned servants were flogged and sentenced to terms in solitary confinement for making threatening language to their master, assaulting him and his overseer, and destroying Hogan's property.[49] On middling to larger estates the mixture of imperious owners, harsh overseers and congregations of workers sometimes proved explosive. A number of estates west and south-west of Sydney experienced repeated waves of absconding mixed with other forms of dissent including absences, insolence, abuse, strikes, petty larceny, assaults on overseers, sabotage and killing animals for food.[50] Frequent resort to the lash to punish Francis Mowatt's servants by the Campbelltown bench failed to deter rising levels of dissent on his property.

As with the revolt that occurred at Castle Forbes in the Hunter Valley in 1833, the build-up to more violent incidents is often evident in the court records with a succession of escalating charges and punishments. In December 1832, following several earlier collective prosecutions on the Minto estate of William Howe, George Ball, Austin Warner and John Hughes were charged with 'mutinous and insubordinate conduct and in particular a violent assault upon the overseer in the execution of his duty and kicking and striking Mr E. Howe'.[51] This attack was not an assault which came out of nowhere. It was provoked by both the failure to address a series of longstanding grievances, and the way in which the lop-sided operation of the law had already resulted in the infliction of considerable violence on the bodies of Howe's workers. Such outbursts become more comprehensible when put in the context of other events. They were a manifestation of the festering resentment associated with attempts to deny convicts access to what they regarded as their own time and adequate payment in the form of rations.

That the tools of work could often be turned into weapons made life particularly dangerous for masters, overseers and other convict administrators. John Edwards was sentenced to receive 50 lashes when he knocked down W.E. Lawrence's overseer with a whip stick in September 1829.[52] Joshua Seaburn was sentenced to receive 150 lashes when he struck a

[49] *Hobart Town Gazette and Southern Reporter*, 25 November 1820.

[50] See for example AONSW., 2482/6 CY Reel 954, Campbelltown Benchbook, 22, 25, 27 February 1834 and 3, 7, 10 January 1835.

[51] AONSW., 2482/6 CY Reel 954, Campbelltown Benchbook, 12 December 1832.

[52] John Edwards, per *Woodman*, Police No. 168, T.A., Con 31-1-9.

constable at Macquarie Harbour with an iron maul.[53] Richard Lennard was sentenced to three years at Port Arthur when he hit his road party overseer with a hammer. He earned an additional 75 lashes when he again threatened his overseer when brought before the magistrate for the first offence.[54]

Tyrannical discipline in some gangs sparked waves of threats and assaults on overseers. In 1834 complaints about the inadequacy of rations supplied to the Sorell Rivulet Road Party in Van Diemen's Land spilled over into a series of strikes and prosecutions for stealing food. These were accompanied by increasingly violent threats against the gang's overseer, Kelsh. One convict, Roberts, told the bench, 'if I go back to the party I will take Mr Kelsh's life', while another responded to Kelsh's order to get on with his work by telling him 'I'll give you something you won't get over very easy.'[55] Those who supervised punishment details were on occasion targeted by convicts other than those that they were tasked with minding. An unnamed overseer of Notman's Road Party was abused by four public works convicts in the streets of Launceston for example.[56] In convict Australia, a bad reputation followed you even when off duty. While it is incorrect to argue that the large proportion of the inhabitants of the Eastern Australian colonies who had arrived as convicts ensured that these developed as classless societies, it is correct to point out that the sympathies of those who had experienced labour exploitation did not lie with overseers, constables, masters, magistrates and others who occupied positions of power.[57]

Some officials felt sufficiently intimidated to carry weapons by way of protection. Pearson, the Superintendent of the Launceston Female Factory felt 'obliged to carry pistols' on account of being 'set at defiance' by his female charges.[58] Richard Hughes, an overseer in Notman's road party, carried a sword for his protection. When he drew this to strike the convict Robert Butler, however, it proved to be of somewhat limited use.

[53] Joshua Seaburn, per *Asia* IV, Police No. 842, T.A., Con 31-1-38, 23 July 1831.

[54] Richard Lennard, per Persian, Police No. 558, T.A., Con 31-1-28, 11 July 1833.

[55] T.A., LC375-1-1, New Norfolk Benchbook, 18 August 1834 and 2 November 1834.

[56] T.A., POL 451/3, Launceston Police Charge Book, 1 January 1832.

[57] Smith, B. (2009) *Australia's Birthstain: The Starling Legacy of the Convict Era*, Allen and Unwin, Sydney, 613.

[58] Frost, Lucy, *Abandoned Women*, 89.

Butler, who had been charged the previous month with 'Assaulting his overseer and threating the Life of him and his children', threw a pickaxe at Hughes and then followed this up by hurling a shovel. In the case that immediately followed John Pratt was charged with striking and using threatening language to another overseer, Samuel Smith. Pulled before the bench Pratt was unrepentant, telling the magistrate he was determined to knock out Smith's brains with a hammer at the first opportunity. For this he received 75 lashes. The bench recommended that both men be sent to Port Arthur. The same day Richard Cloak, another overseer, charged John Davis with repeated disobedience and threatening language. Davis had complained that his irons were too tight to work. He bluntly told the magistrate he would rather do away with himself, or if unable to do that, be hung for hitting his overseer with a hammer. He too was awarded 75 lashes.[59]

Assaults on overseers and masters either by a group of convicts or by one during a strike or riot were not the norm, but certainly occurred—especially in convict gangs. In January 1833 six members of the No. 6 Iron Gang near Bathurst were charged with assaulting their overseer John Hamilton.[60] In May 1842 Thomas Todd received 80 lashes and was ordered to be sent to a distant part of Van Diemen's Land after striking his overseer during a dispute involving members of the Campbell Town Chain Gang.[61] Nor were such attacks limited to male convicts. Mary Sherriff and two other women stabbed Dr. Maddox with a knife in the Launceston Female Factory in October 1842 after he passed her fit to serve a sentence of solitary. All three were sentenced to death for this assault, although this sentence was later commuted to transportation for life.[62]

As can be seen from Fig. 9.1, reconstruction of the timing of threats and actual acts of violence and other prosecutions for restricting output or downing tools, indicate that these different forms of action were all linked. In the case of Notman's Road Party, threats of violence often

[59] M.L., Tas Papers 277, Launceston Benchbook, 23 June 1834.

[60] Rosen, S. (2006) "That Den of Infamy, the No. 2 Stockade Cox's River" An Historical Investigation into the Construction, in the 1830s, of the Western Road from Mt Victoria to Bathurst by a Convict Workforce, PhD thesis, University of Western Sydney, 247–248.

[61] T.A., LC83-1-5 Campbell Town Benchbook, 18 May 1842.

[62] Frost, *Abandoned Women*, 76–77.

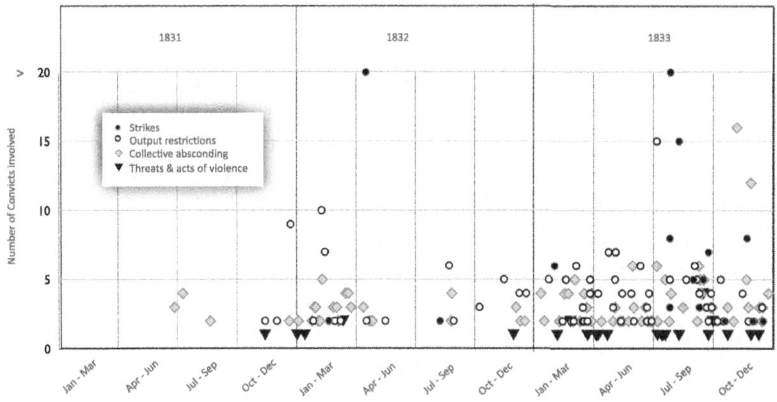

Fig. 9.1 Threats and acts of violence plotted against other forms of collective action—Notman's road party, 1831–33 (*Sources* T.A., Con 31, 32, 33, 40, and 41, POL 451, Launceston Charge Book)

preceded actual assaults and both coincided with increase in output restrictions and strikes. Indeed, attacks on overseers were particularly common in the aftermath of failed strikes. In all cases, those who threatened or struck managers also had a record of participation in collective output restrictions or strikes.

Compensatory Theft

Despite an emphasis on the criminal nature of those prisoners who were ordered to road gangs, chain gangs, penal stations and female factories, a breakdown of all cases brought against convicts reveals that, as with prosecutions for violence, comparatively few charges were laid for offences against property. As can be see from Table 9.1, such charges made up 5.1 percent of all prosecutions brought against female convicts and 7.6 laid of those against males. These totals include charges for destruction of property as well as many brought against prisoners for being in possession of articles for which they could not satisfactory account—a common charge laid against those accused of trafficking. This included items that ganged convicts might have acquired through exchange or barter. Three prisoners in the Launceston chain gang were punished in June 1833 for 'Disobedience of orders in purchasing bread'. While one of these was reprimanded, the other two were sentenced to receive 20 lashes. Four Launceston public works convicts were punished on the same day for 'disobedience of orders in conveying things to the chain gang'—presumably this was the bread bought by three prisoners in irons to supplement their short rations.[63] The four public works convicts were punished even more sternly. They were sentenced to six months hard labour, a period of time in which they too would be placed on a short ration.

If the key to controlling thieves was their stomach, it was crucial that ration scales were not undermined through unauthorized trading. Charity had no place in such a system. Convicts who gave part of their ration to those undergoing punishment were dealt with severely. When Samuel Oxford threw meat over the wall of the Hobart Town treadwheel yard, he was sentenced to 25 lashes and ordered to spend a week engaged in the same species of punishment as those he had endeavored to aid.[64] Overseer William Handcock was sentenced to four months hard labour in the Westbury Road Party for permitting members of his gang to obtain milk for a man in irons.[65] When a tailor threw two loaves of bread into the midst of the Launceston Invalid Gang, the overseer was prosecuted for disobedience for failing to control his charges as they scrambled to gather up the unexpected indulgence. Six of his men were also prosecuted, two receiving 25 lashes, another two three months hard labour (one in the Bridgewater Chain Gang) while the remaining two were deemed to be in such a poor state of health that they were forgiven.[66]

On many occasions convicts in gangs were collectively prosecuted for small scale theft of food items or for otherwise procuring items to supplement their diet. In March 1825 three members of a clearing gang were brought before the Cawdor bench after being charged by their overseer with milking a cow. Two were ordered to be flogged for this offence while the third was acquitted.[67] In May 1833 ten convicts in Notman's Road Party were charged with having potatoes in their possession for which they could not account. Of these, two were discharged, one was

[63] Launceston Police Charge Book, T.A., POL451/1/4, 6 June 1833.

[64] Samuel Oxford, per *Princess Charlotte*, Police No. 56, T.A., Con 31-1-29, 12 February 1829.

[65] M.L., Tas Papers 277, Launceston Benchbook, 20 October 1834.

[66] M.L., Tas Papers 277, Launceston Benchbook, 28 October 1834.

[67] AONSW., Cawdor Benchbook, 15 March 1825.

sentenced to receive 30 lashes and the remainder were placed on the chain gang ration allowance for one month.[68] Convicts working in the coal mines in the Tasman Peninsula were serially prosecuted for procuring fish from the Government seine net, privately fishing, or tossing fish into the barracks yard, while several members of the Grass Tree Hill Chain Gang received 36 lashes in February 1839 for absenting themselves and pilfering apples.[69] In October 1825 seven convicts in the Orphan School Gang were charged with stealing food from a garden (four pled guilty and the other three were discharged), while in July 1828 six convicts working on the Port Macquarie Agricultural Plantation were charged with stealing corn and neglect of work, their overseer complaining they only did half the work they could.[70]

While the colonial administration went to extraordinary levels to police ration scales, convicts did so too. As we have seen, cuts to the ration or a deterioration in ration quality were a common trigger for output restrictions, gang strikes and other protests. This was particularly the case where convicts attributed the decline to local corruption. Complaints that rations were siphoned off by overseers or used to feed livestock were rife. William Green complained bitterly of conditions he experienced at Port Arthur during his Supreme Court trial. Arraigned on a charge of being illegally at large while under arms he insisted that the 'superintendents and gaolers' robbed prisoners of their rations to feed their livestock. He continued, 'I can prove that we do not get anything like our regular ration of bread, which goes to feed these animals.'[71] William Gates reported that similar conditions prevailed at Green Ponds Probation Station four years earlier.[72] While one way to redress such real or imagined grievances was to appeal to higher authority or organise collective action, another was to steal. As William Ullathorne told the Molesworth Committee, 'when the men find that they are under constraint, and that they receive no wages in return for their work, they very soon get the idea into their minds (it is

[68] Launceston Police Charge Book, T.A., POL 451-1-4, 4 May 1833.

[69] M.L., A584 Coal Mines Benchbook, 27 December 1836, 3 January 1837, 22 January 1838, 27 February 1838; M.L., Tas Papers 326, Richmond Benchbook, 20 February 1839.

[70] AONSW., Liverpool Benchbook, 23 October 1825 and Port Macquarie Benchbook, 26 July 1828.

[71] *True Colonist*, 15 March 1844.

[72] Gates, *Recollections of Life in Van Diemen's*, 67.

astonishing how quickly they get that idea) that they are entitled to pilfer from their masters the amount of what their wages would be at home.'[73]

Compensatory pilfering was certainly not restricted to convicts. Such practises featured, for example, in many Caribbean trickster tales. To quote a Jamaican proverb, 'Massa's horse, Massa's grass'. In other words, if I am property—and as such no different from a beast of burden—then I have the right to graze in my master's paddock.[74] Convicts put the Australian version of this to the test early on in the life of the colony. Thomas Hill was prosecuted for theft within a fortnight of the arrival of the First Fleet when he took twopence worth of bread from the general supply. When apprehended he claimed that he had no idea that he had committed a robbery.[75] While convicts regarded supplementing their diet at their employer's expense as fair game, employers' attitudes differed. Some allowed their assigned servants to augment their rations as it was generally recognised that if the rate of production was to be maintained a degree of leakage from the stores had to be tolerated. Private employers, especially, appear to have frequently turned a blind eye to the 'depredations' of their convict servants. Alexander Harris reported a stay in a New South Wales stock hut where the convict occupants had strung a carcass from the lintel. When their master paid an unexpected visit he almost collided with the expropriated sheep, yet, although he could not have failed to notice the animal, he turned his back on the evidence and spoke to the men as though he had seen nothing.[76]

Other masters prosecuted in an attempt to eliminate pilfering altogether, or in order to put a halt to the practice where levels of loss passed acceptable limits. In October 1835 Ben Lomond farmer, Simeon Lord Junior, prosecuted five servants for pilfering milk and potatoes for their own use. Two of these received 25 lashes while the others were sentenced to three months hard labour in different road gangs.[77] The splitting

[73] Minutes of Evidence, Rev. W. Ullathorne, 8 February 1838, *British Parliamentary Papers,* XXII (1837–8), 17.

[74] Duffield, I. (1986) From Slave Colonies to Penal Colonies: The West Indian Convict Transportees to Australia, *Slavery and Abolition*, 7, 1, 30.

[75] Atkinson, *The Europeans in Australia, Vol. 1*, 115.

[76] Harris, A. (1977) *Settlers and Convicts: Recollections of Sixteen Years Labour in the Australian Backwoods by an Emigrant Mechanic*. London, 1847 reprint Melbourne University Press, Carlton, 185–186.

[77] T.A., LC83-1-1, Campbell Town Benchbook, 13 October 1835.

of offenders between punishment locations reveals the serious light in which this act of collective theft was perceived. Despite the inconsequential value of the items purloined by Lord's servants, the act posed a wider threat to a system of remuneration that was pegged to the government ration scale. While masters might reward their servants with small indulgences, servants who helped themselves could be singled out for severe punishment.

A problem that dogged attempts to prosecute convicts is that the evidence upon which a case hinged had often been consumed. In July 1833 York farmer Daniel Stanfield charged three of his assigned servants with taking some beef from a carcass that he had ordered to be slaughtered. Without a forensic reassembly of the butchered animal, this was a charge that was difficult to prove and the men were accordingly acquitted.[78] In a similar case William Bradshaw charged William Thompson and John Harris for taking a fowl for 'their own use' when he discovered bird bones in the fireplace of the men's hut. While the bench found the evidence insufficient to secure a prosecution, it nevertheless ruled that the two assigned servants should be returned to the Crown with a recommendation that they be sent to a road party for six months.[79]

As the case highlights, legal proof was not required in order to exercise retributive punishment. A convict could be ordered to any location, irrespective of the verdict of a court. This included terms in female factories and penal stations—a reminder that it is misnomer that all inmates of these ultra-coercive institutions were doubly convicted felons. It was important, however, to use the sanction of the law where possible, as this provided masters and state with all the conveniences afforded by 'convictism'. The ability to argue that those who laboured in punishment details were there to 'expiate' past crimes, rather than as a result of challenging the conditions under which they were held as prisoners, was a considerable power that should not be underestimated. The operation of the law could be used to justify high levels of punishment as a necessary means of controlling criminal acts although, as Table 9.1 revels, the vast bulk of the offences for which convicts were charged were not criminal.

[78] M.L., Tas Papers 325, Richmond Benchbook (Clarence Plains), 20 July 1833.

[79] M.L., Tas Papers 238, New Norfolk Benchbook, 17 October 1839.

Workplace theft could attract heavy penalties for other reasons too. Convicts were expected to see their masters as social superiors as well as employers—a relationship that was once more underpinned by the operation of the colonial law. Masters and mistresses had the right to prosecute their charges for insolence if they did not pay due respect. Expropriation designed to redress ration or other payment shortfalls cut right through the deferential dialectic that was supposed to underpin the appropriate way to conduct relations with social superiors. In fact, a considerable number of those lagged to the colonies were transported for stealing from employers. Indeed, 'larceny by a servant' was a specific offence which attracted higher penalties precisely because the act of theft involved a breach of trust. Such prosecutions could also result from changes in the way that work was renumerated.[80]

Many convicts were transported for stealing goods and tools that were associated with their occupation.[81] Such practices were always likely to characterise master-servant relations in the colonies, precisely because convicts were not paid. In addition to food assigned servants took materials and goods that were associated with the task that they were instructed to perform. Many of these prosecutions overlapped with charges for privately working. After the end of government hours, convicts used their own time and their employer's tools and raw materials to manufacture articles for sale. Unpicking such acts could be messy, as they often involved conflicts over control of both the start and the finish of the working day, as well as the scraps and bi-products of the workplace. James Murdoch prosecuted Jasper Jones for converting one of his master's towels into a bag for his own use. When the case came to trial Murdoch spent some time describing Jones' neglectful behaviour. In his defence, Jones argued that he thought the towel had been discarded and could be legitimately reclaimed and that he had done so on a Sunday, the only time he had to himself to clean his shirt. He was sentenced to three months hard labour in the Richmond Chain Gang.[82]

Some prosecutions for theft were biproducts of other forms of resistance activity. John Collins was prosecuted in 1846 for absconding and

[80] See Emsley, Crime and Society, 115.

[81] Nicholas, S. and Shergold, P. (1988) Convicts as Workers, in Nicholas, ed. *Convict Workers*, 64–65.

[82] M.L., Tas Papers 325, Richmond Benchbook, 27 November 1833.

making away with a pair of leg irons for example.[83] Absconding was a non-indictable offence. As such it could not be tried in a higher court limiting the array of punishments that could be inflicted on those who challenged the authority of the colonial estate by downing tools and running. Adding a charge of theft provided a means of elevating a prosecution to a higher court ensuring that a new sentence of transportation could be passed upon the absconder. This was an effective means of ensuring that attempts to cut a sentence prematurely could end in a considerable lengthening of the amount of time the convict had left to serve. An example from Macquarie Harbour penal station shows how this operated in practice.

On 2 September 1825 the gang boat arrived at its usual station at the mouth of the Gordon River. The gang had no sooner disembarked than the vessel was seized by four runaway convicts who had been hiding in the scrub. The four men 'compelled' six of the gang, including the coxswain, to row them across the Gordon River. On reaching the southern bank the absconders abandoned the boat and disappeared once more into the scrub. As a parting gesture they partially disrobed the coxswain, an American sailor named William Simpson Lindon. Being a skilled prisoner, Lindon wore his own clothes, rather than ill-fitting government slops. The four absconders relieved him of his jacket and a scarf. Several days later they were all apprehended.

The settlement commandant, James Butler, wrote to Arthur explaining that instead of flogging three of the absconders he would send them to Hobart Town for trial so that they could be returned to the Settlement under an additional sentence of at least seven years. He reckoned that such a measure would act as a deterrent to others who might contemplate 'such villainy'. On 2 November 1825 the three men were duly placed on trial in the Supreme Court charged with stealing one boat value £20 the property of the Crown and a scarf valued at one shilling, and one jacket valued at 10 shillings, the property of the coxswain William Simpson Lindon. They were all sentenced to death, although they were subsequently pardoned on condition of transportation for seven years.

From start to finish the case was a legal sham. Buckley, who had absconded with the three men, was not put on trial because there was no point in doing so. He was already a convict for life and there was no

[83] John Collins, per *Maria Soames*, Police No. 13406, T.A., Con 33-1-57.

advantage to be had by imposing a further sentence upon him—so instead he was flogged. The boat that the other three were said to have stolen had never been in their sole possession—they had only occupied it for the time it took for the boat crew to row across the mouth of the Gordon River. Besides, as Butler had already confided to Arthur, the circumstances strongly suggested that the absconders had the tacit, if not active, support, of the ganged prisoners they were supposed to have robbed. In fact, six of the latter were punished with 75 lashes 'for aiding and abetting the escape' in using 'their utmost efforts' to row the prisoners to the opposite bank of the river. For good measure, the theft of Lindon's jacket and scarf had been added to the Supreme Court charge—just in case the military jury decided that the escape across the river mouth in the government boat did not constitute a larceny. The trouble was that Lindon was one of the prisoners whom Butler had punished for assisting the escape. How, one might ask, could a man be flogged for aiding and abetting a theft perpetrated on his own person? Either he had been falsely punished, or no robbery had taken place.[84] The case illustrates the complex ways in which charges of theft could be used to steal time from convict protestors by extending their sentence. In short, retaliatory theft was not a practice that was limited to convicts.

Conclusion

When Sarah McGregor and Mary Maloney were brought to trial for the murder of Charles Vaughan Waldron, two of the four assigned servants who Jemima Waldron had accused of refusing to come to her husband's assistance gave evidence. William Wade stated he had not seen Maloney strike her master, while James King said he had only seen her extend an arm to push him back.[85] Medical opinion was also called. Dr. Glover, who was Waldron's regular physician, was able to add little to the proceedings. Another medical practitioner, Dr. Husking, was of the opinion that paralysis was unlikely to have resulted from the confrontation with the assigned servants.[86]

[84] Commandant to Lieutenant-Governor, 19 September 1825, T.A., CSO1/226/5514; SC 41/1, 2 November 1825; William Simpson Lindon, per *Competitor*, Police No. 275, T.A., Con 31-1-27.

[85] *Australian*, 24 February 1834.

[86] *Australian*, 24 February 1834.

After retiring for only 15 minutes the military jury found both defendants guilty of murder with a recommendation of mercy.[87] Presiding Judge Burton asked the jury to reconsider, suggesting that manslaughter might be more appropriate. According to the *Australian* the jury put their heads together for a few seconds but decided not to change their original verdict. Burton acknowledged this and made a note of their recommendation for mercy. Then placing a black cap upon his head he sentenced both women to death, ordering that they be executed on Monday morning—that is within a few days of being convicted. In addition, he directed that their bodies be delivered to the surgeons for dissection and anatomy. The prisoners were taken from the court pleading that they had no intention to commit murder. Wade and King, the two male assigned servants whose evidence had conflicted with that provided by Jemima Waldron and her son, were committed to stand trial for wilful and corrupt perjury.[88]

A matter of days after the judgement the *Sydney Herald* reported that the sentence had been referred to the Executive Council and after mature deliberation the matter had been again referred to the King (or at least his London-based advisors). In April both women were removed to Windsor gaol to await the outcome and in January of the following year they received news that their death sentences had been commuted to three years in gaol.[89]

In May 1837 the *Sydney Herald* stated that a letter from 'a respectable gentlemen' in the interior complained that, unbeknown to him, Maloney had been assigned into his service. The paper took this opportunity to remind its readers of the Waldron case arguing that Maloney had only been reprieved on a technical point—at best a contestable reading of the evidence. It expressed dismay that any government could place a woman of such 'vicious and abandoned habits' in a situation from which she could possibly be introduced into a respectable family. As the paper elaborated, 'two females destroyed their master' and 'four male convict servants close at hand refused to listen to the common claims of humanity, when called

[87] For a more detailed examination of the trial and its wider context in terms of capital offences see Plater, D. and Milne, S. (2012) The Capital Case of Sarah Mcgregor and Mary Maloney in New South Wales in 1834: 'Justice Is Due Even to Them', SSRN: http://dx.doi.org/10.2139/ssrn.2363780.

[88] *Australian*, 24 February 1834.

[89] *Sydney Monitor*, 30 April 1834 and *Sydney Herald*, 1 May 1837.

upon by their mistress to save her husband's life.' This, the article claimed should be a reminder to the 'incredulous Settlers of the fate they should experience if, by any unforeseen circumstance, or laxity of discipline, the reins should be taken from them'.[90]

In fact, before his demise Waldron had been in the habit of hammering home a similar message. As a presiding magistrate he had prosecuted a number of assigned servants who had been brought before him for combining in order to protest against the conditions under which they served. In passing sentence on three such men Thomas McQuaid, William Quain and Thomas Darby in June 1833 he had observed 'that it was with extreme regret' that he had noticed 'a spirit of insubordination existing among the assigned servants of this district'. He announced that this was something he 'was determined to suppress.'[91] Others seem to have been just as keen to make Waldron pay for the violence he meted out in his capacity as master and magistrate. In January 1834 while absent from his Spring Hill property a man armed with an incendiary set fire to his barn (no doubt filled with the recent harvest). Although the fire destroyed both the building and its contents there is no record of the perpetrator being apprehended for what the *Sydney Monitor* labelled 'so diabolical an act.'[92] As it turned out, the confrontation with his male and female assigned servants that occurred shortly before his untimely death was merely one act in a more protracted campaign in which violence authorised by law was met with orchestrated violence from below.

[90] *Sydney Herald*, 10 March 1834.

[91] *Sydney Gazette*, 9 July 1833.

[92] *Monitor*, 5 December 1832.

CHAPTER 10

Riot, Bushranging, Piracy and Revolt

Some slave societies, especially in the Caribbean sugar islands, were prone to violent uprisings. As a result, there was an ever-present fear of rebellion. New South Wales and Van Diemen's Land were not immune to similar fears. The arrival of substantial numbers of Irish convicts caused Governor Hunter particular consternation. In 1798 he ordered 20 of the most refractory to be flogged. In early September 1800 a priest, James Harrold, revealed plans for a revolt to Dr. William Balmain, but divulged few details when further interrogated. Harold was gaoled for prevarication and a further 17 suspects received between 100 and 1000 lashes. In an attempt to snuff out further trouble the ringleaders were despatched to Norfolk Island.[1]

This merely succeeded in relocating the problem. Later in the same year a planned uprising on this distant outpost was again betrayed by an informer. Around 100 convicts were implicated and it was revealed that they had hopes of settler support. The discovery of 30 pikes provided evidence of substantial planning. Two ringleaders were identified. One Peter McLean had been transported for sedition, and the other, John Wollaghan, had been heavily implicated in the previous foiled plot in Sydney. Both men were summarily executed and the military guard on the

[1] McQueen, H. (1968) Convicts and Rebels, *Labour History*, 15, 5.

H. Maxwell-Stewart and M. Quinlan, *Unfree Workers*, Palgrave Studies in Economic History,
https://doi.org/10.1007/978-981-16-7558-4_10

island increased.[2] In a further attempt to suppress an uprising, Loyal Associations were established in Sydney and Parramatta, many of the recruits to which were former members of the military. As well as being provided with a uniform, volunteers were placed on the government victualling list, thereby providing them with free provisions.[3]

In February 1802 Governor King issued a General Order authorising a 'search throughout the dwellings and other premises of the inhabitants of this colony' for offensive weapons following attempts 'made by certain desperate characters to stir up tumult and confusion'.[4] This was followed by a further order in April of the same year that made possession of a pike punishable by immediate execution. Fears of a rebellion intensified with the news that war had once more broken out with France. A further General Order in December 1803 called for additional volunteers to supplement the ranks of the Loyal Association.[5]

Rebellion followed. In March 1804, barely 16 years after the penal settlement had been founded the convicts at the Government farm at Castle Hill rose up. The insurrection was led by Phillip Cunningham, the overseer of stone masons and a veteran of the 1798 Irish rebellion. Between 400 and 600 convicts joined Cunningham, breaking into government buildings and farms to secure guns and ammunition. They also set fire to a number of neighbouring farms which they hoped would spark an uprising encompassing much of the agricultural districts west of Sydney, including Parramatta. Their aim was to plant a tree of liberty at Government House before marching on Sydney where they intended to embark upon ships which Cunningham assured the rebels were waiting to take them home. It was later revealed that at least some of the rebels intended to revive Emmet's failed 1803 Irish rebellion.[6]

A rapid response by the colonial administration, who had already been alerted to the plans, quickly dissipated support for the rebels. In the end 233 were cornered by troops led by Major George Johnston at a hillock

[2] McQueen, H. (1968) Convicts and Rebels, *Labour History*, 15, 14.

[3] Ramsey Silver, L. (2002) *Australia's Irish Rebellion: The Battle for Vinegar Hill*, Watermark Press, Sydney, 54.

[4] McQueen, H. (1968) Convicts and Rebels, *Labour History*, 15, 6.

[5] McQueen, H. (1968) Convicts and Rebels, *Labour History*, 15, 7.

[6] Whitaker, M. (1998) Swords to Ploughshares? The 1798 Rebels in New South Wales', *Labour History*, 11; Moore, T. (2010) *Death or Liberty: Rebels and Radicals Transported to Australia 1788–1868*, Pier 9, Millers Point, 116–117.

near Castle Hill. It was at this Antipodean Vinegar Hill, that the New South Wales Corps and Loyal Association opened fire while Cunningham was attempting to negotiate terms. At least 15 convicts died in the ensuing conflict and while many tried to escape, most were captured on the field of battle or shortly afterwards. Nine convict leaders were subsequently executed. Cunningham was hung without trial on the night he was taken. The remains of the leaders were gibbetted at various locations as a warning to others. The rank and file of the rebellion were flogged, receiving between 200 and 300 lashes each. As an additional precaution, 34 were sent to Newcastle to work in chains, effectively establishing the site as Australia's first penal station. Others were despatched to Norfolk Island and Van Diemen's Land.[7] Martial law was also declared and for the week that this was enforce it was alleged that additional arbitrary reprisals were meted out by some settlers against convicts thought to have been involved.

It has been argued that the Castle Hill uprising marked the 'last chapter' in the Irish 1798 rebellion, rather than the starting point for organised resistance to convict labour.[8] Indeed, the cry of 'Death or Liberty and a ship to take us home', might suggest that the 1804 rebels had their eyes fixed on political matters on the other side of the globe. Some have even argued that since mass escape was the principal objective, this was not a rebellion at all, in the sense that it did not constitute an attempt to establish an Antipodean commonwealth of thieves.[9] Others have viewed the violence at Castle Hill as an isolated flash in the plan, proof that Government authority in New South Wales was never seriously threatened.[10] Yet, not all of those involved were Irish. Nor was this the last time that armed convict would shout 'death or liberty'. It was also by no means the last occasion when the remains of those who opposed colonial authority would be hung in chains. It is also surely no coincidence that the revolt occurred on a Government farm that was part of the first attempt to confine convicts within a barracks at night and to use ganging to increase labour intensity. As Grace Karskens has argued, Castle

[7] Moore, *Death or Liberty*, 119.

[8] Whitaker, 'Swords to Ploughshares?', 9–21; Moore, A. (2009) Vinegar Hill/Castle Hill Rebellion, 1804, in Ness, I. ed. *The International Encyclopedia of Revolution and Protest*, Wiley, https://doi.org/10.1002/9781405198073.wbierp1539.

[9] Karskens: *The Colony*, 292.

[10] Hirst, J. (2008) *Freedom on the Fatal Shore*, Black Inc, Melbourne, 123–139.

Hill farm was Hyde Park barracks mark one. It was an attempt to reign in convict rights which provoked an instant and massive reaction.[11]

This chapter examines the many subsequent occasions when groups of convicts combined in order to use force to address grievances, enact reprisals or engage in self-liberational acts. It will start with an examination of riots, before moving on to explore actions that involved the collective use of firearms and other weapons before ending with piratical attempts to take vessels.

Riot

In October 1827 the inmates of the Parramatta Female Factory confronted the matron, Mrs. Raine. Although it was Raine's last day in the post she had attempted to put a halt to the supply of tea and sugar, in consequence of which, 'a general spirit of discontent was excited'. The assault on her person was serious enough to require the intervention of a party of constables. The first act of Raine's replacement, Mrs Gordon, was to reduce the women's bread allowance—a punishment calculated to quell the disorder of the previous day. A large group of women immediately broke out of the factory but were persuaded to return. The women warned, however, that if the full ration was not restored they would 'tear down all before them'. True to their word a 'numerous party' of inmates 'assailed the gates' with pick-axes, crow bars and other implements when it became clear that Gordon had no intention of conceding ground. When the gates yielded they 'poured forth, thick as bees from a hive, over Parramatta and the adjoining neighbourhood'. A detachment of around 40 soldiers were sent to round them up with 'fixed bayonets'. Having secured a large number, the rioters were marched back to the factory. By this stage many of them had successfully obtained provisions from the inhabitants of Parramatta. Accompanied by their military escort they resembled a 'conquering army', singing as they went along 'their aprons loaded with bread and meat'. Once they had been safely resecured within the confines of the factory, Major Lockyer, the Superintendent of Police at Parramatta, directed the ring leaders to be selected and confined in the cells. This, however, the rioters resisted. Though 'opposed by a military force, they

[11] Karskens, *The Colony*, 89.

succeeded in rescuing their companions, declaring, that if one suffered, all should suffer'.[12]

As Joy Damousi has stressed, the protests led by convict women were often described in language that sought to both trivialise and sexualise resistance.[13] This is a reminder of the manner in which convictism was applied with particular force to female prisoners in a largely successful attempt to obscure the many concerted and impressive ways they resisted labour exploitation. As Kay Daniels put it: 'Convict women have been thought of as "non-political", less likely than male convicts to be involved in large-scale acts of rebellion or challenges to authority and more likely to act from personal interest'. As she argued, however, there was plenty of evidence that women combined on the occasions that they were worked together in numbers.[14] We concur, indeed our survey of conduct records and benchbooks reveals that female convicts were more likely to abscond than their male counterparts, were particularly prevalent in actions designed to assert convict rights to a Sunday free from labour. They were also militant when it came to refusing to remain in the service of masters and mistresses who transgressed what might be termed the moral economy of unfreedom. They were also prevalent in actions that employed collective force to address grievances.

In 1831, four years after the inmates at Parramatta had forcefully left the institution in order to restore ration levels, hundreds of women rioted after some of the inmates had their heads shaved. This time they threatened to march on Sydney and shave the Governor. In all, 37 of those involved were sent to the female factory at Newcastle penal settlement for three years.[15] A smaller incident occurred in 1832 followed by a larger riot in 1833, also sparked by hair-cutting.[16] Once more this was only suppressed by the combined efforts of soldiers and constables. Another 19 rioters were sent to Newcastle and a further 15 to the female house of correction at Bathurst, their arrival considerably unnerving residents of the latter district.[17] Attempts to humiliate and defeminise female convicts

[12] *Sydney Gazette*, 31 October 1827.

[13] Damousi, *Depraved and Disorderly*, 79–84.

[14] Daniels, K. (1998) *Convict Women*, Allen and Unwin, Sydney, 145.

[15] *Monitor*, 5 February 1831.

[16] *Sydney Gazette*, 6 October 1832.

[17] *Sydney Gazette*, 6 October 1832; Hendriksen et al., *Women Transported*, 43, 49.

by close cropping or shaving their hair was violently resisted across all institutions.

Unlike strikes, riots and mutinies were not everyday affairs but they were reasonably frequent occurrences in more coercive work locations. This was especially true of female factories.[18] There were further riots at Parramatta in 1830, 1836 and 1843. Others occurred at the Hobart Town factory in 1824, 1826 and 1828 at its replacement at Cascades in 1829, 1839, 1842 and twice in 1843. George Town also experienced a riot in 1828 and Launceston in 1843 and 1844. This tally is almost certainly an underestimate. On a number of occasions individuals or small groups of women in factories were tried for 'insubordination' who may have been ringleaders in protests involving others. Repeat 'appearances' before the courts add some credence to this interpretation. For example, Anne Bennett was charged with insubordination in June 1832 and two months later with inciting others to fight and insolence to the matron of the George Town Factory. Mary Davis sent to the same factory for her part in the February 1829 Hobart riot was charged with insubordination in April 1833. Rosina Gavilin was convicted of insubordination at George Town in May 1834 and then 'impertinence and trying to create dissatisfaction among the women' six weeks later. There is also evidence that the splitting up of ring leaders between institutions may have spread dissent. As Hendrickson et al. note, riots occurred at both Newcastle and Launceston after groups of women who had rioted at larger female factories were sent to these institutions.[19]

Strikes often escalated into riots like one involving 50 women at the Cascades Factory in May 1839. *Bents News* attributed this action to the inadequate supply of rations.[20] Eight of those involved were charged with 'insubordination in forcibly violently & in a turbulent manner resisting Mr Hutchinson & with openly refusing to obey his orders.'[21] Five of these had arrived on the *Atwick*, suggesting that bonds built during the long sea voyage to Australia were maintained on land. Ellen Scott was singled out for special punishment for 'violently assaulting Mr

[18] Smith, B. (2008) *A Cargo of Women: Susannah Watson and the Convicts of the Princess Royal*, Allen and Unwin, Sydney, 83.

[19] Hendriksen et al., *Women Transported*, 15.

[20] *Bents News*, 1 June 1839.

[21] Hendriksen et al., *Women Transported*, 62.

Hutchinson with intent to kill or do him some bodily harm.' Scott had been charged with gross insubordination two weeks prior to the riot and again on 16 May, twelve days after it. This, and other prosecutions of those involved in collective protests serve as a reminder that riots were not isolated actions but were episodic culminations of festering grievances. Kay Daniels makes a similar point in relation to the 1827 prosecution of Ann Wilson who, upon hearing her hair was to be cut off, seized a pair of scissors and cut it off itself. Daniels argues that this individual act of protest needs to be read in the context of its aftermath, particularly the collective attempt by other women in the factory to rescue Wilson from a punishment cell.[22]

There were further riots at both the Cascades Factory and its Launceston counterpart in 1842 and 1843. In the first incident in Launceston three women—Catherine Lowry, Ellen Miles and Mary Sheriff—were charged with creating a disturbance and breaking a table and stools in June 1842, less than two months later, Mills and Sheriff were again brought before the bench, this time for gross insubordination and destroying articles.[23] Deliberate damage to property was a feature of female factory riots, just as it was with revolts by unfree labour more generally. In October 1830 the inmates of the third-class yard in the Parramatta factory 'destroyed all the spinning jennies and spinning wheels, together with everything that appertained thereunto' before making an unsuccessful attempt to force the gates of the institution.[24] After a riot in the same institution in 1843 stronger hinges were supplied to the doors but this did not prevent the inmates breaking the padlocks used to secure the building.[25]

In October 1842 a particularly serious riot broke out in the Launceston factory. The action commenced when 85 women from the crime class combined to rescue Catherine Owens from a solitary cell. Owens had been sentenced to serve two stints of 14 days each for absconding—a prolonged and dangerous punishment. Although she had complained that she was unwell, a medical examination passed her fit to serve out

[22] Daniels, *Convict Women*, 144–145.

[23] T.A., LC346-1-12 Launceston Magistrates Court Benchbook 21 June and 16 August 1842.

[24] *Sydney Gazette*, 5 October 1830.

[25] Damousi, *Depraved and Disorderly*, 82.

her sentence. When the matron went to check on her later in the day, she was seized and Owens rescued. The women then barricaded themselves in, announcing that they would not permit the punishment to continue. A first attempt to quell the riot failed when the inmates used broken-off spindles, knives and forks, medicine bottles and bricks to repel a party of constables who attempted to secure the building. The women then opened negotiations. They offered to break off the action if Owens' punishment was cancelled. When these terms were refused, they systematically broke the furniture in the factory and set light to parts of the building. Although they had now been without food and water for over a day the women refused to submit.

In order to quell the revolt thirty male convicts in the prison barracks were sworn in as special constables and furnished with sledgehammers and crowbars. Together with a similar number of convict constables, they assaulted the building by making a breach through the wall. Despite further sustained resistance, the female insurgents were said to 'have fought like demons', the augmented force was finally able to secure the building. Of 103 women who were under sentence in the factory, only 17 had refused to participate in the action. These were all rewarded with tickets of leave. While the leaders were brought to trial this did not break their determined resistance. As well as participating in the riot they were charged with 'the most outrageous conduct abusing and threatening the magistrates to their face'.[26] In order to try and break-up this confederacy, some of these women were transferred to the Cascades Factory.[27] This major disturbance was described by the *Cornwall Chronicle* as a 'rumpus' and was barely reported in the press.[28]

While the congregation of women in female factories facilitated collective dissent there is evidence of riots by female convicts at other workplaces. In January 1844, for example, nine women at the New Town Probation Farm were charged with insubordination in resisting in a turbulent manner and with violence opposing the lawfully constituted authorities. All nine had recently arrived on board the *East London* and

26 Frost, *Abandoned Women*, 75–76; Damousi, *Depraved and Disorderly*, 82.

27 *Launceston Advertiser*, 1 December 1842.

28 *Cornwall Chronicle*, 22 October 1842.

the protest was triggered by an attempt to punish one of their shipmates, Catherine Kemp.[29]

Groups of male convicts were charged with riotous conduct on road and bridge construction gangs in Van Diemen's Land in 1833, 1834, 1835, 1839, 1844 and in New South Wales in 1826 and 1832. On Christmas Day 1843, a group of constables were assaulted in Liverpool Street, Hobart by a large number of convicts from the prison barracks armed with sticks and stones, when they attempted to arrest one of their number for larceny.[30] There were also reported instances involving Point Puer boys in 1835, Parkhurst boys at New Town 1843 and New Town Government Farm probationers twice in 1844. Riots also occurred amongst convicts at Hyde Park and Sydney Military Barracks in 1826 and 1843, Liverpool Barracks in 1827, Port Macquarie Barracks in 1832 and on Cockatoo Island in 1842. Norfolk Island was particularly prone to this form of violent protest. Three riots occurred there during the first settlement in 1789, 1790, 1794. The subsequent penal station experienced a series of bloody mass riots and insurrections in 1826, 1834, 1842, 1845 and 1846.

Riots also occurred amongst assigned convicts, particularly on rural estates or large urban businesses like Degraves' Hobart brewery operation, where more than a dozen convicts might be employed. Clearing gangs charged with breaking in new country were particular prone to this form of action. Riots were reported amongst private sector convicts in Van Diemen's Land in 1832, 1835 (three times), 1836, 1844, 1846, 1853 and 1854, while in New South Wales similar incidents occurred in 1798, 1825, 1826 (two instances), 1827 (three instances), 1829, 1833 (two instances), and 1836. It is likely further research will uncover more cases.

Riots were frequently followed by mass attempts to abscond as occurred amongst the rank and file of the third class gang at Grass Tree Hill when they received the news on 1 August 1835 that henceforth they would be guarded by soldiers with loaded muskets.[31] In August

[29] For court proceedings associated with this case see https://www.femaleconvicts.org.au/index.php/convict-institutions/probation-stations/new-town-farm (accessed 27 February 2018).

[30] *Hobart Town Courier*, 29 December 1843.

[31] T.A., CSO1/2/819 17506, Statement of Corporate John Shaw, 21st Regiment 2 August 1835 and correspondence to CPM Hobart 3 August 1835.

1842 convicts at Cockatoo Island in Sydney Harbour rioted as part of an escape attempt resulting in the flogging of 20 participants.[32] In the following year a riot at Hyde Park Barracks was quelled through the use of the mounted police, constables and several companies of the 80th Regiment. The five ringleaders were sentenced to 14 days in the cells and then transferred to Cockatoo Island to allay their 'colonial bounce.'[33] Two months later the *Parramatta Chronicle* reported a serious riot at the Sydney Military Barracks' Convict Stockade where the overseer was pelted with stones. Three ringleaders were prosecuted for this disturbance.[34] There is also evidence of actions by large groups that could have been the precursor to open revolt. On 19 July 1838, 47 Point Puer boys were variously charged with absence, disobedience, insolence, sabotage (including defacing their cells) and misconduct in their gangs.[35]

Bushranging

Assignment was designed to foster a particular form of master-servant relationship. Above all, convicts were expected to be obedient and deferent. As thousands of prosecutions testify, those who spoke out, failed to curtsy, tug forelock, or in other ways perform their duty were liable to be prosecuted. Private sector masters and convict administrators put much emphasis on the degree to which paternalism, suitably supported by the authority of the bench could transform criminal lives. Like wayward children, it was thought that unruly, work-shy thieves could be stewarded into more productive roles through a combination of benevolence and discipline. It was argued that assignment was calculated to foster a wider public good. As George Arthur, Lieutenant-Governor of Ven Diemen's Land, put it: 'Bentham's notion that gaolers should possess a personal interest in the reform of convicts is beautifully realised in Van Diemen's Land'.[36] Through unpaid work for private masters, assignment sought to transform those perceived as dissolute and idle into compliant workers.

[32] *Australian*, 3 August 1842.

[33] *Morning Chronicle*, 25 October 1843.

[34] *Parramatta Chronicle*, 23 December 1843.

[35] M.L., Tas Papers 33, Morven records, Tasman Peninsula correspondence/case extracts 19 July 1838.

[36] House of Lords papers, 1837, xxxvi, Appendix i.

In short, convict labour was a species of punishment designed to produce 'docile', and one might add, dutiful bodies.[37]

There was nothing novel in this. Supporters of slavery made similar claims about the benefits of plantation paternalism. As master of the estate, slave owners argued that it was their duty to look after the interests of slaves, just as the slave was obliged to obey them in their capacity as head of the household. This was a system of management designed to manufacture a form of 'wilful obedience'. The guiding hand of the owner would ensure the moral improvement of the slave, while inculcating the unruly with the habits of industry and deference preparing the way for the conditions that would eventually render the institution of slavery unnecessary.[38] Of course, the subtext was that it was the failings of the slave (or for that matter convict) that necessitated labour exploitation. Yet, once locked in place the disorderly could be rendered safe.[39] The unfree worker who kept 'a still tongue' in their head and did as they were bid, identifying their continued well-being and eventual deliverance from bondage with their employer's interest, posed little risk. Of course, as Howard Newby put it, such systems of deference are also calculated to 'ensure the long-term maintenance of the power and privileges on which élites can continue to draw.'[40]

Riot, rebellion, bushranging and other outright assaults on authority shocked masters and convict administrators as they exposed the limits of such systems of management. Large rural properties that relied heavily on paternalist management were the site of many such encounters. To an extent this was an issue of geography. Rural estates were difficult to protect from external threat, as Donald McLeod and his family discovered when their former assigned servants came to pay a visit to their northern Van Diemen's Land property of Claggan in August 1829.

McLeod's son, Magnus, reported that the bushrangers commenced their attack at one in the morning, the household being awoken by 'the report of a gun, and a rattling against the shingles, as if occasioned by shot'. Donald, Magnus and Alexander, another son, immediately got up

[37] Foucault, *Discipline and Punish*, 293–308.

[38] Ford, L. (2008) Reconfiguring the Old South: "Solving" the Problem of Slavery, 1787–1838, *The Journal of American History*, 95(1), 95–122.

[39] Craton, M. *Testing the Chains*, 16.

[40] Newby, 'The Deferential Dialectic', 146.

and armed themselves. They then heard their former assigned servant Thomas Lawton shout from the back of the house, 'open the door or we will slaughter you all'. The threat was shortly followed by John Morton from a different quarter, 'come out you old scoundrel and have fair play' and by William Sainter from the front of the house 'we want some supper, we want Tucker'. When none of the McLeods responded, Samuel Cowden, also at the front of the house shouted: 'here is little pincher, he will pinch some of you tonight; he is called by the rich name of little pincher'. Between thirty and forty shots were then directed at the house, five musket balls passing clean through the double weather boarding. Before departing, the bushrangers told Ruth Price, an assigned domestic servant that they would next go to the McLeod's other property, Talisker. They claimed that they intended to fire the house and shoot the tenants, George and John Stewart, as they attempted to quit the burning building.[41]

The following year convicts at a number of estates in the Bathurst District of New South Wales rebelled and took up bushranging, seizing arms and enrolling recruits until somewhere between 50 and 83 were involved. Some of the members of this group took to sporting white ribbons, a habit that earned them the local sobriquet of the Ribbon Boys. While the leader of this regional rebellion, Ralph Entwistle, was from Bolton, many of the others who participated were from Ireland. It seems likely that the group drew inspiration from the Ribbonmen, a secret society of the agrarian Catholic poor in Ireland.[42]

Consistent with more general bushranging protocols landholders were treated differently, depending on their perceived performance as masters. Some magistrates and landholders like Thomas Evernden, were singled out. Evernden was fortunate to be absent from his farm when the Ribbon Boys attacked, but his overseer James Greenwood was shot dead after he attempted to prevent Evernden's convicts joining the insurrection. Learning of Greenwood's death, a group of 12 volunteers led by pastoralists William and Charles Suttor as well as six troopers commanded by Major Donald McPherson assisted by two Aboriginal trackers pursued the rebels who had in the meantime been reduced as most convicts returned

[41] Information on oath of Mr. Magnus McLeod, T.A., CSO 1/411/9270.

[42] Atkinson, A. (2004) *The Europeans in Australia: Vol. 2*, Oxford University Press, Oxford, 84–85. See also Thompson, J. (2020) *Bone and Beauty: The Ribbon Boys' Rebellion*, University of Queensland Press, St Lucia.

to their farms. A core of around 20 headed for Abercrombie Caves. Cornered near sundown a shoot-out ensued with casualties on both sides (two mortally amongst the convicts) and the volunteers retired in the face of this stiff resistance.

For their part the Ribbon Boys moved from the caves to a bald hill (now known as Bushranger's Hill) where they fought a second battle with a party of police led by Lieutenant James Brown of the 57th Regiment of Foot. Again, the police were forced to retreat after two constables and five horses were killed, calling for reinforcement. A company of 130 soldiers of the 39th Regiment was marched from Sydney as well as a detachment of mounted police from Goulburn commanded by Lieutenant John McAllister.

The Ribbon Boys continued raiding and recruiting as they moved through Cowra until they met and battled McAllister's force near Boorowa. Both sides suffered casualties (including McAllister shot in the thigh), the police retreating to the Bong Bong barracks with three captured convicts. Faced with military reinforcements from both Bathurst and Sydney the rebels splintered or surrendered. Those who surrendered were tried in Bathurst by a Special Commission and a jury of military officers. Ralph Entwistle, William Gahan, Michael Kearney, Patrick Gleeson, Thomas Dunn and John Shepherd were convicted and hanged for murdering James Greenwood, while Robert Webster, James Driver, Dominic Darby and John Kenny were hanged for plundering farmhouses. The men were executed at what is now known as Ribbon Gang Lane, Bathurst, and left on display for a day 'as a warning' before being buried in two mass graves.[43]

The Bathurst incident received little coverage in the colonial press. References in print were mainly restricted to later editorial asides, perhaps because the causes and size of the rebellion were seen to set a potentially dangerous precedent that should not be publicised. A rising tide of convict insubordination and a new administration in the form of Bourke may help explain why a smaller incident three years later received considerably more press coverage. This occurred in November 1833 at ex-Lieutenant (although he liked to title himself Major) James Mudie's Castle Forbes estate. After an undistinguished military career and failed business venture, Mudie took up a 2000-acre grant in the Hunter Valley

[43] Gordon, N.S. (1983) Convict Rebel: Ralph Entwistle, in Fry, E. ed. *Rebels and Radicals*, Allen and Unwin, Sydney.

near Maitland in 1822. By all accounts except his own, he treated his convicts poorly (including breaching customary practices like not working on Sundays). He adopted the same approach to the assigned servants of other regional masters when appointed a magistrate by Governor Ralph Darling. He saw harsh discipline as essential for the maintenance of regional order.

Some of the assigned servants on Mudie's estate rebelled. They first released three convicts (including two from Castle Forbes) who were en route to a chain-gang. Returning to the property they threatened female members of Mudie's family (Mudie was absent) and shot at Mudie's brother-in-law, John Larnach. Six escaped into the bush, but were apprehended after a fire fight in Lamb Valley by a party of troopers led by prominent landholder Robert Scott. Tried in Sydney, evidence of their ill-treatment got a rare public airing, exciting much discussion in the colonial press. Nonetheless, five of the insurgents were sentenced to death and executed, while David Jones, held to be least culpable, was transported to Norfolk Island for life.[44]

While the displays of state power that followed these regional insurrections were savage, executions and long sentences to penal servitude could not unwind the damage wrought by the intrusion of armed convicts into the homes of their former masters. For the McLeod family, who were discovered cowering on the floor by their domestic servants, the experience was intensely humiliating. The authority of the master or mistress over their 'loyal' servants could suffer irreparable damage, this was particularly the case where masters were ordered to strip in front of their station hands. On other occasions, the bushrangers questioned assigned servants as to the character of their masters and or overseers. William Faber, an emancipist herdsman, reported that when Richard Dry's house at Quamby's Brook was attacked by armed absconders led by Matthew Brady, the bushrangers seized Dry's nephew. In a complete reversal of dominant power relations, they enquired of the assembled assigned servants as to their captive's character. For a brief moment, the unfortunate nephew's fate hung in the hands of the estate's unfree workers. The latter pronounced him a 'good man' and he was released, the convicts having exercised a paternalist pejorative which was usually the preserve

[44] Roberts, Masters, Magistrates and the Management of Complaint, 65 and Dunn, M. (2020) *The Convict Valley: The Bloody Struggle on Australia's Early Frontier*, Allen and Unwin, Sydney, 188–190.

of the master class.[45] Such mimicking of the operation of the bench cut deep into the ruling ideology, but left the assigned convicts free from prosecution.

Bushrangers also carried out retributive attacks on other officials. Of the raid by Matthew Brady and ten others on W. E. Lawrence's property at the Lake River in February 1826, Mr. Robert William Lawrence reported:

> I heard two shots fired while I was in the Kitchen, they told me that Bramsgrove (the overseer) had been wounded by Brady – but that if that did not kill him he should not live six months, as his Character was so bad all over the Country for ill-treating the Men.[46]

Thomas Bramsgrove, who survived the attack, had already been cautioned for a 'violent assault' on an assigned servant and was later dismissed from Lawrence's service for a similar offence.[47] Before departing, the bushrangers exacted a heavy toll on Lawrence, setting fire to and completely destroying his wheat fields, house and outbuildings. Bramsgrove was not the only overseer to suffer at the hands of the bushrangers. Edward Williams who worked for G. F. Read was beaten up 'in a most inhuman manner, so as to leave him for dead' by the bushrangers William Oldrey and William Taylor.[48] In a case which has distinct parallels with the attack on Dry's property at Quamby Brook, Mr. Field's overseer received a shock when he addressed three strangers. His enquiries were met with an order to dismount. He indignantly refused and was told 'Come on humbug; we are bushrangers, and have walked sixty miles to come here to blow your brains out.' As the overseer was bound he pleaded for his life, but his assailants were not impressed. They told him that he had been 'represented as an unkind master to prisoner servants, and they would murder him and any others they knew of, who treated their servants unkindly.' However, after discussion with the

[45] Calder, J. (1979) *Brady, McCabe, Dunne, Bryan, Crawford, Murphy, Bird, McKenney, Goodwin, Pawley, Bryant, Cody, Hodgett's, Gregory, Tilley, Ryan, Williams, and Their Associates, Bushrangers in Van Diemen's Land, 1824–1827*, in Fitzsymonds, E. ed. Sullivan's Cove, Hobart, 57.

[46] Calder, *Brady*, 109.

[47] Calder, *Brady*, 107, note 5.

[48] *Hobart Town Gazette*, 27 April 1822.

estate's twenty-six assigned servants, the bushranger George Jones told his prisoner that 'in consequence of the good character the men had given him' his life would be spared. He added, 'that if he ever heard of any harsh treatment' he would return and shoot him.[49] As Byrne argues, such events were similar to the British custom of charivari, where the poor paraded in order to express disapproval of the violation of community norms while dressed as figures of authority.[50]

Officials who presided over convict labour were vulnerable to such attacks as nearly all of them had rural property. Indeed, at times it was difficult to determine whether those targeted by bush-ranging had been singled out for reprisal in their capacity as master or because they were a magistrate. A notice written on a piece of calico that appeared on Dr. Gibson's Mulwaree Ponds estate in 1833 read: 'Donahoe is come alive again — Ten pounds reward for the heads of two Scotch tyrants'[51] The tyrants in question were Gibson and Lachlan Macalister, a landholder and a justice of the peace who was also a lieutenant in the mounted police. In his latter role Macalister had been particularly active in the suppression of bushrangers and the rounding up of runaways including the 1830 Ribbon Boy rebellion.[52] Notably, he had assisted in the capture of the bushranger Jack Donahue who had been shot dead in September 1830. Donahue had acquired a degree of notoriety for the high-profile attacks he led on landholder élites. As well as referencing local events, the wording on this warning placard were thought to have been inspired by the Rockites—a secret society active in south-west Ireland in the early 1820s. The posting of public declarations was a common Rockite tactic. These offered rewards or were often phrased in other ways that implied that the organization was the legitimate source of authority, as opposed to the 'illegitimate' power exercised by local British and Anglo-Irish landholders. Arson and assault were other favored weapons. A direct connection is

[49] *Cornwall Chronicle*, 3 January 1844.

[50] Byrne, P. (2004) *Criminal Law and Colonial Subject*, Cambridge University Press, Cambridge, 138.

[51] *Monitor*, 2 October 1833.

[52] *Monitor*, 23 October 1833.

possible since around 330 followers of Captain Rock were transported to New South Wales in the years 1822–25.[53]

Threatening letters were posted in association with other attacks on prominent public officials. A note was left in March 1815 after the wheat stacks and barns of Police Magistrate A. W. H. Humphrey and District Constable Bartholomew Reardon had been set fire to. These two properties lay about a mile distant from each other in the Pittwater district of southern Van Diemen's Land. This warning read: 'For injustices and we begin the next is ... for you all'. Between the words 'is' and 'all' was a sketch of a musket pointed at a man's head.[54]

While the managers of both slaves and convicts were quick to characterise actions that threatened the distribution of power as criminal, some bushrangers attempted to counter this through displays of civility designed to mirror the mores of those they sought to threaten.[55] The conflict that some armed runaways engaged in was far more than physical. For the ruling élite, it was one thing to be attacked by thugs—to be robbed by convicts dressed in frock coats, sporting top hats and mimicking the manners of the 'big house', was entirely another.

As Paula Byrne has argued, clothing mattered in the colonies. Convict bushrangers in New South Wales wore long white coats, decorated their hats with green and white ribbons and sported red capes.[56] Other bushrangers were said to display a 'strong inclination to assume the *habits* of a gentleman'. When George Clay was apprehended on the bridge at Ross, he was wearing officer's regimentals, a sword, duelling pistols, and had three silk handkerchiefs around his neck.[57] This is remarkably similar to Paul Roberts' description of Caravat tactics in early nineteenth-century Southern Tipperary. Personification of the target group's mores and cultural attributes was clearly a most powerful and effective weapon.[58] While many convict bushrangers did not attempt to escape recognition

[53] Donnelly, J. (2009) *Captain Rock: The Irish Agrarian Rebellion of 1821–1824*, University of Wisconsin, Madison, 119–145 and 310–312. *Australian* 4 October 1833.

[54] HRA., Ser. III, Vol. 3, 89–92.

[55] For a similar discussion in relation to slavery, see Craton, *Testing the Chains*, 251.

[56] Byrne, *Criminal Law and Colonial Subject*, 133–134.

[57] *Hobart Town Gazette*, 17 September 1825.

[58] Roberts, P. (1983) Caravats and Shanavests: Whiteboyism and Faction Fighting in East Munster, 1802–11 in Clark, S. and Donnelly, J. eds. *Irish Peasants, Violence and Political Unrest 1780–1914*, Gill and Macmillan, Dublin, 66–73.

some nevertheless adopted a form of social disguise. This enabled them to appear on stage, no longer tugging forelock and saluting class superiors, but as a person who commanded authority.

It might be argued that the actions of bushrangers were driven by personal agendas. They raided to secure provisions, powder and shot, settle personal grudges and ultimately to escape. The theatrical way in which some attacks were staged, however, reveals a broader agenda aimed at asserting convict rights and designed to strike at the paternalism that lay at the heart of estate management. When bushrangers assaulted properties, they performed in front of an audience of assigned servants. The reporting of these events ensured that these performances edified colonial society as a whole.

Such activities provoked a 'great state of anxiety and alarm' in rural districts.[59] Settlers were driven in from the interior, farmhouses were provided with loopholes and Governors were bombarded with pleas for parties of soldiers to be billeted in outlying districts.[60] But perhaps the most important effect was the uncertainty the actions of armed runaways engendered. In the early 1820s the district constable at Swanport, Adam Amos, recorded the sighting of two suspected bushrangers in his diary. He lamented that the neighbouring settler, George Meredith, was away in Hobart, for 'there is no one that I can put much trust in'.[61] Amos was referring to the remaining able-bodied male population which consisted almost entirely of assigned servants. For the truth was, that when the bushrangers came to pay a visit, the notion of the 'safe' convict was sorely tested.

While the example of those assignees who defended their master's property was lauded in the colonial press and rewarded through the provision of tickets and pardons, the faith that many employers had previously placed in their charges was replaced by profound unease. As Newby observes, workers were passed 'safe' solely on the judgement of a social élite which they curtseyed and touched hats to in the course of the working day. Such a judgement was based on an appraisal of the workers' 'on stage' behaviour, it said nothing about employees' attitudes 'off

[59] *Cornwall Chronicle*, 13 May 1843.

[60] Robson, L. (1983) *A History of Tasmania: Van Diemen's Land from the Earliest Times to 1855*, Vol. 1, Oxford University Press, Melbourne, 143.

[61] Diary of Adam Amos, 27 April 1823, T.A., NS. 323/1.

stage' behind the master's back. As he argues, deference describes what the master wanted, while quiescence is a better word for what he actually got.[62]

When bushrangers struck a property, the assignees had to decide how much of their 'off stage' behaviour it was prudent to reveal 'on stage'. They could back the master and repel the attack or join the bushrangers. Both paths were dangerous. Those who chose to collaborate risked reprisals from both the bushrangers themselves and the 'back-stage' wrath of their fellow servants. Those who threw their lot in with their master's assailants were dicing with the gallows, and if lucky enough to escape the scaffold, a long stint in a penal station. Nevertheless, a few did choose this path, swapping their outward deference for total repudiation of all the master stood for. On at least one occasion a party of bushrangers had to forcibly restrain two assigned servants from shooting the owner of the house in his living room. The *Hobart Town Gazette* reported the actions of another assignee who when bushrangers came to rob his master's house 'ardently joined them, dressed himself in his master's clothes, and sat himself down in his chair as lord of the house.'[63] Such events remained long in memory. They exploded the myth of the deferential worker demonstrating that every assignee was a potential threat.

The point is apply illustrated by the petition of the North-East Van Diemen's Land settler, John Batman, to Lieutenant-Governor Arthur in December 1833. Batman held extensive sheep walks in the Ben Lomond district and employed 22 convicts. Arthur had recently ordered the withdrawal of a party of troops and a constable who had been stationed for Batman's protection who had been considered vulnerable on account of the part he had played in the apprehension of the bushranger Matthew Brady seven years earlier. Despite the passage of time, the withdrawal of troops concerned Batman. As he explained, 'this being the most exposed part of the district, and no land being located between my farm and the south-east coast [the whole formed] an immense extent of Country, and an unmolested retreat for bushrangers.' What concerned Batman, was not so much the level of bushranging, but the fact that one of his own assigned servants had joined 'two armed runaways'. He considered that in the light of this circumstance no faith could be placed in his remaining

[62] Newby, 'The Deferential Dialectic', 142.

[63] *Hobart Town Gazette*, 25 August 1827.

convicts and despite the fact that his free workers out-numbered the unfree by a ratio of two-to-one, he still thought that he required the services of at least a local constable. Ideally, however, he wished for the return of the military post. As he put it: 'I therefore take the Liberty of Soliciting your Excellency that you will be pleased to grant me the protection I formerly enjoyed.'[64]

Yet, far from aiding the master and attempting to repel attackers or throwing in their lot with the bushrangers most assigned servant stood by and did nothing when their master was attacked, meekly surrendering at the first appearance of armed runaways. This posed masters with a problem of a different nature. While they could not prove that their servants had assisted the bushrangers, they could not be sure that they had not. Occasionally the inaction of assigned servants put masters' lives in jeopardy. At nine o'clock in the evening the front door of Philip Pitt's farm at Greenwater Holes burst open. Three bushrangers, John Higgins, Michael Riley and John Hill, rushed into the house and shouted 'Don't be afraid'.[65] Pitt grabbed an adze and made for the leading assailant, at which point one of the other bushrangers shouted 'Fire'. A gun was discharged, but Pitt was able to make an escape through a window. Yet what really alarmed the latter was that he had three assigned servants in the house, not one of whom had attempted to assist him. At the subsequent Supreme Court Trial, the judge 'passed very high eulogium on the conduct of Mr. Pitt, the settler, who had endeavoured to defend his property at the risk of his own life, while the conduct of his servants was no less liable to censure ... in quietly submitting to the demands of a lawless banditti instead of seconding the efforts of their master.' He concluded, that 'Such servants were subject to no light suspicions ... [and] would be looked to and properly disposed of.'[66] Where masters and mistresses were physically hurt servants who stood by and did nothing were sometimes severely punished. However, despite the example made of the few, convicts continued to submit in large numbers at the first appearance of the bushrangers. John Wilson and William Driscoll had no difficulty in tying up twelve assignees when they visited a sawing establishment at

[64] John Batman to Lieutenant Governor Arthur, 28 December 1833, T.A., CSO. 46/2.

[65] John Higgins, per *Daphne* (NSW) and *Admiral Cockburn* (VDL), Police No. 141, T.A., Con 31-1-18; John Hill, per *Dromedary*, Police No. 174, Con 31-1-18; Michael Rilley, per *Tyne* (NSW) and *Prince Leopold* (VDL), Police No. 88, Con 31-1-34.

[66] *Hobart Town Gazette*, 3 February 1821.

Swan Bay on the Tamar River. On another occasion Francis Fitzmaurice and John Smith bound up eight assignees when they attacked Mr. Johnson's property at Green Ponds.[67]

A habit of the bushrangers was to use assigned servants as porters, carrying stolen property and provisions away from raided farms and estates to safer locations. Masters' suspicions were raised by the number of such servants, who although marched away at musket point, returned days later unharmed and unable, or unwilling, to give precise accounts of their movements. In 1843 three convicts, Joseph Selby, George Pearse and James Rushbrook, were tried at the Supreme Court in Launceston 'with making false representation of the movements of the bushrangers'. Despite much evidence that all three had misdirected search parties after their services had been purloined by the bushrangers Jeffs and Conway, they were acquitted for lack of sufficient evidence.[68] It was difficult to prove that convicts' 'off stage' behaviour differed from their 'on stage' behaviour but tantalisingly, circumstances suggested that there was much acting in the master's front parlour. In similar fashion, John Connell was prosecuted in September 1839 for 'Neglect of duty in not reporting to his master the appearance of several armed men whom he represented had met him on his run & questioned [him] upon the state of defence of his masters house'.[69]

There are many parallels here with slave society. As Eugene Genovese argued, time and again questioning slaves failed to elicit information, all professed their ignorance and 'the matter assumes the sacredness of a "professional secret"'.[70] Occasionally subsequent events exposed the nature of this secret. When Mr. Haywood's house at Macquarie Plains was plundered he was fortunate to escape with his life. In the initial onslaught a shot from one of the five assailants took the shoulder of his coat clean off. Four of the bushrangers were subsequently apprehended at a public house owned by a man named John Ray. Amongst those arrested for harbouring and receiving was a public works convict named Charles Jackson who had been a shepherd to the Haywood's at the time

[67] *Launceston Examiner*, 8 July 1846 and *Hobart Town Courier*, 30 August 1844.

[68] *Cornwall Chronicle*, 8 July 1843.

[69] John Connell, per *Marquis of Hastings*, Police No. 2483, T.A., Con 31-1-8.

[70] Genovese, E. (1974) *Roll Jordan Roll: The World the Slaves Made*, Pantheon, New York, 622.

of the robbery. The *Hobart Town Gazette* also noted that another of the bushrangers, William Buckley, was recognised by Mrs Haywood. In her words; 'Buckley was the third man who attempted to rush in; I kept him out; I knew him well being our servant so long.'[71]

For the master this was profoundly un-nerving. Many followed Donald McLeod's lead, and suspecting the worst petitioned for the replacement of their servants. The latter wrote to Lieutenant-Governor Arthur as follows:

> … relative to my assigned servants who with a few exceptions have all (we have certain reasons to believe that it might be difficult to prove so as to punish) been connected with the bushrangers who have lately made such attacks on us. My wish is that his Excellency would be pleased to take all of these men and women in my service into the employ of the govt or to assign them on the other side of the country with a few exceptions.[72]

As McLeod's request ran contrary to the regulations governing assignment, Arthur felt unable to comply. He made it clear, however, that if McLeod brought his complaint before a magistrate, and if the charges against any assigned servant were found strong enough to merit punishment, he would ensure that the servant was removed and a replacement speedily delivered. Despite Arthur's reluctance to bend the assignment regulations, subsequent outbreaks of bushranging were followed by similar requests. A written report submitted to Arthur in mid-1834 recommended 'the return of the whole of the assigned servants in that part of the country infested by the bushrangers — and their being replaced by men of a similar description without experience to the settlers from the next arrival of convicts.'[73] Arthur eventually rejected this proposal as it would cause great inconvenience, yet, that he was prepared to give such a drastic measure serious consideration is a stark reminder of the disruption bushranging occasioned.

[71] *Hobart Town Gazette*, 16 July 1825 and August 27, 1825. For other references to former assigned servants planning robberies and retaliatory raids see *Hobart Town Gazette*, 5 August 1826.

[72] Major Donald McLeod to Governor Arthur, Claggan, 7 September 1829, T.A., CSO 1/74/1632.

[73] [Illeg.] to The Colonial Secretary, 1 August 1834, T.A., CSO 1/739/17855.

Following the apprehension of the five bushrangers who had absconded from Major Donald McLeod's property, Claggan, the *Hobart Town Courier* noted that 'They are all fine able young men, and complain bitterly of the treatment they had received previous to them taking to the bush, and state that want of sufficient clothing and wholesome provisions' together with high levels of punishment had 'caused them to abscond.' The *Colonial Times* responded in the following terms: 'We cannot, however, help making one remark, that notwithstanding the severity of their treatment, ... nothing can possibly excuse them taking to the bush, ... because we cannot suppose for one moment, that there is a Magistrate in the whole Island who would be so indifferent to his duty, as to refuse hearing their complaints, and of doing equal justice to the servants as well as to their masters.' William Stewart, one of the aforementioned 'misguided men', had good grounds to disagree. According to the *Launceston Advertiser*, he had lodged a complaint against his master only days before the outbreak. When he arrived before the bench his face was covered with blood and his body bore the marks of extensive bruising, evidently inflicted with a stick. The Deddington Parish magistrate, a Mr. Walker, refused to believe Stewart's account that his injuries had been inflicted at the hands of Donald McLeod's eldest son, Alexander. Walker dismissed the case, ordered Stewart back to his master and told him to consider himself lucky that he had not received 50 lashes.[74] There appears to have been no enquiry.

Similar complaints were made by James Mudie's assigned servants. The five men tried for the November 1833 attack on his property, Castle Forbes, complained of a regime of 'tyranny and oppression' characterised by high rates of flogging. They alleged that Mudie had bought the compliance of the local bench by providing magistrates with gifts of loaned convict labour, effectively cutting off convict access to a fair hearing. While five of the participants were executed, two of them at Castle Forbes in a show of strength designed to intimidate other would-be rebels, this regional insurrection succeeded in triggering an inquiry. This revealed that the outbreak had been preceded by a long-running history of workplace struggle.[75]

[74] *Lauceston Advertiser*, 14 September 1829.

[75] Roberts, 'Masters, Magistrates and the Management of Complaint', 69.

Mudie's convicts complained of being forced to work on Sundays and being supplied with short rations. When these were forthcoming, they alleged that the meat was often maggoty and the flour contaminated with grass seed and smut. In an attempt to address such inadequacies and to regain control over non-government work hours, they had withdrawn their labour. In a pattern that was repeated on many other properties, when Mudie and Larnach responded by cutting incentives of alcohol, tea and sugar, labour participation was further reduced. When asked why they had not made their dissatisfaction known, the estate's servants replied that any attempt to speak out resulted in punishment. As James Harvey put it: 'If any man spoke of it, Mr Mudie would call him an insubordinate character and hunt him down'.[76] The withdrawal of labour was accompanied by escalating violence. As well as threats and assaults on overseers and managers, the estate's workers were attacked. They alleged that the younger convicts were singled out, being kicked and punched. The convicts on the receiving end of such illegal beatings thought about lodging court actions but were counselled against making formal complaints before the local bench by their fellow workers. In Richard Nagel's words 'the men told me that if I complained I would get flogged, that insolence would be sworn against me'.[77]

Other convict runaways who took up arms claimed that they had done so as a result of poor treatment. James Regan was scathing about his former master G. C. Clarke of Ellenthorpe Hall.[78] John Morrel, recognised by one of Charles Reed's servants as a former employee, stated at his trial 'that bad usage drove him into the bush; that he had no clothes or anything.'[79] Concerned at this violent trend, the colonial press repeatedly stated that bushranging was a product of abuses of the assignment system. The *Hobart Town Gazette*, for example, gave prominent coverage to the statement of the bushranger John Plumb. Plumb and his fellow stock-keeper Walls had lived in a state of near starvation in a stockhut on Mike Howe's Marsh while in the employ of a Mr. Franks. Deprived of adequate rations by their master, the paper disclosed that they were kept

[76] Roberts, Masters, 'Magistrates and the Management of Complaint', 69–70.

[77] As quoted by Roberts, Masters, 'Magistrates and the Management of Complaint', 71.

[78] *Hobart Town Courier*, 20 June 1838.

[79] *Hobart Town Gazette*, 9 June 1821.

Table 10.1 Last recorded work location for Van Diemen's Land bushrangers, 1820–1846

Location	*No.*	*(%)*
Free by servitude or ticket-of-leave	4	1.7
Assigned service, passholder or on loan	23	9.8
Public works grades one and two and hiring depots	31	13.2
Road, probation gangs and working parties	67	28.6
Chain gangs and confinement	41	17.5
Penal stations	68	29.1
Total	234	99.9

Source Con 31, 32, 33 and *Hobart Town Gazette* 1816–1846

alive by the supply of provisions maintained by Matthew Brady and his fellow bushrangers. When this connection was discovered, Plumb opted for a life in the bush rather than explain his association to the district magistrate, a story which the *Colonial Times,* considered a near 'justification' of his conduct.'[80] A group of runaway convicts in the Hunter Valley known as 'Jacob's Irish Brigade' were also said to have taken to the bush out of desperation and hunger.[81]

Most bushrangers, however, commenced their career by escaping from a government gang or penal station (see Table 10.1). Many cited the poor conditions they had encountered there as the cause of their decision to bolt. John Dyarmott, for example, exclaimed 'I am driven more like a brute than a Christian by my overseer, and I am forced to abscond.'[82] And John Higgins stated 'that he was compelled to fly to the bush in consequence of ill-treatment he had received in the gaol-gang.'[83]

As with other forms of protest, many bushrangers attempted to address their grievances through more traditional channels, resorting to firearms only after other methods of protest had failed to alleviate localised abuses. John Plumb first took his complaint to a magistrate, as did William Stewart, who accused his master's son of ill-treating him, and the breakout from Deloraine Probation station in 1845 occurred only

[80] *Colonial Times*, 25 March 1825.

[81] Dun, *The Convict Valley*, 198.

[82] *Cornwall Chronicle*, 24 October 1844.

[83] *Hobart Town Gazette*, 3 February 1821.

after a gang strike had failed to reinstate the station ration to its official level. The colonial press provided prominent coverage of accusations of harsh treatment wherever they were perceived to have fuelled the rate of bushranging. Concerned that the actions of a few misguided private employers and public officials jeopardised the property and safety of the many, newspapers aired the reported grievances of bushrangers and called for official investigations of the charges the latter levelled at the system.[84] While the price paid by bushrangers was high—large numbers were executed or killed in action—bushranging did serve to focus public attention on convict grievances.

Piratical Seizures

In January 1835 ten prisoners assigned to the Van Diemen's Land Company conspired to seize the settlement at Circular Head by force and imprison all the free persons and convicts that refused to join in their plot within the confines of the Company storehouse. They then intended to plunder the settlement before making their escape in the schooner *Edward*, expected to arrive shortly from Launceston. The plan was then to 'make all sail' for America. The forming of this conspiracy followed an attempt to withdraw labour on New Year's Day. Revealingly, the conspirators had deliberately concealed the plan to take the *Edward* from their fellow prisoners who had refused to participate in the prior strike action, reasoning 'that by their obedient conduct thus exhibited' they were 'unfit to be trusted with any part of the plot'.[85]

Prior to hatching the plan to take the Schooner, the party had debated whether to abscond from the settlement in order to lay a complaint about their treatment before the bench in Launceston. They considered the punishment meted out by the Van Diemen's Land Company to be particularly severe. As Hugh Holland rhetorically put it to one of his fellow assignees, 'What would the Port Arthur men think of this place!'.[86] Penal station regimes were a subject in which Holland was well versed. He had previously served for five years at Macquarie Harbour.

[84] See for example *Launceston Advertiser*, 14 September 1829.

[85] Malcolm Laing Smith and Statement of Hugh Holland, 2 April 1835, T.A., CSO1/1/800 file 17088.

[86] Statement of James King, 2 February 1835, T.A., CSO1/1/800 file 17088.

However, he also knew the dangers of lodging an objection. While serving at that settlement he had been punished for complaining to the serving medical officer, rather than the commandant, that he was 'tyrannically and oppressively treated'.[87] Rather than take their chance with the bench, the Company servants determined to affect a release from tyranny through other means.

Some thought appears to have gone into the plan to take the *Edward*. Hugh Holland was to be the 'Captain of the land forces', while at least one of those involved, John Knowland, had experience at sea. A boatman by calling, Knowland, claimed to have seen a vessel taken by force before when he was in the 'Patriot Service'—suggesting he had served in the United States navy. The conspirators also recruited Harewood, a carpenter, in case they needed to repair the schooner while at sea.[88] In the event, however, Holland who was serving a life sentence for highway robbery, turned King's evidence—dobbing in his fellow conspirators. Four of the latter were sent to Port Arthur, while the remainder were scattered amongst various chain gangs.[89] As a reward for revealing the plot which he had played a central role in hatching, Hugh Holland was removed to Oatlands with instructions that he was to be 'well looked after'.[90] Just as on board the transport vessels that conveyed prisoners into Antipodean exile, the rewards for turning in conspirators considerably added to the dangers associated with self-liberational schemes.

It is precisely this that makes the record of successful piratical seizures so impressive. As Ian Duffield and Graeme Broxam have shown, in the period from 1790 to 1859 convicts combined to take boats and ships of all different types and sizes on at least 211 occasions. Here success is judged as securing control over a vessel for a sufficient period of time to take command, although on many occasions this did not result in a permanent escape.[91] Not only were these relatively common events, but

[87] Hugh Holland, per *Medina*, Police No. 666, Con 31-1-19.

[88] Statement of Hugh Holland, 2 April 1835, T.A., CSO1/1/800 file 17088.

[89] Malcom Laing Smith, 2 April 1835, T.A., CSO1/1/800 file 17088.

[90] John Montagu, 12 April 1835, Tasmani T.A., CSO1/1/800 file 17088.

[91] Duffield, I. (2013) Cutting Out and Taking Liberties, Australia's Convict Pirates, 1790–1829, *International Review of Social History*, 54, 197–227; Nicholson, I. (1983) *Shipping Arrivals and Departures, Tasmania 1803–1833, Vol. I*, Roebuck, Canberra; Nicholson, I. (1985) *Shipping Arrivals and Departures, Tasmania 1834–42, Vol. II*, Roebuck, Canberra; Broxam, G. (1997) *Shipping Arrivals and Departures, Tasmania*

as Duffield argues, each was a revolutionary act. By definition any attempt to take a vessel was dependent on collective organisation and liberational in that the unfree became masters of their own destiny.[92]

The point can be illustrated through the reported actions of the convicts who successfully took command of vessels. The 40 prisoners who seized the *Wellington* bound for Norfolk Island in 1826 selected one of their number, an ex-army officer named John Walton, to command the captured brig. They also elected a 'council of seven' to judge and punish misdemeanours and ensure the equitable distribution of provisions and other supplies. This was an unmistakable revolutionary moment. As Erin Ehde notes, it was also a form of practice that mirrored the governance of pirate vessels where a captain was provided with the authority to issue orders in battle, but was otherwise subject to democratic control of the crew.[93] As Paula Byrne notes of bushrangers 'There was a consciousness of being engaged in an activity which had a past' and one which they naturally hoped would deliver a future, albeit one that they would probably have to sacrifice their lives to secure.[94]

The *Wellington* might be aptly described as engine of the state. While important for transporting goods and personnel between colonial settlements, it doubled as a prison—a secure environment for transferring convicts to the remote Norfolk Island penal station.[95] Its seizure marked a symbolic moment, a reversal of power not lost on those who took part in such events. When the *Cyprus* brig was taken *en route* to Macquarie Harbour, Leslie Fergusson—a servant from Colerain in Ireland—put on Lieutenant Carew's regimental uniform and sword. He then strutted on the deck in view of the commander of the deposed military detachment while the convicts shouted 'the ship's our own'. When Carew tried to impress upon the rebels the dangers of continuing in their bold enterprise, they replied 'we have our liberty, and we shall die to a man before we

1843–1850, Vol. III, Navarine, Hobart; Broxam, G. and Nash, M. (1997) *Tasmanian Shipwrecks, Vol. 1 1797–1900*, Navarine, Hobart.

92 Duffield, Cutting Out and Taking Liberties, 198.

93 Ihde, E. (2008), Pirates of the Pacific: The Convict Seizure of the "Wellington", *The Great Circle*, 30, 17; Rediker, M. (1987) *Between the Devil and the Deep Blue Sea: Merchant Seaman, Pirates and the Anglo-American Maritime World 1700–1750*, Cambridge University Press, Cambridge, 261–264.

94 Byrne, *Criminal Law and Colonial Subject*, 139.

95 Ihde, 'Pirates of the Pacific', 6.

give her up'. To reinforce the point, Matthew Pennell levelled a primed, but otherwise unloaded musket, pulling the trigger to burn powder in the deposed lieutenant's face.[96] When the *Wellington* was seized the convicts also donned the uniforms of the vanquished military detachment, emphasising the reversal of roles and the arrival of a new system of governance.

Notions that escape, especially when it involved the seizing of a vessel, was not an act of resistance would appear strange to a historian of slavery. As Marcus Rediker emphatically puts it, the seizure of the *Amistad* by its enslaved cargo was not only a rebellion, but a particularly important moment of collective self-liberation.[97] The confused way in which escape by convicts and slaves has been viewed is aptly illustrated by reactions to the lives of those who experienced both institutions. Thomas Day, a former slave from Spanish Town, Jamaica affected a successful escape from the plantation world of his youth and made a subsequent daring, but ultimately unsuccessful attempt, to slip the shackles imposed upon him by a sentence to seven years transportation. He was one of the five members of the pilot's boat crew at Macquarie Harbour who seized a whale boat in 1828 and managed to temporarily escape by sea. While the missionary William Schofield approved Day's self-liberation from the 'degradation' of slavery he saw his second attempt to escape the degradation of penal servitude as merely a crime.[98]

Yet, both slavery and convict servitude were legally defined states. Thomas Day broke laws on the two occasions he slipped his metaphorical shackles. If one was a crime, then so was the other. That the second attempt at self-liberation should be viewed differently serves as an illustration of the power of convictism. Any action by a convicted criminal could be used to reinforce their 'hardened' state. An account of the taking of the *Cyprus* circulated in verse provides an alternative reading. In the eyes of the penal colony's lower orders, the event was an occasion to be celebrated:

[96] *Colonial Times*, 4 September 1829; Proceedings of a Garrison Court of Enquiry, 5 September 1829, T.A., CSO1/415/9352 and Hirst, W. (1999) *Great Escapes by Convicts in Colonial Australia*, Kangaroo Press, East Roseville, 65–86.

[97] Rediker, M. (2013) *The Amistad Rebellion: An Atlantic Odyssey of Slavery and Freedom*, Penguin, New York.

[98] Duffield, I. (1999) Daylight on Convict Lived Experience: The History of a Pious Negro Servant, *Tasmanian Historical Studies*, 6(2), 29–62.

Come all you sons of Freedom, a chorus join with me,
I'll sing a song of heroes and glorious liberty.

This has a somewhat different ring to Schofield's take on convict piratical seizures. While two of those who took the *Cyprus* were the last men to be hung in Britain for piracy, the convict version of events turns the law on its head:

By tyranny we've been oppressed, by your colonial laws
But we will bid adieu to slavery, or die in freedom's cause.

As Duffield puts it, the ballad of the *Brig Cyprus* extols 'piracy as anti-tyranny and pro an egalitarian and liberational order'.[99] The song ends on a particularly triumphant note.

Then sound your golden trumpets boys, play on your tuneful notes,
The Cyprus Brig is sailing, how proudly now she floats.
May fortune help th' Noble lads, and keep them ever free
From Gags, and Cats, and Chains, and Traps, and Cruel Tyranny.

Death or Liberty

On 2 June 1826 Thomas Scott was asleep in his house at Port Macquarie when he was attacked by convicts armed with cutlasses. As well as raiding the premises and putting Scott in 'bodily fear', his assailants told him that they were going to murder two of the penal station's overseers before joining others in arms against the establishment. On the same night another overseer was robbed in what had all the hallmarks of a coordinated operation. When Scott's assailants departed, they shouted the same cry that had been heard at Castle Hill in 1804—'Death or Liberty'.[100] In all 23 convicts joined this outbreak which succeeded in overpowering a soldier and district constable and seizing their muskets and ammunition. The revolt was only suppressed after the leader of the rebels, 'Captain Brown', and an Irishman named Michael Clancy had been shot and killed. Many of those who participated had a long history of opposing authority. The convict 'Black' John Goff had already received 3000 lashes and had

[99] Duffield, 'Cutting Out and Taking Liberties', 199.

[100] Byrne, *Criminal Law and Colonial Subject*, 129.

lost all his teeth when he caught a musket ball in the face which also shot away most of his lower jaw. Goff had been sent to Port Macquarie after successfully escaping from Macquarie Harbour where he had also previously led an armed breakout which ended when the absconders were overwhelmed by a party of soldiers on the remote west coast of Van Diemen's Land.[101]

The initial target of the Port Macquarie insurrection, Thomas Scott, had been directed to the settlement in order to oversee the production of sugar. As tobacco was also grown in this remote penal station, this appears to have been part of a concerted plan to use secondary convicted labour to drive the creation of a plantation economy. Although a Glaswegian by birth, Scott had studied cane cultivation and plantation management in Antigua. As Ian Duffield argues, however, the true pioneer of sugar cultivation at Port Macquarie was more likely to have been the Antiguan convict John Williams. Along with Goff, Williams was one of a number of black convicts sent to this Antipodean penal proto-plantation. In the end the experiment failed when frost killed off the cane crop. Unlike Queensland, northern New South Wales did not have a climate that would support sugar cultivation.[102] The project, however, recalled Commissioner Bigge's recommendation to Earl Bathurst: 'After much reflection on the mode of employing convicts, I am disposed to believe the labours of a sugar estate, excepting always the manufacture of rum and spirit, offer the best means of constant and profitable employment'.[103]

The men who challenged Scott did so in the expectation that they might die.[104] These were not trivial or unconsidered actions. The cry 'liberty or death' was no threat—it was statement of fact—a declaration that a life of servitude was worth staking for liberty. As those who ran in arms in company with John Donohue described themselves, they were 'a box of dead meat already'.[105] In part, this was because for some death was a form of escape. The risks associated with insurrection were too great

[101] McLachlan, I. (1988) *Place of Banishment: Port Macquarie 1818*–1832, Hale & Iremonger, Sydney, 120–121.

[102] Duffield, I. (1987) The Life and Death of "Black" John Goff: Aspects of the Black Contribution to Resistance Patterns During the Transportation Era in Eastern Australia, *Journal of Australian Politics and History*, 33(1), 30–34.

[103] McLachlan, *Place of Banishment*, 151.

[104] Ihde, E. Pirates of the Pacific, 4.

[105] Byrne, *Criminal Law and Colonial Subject*, 138.

for most, however. As the *Hobart Town Gazette* reported in December 1825, when three bushrangers stopped on the Bagdad road to talk to a construction gang 'they called on the men … and asked them one by one to join them, but all unanimously refused'.[106]

This does not mean that convict sympathies did not lie with those that took up arms, or in other ways put their life on the line in order to protest about the inequity of labour exploitation. There are many indications that the factors that motivated those who took up arms or seized vessels were similar to those that triggered other forms of protest. In April 1830, five months before the Bathurst revolt, the Sydney *Monitor* reproduced a statement by Thomas Matthews discovered in his cell after his execution for murdering another member of his gang at Moreton Bay. This killing appears to have been undertaken as part of a suicide pact. As the *Australian* reported: 'it would not at all surprise us, had the massacre been executed at the murdered man's individual request!'.[107] Such events were not uncommon in penal stations—a stark reminder of the brutality of such places.[108]

The note Matthews left was a literate and documented account of the ill-treatment of convicts, including unreported murders alleged to have been committed by overseers, and the use of arbitrary and inconsistent punishment he had witnessed at Moreton Bay. Matthews claimed that he had seen convicts who were so incapacitated from receiving the first half of their allotted judicial beating that they had to be carried to the triangle in a wheelbarrow in order for the flagellator to complete the task. On another occasion he alleged that the commandant ordered all the invalids in the hospital to be flogged, although some of them were on crutches.[109] As we have seen, disciplinary actions taken against sick convicts were common triggers for riots in female houses of correction.

Like strikes and other forms of convict action, riots, mutinies, revolts, bushranging and piratical seizures shared a common set of casual factors. This included claims of ill-treatment, especially the punishment of the sick, and the refusal to listen to convict complaints brought before the bench and other legally constituted figures of authority. Attempts

[106] *Hobart Town Gazette,* 31 December 1825.

[107] *Australian*, 21 April 1829.

[108] Maxwell-Stewart, *Closing Hell's Gates*, 203–220.

[109] *Monitor*, 24 April 1830.

to extract labour from convicts on traditional holidays and outside of government working hours was another issue that could result in wider repercussions. It is no accident that the temporary convict republic installed upon the brig *Wellington* celebrated Christmas with particular gusto. The mutineers slaughtered four geese and three sheep as well as consuming 'moderate' quantities of gin and brandy.[110] Such feasting underscored the importance unfree workers placed on restricting the hours of work.

There was also much overlap between different forms of action that involved the collective use of violence. Some bushranging outbreaks commenced with the piratical seizure of vessels, especially in penal stations. The escape by Matthew Brady and 12 other convicts from Macquarie Harbour in 1824 in a whale boat is a case in point. This sparked a bushranging outbreak that lasted two years and was only suppressed through the use of around 400 troops and 150 special constables.[111] On other occasions bushrangers seized boats as part of raids or in a final attempt to secure freedom. After the failed 1826 uprising on Norfolk Island, for example, 50 of the 115 convicts on the island escaped by boat. It was later revealed that this uprising and the fall-back plan of escape by boat had been three months in planning. Those who survived this event went on to participate in further insurrectionary moments. Patrick Clynch, for example, subsequently absconded and attempted to kill the new commandant, Captain Allman. A few days later he himself was killed by a patrol of soldiers.[112] The convict term for men like Lynch was an 'out and outer'. These were individuals prepared to stake their lives in an attempt to bring the colonial estate to account.[113] When put on trial for leading the first Norfolk Island uprising John Goff 'detailed to the court a long complaint' of the hardships he had undergone and his 'love of liberty' and the 'degree of violence' he thought 'justified in using to obtain it'.[114] While the revolt at Castle Hill may have posed

[110] Ihde, 'Pirates of the Pacific', 9.

[111] Maxwell-Stewart, Hamish (1991) The Bushrangers and the Convict System, PhD thesis, University of Edinburgh, 227.

[112] Duffield, 'Life and Times', 34.

[113] Lempriere, *The Penal Settlements*, 51.

[114] Duffield, I. (1987) The Life and Death of "Black" John Goff: Aspects of the Black Contribution to Resistance Patterns During the Transportation Era in Eastern Australia, *Journal of Australian Politics and History*, 33(1), 30.

the greatest individual threat to the colonial establishment, it was by no means the last time that convicts combined, risking all to resist the state.

For all of that, outright armed resistance to the colonial state was relatively rare. While convicts collectively downed tools, slowed the pace of work, or ran away on thousands of occasions, they took up arms against the state sporadically. In part this can be put down to the nature of convict society. The use of an elaborate system of rewards and associated surveillance regimes rendered any form of conspiracy dangerous. While some have argued that the willingness of convicts to betray the plans of other transported workers provides evidence of their generally depraved nature, such betrayals were not unique to convict society.[115] Informers revealed the details of many planned slave rebellions before they could be put into action.[116] In fact, despite the historical importance they have assumed, revolts by unfree workers were rare events. To put the Australian record of armed insurrection into comparative perspective, slaves in Virginia took up arms on fewer occasions than convicts. Although it had a much larger bond population, and a longer history of unfree labour, Virginia experienced only one full rebellion (Nat Turner's) and one major plot (Gabriel Prosser's). As Kolchin has written of the North America, 'of the handful of "major" slave rebellions, none involved more than a few hundred slaves or encompassed more than a local geographical area.'[117] As with other unfree societies, the dangers associated with tackling the state head on largely explain why convict protestors turned to other forms of action.

[115] Hirst, *Freedom on the Fatal Shore*, 126–128.

[116] Craton, *Testing the Chains*, 13.

[117] Kolchin, P. (1978) The Process of Confrontation: Patterns of Resistance to Bondage in Nineteenth-Century Russia and the United States, *Journal of Social History*, 11, 457.

CHAPTER 11

Nothing to Lose but Your Chains

Those transported to Eastern Australia's penal colonies experienced a peculiar form of incarceration. Rather than being hemmed in by the forbidding walls of a penitentiary, they were legally bound to the workplace. The instruments that held them captive were not entirely novel. They had their antecedents in the plantation world of the Atlantic and while there were technical differences between convict transportation and other forms of unfreedom, the parallels were ever present.[1] For many, penal transportation was slavery in the sense that it was a legally constituted form of bondage—albeit one that was limited by the length of a sentence. That sentence was rendered into property through an indent, a legal document of ownership. This system of judicial indenture was never fully commodified as it had been in the seventeenth and eighteenth century Atlantic. The rights to convict labour conferred via an indent were loaned out by the colonial state, however, a practice that created a peculiar form of carceral archipelago. Early colonial Australia was therefore a gaol that straddled both the public and private sector. This was a genuine innovation that created a complex geography of confinement.

[1] Lydon, *Anti-Slavery and Australia*, 71 and 92; Ford, L. and Roberts, D.A. (2021) The Convict Peace: The Imperial Context of the 1833 Convict Revolt at Castle Forbes, *Journal of Commonwealth and Imperial History*, 49, 1, 2.

H. Maxwell-Stewart and M. Quinlan, *Unfree Workers*,
Palgrave Studies in Economic History,
https://doi.org/10.1007/978-981-16-7558-4_11

Rather than being contained within the bounds of a penitentiary, the form of incarceration exercised in Australia was defused through the entire colonial social body. Convicts were confined in places as diverse as penal stations, female factories, road construction sites, quarries and mines, breweries, tailoring establishments, pastoral stations, farms and haberdashery shops. An elaborate system of control and exchange was imposed across this landscape of production to manage labour extraction and its associated system of rewards and punishment.[2] Rather than a set of discreet sites, each place of labour was linked by the constant circulation of prisoners. Confinement was configured so as not to restrict such geographical mobility. Paper played a crucial part in that process. Records indexed via ship of arrival and police number were used to track the physical and social movement of prisoners across both sites and states of incarceration. Charge and benchbooks, passes, identification documents and conduct records were used to distinguish and manage ticket-of-leave bearers, passholders and assignees, who were in turn marked out from those undergoing probation or punishment labour.[3] This was a form of panoptic power that used an archival central observation tower to extend the reach of the state. Any attempt to test the bounds of these bureaucratic controls could lead to physical repercussions that would in turn generate further documentation. As Alan Atkinson poetically put it: 'Print in black and white had its reverberations in flesh and blood'.[4]

This process of labour extraction was grounded in the assumption that a judicially imposed sanction, a sentence to transportation, could be commodified. As Rusche and Kirchheimer argue: 'Every system of production tends to discover punishments which correspond to its productive relationships'.[5] When labour markets are flooded, prisons tend to become more austere and restrictive environments cut off from the external world. Conversely, when labour is scarce, carceral institutions develop more fluid boundaries. Such elasticity enables access to cheap and expendable convicted labour, as well as providing opportunities to

[2] Tuffin, et al., 'Landscapes of Production', 50–76.

[3] Tuffin, R., Maxwell-Stewart, H. and Quinlan, M. (2020) Reintegrating Historical Records Through Digital Data Linking: Convicts Prosecuted for Collective Action in Van Diemen's Land, *Journal of Australian Colonial History*, 22(2), 55–60.

[4] Atkinson, *The Europeans*, Vol. 1, 30.

[5] Rusche, G. and Kirchheimer, O. (1939) *Punishment and Social Structure*, Columbia University Press, New York, 5.

reduce free wages and impose restrictions on working conditions generally.[6] Transportation was a sophisticated variation of this which removed the convicted from an area of relative labour oversupply to colonial sites of shortage. It was simultaneously an experience that was exclusionary, in that it isolated the prisoner from the world of metropolitan work, and inclusionary in that it rendered their labour exploitable on the other side of the world.[7] In George Arthur's words, the Australian penal colonies were a 'Gaol to the Empire'.[8]

That system of exploitation was hammered out over time and was in a constant state of flux. Crucially, the bureaucratic controls that came to characterise the deployment of both free and unfree labour in the Australian colonies did not arrive neatly packaged with the First Fleet. Indeed, in the early years of the colony convicts and emancipists were able to achieve a number of notable victories as both free and convict labour remained commodities that were in demand. The concessions wrought included: payment of wages to the unfree; limits on the work obligations that could be imposed on serving convicts; the right to work unfettered by the controls imposed by a sentence outside of government hours; and freedom dues in the form of land grants and other financial supports and incentives for emancipists. The increase in the number of those transported that accompanied the post-Napoleonic War demobilisation of the armed forces coincided with a concerted attempt to wind these concessions back. Starting with the completion of Hyde Park Barracks, the colonial state used public control over a significant component of Australia's convict labour force to regulate conditions of service in the private sector. This was a system of partial confinement that attempted to stem convict access to cash in hand (as opposed to cash in state-administered bank accounts), increase the hours of labour, and restrict freedom of movement during whatever 'leisure time' was left. It was also a species of incarceration designed to impose fetters on metropolitan and colonial free workers. The spectre of being spirited into a form of indenture on the far side of the world was designed to temper agitation at

[6] Melossi, D. (2003) A New Edition of "Punishment and Social Structure" Thirty-Five Years Later: A Timely Event, *Social Justice*, 30(1), 250.

[7] Braithwaite, 'Crime in a Convict Republic', 45–46.

[8] As cited in Cary, H. (2019) *Empire of Hell: Religion and the Campaign to End Convict Transportation in the British Empire, 1788–1875*, Cambridge University Press, Cambridge, 55.

home—while the deployment of cheap convict labour undercut free wage rates in the colonies.[9]

A magisterial code largely borrowed from the British Caribbean was used to drive this system of labour exploitation. This proscribed attempts by prisoners to challenge the power invested in the managers of convict labour. This legislation indirectly impacted upon free workers too as it informed colonial Master and Servant Acts that were framed against the benchmark of the controls put in place to manage the unfree.[10] The administration of these labour laws was placed in the hands of the private sector masters of convict labour who served as magistrates. A system of colonial labour exploitation could be disguised as a means of checking lower order excess. Managers argued that they were unpaid gaolers—thereby masking the benefits that accrued from the employment of the unfree. This mirrored a common defence of slavery. Both prisoner and slave were unruly children who could be rescued from barbarism through the application of appropriate paternal management. The manufacture of compliant docile workers could be disguised as an exercise in tutelage. In the words of Richard Ely: 'Thus "minded" shamed as well as hurt by punishment, the convict would be led step by step, to develop the "inward regulator", which conforms conduct of the laws of God and man'.[11] That 'inward regulator' included acceptance of workplace laws designed to lock a social ordering in place based on the principles of deference and obligation. Those who spoke out, remained sullen, downed tools or ran away could expect to be severely punished.

Any attempt to quantify resistance to this colonial carceral archipelago must necessarily be provisional and qualified. For one, there are critical limits to the evidence that we have at our disposal. The archive is a public space in which private victories are rarely inscribed. We suspect that convict negotiations with masters and other managers often succeeded in wringing concessions that went undocumented. The vast bulk of the evidence upon which this book is based has been extracted from absconding notices, conduct records and benchbooks. These are records of indiscretions and proscribed acts defined by those in power. To be sure,

[9] Nicholas, The Convict Labour Market, 111–126.

[10] Ford and Roberts, The Convict Peace, 2–5.

[11] Ely, R. (2004) Arthur, Sir George, in *Blackwell Dictionary of Evangelical Biography*, Vol. 1, 30.

this archive contains convict 'micro-narratives' that serve to query each offence's 'fundamental social location' as a misdemeanour or crime.[12] Each of these needs to be excavated, although we suspect that in doing so we have under-counted, rather than over-estimated, the extent to which convicts fought back. As Tamsin O'Connor memorably put it:

> … we continue to berate the convicts for their apparent political nullity. We scrutinise their actions with our protest check list — more sceptical than any magistrate. The convicts are expected to prove their motives, hoist a figurative banner stating loud and clear, 'I am resisting now'.[13]

While we have used the reported acts of individual protestors as illustrations, we have limited our estimate of the scale of resistance to collective prosecutions—or, in the case of absconding, incidences where multiple convicts were gazetted for running from the same place on the same day. While there is no iron-fast rule that a joint endeavour is more likely to have been seen as a political challenge by those who participated in such combinations, collective challengers are more likely to have been interpreted as threats by the colonial social order. We are conscious this conservative approach, combined with the gaps in the available archival record outlined in chapter two, means that we have considerably underestimated the scale of protest.

To employ a term coined by Peter Linebaugh, any attempt to oppose a state of incarceration constitutes an act of excarceration.[14] Even our conservative account suggests that in convict Australia acts of excarceration were legion. The attempt to harness the labour of thieves for public and private profit was systematically resisted. Transported prisoners combined in defence of a moral economy of unfreedom. In particular they contested attempts to: translate a sentence into a seven-day working week; restrict movement after the end of the working day; reduce the quality of the ration provided; and punish the sick. These acts were not isolated frustrations expressed through explosions of anger. If convict protestors

[12] Duffield, I. (2001) "State This Offence": High-Density Convict Micro Narratives, in Frost, L. and Maxwell-Stewart, H. eds. *Chain Letters Narrating Convict Lives*, Melbourne University Press, Melbourne, 135.

[13] O'Connor, T. (1999) Buckley's Chance: Freedom and Hope in the Penal Settlements of Newcastle and Moreton Bay, *Tasmanian Historical Studies*, 6(2), 118.

[14] Linebaugh, *The London Hanged*, 23–30.

failed at first to obtain satisfaction through one form of agitation, they turned to another. Common cause linked all five patterns of convict resistance: the issuing of demands; appeals to authority; withdrawal of labour; compensatory retribution; and outright collective attacks. Just as, much can be learned from an examination of the sequence of events that played out in different sites of labour extraction, a collective reading of these actions is revealing.

Counting the Protesters

In the period from 1788 to 1860 we have counted 10,903 instances of collective action involving at least 43,275 convicts (an average of just under four per action). Note, however, that the practice of selecting ringleaders for punishment will necessarily render any attempt to quantify resistance based on prosecutions an undercount.[15] A breakdown of these by method is listed in Table 11.1 although it should be noted that some actions involved multiple methods.

We have used convict population totals in order to calculate a collective action participation rate—the number of convict protestors for every 1000 convicts in the colony. This is plotted as a black line in Fig. 11.1. For comparative purposes we have also plotted the absolute number of convicts involved in actions each year (shown in grey). In terms of the proportion of convicts involved, the Castle Hill rebellion dominates this chart.[16] Almost nine percent of the convicts in the colony were punished for participating in the failed 1804 uprising. Our evidence suggests that the suppression of this revolt was followed by a marked lull in the rate of protest which lasted until the opening of Hyde Park Barracks on 4 June 1819. Thereafter there was an upturn in both the rate and absolute number of convict protestors which turned into a flood of go-slows, strikes, mass withdrawals of labour following the tabling of the first volume of the Bigge Report in 1822.

[15] As some convicts participated in multiple actions the number of unique protesters will be lower than these totals imply.

[16] Estimates for the number who participated in this event vary. While it is possible that as many as 600 may have been involved we have only counted the 233 known to have taken up arms. This is consistent with the measure that we have used subsequently which is based on the number of absconders gazetted or convicts prosecuted and not on larger claims made, for example, in newspaper reports.

Table 11.1 Collective protests by methods used in New South Wales and Van Diemen's Land 1788–1860

Main category	*Sub-category*	*No. Incidents*
Issue of demands	Demands	53
	Threats	83
Appeal to authority	Petitioning	8
	Court action	70
Withdrawal of labour/cooperation	Go-slows	793
	Insolence	342
	Misconduct and Bans	493
	Strikes	1756
	Collective absconding	6470
Compensatory retribution	Sabotage	116
	Theft	146
	Assault on individuals	123
Attack	Riot	38
	Bushranging[a]	117
	Piracy	211
Action but type unknown		84
Total		10,903

[a]This is an underestimate. In the years to 1846 at least 64 groups of convicts were charged with being illegally at large with firearms in Van Diemen's Land. We have added 53 'runaway gangs' identified as bushrangers by Paula Byrne in her study of New South Wales 1810–30, Byrne, *Criminal Law and Colonial Subject*, 133

Convict Australia could never have become an Antipodean Barbados. The frost that destroyed the sugar crop at Port Macquarie put pay to that. Nevertheless, the Bigge report was designed to tilt the penal colonies in the direction of the Caribbean. Lacking the appropriate climate to cultivate planation crops, fine wool production developed as the main export commodity. Pastoralism required the antithesis of ganged labour management. As the experience of the Cape Colony demonstrates, unfree labour could be successfully deployed in mixed agricultural production.[17] In general, however, non-ganged workers have considerably more bargaining power than ganged. The post-Bigge reorganisation of labour in Australia attempted to limit bargaining opportunities for assigned servants and ticket-of-leave convicts, through the creation of series of de facto public

[17] Worden, N. (1985) *Slavery in Dutch South Africa*, Cambridge University Press, Cambridge, 19–40.

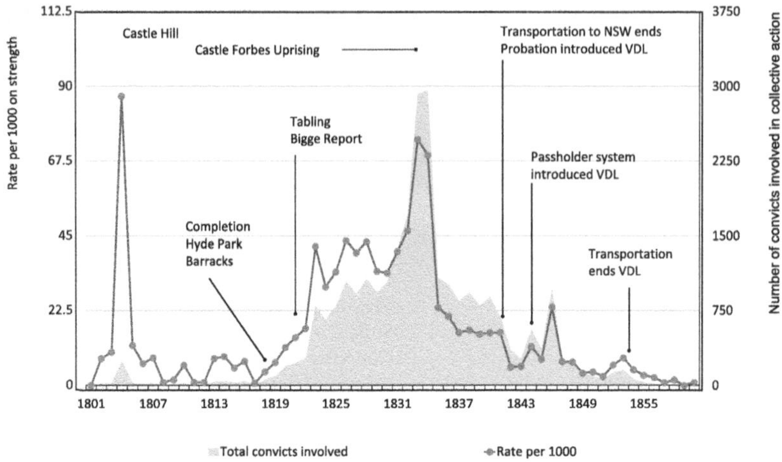

Fig. 11.1 Collective actions in New South Wales and Van Diemen's Land, 1801–1860 (*Sources* Convict population totals, Butlin, N.G., Ginswick, J. and Statham, P. [1987], 'The Economy Before 1850' in Wray Vamplew [ed.], *Australians: Historical Statistics*, Cambridge University Press, Cambridge: 104; Sturma, Michael [1983], *Vice in a Vicious Society: Crime and Convicts in Mid-Nineteenth Century New South Wales*, University of Queensland Press, St Lucia: 188; *Statistical Returns of Van Diemen's Land*: Hobart Town, 1838, 1841–44 and 1853; *Statistics of Tasmania 1804–1854* [Hobart, 1856]—[1804–1823]: 9–11—[1824–38] Enclosure No. 17. [1838–41]: 10, [1841–44]: 9; *Statistics of Tasmania for the Year* 1855–60. *Note* Data for Van Diemen's Land subsumed within New South Wales total prior to 1816)

sector plantations.[18] Road gangs, factories, chain gangs and penal stations were designed to generate the terror required to wring compliance from convict shepherds and other unfree agricultural and urban workers not engaged in repetitive labour under the constant eye of an overseer. These measures failed to quell convict resistance despite the levels of punishment meted out. By our count 4152 convicts were flogged for participating in collective actions receiving a total of 153,431 strokes—an average of

[18] Evans, R. and Thorpe, Bill (1996) Freedom and Unfreedom at Moreton Bay: The Structures and Relations of Secondary Punishment, in Dyster, B. ed. *Beyond Convict Workers*, University of New South Wales, Sydney, 64–82.

37 per beating. Many more convict protestors were sentenced to solitary confinement or hard labour and at least 280 were executed.

While the insurrection in 1804 marked the greatest political challenge faced by the colony, many more convicts downed tools in subsequent years than took up arms at Castle Hill.[19] In 1833, the year of the Castle Forbes revolt, nearly 4000 convicts participated in protest actions across New South Wales and Van Diemen's Land. The attack on Mudie's property was not an isolated event. Thereafter, the rate of action peaked before falling below 1820s levels. It fell again following the abolition of transportation to New South Wales and the introduction of probation for men in Van Diemen's Land, before temporarily rising in 1844—the year the passholder wages system was overhauled and probation extended to female convicts. After the arrival of the last convict vessel in Van Diemen's Land the rate of collective action by serving convicts tailed away.

The scale at which convicts collectivised in an attempt to ameliorate their conditions of service is revealed when plotted against later participation in non-union and union organised protests by free workers. As Fig. 11.2 details, the years from 1822–1833 marked Australia's first, and arguably one of its biggest, industrial relations crises. Convicts organised in order to change the conditions under which they served at levels that were not matched by free workers in Australia until the titanic maritime and pastoral strikes of the early 1890s. The intense convict resistance of the 1820s and 1830s—a decadal crisis in labour relations—reflects the one advantage that convict protestors had over their free counterparts. When they took action, it was in the knowledge that they would continue to be fed—the state in effect provided them with strike pay. Nevertheless, those that participated in such organised resistance knew that in all-likelihood their daily calorie intake would be reduced as punishment.

The number of individual protests organised by convicts dwarfed formal and informal actions initiated by free workers in Australia in the years to 1900 (see Fig. 11.3). Non-union organised protests involved fewer workers on average. This was true of both convict actions and informal free protests. Over the course of the nineteenth century there was a marked increase in the mean number of workers engaged in disputes reflecting the rise of formal unionism and the development of better coordination across workplaces, regions and industries. By contrast convict

[19] Hirst, *Freedom on the Fatal Shore*, 124.

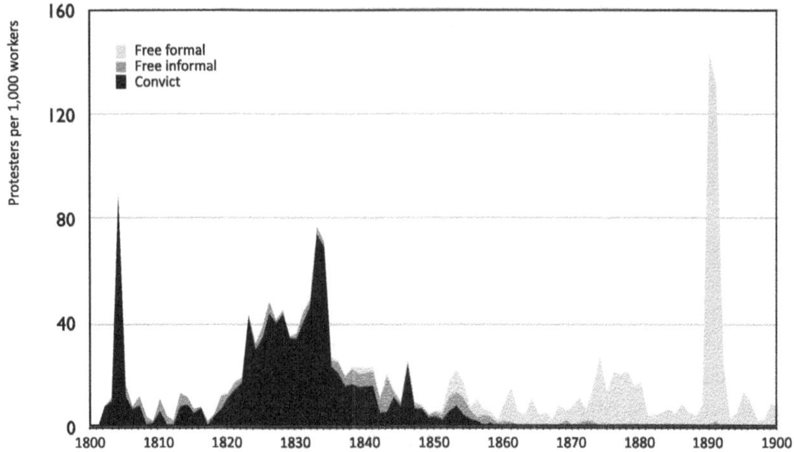

Fig. 11.2 Rates of convict participation in collective action (per 1000 under sentence) and rates of free worker participation in informal and formal collective action (per 1000 in the free workforce)

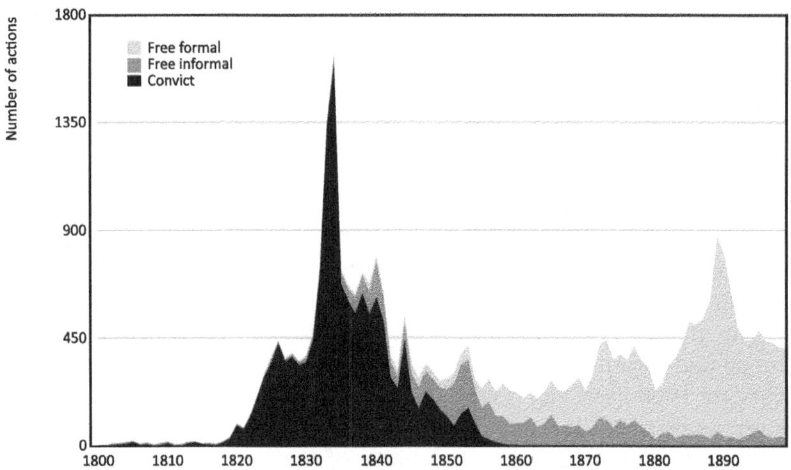

Fig. 11.3 Number of protest actions per year Australia 1800–1900

protests were small affairs and were usually short in duration. They were, however, frequent events. As we have shown, one form of action often followed another.[20] With the exception of absconding, convicts did not attempt to fight a war of attrition by downing tools for a protracted period of time. Instead, they punctuated their negotiations with managers with repeated blows—slowing production, withdrawing labour, expropriating victuals, and attacking both property and those tasked with managing them. While each individual collective assault on authority was small, stacked one on top of the other, they amounted to an impressive and sustained campaign of resistance.

Organising the Convicted

In the past it has been assumed that the mass of convicts lacked the political leadership to fight back. With the exception of a few United Irishmen, it has long been accepted that those transported for political and industrial offences stayed aloof from 'their fellow convicts whose crimes and characters they found as repellent as other respectable people'.[21] Yet, our research found transported dissenters who subsequently resisted their convict managers. Several examples illustrate this.

In 1832 two years before the conviction of the Tolpuddle martyrs, ten leading activists in the United Colliers of Northumberland and Durham Association were charged with robbing a house. The case and subsequent harassment of the families of the accused suggests the charges were aimed at suppressing dissent. In 1830 the Association had successfully struck for a reduction of daily working hours (from 18 to 12). This sparked a hostile response from employers, aided by armed police and the local magistracy. Only two of the accused were linked by witnesses to the assault and stealing of meat and a pistol. Three of the ten fled and the remaining seven—John Smith, John Stewart, Thomas Armstrong, David Johnson, John Barker, Bartholomew Stephenson, and Isaac Ecclestone—were transported on the *Isabella* to New South Wales. In Australia they were assigned to the Australian Agricultural Company coal mine in the Hunter Valley. Unlike the Tolpuddle Martyrs transported for taking

[20] For a broader discussion see Quinlan, M. (2020) *Contesting Inequality and Worker Mobilisation: Australia 1851–1880*, Routledge, New York.

[21] Hirst, *Freedom on the Fatal Shore*, 124.

'unlawful oaths' two years later, none ever returned.[22] Although their prosecution was linked to an industrial struggle they were charged with a property offence and were not included amongst the transported industrial protesters identified by George Rudé.[23] We suspect this applies to a significant number of other protestors that have hitherto gone unenumerated. In 1836, while employed by the Australian Agricultural Company, the Jarrow Seven participated in a go-slow protest after monetary incentives were removed in favour of orders redeemable for goods in local shops.[24]

James Simms, who participated in a series of collective protests while assigned to David Lord, had been transported for participating in the Bristol Riots.[25] This event, triggered by House of Lords rejection of the 1831 Reform Bill, was described as the worst public disturbance since the 1780 Gordon Riots. In three days the rioters laid waste to a large part of the centre of Bristol, destroying the Mansion House, Excise Office and Customs House in Queen's Square and the toll houses along the banks of the river. They also set fire to the Bridewell and the city's two gaols as well as the bishop's palace.[26] Sims and his co-accused Thomas Evans Bendall were seen throwing books and furniture into the flames during the destruction of the palace. Witnesses confirmed that Bendall, who had tied a piece of white tape round his arm, 'had been previously engaged in going about for signatures for a Reform petition' equipped with a constable's staff and declaring that 'he belonged to the Union'.[27] Like Sims, he continued to agitate in the colony. On 28 August 1833 he was tried while in a road gang for 'Mutinously assembling with others and declaring his Resolution to abstain from Labor.'[28]

22 *Newcastle Morning Herald*, 2 February 1894.

23 Rudé, G. (1978) *Protest and Punishment: The Story of the Social and Political Protesters Transported to Australia, 1788–1868*, Oxford University Press, Melbourne, 9–10.

24 Turner, J. (1982) *Coal Mining in Newcastle 1801–1900*, Newcastle regional Public Library, Newcastle, 40, 142.

25 James Simms, per *Katherine Stewart Forbes*, Police No. 1516, T.A., Con 31-1-39.

26 Thomas, Susan (1974) *The Bristol Riots*, University of Bristol, Bristol.

27 *North Devon Journal*, 12 January 1832.

28 Thomas Evans Bendall, per *Katherine Stewart Forbes*, Police Number 1695, Con 31-1-4.

Cotton spinners Henry McConnell and John Sharp were transported from Glasgow for firing shots at factory owners in order to intimate them after a failed strike.[29] Both participated in armed collective actions in Australia. McConnell was executed for the part he played in the bushranging revolt led by Matthew Brady, while John Sharp was sentenced to receive 100 lashes and serve six months in irons after he combined with Black John Goff and four other convicts to rob two soldiers of their muskets. The two firearms were seized during a daring attempt to escape from Macquarie Harbour penal settlement in 1823. The absconders managed to make it to the Pieman River heads before they were apprehended after a firefight with a party of soldiers.[30]

Several Swing rioters also participated in collective convict protests. David Heath, a machine breaker transported on the *Eliza*, combined with Charles Pizzie and three other convicts to confront their master, Thomas Parker, on his South Esk property. All five were charged with gross insubordination. Pizzie, who had originally been sentenced to death by a special commission in Salisbury for shouting 'We'll have blood or money' during the Wiltshire riots was award 50 lashes, while Heath's sentence to transportation was extended by three years.[31] Alfred Toogood who was transported on the *Georgina* in 1832 for machine breaking was sent to Notman's Road Party in July 1833 for striking a constable. There he was punished with 100 lashes when he was charged with insubordination alongside 32 of his gang in July 1831.[32] Another machine breaker, Thomas Grant, was awarded 50 lashes when he absconded from the same gang in company with three other convicts in January 1833. Likewise, women transported for participating in machine breaking also took part in collective action in the colonies.[33] Ann Entwistle was transported in 1827 for destroying shuttles in a Lancashire mill and Mary Hindle, who

[29] Precognition against John O'Donnell (as witness), Hugh Lafferty, Henry McConnell, Malcolm Cameron, Owen Callaghan, 1821, Scottish Records Office, AD14/21/64.

[30] Henry McConnell, per *Lord Hungerford*, Police No. 435, T.A., Con 31-1-6; John Sharp per *Lord Hungerford*, Police No. 404, Con 31-1-38.

[31] David Heath, per *Eliza*, Police No. 1219, T.A., Con 31-1-20 and Charles Pizzie, per Proteus, Police No. 728, Con 31-1-25; *Salisbury and Wiltshire Journal*, 17 February 1831.

[32] Alfred Toogood, per *Georgiana*, Police No. 695, T.A., Con 31-1-43.

[33] Thomas Grant, per *Eliza*, Police No. 739, T.A., Con 31-1-16.

accompanied her to New South Wales, for 'shouting encouragement to the rioters'. Both were active in female factory protests.[34]

On occasion the tactics employed by convict protestors mirrored those used elsewhere. When the women in the Parramatta Factory broke down the gates in a protest over ration levels they expropriated food from nearby shops—an act of reappropriation that bore similarities to British food riots.[35] Other forms of action in the colonies resembled traditional British and Irish protests designed to maintain rights to perks and privileges. Some colonial actions were theatrical events. The donning of uniforms, displays of civility, and the use of mock trials were all traditional protest features. While more could be said about continuities, particularly amongst those transported from Ireland, surely this would risk missing a point. Political leadership was not necessary in order to affect local resistance. Few women, for example, were transported for overtly political crimes, and yet some of the most organised colonial protests occurred in female factories. The barricades assembled to defend the 'moral economy' of unfreedom were manned by thieves. In so doing, those thieves unpacked themselves.

Criminals have traditionally been thought of as apolitical. As Humphry McQueen once put it: 'It is misleading to clothe the convicts in the aura of class struggle since for its first fifty years Australia did not have a class structure, but only a deformed stratification which had itself been vomited up by the maelstrom which was delineating class in Britain'.[36] Such assumptions spring from the language employed by the managers of convicts. As James Mudie argued, convicts were 'lower than the brutes, a disgrace to all animal existence'.[37] It was important to essentialise penal workers as a species of sub-human who lived by crime and crime alone from cradle to site of colonial incarceration. Such miscreants had forfeited their rights. Because they were idle, conniving and vicious, managers were justified in applying force in order to inculcate their charges with appropriate and productive values. They were also justified in meeting sullen,

[34] Smith, *Defiant Voices*, 24; Quinlan, *Origins of Worker Mobilisation*, 100–101.

[35] Kent, D. (1994) Customary Behaviour Transported: A Note on the Parramatta Female Factory Riot of 1827, *Journal of Australian Studies*, 18, 40, 75–79.

[36] McQueen, 'Convicts and Rebels', 24–25.

[37] Mudie, *The Felonry*, 122.

brutish and insolent behaviour with force. The myth of the professional criminal class was pervasive because it was useful.

Yet, as a range of studies have shown, there is overwhelming evidence that the vast majority of those transported to the Australian penal colonies had experience of work. Indeed, many were convicted for stealing from the workplace.[38] If there is something remarkable about the scale of collective action in convict New South Wales and Van Diemen's Land, it is not that it was organised by transported thieves, but that those thieves were drawn from many disparate workplaces and were possessed of the full gamut of British and Irish regional accents. Unfree workers did not just defy the language of convictism in Australia, they reorganised across trades and regional divides to make common purpose.

That common purpose coalesced around a counter ideology. While the likes of George Arthur talked of the penal establishment as a 'moral mechanism', the common parlance of the colonial lower orders sought to throw this on its head.[39] Those who had been lagged to Australia were referred to as 'legitimates' and those who had come free as 'illegitimates'. A man 'who was ready to perform his duty was generally called a bad man' while one refusing to kowtow, good. As Amanda Laugesen argues, prisoners inverted the terms used to 'stigmatise them', redeploying the language of penal management to match 'their own sense of morality or justice'.[40] In 'A Convict's Tour to Hell' penned by Francis MacNamara in 1839, a deceased bushranger is refused access into the infernal regions by a devil who proclaims to 'detest and hate the poor'. In this moral landscape, those condemned to eternal damnation include masters, magistrates, penal station commandants, overseers, constables, flagellators, informers and spies. All of these suffer in the fires of hell alongside 'Cook who discovered New South Wales and he who first invented gaols'.[41] Convicts were used to being preached at. In a colony which,

[38] Oxley, D. (1996) *Convict Maids: The Forced Migration of Women to Australia*, Cambridge University Press, Cambridge, 98–128; Nicholas, S. and Shergold, P.A Labour Aristocracy in Chains, in Nicholas, S. ed. *Convict Workers: Reinterpreting Australia's Past*, Cambridge University Press, Cambridge, 98–110.

[39] Carey, *Empire of Hell*, 75.

[40] Laugesen, 'The Politics of Language', 29–30.

[41] Murray, L. (1997) *A Working Forest*, Duffy and Snellgrove, Sydney, 365–370. See also Brownrigg, Jeff (2016) The Legend of Frank the Poet: Convict Heritage Recovered or Created? *Journal of Australian Colonial History*, 28, 1–22.

for Europeans, was geographically inverted—pulpit words could also be turned on their head. In this upside-down world, it was the thief who was next to Christ and the master whose soul was in jeopardy.[42] There was no need for imported radicalisation in colonial Australia. Those who experienced labour exploitation Antipodean style did not need others to tell them right from wrong since the disjuncture between the actions and words of their penal managers made this abundantly clear.

The Consequences of Protest

Whatever else it achieved the resistance of convicts cut into profits. Time lost through strike action, go-slows and other collective endeavours to reduce output, absenteeism and absconding were costly. As in slave societies, day-to-day resistance gnawed away at the apparatus of unfreedom from within.[43] While on average the cost of rationing and accommodating convict workers amounted to only 59 percent of a free pastoral sector wage, the actions of convicts did much to bridge that gap.[44] As John West observed: 'True, he [the convict] was well fed, while many in England laboured hard, and yet went hungry and poor; but nothing reconciled the prisoner to his bondage: he compared his condition not with the British pauper, but those who though working in the same field, were masters of their own labour'.[45] In particular convicts sought to, either restore a wage, or extract the equivalent from private sector masters. The evidence suggests that this was a battle which they largely won.

The abolition of convict wages formed a cornerstone of the post-Bigge report changes. Not all private sector masters welcomed the move. While Minto landholder William Howe opposed all payments, Robert Lowe adopted a nuanced approach arguing that some assigned workers, notably shepherds, should receive remuneration in consequence of their

[42] Maxwell-Stewart, H. and Duffield, I. (2000) Skin Deep Devotions: Religious Tattoos and Convict Transportation to Australia, in Caplan, J. ed. *Written on the Body: The Tattoo in European and American History*, Princeton University Press, Princeton, 118–135.

[43] McGary, Reistance and Slavery, 35–54.

[44] Panza and Williamson, 'Australian Squatters, Convicts, and Capitalists', 582–583.

[45] West, J. (1852) *The History of Tasmania*, Henry Dowling, Launceston, reprinted Libraries Board of South Australia, Adelaide, 1966, Vol. 2: 231.

responsibilities and capacity to affect their master's prosperity.[46] It is not coincidental that Howe brought his assigned servants before the Campbelltown magistrates' bench on more occasions than Lowe and that a number of these prosecutions were for collective dissent. Other masters like Hannibal Macarthur publicly opposed payments, but conceded to convict demands in private.[47]

In the late 1830s the Molesworth Committee collected evidence of the widespread payment of illicit wages to assigned agricultural workers and mechanics. The Van Diemen's Land farmer Peter Murdoch was particularly forthcoming. He argued that wages were essential in order to extract work from convicts. He paid his skilled dairymen and shepherds according to their commercial value. When Governor Arthur attempted to crack down on the practice in 1833, Murdoch refused to comply, and as a result was threatened with the removal of his assigned servants. When he visited Hobart to plead his case he met a senior public official who assured him that, as 'Colonel Arthur's own servants are paid', we shall hear no more about this matter.[48] The Australian Agricultural Company was also reported to pay its assigned domestic servants £10–15 per year, a practice which the Molesworth Report interpreted as suggesting that payments were widespread in New South Wales.[49] Kirsty Reid has argued some assigned convict women negotiated £12–30 per annum, or close to the wages earned by free labour.[50] Meg Dillon's detailed examination of the Campbell Town Police District in Van Diemen's Land provides further evidence that payments to convicts were frequent, especially for

[46] Ritchie, J. (1971) *The Evidence to the Bigge Report: New South Wales under Governor Macquarie*, Volume 2 written evidence, Heinemann, Melbourne, 44–52.

[47] Ritchie, J. (1971) *The Evidence to the Bigge Report: New South Wales under Governor Macquarie*, Volume 2 written evidence, Heinemann, Melbourne, 70.

[48] For a discussion of this evidence, and its relationship to the wider district where Murdoch farmed, is discussed in some detail see Dillon, 'Convict Labour and Colonial Society', 234–235.

[49] Priestley, A. (1967) The Molesworth Committee and New South Wales, MA thesis, Australian National University, 164, 215.

[50] Reid, K. (2003) Setting Women to Work The Assignment System and Female Convict Labour in Van Diemen's Land, 1820–1839, *Australian Historical Studies*, 34(121), 4–8.

convicts with skills that were in demand.[51] As the Molesworth Report put it:

> As a mechanic can scarcely be compelled by punishment to exert his skill, it is for the interest of the master to conciliate his convict mechanic, in order to induce him to work well; in too many cases this is effected by granting to the skilled convict various indulgences; by paying him wages, by allotting to him task-work, and by permitting him, after the performance of the task, to work on his own account; and, lastly, by conniving at or overlooking disorderly conduct; for the most skillful mechanics are generally the worst behaved and the most drunken.[52]

They were of course the most drunk because they were the most cashed-up. Indeed, in the absence of a black market in convict wages it is difficult to explain the frequent prosecution of convicts for drink-related offences. Like publicans everywhere, it seems unlikely that the colonial purveyors of spirits and beer were in the habit of giving away their merchandise free of charge.

The success of wage bargaining in the private sector had repercussions for convicts in public service. In 1835 the *Cornwall Chronicle* complained that the poor performance of the convict police could largely be attributed to the ways in which their wage, one the few forms of convict payment that was officially sanctioned, contrasted unfavorably with the illicit payments masters provided to their assigned servants.[53] Other public sector convicts worked for local traders and farmers on Saturday afternoons or at other times, not only providing a source of income (and helping to fund some absconding attempts) but boosting local sales of goods.[54] Some even absconded to reclaim wages. Paul Peers left Notman's Gang in order to go to Campbell Town to claim £6, 17 shillings and nine pence owed by the local postmaster for services rendered while he was a member of the Ross Bridge gang. Meg Dillon argues the work undertaken for side-pay by those on public works created a black economy of production and consumption. This included the hire

[51] Dillon, 'Convict Labour and Colonial Society', 235.

[52] Molesworth, W. (1838) Report of the Select Committee of the House of Commons on Transportation, Henry Hooper, London, 9.

[53] Cited in Dillon, 'Convict Labour and Colonial Society', 87.

[54] Dillon, 'Convict Labour and Colonial Society', 135–136.

of convict runaways from road gangs by farmers who welcomed the opportunity to reduce their wage bill.[55]

In the end the colonial state conceded to the inevitable. The changes that accompanied the introduction of probation included the payment of passholder wages. While the concession was politically convenient as it weakened the association between transportation and slavery, it also loosened the state's grip on its convict charges. They had more room to negotiate conditions of service in the 1840s. The short period in which they were contracted, which could be as little as a month in duration, handed greater bargaining power to passholders. These were hard-won gains, but they were gains none the less. This helps to explain the reduction in the levels of convict protest in the 1840s.[56]

Bargaining over wages and conditions of service in the private sector, however, formed only part of the struggle fought by convict protesters. The transported also railed against levels of labour extraction and associated punishments, hours of work and the quantity and quality of rations. Some of the most protracted fights centred on these issues occurred in public sector gangs, penal stations and female factories. Such penal labourers, to use the term coined by Ray Evans and Bill Thorpe, had less room to manoeuvre than their assigned counterparts and their protests were met by bloody levels of repression. Yet they too won a victory, albeit one that was less easy to see than the concessions granted over convict wages and assigned and passholder conditions of service.

As David Meredith and Deborah Oxley argue, all penal transportation systems contain the seeds of their demise at the point of their birth.[57] The logic that powered the overseas deployment of convicted labour was that this would encourage growth, attracting free migration. This is Rusche and Kirchheimer's dictum in action—inclusive penal systems will give way to more exclusive institutional forms of confinement as labour markets tighten. Nevertheless, transported workers played a considerable role in speeding up that process. Some forms of punishment are particularly suited to field labour. Flogging, for example, was relatively easy to implement. So was head shaving and hair cutting—or at least it was in theory. Scissors and triangles are inexpensive pieces of equipment, yet the

[55] Dillon, 'Convict Labour and Colonial Society', 136–137.

[56] Meredith and Oxley, 'Contracting Convicts', 46–52.

[57] Meredith and Oxley, 'Condemned to the Colonies', 36.

use of both declined in the penal colonies. By the mid-1830s the landscape of punishment had tilted decidedly in favour of the use of solitary confinement. We argue that, at least in part, this was because physical punishments failed to subdue the wave of protest that confronted convict administrators in the 1820s. In effect the state was forced to increase levels of incarceration to counter levels of excarceration.

Protest further exacerbated the issue by increasing the need to circulate labour. Refractory prisoners required moving to places of trial and between sites of punishment. This necessitated the construction of watch-houses and local lockups, sites of confinement where workers on the move could be housed. All of this substantially added to the costs of maintaining the penal colonies—costs that the British government argued should be paid locally.[58] As the expensive of the infrastructure designed to manage convict labour was weighed against the economic benefits that stemmed from exploiting prisoners, opposition to continued transportation grew. Industrial action by convicts may have been aimed at improving conditions, but in the end it decisively contributed to the abolition of transportation itself. As the benefits that accrued from hiring convict labour over free were eliminated, transportation lost private sector support.

In the end, convict labour did not prove as tractable as employers hoped. In large part this was because convict bargaining and resistance narrowed the relative costs of employing prisoners over free workers far more than the formal conditions of convict service would suggest. The narrowing gap in labour costs was paralleled by growing opposition to transportation, an opposition led in practice by an increasingly industrially and politically-mobilised free workforce composed of emigrants, the colonially born and emancipists. As a result of effective political lobbying, transportation to New South Wales was abolished in 1840 and to Van Diemen's Land in 1853.[59]

[58] Tuffin and Gibbs, 'Uninformed and Impractical', 98–99.

[59] For an examination of worker anti-transportation struggles see Quinlan, *Origins of Worker Mobilisation*.

The Emancipation of the Free

In England and Wales anti-combination laws to suppress journeymen societies and unions were enacted from the fifteenth century on. These were expanded in scope and activity in the early eighteenth century before their coverage was restricted in 1825 just as the first known unions were formed in the Australian colonies. In 1824, coopers working for Icely and Hindson in Macquarie Street, Sydney, were remanded to stand trial for combination and conspiracy after demanding increased wages and allowances.[60] Charges of conspiracy and illegal combination continued to be used periodically until at least the 1850s. However, these actions were atypical, the vast majority of free workers were charged under master and servant (related assisted emigrant or indentured labour) and maritime labour laws (for seamen and whalers) for offences such as refusing work. Notably, workers belonging to unions were far less likely than informal groups to be prosecuted for their actions under any type of legislation.[61] In England and Wales the relative significance of the Combination Acts in the eighteenth and early nineteenth centuries as class-based laws to subordinate workers has been the subject of some debate, especially since the 1980s. Some have argued that the laws were symbolic and were seldom used in practice. This debate has largely occurred in isolation of any assessment of the use of master and servant and maritime labour laws against collective action by workers.[62] Our analysis reveals that such legislation was applied with force to unfree workers and this helped in turn to shape later legislation designed to regulate free labour.

Convicts under sentence in the Australian colonies constituted a highly exploitable and subordinated form of labour. They could neither form nor join unions. Those who engaged in such formal combinations risked being charged with criminal conspiracy or illegal combination. The majority of those prosecuted for engaging in collective action were, however, sentenced under provisions designed to regulate unfree master and servant relations. This included refusing work, insubordination and breaking contracts through acts like absconding. The degree of resistance this process encountered was largely unanticipated. As we have seen, the

[60] *Sydney Gazette*, 24 June 1824.

[61] Quinlan, *Origins of Worker Mobilisation:* Quinlan, *Contesting Inequality.*

[62] For a summary of this debate see Orth, J. (1987) English Combination Acts of the Eighteenth Century, *Law and History Review*, 5(1), 175–211.

post-Bigge changes to the way the labour-extraction system was organised triggered thousands of collective actions and resulted in tens of thousands of individual prosecutions for workplace-dissent. It was perhaps inevitable that an industrial war fought at scale between prisoners and their managers would spill over into the free workforce.

Here the semi-free status of ticket-of-leave holders was crucial. Since their experience bridged both the free and the unfree sections of the labour force, they acted as a conduit enabling laws designed to control convicts to be applied by stealth to free workers. This transition began before the first colonial master and servant laws were enacted. In 1819 William Holmes hired to James Gordon forfeited his ticket-of-leave for insolence and refusal to work.[63] The convict regime left its echoes on Australian labour legislation for decades after transportation ceased, influencing all colonies as those that did not directly experience penal transportation copied legal provisions from New South Wales and Tasmania.[64] This was especially true of colonial master and servant laws which had wider coverage than English law. Domestic servants were covered by their provisions for example. The colonial application of these laws also differed from metropolitan practice, enabling the offence of 'insolence' to be applied to free workers.

Longer term effects included a greater level of state regulatory control of work arrangements. Convict transportation entailed a large state-apparatus and the type of capitalist society that evolved in Australia continued to be marked by the pivotal role of the state. In the Australian colonies government extended its interests into all manner of activities in ways that were unusual in nineteenth century Britain and Ireland. This included the application of tariffs, education, labour regulation (including compulsory arbitration from 1896), transport infrastructure, utilities, healthcare, scientific research and agricultural marketing bodies. The struggle over work involving convicts—what might be termed the industrial relations of convict labour—was not simply a precursor to the rise of unions and worker mobilisation more generally in Australia, but a significant and integral part of this country's industrial relations history.[65]

[63] ML Tasmanian Papers 271 Hobart Benchbook 2 October 1819.

[64] See Quinlan, M. (1989) Pre-Arbitral Labour Law in Australia and Its Implications for the Adoption of Compulsory Arbitration, in McIntyre, S. and Mitchell eds. *Foundations of Arbitration*, Oxford University Press, 25–47; Quinlan, 'Australia 1788–1902', 219–250.

[65] Vito and Lichtenstein, 'Writing a Global History of Convict Labour', 285–325.

As ticket-of-leave holders and emancipists formed a significant part of the free workforce in New South Wales and Van Diemen's Land prior to 1850, they played a role in the organization of trade and benefit societies, unions and other political bodies formed in this period. Some took on leadership roles, like London-born printer Peter Tyler who became the secretary of the first compositors union in Sydney in 1835. Others who were transported for involvement in industrial or political dissent like tailor, unionist and Chartist William Cuffay, remained active in protesting against transportation and oppressive master and servant legislation.[66] The Hobart Town Trades Union and Committee of Free Working Classes which included specific union representative represented the working class on a number of issues, campaigned powerfully against convict transportation from the mid-1840s into the 1850s. This organisation included a number of former convicts in its leadership. It strongly resisted the efforts of pro-transportation groups to create division between free emigrants and emancipists.[67] The same rationale operated within early craft unions, which included both emigrant and emancipist members, notwithstanding their strident opposition to the engagement of probationers. Political alliance between emancipists and free migrants with union interconnections can be identified in Launceston too.

The principle of silence or 'don't-ask-don't-tell' integration was also manifest in New South Wales and for the same reasons. There was nothing to distinguish the social and ethnic origins or class-background of Peter Tyler from a free emigrant—as free workmen they had the same needs and interests. They also recognized that institutionalising a division between free migrant and former convict workers would have meant organisational death for both unions and political movements given the significance of ex-convicts and their children within the working class. The wave of free emigrants who unionised in the 1850s built on a base of organisation that began in the late 1820s and included many ex-convicts in New South Wales, Tasmania and later Victoria. This ensured that there was no sharp divide between pre- and post-gold-rush unionism.

[66] Quinlan, *The Origins of Worker Mobilisation*, 101, 108; Moore, *Death or Liberty*, 207.

[67] Quinlan, M. (1986) *Hope Amidst Hard Times: Working Class Organisation in Tasmania 1830–1850*, Industrial Relations Research Centre Monograph, University of New South Wales, 58–74.

Some industrially-active convicts like transported machine-breakers Ann Entwistle and Mary Hindle or Captain Swing rioter and shepherd Isaac Hurrell had no opportunity of transitioning into unions for a simple reason. The effective unionisation of female factory operatives did not begin until the 1870s (when larger scale manufacturing became more common). The same timeline applies to rural workers, and even then was predominantly confined to shearers and shed-hands that were easier to organise than shepherds. Ex-convicts were also active in other predominantly working-class institutions like friendly societies. Edward Bettison, transported to Van Diemen's Land on the *Fairlie* in 1852, played a leading role in the founding of the Oddfellows in Tamworth New South Wales for example.[68] Similar overlapping interconnections can be identified in Western Australia where transported-convict and social agitator Leopold Redpath played a prominent role in forming the Western Australian Working Men's Association in 1862.[69]

As the last point indicates, the contribution of former convicts to working-class organization in Australia extends beyond New South Wales and Van Diemen's Land. Many former convicts moved to the Port Phillip District where some participated in unions formed by sawyers and others from the late 1830s. The movement to what became Victoria was especially pronounced from Van Diemen's Land, where a flooded post-1840 labour market and better job prospects and wages in the rapidly growing Port Phillip District enticed many to cross the Bass Strait. This was especially the case following the discovery of gold in 1852. It is estimated that as many as 30,000 former convicts left Van Diemen's Land, the vast majority moving to Victoria.[70] It is not surprising that there were links between Hobart and Melbourne unions. The tailors and bootmakers, organized across the Bass Strait from the early 1840s with the Hobart bodies at least, included considerable numbers of ex-convicts. It seems reasonable to suggest that at least some of the mechanics who left Van Diemen's Land had experience of collective action as convicts that helped

[68] *Northern Star*, 4 September 1928.

[69] Quinlan, *Contesting Inequality and Worker Mobilisation*, 275.

[70] Alexander, A. (2010) *Tasmania's Convicts: How Felons Built a Free Society*, Allen & Unwin, Sydney; Maxwell-Stewart, H. and Kippen, R. (2014) What Is a Man That Is a Bolter To Do? I Would Steal the Governor's Axe Rather Than Starve": Old Lags and Recidivism in the Tasmanian Penal Colony, in Campbell, J. and Miller, V. eds. *Transnational Penal Cultures*, Routledge, London, 75–76.

inform the unionisation of stonemasons, tailors, bricklayers, carpenters and other skilled workers in Victoria in the 1850s. In the absence of detailed research into surviving union records, the extent of this link will remain fragmentary.[71] While following convicts post emancipation is notoriously hard, individual examples illustrate the ways in which those who engaged in industrial action during their sentence continued to be active in industrial disputes and working-class politics after they became free.

Isaac Ecclestone, one of the Jarrow Seven, continued to work for the Australian Agricultural Company after he became free.[72] Even as convicts the Jarrow Seven took collective action at the Company mine and Ecclestone was pivotal to the introduction of a token system to better monitor the filling of coal skips. Individual miners' output and reward were calculated on the number of skips and the quality of the coal they were filled with. Ultimately union-appointed checkweighmen scrutinised skips to ensure fairness and avoid favouritism by management. Ecclestone formed a strong friendship with James Fletcher, an emigrant Scottish miner who helped establish the Hunter Valley Coalminers Union in 1870 (which survives to this day), founded the *Newcastle Morning Herald and Miners Advocate*, and was elected to parliament representing coalminers where he advocated for improved safety legislation. When Ecclestone was no longer able to work, Fletcher provided him with an allowance of 12 shillings a week.[73] While Fletcher's gesture may have been purely philanthropic, it is likely Ecclestone's unionist principles appealed to the Scot. The former convict had a long involvement in collective action and unionism in the Hunter Valley as well as Jarrow. Fletcher may also have had some knowledge of the heritage of collectivism by convict coalminers in the Hunter—a district which rapidly developed a strong working-class identity and history of struggle.[74]

[71] For an examination of union growth in Victoria and some evidence of union links between Victoria and VDL see Quinlan, M. (2018) *The Origins of Worker Mobilisation: Australia 1788–1850*, Routledge, New York; Quinlan, M. (2020) *Contesting Inequality and Worker Mobilisation: Australia 1788–1850*, Routledge, New York.

[72] *Maitland Mercury* 25 April 1894.

[73] *Newcastle Morning Herald* (UK) 2 and 3 February 1894.

[74] Gollan, R. (1972) Fletcher, James (1834–1891), Melbourne University Press, https://adb.anu.edu.au/biography/fletcher-james-3538.

The lack of evidence of acrimony, tensions or schisms between transported and free-immigrant workers is remarkable testimony to the conscious efforts of people like William Jeffrey and John Williams in Van Diemen's Land and many others not to allow a potentially debilitating split to develop. In Thompsonian terms, the Australian working class was a conscious agent in its own creation resisting employer attempts to build internecine divides.

As this book has shown, convict dissent while informal was not lacking calculation or wider collaboration. Clear patterns are discernible that both drew on, and 'invented' customary expectations. While not codified, some customs carried over to the free labour market. These included demands for extra-rations, grog and other rewards during harvest and shearing, efforts to combat work intensification and go-slows as a calculated industrial tactic. The transition to a free labour market did not mark the beginning of intense industrial struggle for the simple reason that mass conflict over the terms and conditions of work had established itself decades earlier.

Other issues that dominated the struggle between convicts and their managers remained central to workplace relations in Australia. This included the length of the working day as well as provision for meal-breaks and the observance of public holidays—especially Christmas, Boxing Day, New Year's Day and Good Friday. From 1840 the campaign to shorten hours became the lynchpin of worker mobilisation in Australia, beginning with the early closing movement. This later merged into the half-holiday movement that commenced in the early 1850s which was an especially significant for manual workers. The eight-hour day movement that initiated in New South Wales in 1855 before spreading to other colonies, became a foundation of union organization and achieved a level of success not mirrored in Europe and North America until decades later.[75] While all three hour-movement principles (early closing of shops, half-holidays and eight-hours) originated in Britain and Ireland, the importance that convict workers and free workers (many ex-convicts) placed on shortening their hours was well-established long before union mobilisation over hours in the 1850s. We contend that it set an important

[75] Quinlan, *Contesting Inequality and Worker Mobilisation*.

context for these later struggles. This is evident not only in extensive evidence of bargaining and resistance relating to working hours documented in this book, but also in contemporary observations.

Different attitudes and practices relating to working hours compared to Britain and Ireland were noted early in the life of the colonies.[76] A series of researchers have pointed to the shorter hours of many convicts when compared to agricultural and other workers in Britain and Ireland. This included an effective half-holiday on Saturday for those in public works.[77] This, and its carryover to free workers, was also noted by contemporary observers. In 1846 Godfrey Mundy mused:

> … the fortunate man who enjoys what may be called full wages at Home, is only half fed and clothed, if he have a numerous family. In England and Ireland the permission to work hard from Monday morning to Saturday night, is a great boon. In Australia, the artisan and labourer has leisure as well as work. Contrast, I repeat, such facts as the above with the preceding statement of Australian wages and rations, and the well-known Australian profusion of human food.[78]

The reference to being better fed is important as it helps explain the aversion to longer hours. While some convicts went hungry and protested over this, the vast majority were better fed than they had been in Britain and Ireland, not a few writing to relatives to inform them of this.[79] As our research shows, much of the convict struggle over food was not about starvation, but additional rations—especially sugar, tea and alcohol and other allowances at harvest and shearing time. When convict workers took action over rations, it was usually because landholders or other employers sought to breach customary expectations or use items deemed as inferior substitutes like maze instead of wheat flour.

The goldrushes of the early 1850s have traditionally been viewed as a turning point in Australian history, although economic historians have long known that the trajectory of rapid economic development began

[76] Ward, R. (1956) The Ethos and Influence of the Australian Pastoral Worker, PhD thesis, Australian National University, 132.

[77] McKay, The Assignment System of Convict Labour, 28.

[78] Mundy, G. (1852) Our Antipodes or, Residence and Rambles in the Australasian Colonies, with a Glimpse of the Goldfields, Richard Bentley, London, 459.

[79] Quinlan, *Contesting Inequality and Worker Mobilisation*, 168.

three decades before this. Between 1820 and 1870 GDP per worker in Australia grew twice as fast as the United States and three times that of the United Kingdom. Laura Panza and Jeff Williamson found that, unlike the United States, there was a 'revolutionary leveling of incomes up to the 1870s.'[80] In explaining why Australia was an exception to the frontier inequalities common to other land-abundant settler societies, they point to particular features of Australia's commodity exports (notably wool), as well as two aspects of the colonial labour market. As they argue, both the rapid transition of coerced convicts to free waged labour in this period, and the post-goldrush emigration of mechanics that outran demand, were significant. These combined to ensure that a more egalitarian wage structure developed in Australia compared to other settler societies. As they note, while both Australia and the United States made extensive use of unfree labour (serving convicts made up over half the workforce prior to 1850 while slaves constituted a fifth of the United States labour force) Australia transitioned more rapidly to free labour.[81]

We would point to several additional factors that helped shape that transition. First, as Barry Dyster has noted, many convicts in the Australian colonies gained access to money and other property through effective workplace bargaining. We argue that this remained a feature of assigned service post-1822, despite a concerted campaign to stamp out cash payments to convicts. Here hard-won convict victories had important spin offs. Such sources of income aided the transition to free work, including post-emancipation migration to colonial areas of labour shortage, as well as boosting overall consumption.[82]

Second, the engagement of convicts in public works in the Australian colonies (in the United States the use of slaves was largely limited to private production) facilitated faster economic growth in the private sector. As we have seen, the dynamic between the private and public sector was an important feature of convict labour exploitation. It enabled the punishment of labour, as well as the shifting of unfree workers between sectors in order to suit market demand. It also ensured the development of the necessary infrastructure in terms of public buildings, roads and port facilities, to foster wider growth.

[80] Panza and Williamson, 'Australian Squatters, Convicts, and Capitalists', 568–594.

[81] Panza and Williamson, 'Australian Squatters, Convicts, and Capitalists', 569–570.

[82] Dyster, Argentine and Australian Development Compared, 91–110.

Third, the relatively small gap between skilled and unskilled wages in Australia arose from an array of factors, including the nature of rural production. This was more capital intensive than plantation labour in the South, a factor that made unskilled labour more valuable. The bargaining power of skilled labour was also complicated by the oversupply of particular trades, especially tailors and shoemakers—a feature of both convict and free migration flows. Finally, non-skilled workers organised more effectively than their United States counterparts. While greater urbanization and the peculiar features of Antipodean rural production contributed to this, the experience of convict labour organization is likely to have played a part too.[83] Fourth and not least, serving convicts bargained and resisted in ways that established a baseline of conditions and as well as a heritage of industrial struggle. We suspect also that a significant number also rapidly transitioned into union and political leadership as activists, combining with free emigrant workers in ways that were difficult for former slaves. Convictism was effective at exploiting prisoners under sentence. It was, however, a form of ideological control that was easier for emancipists to escape than the shackles of plantation racism used to define and justify the conditions of work in the South that led to a bloody civil war which abolished slavery without setting in place the structures for establishing equality between the races, and hence between workers.

For all of that, convictism has had a powerful reach. Its ideological shackles have helped conceal the extraordinary levels of opposition that transported women and men mounted to the post-Bigge reorganisation of convict labour. It has also effectively concealed the contribution Australia's unfree workers made to the improvement of free working conditions. It did so, not only by highlighting the past conviction history of Australia's unfree workforce, but by atomising them. It has taken the labour of hundreds of academic, local and family historians to digitally excavate and reconstruct that record of protest from tens of thousands of individual conduct records, indents, description lists, benchbooks and absconding notices. It is fitting that many of those who have worked so assiduously to break the grip of the colonial state's ideological shackles are themselves the descendants of convicts. We are conscious, however, that there remains much to do. New technologies, especially spatial mapping

[83] For an examination of these aspects see Quinlan *Contesting Inequality and Worker Mobilisation*.

tools and network analysis will help to explore the links between individual convict protests. They should also aid a more detailed analysis of the ways in which that record of collaboration contributed to subsequent gains won by free workers. Further work is also needed in order to explore the links between Australia's early carceral history and the evolution of subsequent institutional forms of control.

There is an emerging consensus that penal transportation did not cease in the Australian colonies with the arrival of the last convict vessel in 1868. Aboriginal Australians in particular, continued to be subjected to labour extraction systems that borrowed heavily from the convict era.[84] The Aboriginal penal settlement on Palm Island in Queensland, for example, did not close until 1975. The manner in which industrial reformatory schools and other correctional institutions, reservations, mission stations, children's homes and the domestic settings to which Australia's stolen generations were removed, operated as a carceral archipelago is a startling reminder of the dangers of calling a premature end to Australia's experience of penal transportation. It should also remind us of the many ways that we remain blinded by convictism to systems of exploitation.

[84] Roscoe, 'Work on Wadjemup', 79–96.

References

Archival References

State Library New South Wales

Mitchell Library (ML), Tasmanian Papers
Tas Papers 2 Richmond and Brighton Benchbooks
Tas Papers 33, Morven records, Tasman Peninsula correspondence
Tas Papers 196 Hobart Benchbook
Tas Papers 237 New Norfolk Benchbook
Tas Papers 238 New Norfolk Benchbook
Tas Papers 256 Campbell Town Prisoner Records and Sentences
Tas Papers 261 George Town Magistrates Letterbook correspondence
Tas Papers 268 Hobart Benchbook
Tas Papers 270 Hobart Benchbook
Tas Papers, 277, Launceston Benchbook
Tas Papers 278, Launceston Convict Superintendent Letterbook, correspondence
Tas Papers 284 New Norfolk Police Office Letterbook
Tas Papers 285 New Norfolk Police Office Letterbook
Tas Papers, 290, Oatlands Benchbook
Tas Papers, 291, Oatlands and Richmond Benchbooks
Tas Papers, 292, Oatlands Benchbook
Tas Papers 323 Richmond Benchbook
Tas Papers, 325, Richmond Benchbook
Tas Papers, 326, Richmond Benchbook
Papers relating to the *Narinio* MSS 1808/Box 1

H. Maxwell-Stewart and M. Quinlan, *Unfree Workers*, Palgrave Studies in Economic History,
https://doi.org/10.1007/978-981-16-7558-4

Papers relating to the *Isabella Watson* Dixson Library, Add 537
M.L., Coal Mines Benchbook, A584-

Archives Office New South Wales

Colonial Secretaries Correspondence files
Magistrates benchbooks for:
Bathurst
Berrima
Campbelltown
Cawdor
Goulburn
Liverpool
Newcastle
Picton
Port Macquarie
Sutton Forest
Yass

Tasmanian Archives

Con18 Male Convict Description Lists
Con19 Female Convict Description Lists
Con23 Convict Description Lists
Con27 Convict Appropriation Records
Con31 Male Offence Registers for the Assignment Period
Con32 Supplementary Offence Registers for the Assignment Period
Con33 Male Offence Registers for the Probation Period
Con40 Female Offence Registers for the Assignment Period
Con41 Female Offence Registers for the Probation Period
CSO1, Colonial Secretaries Correspondence files 1824-36
CS05, Colonial Secretaries Correspondence files 1837-41

LC 83, Campbell Town Benchbook
LC 247, Hobart Benchbook
LC 346, Launceston Benchbook
LC 362, Longford Benchbook
LC 375, New Norfolk Benchbook
LC 390 Oatlands Magistrates Court Benchbook

POL 481, Copies of Circulars received by the Police Magistrate from the Chief Police Magistrate
POL 451 Launceston Charge Book

Elliston's Hobart Town Almanack and Ross's Van Diemen's Land Annual 1837

Scottish Records Office
Precognitions series AD/14

National Archives UK
ADM 101 Surgeon's journals
HO/10/47 1830 Convict Muster Van Diemen's Land
HO/10/48 1832 Convict Muster Van Diemen's Land
HO/10/49 1833 Convict Muster Van Diemen's Land
HO/10/50 1835 Convict Muster Van Diemen's Land

Newspapers

Australian
Bath Chronicle and Weekly Gazette
Bent's News (Hobart)
Colonial Times (Hobart)
Cornwall Chronicle (Launceston)
Hobart Town Courier
Hobart Town Gazette
Hobart Town Gazette and Southern Reporter
Independent (Hobart)
Launceston Advertiser
Launceston Examiner
Monitor (Sydney)
Morning Chronicle (Sydney)
Newcastle Morning Herald
New South Wales Government Gazette
North Devon Journal
Parramatta Chronicle
Sydney Gazette
Sydney Herald
Sydney Morning Herald
Tasmanian
The Colonist (Hobart)
True Colonist (Hobart)

List of Theses and Published Works

Alexander, A. (2010). *Tasmania's convicts: How felons built a free society*. Allen & Unwin.

Anderson, C. (1997). The genealogy of the modern subject: Indian convicts on Mauritius, 1814–1853. In I. Duffield & J. Bradley (Eds.), *Representing convicts: New Perspectives on convict forced labour migration* (pp. 164–182). Leicester University Press.

Anderson, C. (2009). Convicts and coolies: Rethinking indentured labour in the nineteenth century. *Slavery and Abolition, 30*(1), 93–109.

Anderson, C. (2016). Transnational histories of penal transportation: Punishment, labour and governance in the British Imperial World, 1788–1939. *Australian Historical Studies, 47*(3), 381–397.

Anderson, C. (2018). Introduction: A global history of convicts and penal colonies. In C. Anderson (Ed.), *A global history of convicts and penal colonies* (pp. 1–36). Bloomsbury.

Anderson, C., & Maxwell-Stewart, H. (2014). Convict labour and the Western Empires, 1415–1954. In R. Aldrich & K. McKenzie (Eds.), *Routledge history of Western empires* (pp. 165–183). Routledge.

Anderson, S. (2020). *A history of capital punishment in the Australian colonies, 1788 to 1900*. Palgrave Macmillan.

Arthur, G. (1835). *Defence of transportation in reply to the remarks of the Archbishop of Dublin in his second letter to Early Grey by Colonel George Arthur*. George Cowie.

Atkinson, A. (1979). Four patterns of convict protest. *Labour History, 37*, 28–51.

Atkinson, A. (1998). *The Europeans in Australia: Vol.* 1. Oxford University Press.

Atkinson, A. (2004). *The Europeans in Australia: Vol.* 2. Oxford University Press.

Australian (Sydney), various issues.

Baine, R. (1993). New perspectives on debtors in colonial Georgia. *The Georgia Historical Quarterly, 77*(1), 1–19.

Bamford, P. W. (1956). The procurement of Oarsmen for French Galleys, 1660–1748. *American Historical Review, 65*(1), 31–48.

Banaji, J. (2003). The fictions of free labour: Contract, coercion, and so-called unfree labour. *Historical Materialism, 11*(3), 69–95.

Barker, J. (2016). A history of history through the lens of our digital present, the traditions that shape and constrain data-driven historical research and what librarians can do about IT. In J. White & H. Glibert (Eds.), *Laying the foundation: Digital humanities in academic libraries*. Purdue University Press.

Bateson, C. (1959). *The convict ships*. Brown, Son and Ferguson.

Beckles, H. (1985). From land to sea: Runaway Barbados slaves and servants, 1630–1700. *Slavery & Abolition, 6*(3), 79–94.

Beckles, H. (1985). Plantation production and "white proto-slavery": White indentured servants and the colonisation of the English West Indies 1624–1645. *The Americas, 41*(3), 21–45.

Beckles, H. (1988) *Afro-Caribbean women and resistance to slavery in Barbados*. Karnak House.

Beckles, H., & Downes, A. (1987). The economics of transition to the black labor system in Barbados, 1630–1680. *The Journal of Interdisciplinary History, 18*(2), 225–247.

Beier, A. L. (1978). Social problems in Elizabethan England. *The Journal of Interdisciplinary History, 9*(2), 203–221.

Bennett, J. (1966). *Bigge, John Thomas (1780–1843), Australian dictionary of biography: 99–100.* Melbourne University Press.

Benton, L., & Ford, L. (2013). Magistrates in empire: Convicts, slaves and the remaking of the plural legal order in the British Empire. In R. J. Ross (Ed.), *Legal pluralism and empires, 1500–1850* (pp. 173–197). University Press.

Blackburn, R. (1997). The old world background to European colonial slavery. *William and Mary Quarterly, 54*(1), 65–102.

Bly, A. (2012). A prince among pretending free men: Runaway slaves in colonial New England revisited. *Massachusetts Historical Review, 14*, 87–118.

Boyce, J. (2008). *Van Diemen's land.* Black Inc.

Boyce, J. (2013). *The founding of Melbourne and the conquest of Australia.* Black Inc.

Bradley, J., & Maxwell-Stewart, H. (1997). "Behold the Man": Power, observation and the tattooed convict. *Australian Studies, 12*(1), 71–97.

Braithwaite, J. (2001). Crime in a convict republic. *The Modern Law Review, 64*(1), 11–50.

Brand, I. (1990). *The convict probation system; Van Diemen's Land, 1839–1854.* Blubber Head Press.

Brass, T. (1994). Some observations on unfree labour, capitalist restructuring, and deproletarianization. *International Review of Social History, 39*(2), 255–275.

Brass, T., & Bernstein, H. (1992). Introduction: Proletarianisation and deproletarianisation on the colonial plantation. *The Journal of Peasant Studies, 19*(3–4), 1–40.

Breman, J., & Van der Linden, M. (2014). Informalizing the economy: The return of the social question at global level. *Development and Change, 45*(5), 920–940.

Breton, W. H. (1835). *Excursions in New South Wales, Western Australia and Van Diemen's land during the years 1830, 1831, 1832 and 1833.* Richard Bentley.

British Parliamentary Papers, XLII. (1837–38). Copy of Despatch, Note (G) Testimonials by Messrs. Backhouse and Walker; Minutes of Evidence, Rev. W. Ullathorne, 8 February 1838 and E. Parry, 26 February 1838.

British Parliamentary Papers, House of Lords, 1837, xxxvi, Appendix i.

British Parliamentary Papers. (1972). Instructions to surgeons superintendent on board convict ships proceeding to New South Wales or Van Diemen's land, 1832, *Correspondence and Papers Relating to Convict Transportation 1810–41*, vol. 6, 253–258. Irish University Press.

Brooke, A., & Brandon, D. (2005). *Bound for Botany Bay: British convict voyages to Australia.* National Archives (UK), Kew.

Brownrigg, J. (2016). The legend of Frank the poet: Convict heritage recovered or created? *Journal of Australian Colonial History, 28*, 1–22.

Broxam, G. (1997). *Shipping arrivals and departures, Tasmania 1843–1850, Vol III*. Navarine.

Broxam, G., & Nash, M. (1997). *Tasmanian shipwrecks, Vol 1 1797–1900*. Navarine.

Buckley, R. (1988). *The British Army in the West Indies: Society and the military in the Revolutionary Age*. University Press of Florida.

Burnard, T., & Garrigus, J. (2018). *The plantation machine: Atlantic capitalism in French Saint-Domingue and British Jamaica*. University of Pennsylvania Press.

Bush, B. (1984). Towards emancipation: Slave women and resistance to coercive labour regimes in the British West Indian Colonies, 1790–1838. *Slavery & Abolition, 5*(3), 222–243.

Butler, J. (1896). British convicts shipped to American colonies. *American Historical Review, 2*(1), 13–14.

Butlin, N. G., Ginswick, J., & Statham, P. (1987). The economy before 1850. In W. Vamplew (Ed.), *Australians historical statistics* (pp. 102–125). Cambridge University Press.

Byrne, P. (2004). *Criminal law and the colonial subject*. Cambridge University Press.

Calder, J. (1979). *Brady, McCabe, Dunne, Bryan, Crawford, Murphy, Bird, McKenney, Goodwin, Pawley, Bryant, Cody, Hodgett's, Gregory, Tilley, Ryan, Williams, and their associates, bushrangers in Van Diemen's Land, 1824–1827* (E. Fitzsymonds, Ed.). Sullivan's Cove.

Campbell, G., & Alpers, E. (2004). Introduction: Slavery, forced labour and resistance in Indian Ocean Africa and Asia. *Slavery & Abolition, 25*(2), 9–27.

Casanovas, J. (1995). Slavery, the labour movement and Spanish Colonialism in Cuba, 1850–1890. *International Review of Social History, 40*(3), 367–382.

Casella, E. (2001). To watch or restrain: Female convict prisons in 19th-century Tasmania. *International Journal of Historical Archaeology, 5*(1), 45–72.

Cash, M. (1940). *Martin Cash, the Bushranger of Van Diemen's land in 1843–4*. Walch.

Chartrand, V. (2014). Penal and colonial politics over life: Women and penal release schemes in NSW, Australia. *Settler Colonial Studies, 4*(3), 305–320.

Chase, R. (2012). Slaves of the State Revolt: Southern prison labor and a prison-made Civil Rights Movement, 1945–1980. In R. Zieger (Ed.), *Life and labor in the New South*. University of Florida Press.

Christopher, E., & Maxwell-Stewart, H. (2013). Convict transportation in global context, c. 1700–88. In A. Bashford & S. McIntyre (Eds.), *Cambridge history of Australia*, vol 1 (pp. 88–99). Cambridge University Press.

Colburn, F. (Ed.). (1989). *Everyday forms of resistance*. M.E. Sharp.

Connell, R., & Irving, T. (1984). *Class structure in Australian history: Documents, narrative and argument*. Melbourne University Press.

Cowley, T. (2005). *A drift of 'Derwent Ducks': Lives of the 200 female Irish convicts transported on the Australasia from Dublin to Hobart in 1849*. New Town.

Craton, M. (1978). Hobbesian or Panglossian? The two extremes of slave conditions in the British Caribbean, 1783–1834, *William and Mary Quarterly*, 3rd Ser. *35*, 324–356.

Craton, M. (1982). *Testing the chains: Resistance to slavery in the British West Indies*. Cornell University Press.

Croucher, R., & Didier, M. (2014). "Legal at the Time?" Companies, governments and reparations for Mauritian Slavery. *Journal of African Law, 58*(1), 89–108.

Curthoys, A. (2020). The beginnings of transportation in Western Australia: Banishment, forced labour, and punishment at the aboriginal prison on Rottnest Island before 1850. *Studies in Western Australian History, 34*, 59–77.

Daniels, K. (1998). *Convict women*. Allen and Unwin.

Damousi, J. (2007). *Depraved and disorderly: Female convicts, sexuality and gender in colonial Australia*. Cambridge University Press.

Davidson, A. (1975). *An analytical and comprehensive history of the master and servant legislation in Tasmania*. Masters of Law thesis, University of Tasmania.

Denning, G. (1992). *Mr Bligh's bad language: Passion, power and theatre on the bounty*. Cambridge University Press.

Devereaux, S. (1999). The making of the Penitentiary Act, 1775–1779. *The Historical Journal, 42*(2), 405–433.

De Vito, C., & Lichtenstein, A. (2013). Writing a global history of convict labour. *International Review of Social History, 58*(2), 285–325.

Dillon, M. (2008). *Convict labour and colonial society in the Campbell Town Police District: 1820–1839*. Ph.D. thesis, University of Tasmania.

Dixon, J. (1839). *The condition and capabilities of Van Diemen's land as a place of emigration being the practical experience of nearly ten years residence*. Smith, Elder and Co.

Dixon, J. (1984). *Narrative of a voyage to New South Wales and Van Diemen's Land in the ship Skelton during the year 1820*. Melanie.

Donnelly, J. (2009). *Captain Rock: The Irish Agrarian Rebellion of 1821–1824*. University of Wisconsin.

Donoghue, J. (2010). "Out of the Land of Bondage": The English Revolution and the Atlantic origins of abolition. *The American Historical Review, 115*(4), 943–974.

Doyle, D., & Carballedo, A. (2014). Infertility and mental health. *Advances in Psychiatric Treatment, 20*(5), 297–303.

Duffield, I. (1986). From slave colonies to penal colonies: The West Indian convict transportees to Australia. *Slavery and Abolition, 7*(1), 25–45.

Duffield, I. (1987). The life and death of "Black" John Goff: Aspects of the Black contribution to resistance patterns during the transportation era in Eastern Australia. *Journal of Australian Politics and History, 33*(1), 30–34.

Duffield, I. (1999). Daylight on convict lived experience: The history of a pious Negro servant. *Tasmanian Historical Studies, 6*(2), 29–62.

Duffield, I. (2001). "State This Offence": High-density convict micro narratives. In L. Frost & H. Maxwell-Stewart (Eds.), *Chain letters narrating convict lives* (pp. 119–135). Melbourne University Press.

Duffield, I. (2013). Cutting out and taking liberties, Australia's convict pirates, 1790–1829. *International Review of Social History, 54*, 197–227.

Dunn, M. (2020). *The convict valley: The bloody struggle on Australia's early frontier*. Allen and Unwin.

Dunn, R. (1993). Sugar production and slave women in Jamaica. In I. Berlin & P. Morgan (Eds.), *Cultivation and culture: Labour and the shaping of slave life in the Americas* (pp. 49–72). University Press of Virginia.

Dunn, R. (2007). The demographic contrast between slave life in Jamaica and Virginia, 1760–1865. *Proceedings of the American Philosophical Society, 151*(1), 43–60.

Dunning, T. P., & Maxwell-Stewart, H. (2002). Mutiny at Deloraine: Ganging and convict resistance in 1840s Van Diemen's land. *Labour History, 82*, 35–47.

Dyster, B. (1979). Argentine and Australian development compared. *Past and Present, 84*, 91–110.

Dyster, B. (Ed.). (1996). *Beyond convict workers*. Department of Economic History.

Eddy, I. (1969). *Britain and the Australian Colonies 1818–1831: The techniques of government*. Oxford University Press.

Edmonds, P., & Maxwell-Stewart, H. (2016). 'The whip is a very contagious kind of thing': Flogging and humanitarian reform in penal Australia. *Journal of Colonialism and Colonial History, 17*, 1. https://doi.org/10.1353/CCH.2016.0006

Ekirch, A. (1984). Britain's secret convict trade to America, 1783–4. *American Historical Review, 89*(5), 1285–1291.

Eltis, D. (1993). Europeans and the rise and fall of African slavery in the Americas: An interpretation. *American Historical Review, 98*(5), 1399–1423.

Eltis, D., & Engerman, S. (2000). The importance of slavery and the slave trade to industrializing Britain. *Journal of Economic History, 60*(1), 123–144.

Ely, R. (2004). Arthur, Sir George. In *Blackwell dictionary of evangelical biography*, Vol. 1, 30.

Emmer, P. C. (2005). *The Dutch slave trade, 1500–1850*. Berghahn Books.

Evans, R. (2009). 19 June 1822, creating an 'Object of Real Terror': The tabling of the first Bigge report. In M. Crotty & D. Roberts (Eds.), *Turning points in Australian history* (pp. 53–54). UNSW Press.

Evans, R., & Thorpe, W. (1992). Power, punishment and penal labour: *Convict Workers* and Moreton Bay, *Australian Historical Studies, 25*(98), 90–111.

Evans, R., & Thorpe, W. (1996). Freedom and unfreedom at Moreton Bay: The structures and relations of secondary punishment. In B. Dyster (Ed.), *Beyond convict workers* (pp. 64–82). University of New South Wales.

Emsley, C. (1987). *Crime and society in England 1750–1900*. Longman.

Featherstone, D., & Griffin, P. (2016). Spatial relations, histories from below and the makings of agency: Reflections on the making of the English working class at 50. *Progress in Human Geography, 40*(3), 375–393.

Fenoaltea, S. (1984). Slavery and supervision in comparative perspective: A model. *Journal of Economic History, 44*(3), 635–668.

Finch, A. K. (2015). *Rethinking slave rebellion in Cuba: La Escalera and the insurgencies of 1841–1844*. University of North Carolina Press.

Ford, L. (2008). Reconfiguring the Old South: "Solving" the problem of slavery, 1787–1838. *The Journal of American History, 95*(1), 95–122.

Ford, L., & Roberts, D. A. (2021). The convict peace: The imperial context of the 1833 convict revolt at Castle Forbes. *Journal of Commonwealth and Imperial History, 49*(1), 1–21.

Forsyth, W. (1970). *Governor Arthur's convict system: Van Diemen's land 1824–36*. Sydney University Press.

Forsythe, W. J. (1987). *The reform of prisoners 1830–1900*. Croom Helm.

Foucault, M. (1977). *Discipline and punish: The birth of the prison*. Pantheon.

Franklin, J. H., & Schweninger, L. (1999). *Runaway slaves: Rebels on the plantation*. Oxford University Press.

Frost, L. (1999). "Singing and Dancing and Making a Noise": Spaces for women. *University of Tasmania Occasional Paper, 52*, 1–20.

Frost, L. (2001). Eliza Churchill Tells … In L. Frost & H. Maxwell-Stewart (Eds.), *Chain letters: Narrating convict lives* (pp. 79–90). Melbourne University Press.

Frost, L. (2012). *Abandoned women: Scottish convicts exiled beyond the seas*. Allen and Unwin.

Garvin, T. (1982). Defenders, Ribbonmen and others: Underground political networks in pre-famine Ireland. *Past and Present, 96*, 133–155.

Gaspar, D. (1978). The Antigua slave conspiracy of 1736: A case study of the origins of collective resistance. *The William and Mary Quarterly, 35*(2), 308–323.

Gates, W. (1961). *Recollections of life in Van Diemen's Land by William Gates, one of the Canadian patriots* (Ed. with an intro., notes and commentary by G. Mackaness). Ford.

Geggus, D. (1993). Sugar and coffee cultivation in Saint Domingue and the shaping of the slave labor force. In I. Berlin & P. Morgan (Eds.), *Cultivation and culture: Labor and the shaping of slave life in the Americas* (pp. 73–100). University Press of Virginia.

Genovese, E. (1974). *Roll Jordan Roll: The world the slaves made*. Pantheon.

Gibbs, M. (2006). The convict places of Western Australia. *Studies in Western Australian History, 24*, 71–97.

Gibbs, M. Tuffin, R., Maxwell-Stewart, H., Roberts, D., & Roe, D. et al. (2018). Landscapes of production and punishment: Convict labour management on the Tasman Peninsula 1830–1877. *Antiquity, 92*(362). https://doi.org/10.15184/aqy.2018.58

Gilchrist, C. (2006). The "Crime" of precocious sexuality: Young male convicts and the politics of separation. *Journal of Australian Colonial History, 8*, 57–58.

Gollan, R. (1972). *Fletcher, James (1834–1891).* Melbourne University Press, https://adb.anu.edu.au/biography/fletcher-james-3538

Godfrey, B., & Cox, D. (2008). 'The Last Fleet': Crime, reformation, and punishment in Western Australia after 1868. *The Australian and New Zealand Journal of Criminology, 41*(2), 236–258.

Godfrey, B., Homer, C., Inwood, K., Maxwell-Stewart, H., Read R., & Tuffin, R. (2021). Crime, penal transportation and digital methodologies. *Journal of World History, 32*(2), 241–260.

Godfrey, B., Inwood, K., & Maxwell-Stewart, H. (2018). Exploring the life course and intergenerational impact of convict transportation. In C. Bijleveld & S. Weijer (Eds.), *Intergenerational continuity of criminal or antisocial behaviour* (pp. 61–75). Routledge.

Gragg, L. (2003). *Englishmen transplanted: The English colonization of Barbados, 1627–1660*. Oxford University Press.

Green, T. (2020). *A fistful of shells: West Africa from the rise of the slave trade to the age of revolution*. Penguin.

Greenburg, K. (Ed.). (2006). *Nat Turner: A slave rebellion in history and memory*. Oxford University Press.

Grubb, F. (2001). The market evaluation of criminality: Evidence from the auction of British convict labor in America, 1767–1775. *The American Economic History Review, 91*(1), 295–304.

Hakluyt, R. (1877). A discourse concerning Western planting, 1584. In C. Deanne (Ed.), *Collections of the Maine Historical Society*, 2nd series (pp. 36–38). John Wilson.

Handler, J. (1997). Escaping slavery in a Caribbean Plantation Society: Marronage in Barbados, 1650s–1830s. *New West Indian Guide, 71*(3), 183–225.

Harris, A. (1977). *Settlers and convicts: Recollections of sixteen years labour in the Australian backwoods by an emigrant mechanic*. 1847 reprint Melbourne University Press.

Harvey, M. (2019). Slavery, indenture and the development of British industrial capitalism. *History Workshop Journal, 88*, 66–88.

Hay, D., & Craven, P. (Eds.). (2004). *Masters, servants, and magistrates in Britain and the empire 1562–1955*. University of North Carolina Press.

Hay, D., Linebaugh, P., Rule, J., Thompson, E., & Winslow, C. (Eds.). (1977). *Albion's fatal tree: Crime and society in eighteenth century England*. Penguin.

Haynes, D., & Prakash, G. (Eds.). (1991). *Contesting power: Resistance to everyday social relations in South Asia*. University of California Press.

Heaney, H. (1974). Ireland's penitentiary 1820–1831: An experiment that failed. *Studia Hibernica, 14*, 28–39.

Heinsen, J. (2018). The Scandinavian empires in the seventeenth and eighteenth centuries. In C. Anderson. *A global history of convicts and penal colonies* (pp. 97–121). Bloomsbury.

Hendriksen, G. Liston, C., & Cowley, T. (2008). *Women transported: Life in Australia's convict female factories*. NSW Parramatta Heritage Centre/University of Western Sydney.

Hillier, B., & O'Lincoln, T. (2013). Five hundred lashes and double irons: The origins of Australian capitalism. *Marxist Left Review, 5*, 149–180.

Hilton, P. (2010). *"Branded D on the Left Side": A longitudinal study of military convicts transported to Van Diemen's land*. Ph.D. thesis, University of Tasmania.

Hindmarsh, B. (2001) *Yoked to the plough: Male convict labour, culture and resistance in rural Van Diemen's land, 1820–40*. Ph.D. thesis, University of Edinburgh.

Hirst, J. (2008). *Freedom on the fatal shore*. Black Inc.

Hirst, W. (1999). *Great escapes by convicts in colonial Australia*. Kangaroo Press.

Hobsbawm, E., & Rudė, G. (1972). *Captain swing*. Penguin.

Hordvik, E. (2016). *Mauritius—Caught in the web of empire: The legal system, crime punishment and labour 1825–1845*. Ph.D. thesis, University of Tasmania.

Horne, G. (2014). *The counter revolution of 1776: Slave resistance and the origins of the United States*. New York University Press.

Huf, B. (2018). Making things economic: Theory and government in New South Wales, 1788–1863. Ph.D. thesis, Australian National University.

Humphrys, E. (2012). The birth of Australia: Non-capitalist social relations in a capitalist mode of production? *Journal of Australian Political Economy, 70*, 110–129.

Hyland, J. (2020). 'The vilest and most degraded of human beings': An investigation into why female convicts were not transported to Western Australia. *Studies in Western Australian History, 34*, 147–163.

Ihde, E. (2005). *A manifesto for New South Wales: Edward Smith Hall and the Sydney Monitor 1826–1840*. Australian Scholarly Publishing.

Ihde, E. (2008). Pirates of the Pacific: The convict seizure of the "Wellington." *The Great Circle, 30*, 3–17.

Irving, T. (2018). *Review of Michael Quinlan, the origins of worker mobilisation: Australia 1788–1850*. Routledge: 2017, *Economic and Labour Relations Review, 29*(2), 263–268.

Jarvis, M. (2002). Maritime masters and seafaring slaves in Bermuda, 1680–1783. *The William and Mary Quarterly, 59*(3), 585–622.

Jordan, W. (2012). *White over Black: American attitudes toward the Negro, 1550–1812*. University of North Carolina Press.

Karskens, G. (1986). Defiance, deference and diligence: three views of convicts in New South Wales road-gangs, Australian. *Historical Archaeology, 4*, 17–28.

Karskens, G. (1997). The dialogue of townscape: The rocks and Sydney, 1788–1820. *Australian Historical Studies, 27*(108), 88–112.

Karskens, G. (1999). *Inside the rocks: The archaeology of a neighbourhood*. Hale and Iremonger.

Karskens, G. (2009). *The colony: A history of early Sydney*. Allen & Unwin.

Kay, M., & Cary, L. (1976). "The Planters Suffer Little or Nothing": North Carolina compensations for executed slaves, 1748–1772. *Source: Science & Society, 40*(3), 288–306.

Kent, D. (1994). Customary behaviour transported: A note on the Parramatta Female Factory Riot of 1827. *Journal of Australian Studies, 18*(40), 75–79.

Kippen, R. (2005). *"And the Mortality Frightful" infant and child mortality in the convict nurseries of Van Diemen's Land*. International Workshop organized by the IUSSP Scientific Committee on Historical Demography, the Ecole des Hautes Etudes en Science Sociales, and the Institut National d'Etudes Démographiques, Paris.

Kippen, R., & Maxwell-Stewart, H. (2015). Sickness and death on convict voyages to Australia. In P. Baskerville & K. Inwood (Eds.), *Lives in transition: Longitudinal research in historical perspective* (pp. 43–70). McGill-Queens UP.

Konig, D. T. (1982). "Dale's Laws" and the non-common law origins of criminal justice in Virginia. *The American Journal of Legal History, 26*(4), 345–375.

Kyles, P. (2008). Resistance and collaboration: Political strategies within the Afro-Carolinian slave community, 1700–1750. *The Journal of African American History, 93*(4), 497–508.

Lack, P. (1982). An urban slave community: Little Rock, 1831–1862. *The Arkansas Historical Quarterly, 41*(3), 258–287.

Langen, N. (2019, May 15). Prisons. *The Justice Gap*. https://www.thejusticegap.com/the-cost-of-a-year-in-prison-is-greater-than-fees-for-eton-perhaps-we-should-be-more-ambitious-about-what-we-expect/. Accessed 10 Jan 2020.

Laugesen, A. (2002). The politics of language in convict Australia, 1788–1850. *Journal of Australian Colonial History, 4*(1), 17–40.

Lempriere, T. (1954). *The penal settlements of early Van Diemen's land* (pp. 27–51). Royal Society of Tasmania.

Leppard Quinn, C. (2007). *Why leg irons were not emancipated: The Role of Convict Leg Irons in Van Diemen's Land and New South Wales, 1788–1853*. BA Honours thesis, School of History and Classics, University of Tasmania.

Levy, C. (1970). Slavery and the emancipation movement in Barbados 1650–1833. *The Journal of Negro History, 55*(1), 1–14.

Lichtenstein, A. (1996). *Twice the work of free labor: The political economy of convict labor in the New South*. Verso Books.

Linebaugh, P. (1991). *The London hanged: Crime and civil society in the eighteenth century*. Penguin.

Linebaugh, P., & Rediker, M. (1990). The many-headed hydra: Sailors, slaves, and the Atlantic working class in the eighteenth century. *Journal of Historical Sociology, 3*(3), 225–252.

Linebaugh, P., & Rediker, M. (2000). *The many-headed hydra: Sailors, Slaves, commoners and the hidden history of the revolutionary Atlantic*. Beacon.

Lisle, J. S. (1800) *The life of Major J. G. Semple Lisle containing a faithful narrative of his alternate vicissitudes of splendor and misfortune*. Stewart.

Lydon, J. (2021). *Anti-slavery and Australia: No slavery in a free land?* Routledge.

Maconochie, A. (1838). *Thoughts on convict management: And other subjects connected with the Australian penal colonies*. MacDougall.

Mann, D. (1811). *The present picture of New South Wales*. John Booth.

Marshall, L. (2018). *Surviving the colony, the impact of the Western Australian convict system on prisoner health, 1850–77*. Ph.D. thesis, University of Western Australia.

Marshall, L. (2020). The ticketer's plight: Living standards and mortality among ticket-of-leave convicts in Western Australia, 1850–1877. *Studies in Western Australian History, 34*, 98–121.

Maxwell-Stewart, H. (1991). *The bushrangers and the convict system*. Ph.D. thesis, University of Edinburgh.

Maxwell-Stewart, H. (1997). Convict workers, "Penal Labour" and Sarah Island: Life at Macquarie Harbour, 1822–1834. In I. Duffield & J. Bradley (Eds.), *Representing convicts: New perspectives on convict forced labour migration* (pp. 142–162). Leicester University Press.

Maxwell-Stewart, H. (1999). The rise and fall of John Longworth: Work and punishment in early Port Arthur. *Tasmanian Historical Studies, 6*(2), 96–114.

Maxwell-Stewart, H. (2008). *Closing hell's gates: The death of a penal station.* Allen and Unwin.

Maxwell-Stewart, H. (2010). Convict transportation from Britain and Ireland, 1615–1870. *History Compass, 8*(11), 1221–1242.

Maxwell-Stewart, H. (2012). Isles of the dead: Convict death rates in comparative perspective. *Historic Environments, 24*(3), 26–34.

Maxwell-Stewart, H. (2015). "And All My Great Hardships Endured"? Irish convicts in Van Diemen's land. In N. Whelehan (Ed.), *Beyond the island: Transnational perspectives in modern Irish History* (pp. 69–87). Routledge.

Maxwell-Stewart, H. (2016). The rise and fall of penal transportation. In A. Johansen (Ed.), *Oxford handbook of the history of crime and criminal justice* (pp. 335–654). Oxford University Press.

Maxwell-Stewart, H. (2016). The state, convicts and longitudinal analysis. *Australian Historical Studies, 47*(3), 419–423.

Maxwell-Stewart, H. (2020). Western Australia and transportation in the British Empire 1615–1939. In J. Gregory & L. Marshall (Eds.), *The Carceral colony: Studies in Western Australian History*, 34 (pp. 5–22).

Maxwell-Stewart, H. (2022). Bentham, convict transportation and the great confinement thesis. In P. Schofield & T. Causer (Eds.), *Bentham and Australia: Convicts, utility and empire.* University College London Press.

Maxwell-Stewart, H., Inwood, K., & Stankovich, J. (2015). The prison and the colonial family. *History of the Family, 20*(2), 231–248.

Maxwell-Stewart, H., & Kippen, R. (2014). "What is a man that is a bolter to do? I would steal the Governor's axe rather than starve": Old lags and recidivism in the Tasmanian penal colony. In J. Campbell & V. Miller (Eds.), *Transnational penal cultures* (pp. 165–183). Routledge.

Maxwell-Stewart, H., & Quinlan, M. (2017). Female convict labour and absconding rates in colonial Australia. *Tasmanian Historical Studies, 22*, 19–36.

McConville, S. (1981). *A history of English prison administration, Vol. 1 1750–1877.* Routledge.

McGary, H. (1992). Resistance and Slavery. In H. McGary & B. Lawson (Eds.), *Between slavery and freedom* (pp. 35–54). Indiana University Press.

McGillivary, A. (2004). Seaman's greens and imperial designs at Port Jackson: A maritime perspective of British settler agriculture. *Agricultural History, 73*(3), 261–288.

McIntyre, P. (2011). *Free passage: The reunion of Irish convicts and their families in Australia 1788–1852.* Irish Academic Press.

McKay, A. (1958). *The assignment system of convict labour, Van Diemen's Land 1824–1842.* MA thesis, University of Tasmania.

McLachlan, I. (1988). *Place of banishment: Port Macquarie 1818*–1832. Hale & Iremonger.

McQueen, H. (1968). Convicts and rebels. *Labour History, 15*, 5–14.

Meinzer, N. (2015). The Western Australian convicts. *Australian Economic History Review, 55*(2), 163–186.

Meredith, J. (1988). *The plantation slaves of Trinidad: 1783–1816: A mathematical and demographic enquiry*. Cambridge University Press.

Melossi, D. (2003). A new edition of "Punishment and Social Structure" thirty-five years later: A timely event. *Social Justice, 30*(1), 248–263.

Meredith, D., & Oxley, D. (2005). Contracting convicts: The convict labour market in Van Diemen's Land 1840–1857. *Australian Economic History Review, 45*(1), 45–72.

Meredith, D., & Oxley, D. (2007). Condemned to the colonies. Penal transportation as the solution to Britain's law and order problem. *Leidschrift, 22*(1), 19–39.

Miller, L. (1846). *Notes of an exile to Van Diemen's land*. McKinstry.

Millett, P. (2007). The distribution of an offensive population: Classification and convicts in Fremantle Prison, 1850–1865. *Studies in Western Australian History, 25*, 40–56.

Molesworth, W. (1967). *Report from the Select Committee of the House of Commons on Transportation together with a Letter from the Archbishop of Dublin on the same Subject and Notes by Sir Wiiliam Molesworth, BART Chairman of the Committee 1838*. Wakefield, Adelaide.

Molloy, J. (2000). *The native-born: The first white Australians*. Melbourne University Press.

Moore, A. (2009). Vinegar Hill/Castle Hill Rebellion, 1804. In I. Ness (Ed.), *The international encyclopedia of revolution and protest*. Wiley. https://doi.org/10.1002/9781405198073.wbierp1539

Moore, T. (2010). *Death or liberty: Rebels and radicals transported to Australia 1788–1868*. Pier 9 Millers Point.

Moran, D., Piacentini, L., & Pallot, J. (2011). Disciplined, mobility and carceral geography: Prisoner transport in Russia. *Transactions of the Institute of British Geographers*, New Series, *37*(3), 446–460.

Moretti, F. (2005). *Graphs, maps, trees: Abstract models for a literary history*. Verso.

Morgan, G., & Rushton, P. (2003). Running away and returning home: The fate of English convicts in the American colonies. *Crime, Histoire & Sociétés, 7*(2), 61–80.

Morgan, K. (1989). Convict runaways in Maryland, 1745–1775. *Journal of American Studies, 23*(2), 253–268.

Morris, R. (1948). Labor controls in Maryland in the nineteenth century. *The Journal of Southern History, 14*(3), 385–400.

Moss, K. (2020). The Swan River experiment: Coerced labour in Western Australia 1829–1868. *Studies in Western Australian History, 34*, 23–39.

Mudie, J. (1837). *The felonry of New South Wales: Being a faithful picture of the real romance of life in Botany Bay*. With Anecdotes of Botany Bay Society.

Mundy, G. (1852). *Our antipodes or, residence and rambles in the Australasian Colonies, with a glimpse of the goldfields*. Richard Bentley.

Nash, G. (1998). Reverberations of Haiti in the American North: Black Saint Dominguans in Philadelphia. *A Journal of mid-Atlantic Studies, 65*, 44–73.

Neal, D. (1987). Free society, penal colony, slave society, prison? *Historical Studies, 22*(89), 497–518.

Neal, D. (1991). *The rule of the law in a penal colony: Law and power in early New South Wales*. Cambridge University Press.

Newby, H. (1975). The deferential dialectic. *Comparative Studies in Society and History, 17*, 139–164.

Newman, S. (2015). *In great slavery and bondage: White labour and the development of plantation slavery in British America*. University of Pennsylvania Press.

Nichol, W. (1984). Malingering and convict protest. *Labour History, 47*, 18–27.

Nicholas, S. (1988). The convict labour market. In S. Nicholas (Ed.), *Convict workers: Reinterpreting Australia's past* (pp. 111–126). Cambridge.

Nicholas, S., & Shergold, P. (1988). Convicts as workers. In S. Nicholas (Ed.), *Convict workers: Reinterpreting Australia's past* (pp. 62–84). Cambridge University Press.

Nicholson, I. (1983). *Shipping arrivals and departures, Tasmania 1803–1833, Vol I*. Roebuck.

Nicholson, I. (1985). *Shipping arrivals and departures, Tasmania 1834–42, Vol II*. Roebuck.

O'Connor, T. (1994). *Power and punishment: The limits of resistance, Moreton Bay Penal Station 1824–42*. Hons Thesis, University of Queensland.

O'Connor, T. (1999). Buckley's chance: Freedom and hope in the penal settlements of Newcastle and Moreton Bay. *Tasmanian Historical Studies, 6*(2), 115–128.

O'Laughlin, B. (2002). Proletarianization, agency and changing rural livelihoods: Forced labour and resistance in colonial Mozambique. *Journal of Southern African Studies, 28*, 511–530.

Orth, J. (1987). English combination acts of the eighteenth century. *Law and History Review, 5*(1), 175–211.

Oxley, D. (1996). *Convict maids: The forced migration of women to Australia*. Cambridge University Press.

Panza, L., & Williamson, J. (2019). Australian squatters, convicts and capitalists: Dividing-up a fast growing frontier pie, 1821–71. *Economic History Review, 72*(2), 568–594.

Parham, D., & Noble, B. (1994). *Convict probation stations archaeological survey*. Tasmanian Archaeological Society.

Paton, D. (2001). Punishment, crime and the bodies of slaves in eighteenth-century Jamaica. *Journal of Social History, 34*(4), 923–945.

Pestana, C. G. (2004). *The English Atlantic in the age of revolution 1640–61*. Harvard University Press.

Pestana, C. G. (2005). English character and the fiasco of the Western design. *Early American Studies: An Interdisciplinary Journal, 3*(1), 1–31.

Petrow, S. (2000). Policing in a penal colony: Governor Arthur's police system in Van Diemen's land, 1826–1836. *Law and History and Review, 18*(2), 351–395.

Pike, R. (1978). Penal servitude in the Spanish empire: Presidio labor in the eighteenth century. *Hispanic American Historical Review, 58*(1), 21–40.

Plater, D., & Milne, S. (2012). *The capital case of Sarah McGregor and Mary Maloney in New South Wales in 1834: 'Justice is Due Even to Them'*. SSRN.

Pomeranz, K. (2000). *The great divergence: China Europe and the making of the modern economy*. Princeton University Press.

Priestley, A. (1967). *The Molesworth Committee and New South Wales*. MA thesis, Australian National University.

Prinsep, A. (1833) *The Journal of a Voyage from Calcutta to Van Diemen's land comprising a description of that colony during six months residence*. Smith Elder and Co.

Quinlan, M. (1986). *Hope amidst hard times: Working class organisation in Tasmania 1830–1850*. University of New South Wales.

Quinlan, M. (1989). Pre arbitral labour law in Australia and its implications for the adoption of compulsory arbitration. In S. Macyntire & R. Mitchell (Eds.), *Foundations of arbitration* (pp. 25–47). Oxford University Press.

Quinlan, M. (2004). Australia 1788–1902: A working man's paradise? In D. Hay & P. Craven (Eds.), *Masters, servants, and magistrates in Britain and the empire, 1562–1955* (pp. 219–250). University of North Carolina Press.

Quinlan, M. (2005). Tasmanian trade unions in the nineteenth century. *Tasmanian Historical Research Association Papers and Proceedings, 52*(3), 150–174.

Quinlan, M. (2018). *The origins of worker mobilisation: Australia 1788–1850*. Routledge.

Quinlan, M. (2020). *Contesting inequality and worker mobilisation: Australia 1851–1880*. Routledge.

Quinlan, M., Gardner, M., & Akers, P. (2003). Reconsidering the collective impulse: Formal organisation and informal associations amongst workers in the Australian Colonies 1795–1850. *Labour/le Travail, 52*, 137–180.

Ramsey Silver, L. (2002). *Australia's Irish rebellion: The battle for Vinegar Hill*. Watermark Press.

Rao, J. (1999). Freedom, equality, property and Bentham: The debate over unfree labour. *The Journal of Peasant Studies, 27*(1), 97–127.

Rashid, I. (1998). "Do Dady Nor Lef Me Make Dem Carry Me": Slave resistance and emancipation in Sierra Leone, 1894–1928. *Slavery & Abolition, 19*(2), 208–231.

Read, R. (2020). *Convict assignment and prosecution risk in Van Diemen's land 1830–35*. Ph.D. Thesis, University of Tasmania.

Rediker, M. (1987). *Between the devil and the deep blue sea: Merchant seamen, pirates and the Anglo-American world, 1700–1750*. Cambridge University Press.

Rediker, M. (2007). *The slave ship: A human history*. Viking.

Rediker, M. (2013). *The Amistad rebellion: An Atlantic Odyssey of slavery and freedom*. Penguin.

Reid, K. (1998). "Contumacious, Ungovernable and Incorrigible": Convict women and workplace resistance; Van Diemen's Land, 1820–1839. In I. Duffield & J. Bradley (Eds.), *Representing convicts: New perspectives on convict forced labour migration* (pp. 106–123). Leicester University Press.

Reid, K. (2003). Setting women to work the assignment system and female convict labour in Van Diemen's land, 1820–1839. *Australian Historical Studies, 34*(121), 1–25.

Reid, K. (2007). *Gender, crime and empire: Convicts, settlers and the state in early colonial Australia*. Manchester University Press.

Ritchie, J. (1971). *The evidence to the Bigge report: New South Wales under Governor Macquarie*, Volume 2 written evidence. Heinemann.

Rio, A. (2015). Penal enslavement in the Early Middle Ages. In C. G. De Vito & A. Lichtenstein (Ed.), *Global convict labour* (pp. 79–107). Brill.

Rivers, L. E. (2012). *Rebels and runaways: Slave resistance in nineteenth-century Florida*. University of Illinois Press.

Robbins, W. (2001). *The management of convict labour employed by the New South Wales Government 1788–1830*. Ph.D. thesis, UNSW, Sydney.

Robbins, W. (2005). Spatial escape and the Hyde Park convict barracks. *Journal of Australian Colonial History, 7*, 81–96.

Roberts, D. (2005). A "change of place": Illegal movement on the Bathurst frontier, 1822–1825. *Journal of Australian Colonial History, 7*, 97–122.

Roberts, D. (2006). The valley of the swells, 'Special' or 'Educated' convicts on the Wellington Valley Settlement, 1827–30. *History Australia, 3*, 11–21.

Roberts, D. (2011). The 'Knotted Hands that Set Us High': Labour history and the study of convict Australia. *Labour History, 100*, 33–50.

Roberts, D. (2017). Colonial gulag: The populating of the Port Macquarie penal settlement, 1821–1832. *History Australia, 14*(4), 588–606.

Roberts, D. (2017). Masters, magistrates and the management of complaint: The 1833 convict revolt at Castle Forbes and the failure of local governance. *Journal of Australian Colonial History, 19*, 57–93.

Roberts, P. (1983). Caravats and Shanavests: Whiteboyism and faction fighting in East Munster, 1802–11. In S. Clark & J. Donnerly (Eds.), *Irish peasants, violence and political unrest 1780–1914* (pp. 66–73). Gill and Macmillan.

Robson, L. (1965). *Convict settlers of Australia*. Melbourne University Press.

Robson, L. (1966). Fenton, Michael (1789-1874). *Australian dictionary of biography*. Melbourne University Press.

Robson, L. (1983). *A history of Tasmania: Van Diemen's land from the earliest times to 1855* (Vol. 1). Oxford University Press.

Rodger, N. (2004). *Command of the ocean: A naval history of Britain, 1649–1815*. Norton.

Roe, M. (1965). *Quest for authority in Eastern Australia, 1835–51*. Melbourne University Press.

Roscoe, K. (2020). Work on Wadjemup: Entanglements between aboriginal prison labour and the imperial convict system in Western Australia. *Studies in Western Australian History, 34*, 79–95.

Rosen, S. (2006). *"That Den of Infamy, the No. 2 Stockade Cox's River" An historical investigation into the construction, in the 1830s, of the Western Road from Mt Victoria to Bathurst by a convict workforce*. Ph.D. thesis, University of Western Sydney.

Rudė, G. (1964). *The crowd in history: A study of popular disturbances in France and England 1730–1848*. Wiley.

Rusche, G., & Kirchheimer, O. (1939). *Punishment and social structure*. Columbia University Press.

Rushton, P., & Morgan, G. (2013). *Banishment in the early Atlantic world: Convicts, rebels and slaves*. Bloomsbury.

Sankey, M. (2005). *Jacobite prisoners of the 1715 rebellion: Preventing and punishing insurrection in early Hanovarian Britain*. Ashgate.

Scott, J. (1985). *Weapons of the weak: Everyday forms of resistance*. Yale University Press.

Scott, J., & Tria Kerkvliet, B. (Eds.). (1986). *Everyday forms of peasant resistance in South-East Asia*. Frank Cass.

Sellin, J. (1976). *Slavery and the penal system*. Elsevier.

Shepherd, J., & Maxwell-Stewart, H. (2021). Rites of passage: The voyage to convict Australia and the creation of the penal labourer. *Australian Historical Studies, 52*, 4.

Shoemaker, R., & Ward, R. (2017). Understanding the criminal: Record-keeping, Statistics and the early history of criminology in England. *British Journal of Criminology, 57*, 1442–1461.

Smith, A. (1766). *The wealth of nations*. 1970 edn. Pelican.

Smith, B. (2008). *A cargo of women: Susannah Watson and the convicts of the princess royal*. Allen & Unwin.
Smith, B. (2009). *Australia's Birthstain: The starling legacy of the convict era*. Allen and Unwin.
Smith, B. (2014). *Luck of the Irish*. Allen & Unwin.
Smith B. (2021). *Defiant voices: How Australia's female convicts challenged authority*. National Library of Australia Publishing Canberra.
Smith, M. (Ed.). (2005). *Stono: Documenting and interpreting a southern slave revolt*. University of Southern Carolina Press.
Solow, B. (1987). Capitalism and slavery in the exceedingly long run. *Journal of Interdisciplinary History, 17*(4), 711–737.
Southey, T. (1848). *The rise and present state of Colonial Wools*. Smith Elder & Co.
Stoler, A. (2008). *Along the archival grain: Epistemic anxieties and colonial common sense*. Princeton University Press.
Therry, R. (1863). *Reminiscences of thirty years residence in New South Wales and Victoria*. S. Low, Son, and Co.
Thompson, E. (1967). Time, work-discipline, and industrial capitalism. *Past and Present, 38*, 56–97.
Thompson, E. (1968). *The making of the English working class*. Penguin.
Thompson, E. (1974). Patrician society, plebeian culture. *Journal of Social History, 7*(4), 382–405.
Thompson, E. (1975). Folklore, anthropology, and social history. *Indian Historical Review, 3*(2), 247–266.
Thompson, E., et al. (1975). The crime of anonymity. In D. Hay (Ed.), *Albion's fatal tree; Crime and society in eighteenth century England* (pp. 255–344). Allen Lane.
Thompson, E. (1977). *Whigs and hunters: The origin of the black act*. Penguin.
Thompson, E. (1991). *Customs in common*. Merlin Press.
Thompson, J. (2020). *Bone and beauty: The ribbon boys' rebellion*. University of Queensland Press.
Thornton, J. (1991). African soldiers in the Haitian revolution. *Journal of Caribbean History, 25*(1), 58–80.
Throness, L. (2016). *A protestant purgatory: Theological origins of the Penitentiary Act, 1779*. Ashgate.
Travers, T. (2016). *Samuel Smiles and the Victorian work ethic*. Routledge.
Tuffin, R. (2007). The post-mortem treatment of convicts in Van Diemen's land, 1814–1874. *Journal of Australian Colonial History, 9*, 99–126.
Tuffin, R. (2007). The evolution of convict labour management in Van Diemen's Land: Placing the 'Penal Peninsula' in a colonial context. *Tasmanian Historical Research Association, 54*(2), 69–83.

Tuffin, R. (2008). 'Where the vicissitudes of day and night are not known': Convict coal mining in Van Diemen's Land, 1822–1848, *13*, 35–61.
Tuffin, R. (2013). Australia's industrious convicts: A reappraisal of archaeological approaches to convict labour. *Australian Archaeology, 76*(1), 1–12.
Tuffin, R. (2018). Convicts of the "Proper Description": The appropriation and management of skilled convict labour. *Labour History, 114*, 69–92.
Tuffin, R., & Gibbs, M. (2018). Early Port Arthur: Convict colonization and the formation of a penal station in Van Diemen's land 1830–35. *International Journal of Historical Archaeology, 23*(3), 568–595.
Tuffin, R., & Gibbs, M. (2019). Repopulating landscapes: Using offence data to recreate landscapes of incarceration and labour at the Port Arthur Penal Station, 1830–1877. *International Journal of Humanities and Arts Computing, 13*(1–2), 155–218.
Tuffin, R., & Gibbs, M. (2020). The archaeology of the convict probation system: The labor landscapes of Port Arthur and the Cascades Probation Station, 1839–55. *International Journal of Historical Archaeology, 24*(3), 589–617.
Tuffin, R., & Gibbs, M. (2020). 'Uninformed and Impractical'? The convict probation system and its impact upon the landscape of 1840s Van Diemen's land. *History Australia, 17*(1), 87–114.
Tuffin, R., Gibbs, M., Roberts, D., Maxwell-Stewart, H., Roe, D., et al. (2018). Landscapes of production and punishment: Convict labour in the Australian context. *Journal of Social Archaeology, 18*(1), 50–76.
Tuffin, R., Gibbs, M., Roberts, D. A., Maxwell-Stewart, H., Roe, D., Steele, J., Hood, S., & Godfrey, B. (2019). *Convict labour landscapes, Port Arthur 1830–1877*. www.convictlandscapes.com.au
Tuffin, R., Roe, D., Gibbs, M., Clark D., & Clark, M. (2020). Landscapes of production and punishment: LiDAR and the process of feature identification and analysis at a Tasmanian convict station. *Australian Archaeology*, 1–20.
Tuffin, R., Maxwell-Stewart, H., & Quinlan, M. (2020). Reintegrating historical records through digital data linking: Convicts prosecuted for collective action in Van Diemen's land. *Journal of Australian Colonial History, 22*(2), 53–86.
Turner, J. (1982). *Coal mining in Newcastle 1801–1900*. Newcastle regional Public Library.
Turner, M. (Ed.). (1995). *From chattel slaves to wages slaves: The dynamics of labour bargaining in the Americas*. Indiana University Press.
Turner, M. (2004). The British Caribbean, 1823–1838: The transition from slave to free legal status. In D. Hay & P. Craven (Eds.), *Masters, servants and magistrates* (pp. 303–322). University of North Carolina Press.
Walsh, B. (2007). *Heartbreak and hope, deference and defiance on the Yimmang: Tocal's convicts 1822–1840*. Ph.D. thesis, University of Newcastle.

Ward, R. (1956). *The ethos and influence of the Australian Pastoral worker*. Ph.D. thesis, Australian National University, 132.
Waring, J. (2017). *Indentured migration and the servant trade from London to America, 1618–1718*. Oxford University Press.
Webb, S., & Webb, B. (1914). *Industrial democracy*. Longman Green & Co.
Wegman, I. (2018). Water wise: How rivers shaped a colony. *Tasmanian Historical Research Association Papers and Proceedings, 65*(3), 45–60.
Wells, A. (1981). Social conflict and protest in the English countryside in the early nineteenth century: A rejoinder. *The Journal of Peasant Studies, 8*(4), 514–530.
Wentworth, W. C. (1819). *Statistical, historical, and political description of the colony of New South Wales and its dependent settlements in Van Diemen's land with a particular enumeration of the advantages which these colonies offer for emigration, and their superiority in many respects over those possessed by the United States of America*. London.
Whitaker, M. (1998). Swords to ploughshares? The 1798 rebels in New South Wales. *Labour History, 75*, 9–21.
Widowson, H. (1829). *Present state of Van Diemen's land comprising an account of its agricultural capabilities with observations on the present state of farming etc etc pursued in that colony and other important matters connected with emigration*. S. Robinson et al.
Williams, E. (1964). *Capitalism and slavery*. Andre Deutsch.
Willis, J. (2005). Transportation versus imprisonment in eighteenth and nineteenth century Britain; Penal power, liberty and the state. *Law & Society, 39*(1), 171–210.
Winter, S. (2013). Legislation, ideology and personal agency in the Western Australian penal colony. *World Archaeology, 45*(5), 802–811.
Winter, S. (2016). Coerced labour in Western Australia during the nineteenth-century. *Australasian Historical Archaeology, 34*, 3–12.
Wood, B. (1987). Some aspects of female resistance to chattel slavery in low county Georgia 1763–1815. *The Historical Journal, 30*(3), 603–622.
Woodberry, J. (1972). *Andrew Bent and the freedom of the press in Van Diemen's land*. Fullers.
Worden, N. (1985). *Slavery in Dutch South Africa*. Cambridge University Press.
Young, D. (2020). Layers of visibility: Convict discipline, crime and punishment, King George's sound, Western Australia, 1826–1831. *Studies in Western Australian History, 34*, 41–77.

Index

H. Maxwell-Stewart and M. Quinlan, *Unfree Workers*, Palgrave Studies in Economic History,
https://doi.org/10.1007/978-981-16-7558-4

C

The manufacturer's authorised representative in the EU is Springer Nature Customer Service Centre GmbH, Europaplatz 3, 69115 Heidelberg, Germany. If you have any concerns regarding our products, please contact ProductSafety@springernature.com

Printed and bound by CPI Group (UK) Ltd, Croydon, CR0 4YY
30/09/2026
02225327-0012